SOUL FOOD

ADRIAN MILLER

SOUL
FOOD

THE SURPRISING STORY OF AN

American Cuisine

ONE PLATE AT A TIME

THE UNIVERSITY OF NORTH CAROLINA PRESS   CHAPEL HILL

Designed by Sally Scruggs
Set in Quadraat by Tseng Information Systems, Inc.
Manufactured in the United States of America

The paper in this book meets the guidelines for permanence
and durability of the Committee on Production Guidelines for
Book Longevity of the Council on Library Resources.

The University of North Carolina Press has been a member
of the Green Press Initiative since 2003.

Portions of Chapter 13 appeared previously in somewhat
different form in *Edible Memphis*, Summer 2009, 8–10.

Unless otherwise indicated, all photos are by the author.

Library of Congress Cataloging-in-Publication Data
Miller, Adrian.
Soul food : the surprising story of an American cuisine, one
plate at a time / by Adrian Miller.
pages cm
Includes bibliographical references and index.
ISBN 978-1-4696-0762-7 (cloth : alk. paper)
ISBN 978-1-4696-3242-1 (pbk. : alk. paper)
1. African American cooking—History. 2. Cooking, American—
Southern style. I. Title.
TX715.M6379 2013
641.59′296073—dc23

2013002823

TO MY PARENTS, HYMAN & JOHNETTA MILLER

Thanks for all those years of soul in the suburbs

Contents

PREFACE xiii

1 What Is Soul Food? 1

2 West Africa: The Culinary Source 11

3 From Southern to Soul 29

4 Fried Chicken and the Integration of Church and Plate 49

5 Catfish and Other Double Swimmers 70

6 Chitlins: A Love Story 91

7 Black-Eyed Peas: What's Luck Got To Do With It? 111

8 How Did Macaroni and Cheese Get So Black? 129

9 Sometimes, I Feel Like Motherless Greens 146

10 Candied Yams: West African in Name, but Not in Taste 166

11 Cornbread: Drop It Like It's Hot Bread! 186

12 Hot Sauce: The Best Medicine Ever? 208

13 What's Sweet, Red, and Drunk from a Jelly Jar? Hint: Liquid Soul! 222

14 Give Me Some Sugar: The Glory of Soul Food Desserts 240

15 Whither Soul Food? 255

NOTES 267

BIBLIOGRAPHY 285

INDEX 311

Illustrations & Maps

ILLUSTRATIONS

Home Cooking Restaurant advertisement, 1910, Denver 38

"Straight Ahead" fried chicken, Deborah's Kitchen, Philadelphia 63

Sign advertising Mayo's and Mahalia Jackson fried pies and chicken, Nashville 65

Catfish sandwich, Johnson Street Fish House, Greenwood, Miss. 76

Buffalo fish ribs, Betty's Place, Indianola, Miss. 83

Thanksgiving Crock-Pot of chitlins at the Miller residence 93

Sign at Lema's World Famous Chittlins, Knoxville 104

Black-eyed peas, Red Rooster Restaurant, Harlem 113

African American cook shares a New Year's Day tradition 125

Mac 'n' cheese tray, Bethlehem Bistro, Chattanooga 140

The greens table at Bully's Soul Food, Jackson, Miss. 160

A box of sweet potatoes ready for action, the Country Platter, Cleveland, Miss. 179

Soul Food Cornbread Family Stalk 195

Hot water cornbread, Sands Soul Diner, Nashville 197

The hot sauce collection at Mert's, Charlotte, N.C. 217

Alcenia's Ghetto Aid, Memphis 233

Pear cobbler, "The Cobbler Lady," Los Angeles 245

MAPS

1 West African Culinary Carbohydrate Zones 12

2 Culinary Zones of the American South, 1860 17

3 The Black Belt, ca. 1938 18

4 The Great Migrations, 1920–1970 37

Recipes

Marta's Oven-Fried Chicken 66

Corn Flake Fried Chicken and Cheddar Waffles 67

Nanticoke Catfish 87

Creole Broiled Catfish 88

Catfish Curry 89

Chitlins Duran 108

Deep-Fried Chitlins 110

Black-Eyed Peas 126

Purple Hull Peas 127

Mac 'n' Cheese 143

Nyesha Arrington's Mac and Cheese 144

Classic Macaroni and Cheese 145

Johnetta's Mixed Greens 163

Sweet Potato Greens Spoonbread 164

Candied Yams 184

Momma Cherri's Candied Carrots 185

Hot Water Cornbread 206

Minnie Utsey's "Never Fail" Cornbread 207

Alcenia's Ghetto Aid 238

Hibiscus Aid 239

Banana Pudding 252

Summer Peach Crisp 254

Preface

What comes to mind when you hear the words "soul food"? *Does your mouth water* as you visualize the images of familiar food items taking shape? Do you recall the aromas, sounds, and tastes of a Sunday dinner—all the culinary artifacts of a grandmother's love? Or maybe you picture a celebrity chef or television personality who is an unabashed soul food evangelist? Do you see the facade and neon lights of the last soul food in a restaurant you patronized, or perhaps the cozy interior of someone's home? Or does your mind turn to thoughts of death as if a heart attack, cancer, diabetes, or some other chronic disease could be served to you on a plate? If your mind went completely blank or you had to grope for answers, *don't feel too bad*—it's symptomatic of the current state of this particular cuisine. In our food-obsessed times, soul food—the food most associated with one of America's most conspicuous racial groups—remains unknown to some, unfamiliar to many, and unappreciated by most.

It never occurred to me that soul food needed a biographer until I stumbled across John Egerton's 1993 book *Southern Food: At Home, on the Road, in History.* In that book, Egerton penned the following: "The comprehensive history of black achievement in American cookery still waits to be written. From frontier cabins to plantation houses to the White House, from steamboat galleys and Pullman kitchens to public barbecues and fish fries and private homes without number, black chefs and cooks and servants have elevated the art of American cookery and distinguished themselves in the process, and they and all other Americans need to see the story fully told."[1] Those words instantly piqued my curiosity and inspired me to take a closer look at African American cuisine.

This is the story of soul food. Down through history, African American cuisine has gone by several names since enslaved West Africans arrived in British North America: slave food, the master's leftovers, southern food, country cooking, home cooking, down home cooking, Negro food, and soul food. Those are the more polite names that have been used. Of them, "southern food" and "soul food" are the labels most used, but they also tend to confuse. This book explores where southern food ends and soul food begins, and why soul food became the most recognized aspect of African American cooking. My hope is that by sharing the intriguing story of how soul food developed, people of all stripes will be more apt to try this cuisine. Soul food's not in immediate danger of becoming extinct, but it certainly faces the prospect of being needlessly obscure. That can change if stereotypes of and negative associations with soul food become perishable items instead of something processed for a long shelf life.

Chasing down the soul food story required me to break cornbread in many places—sometimes literally, but mostly metaphorically. I consumed the culinary history works of Jessica Harris, Judith Carney, Fred Opie, Howard Paige, and Diane Spivey. I read and cooked out of too many cookbooks to remember. I drew upon my own memories and mined the memories of others. The most gratifying research was done at the table—in homes where traditional cooking is still practiced and at soul food restaurants whose numbers are thinning.

For the past decade, I've peppered a lot of people—immediate family, countless relatives, the congregation at Campbell Chapel A.M.E. Church (my home church), friends, dates, Facebook friends, Twitter followers, and strangers—with random questions about what they ate during their childhood and what soul food means to them now. Soul food would never have tugged at my curiosity if my parents, Hyman and Johnetta Miller, had not fed me soul food while I was growing up in a suburb south of Denver, but far removed from the South. I dedicate this book to them. All of the above has been a blessing beyond measure. My jar of bacon grease (on the back of the stove) truly runneth over!

I thank the following folks who gave me shelter as I traveled around the United States assessing the state of soul food: Eric Ames, Brett Anderson and Nathalie Jordi, Rachna and Rajeev Balakrishna, Gary Blackmon, Hieu Dang, Joel and Freddi Felt, Martha Foose, Shailu Halbe and Manju Kulkarni, my Aunt Joyce Halsey, Martha Hopkins, Nelson Hsu, Kimberly Kho, Judy and James Justice, Al and Fran Lanier, Mary Beth Lasseter, my loving twin, April Miller-Cook, my cousin Antoinette Miller, Prakash Mehta and Shefali Shah, Terry and Carolyn Murphy, Paul and Joy Martin, Linda Paulson, and Tammy Svoboda and Sandra Wray-McAfee. I truly appreciate Rhonda Andrew, Jim Auchmutey, Sheri Castle, Angela Cooley, Ajay Dandavati, Grace and Damian Dobosz, Charla Draper, Karen Edwards, John Egerton, John T. Edge, Lolis Elie, Fatima Ford, James Foy, Jessica Harris, James Keown and Joette Bailey Keown, Jeannette LaFors and Matt

Kelemen, Kary and Nanette LaFors, Jan Longone, the late David Walker Lupton for graciously sharing his astounding historical bibliography of African American cookbooks, Toni Tipton Martin, LaRuth McAfee, Nancie McDermott, my brothers Hyman Miller Jr. and Kenny Lloyd, Gloria Montgomery and family, Michelle Oakes, Sandy Oliver, Fred Opie, Cathleen Price, Susan Puckett, Katie Rawson, Leni Sorensen, Ellen Sweets, Carol Titley, Bob Underwood, Ari Weinzweig, the staff at the Denver Public Library, and countless others for their willingness to entertain my random questions or impromptu dinner invitations, for their wise on-the-spot counsel, helpful suggestions, support, and not-so-random acts of kindness when I needed them.

To Parijat Desai, Suzanne Koehler MacMillan, Sarah Peasley, Rebecca Caro, Catherine Ricca, Adam Randall, Michael Shea, and Ruth Tobias, thanks for looking at drafts and telling me when my writing or thought process was whacked. Thanks to Steve Fisher for your guidance with the Husted culinary collection at the University of Denver—truly a godsend during the early years of my research. Thanks to Adam Lerner, Sarah Baie, and everyone at the Museum for Contemporary Art at Denver for giving me the opportunities to test my burgeoning soul food theories via the Mixed Tastes lecture series. Thanks to Stacia Cardille for spending hours researching in the Library of Congress in the early days of the project, and to Lori Colburn, Andrew Craig, Ruchika Gupta, Christine Harrell, Diandra Partridge, Michele Parvensky, and Ty Shaw for providing crucial assistance when I most needed it. A big thanks to Sheri Castle, recipe tester extraordinaire, for making my recipes more user-friendly. A special thanks to my friend the late Jake Adam York for his insights that always made me "raise my game."

Thanks to my agent Tony Gardner for believing that there was a market for this book, and for being a great booster. Thanks to Elaine Maisner and Stephanie Wenzel at the University of North Carolina Press for their encouragement, editorial guidance, and tremendous patience.

Finally, I thank God for the opportunity to sift through a rich past that connects me with exceptional cooks long gone, bears witness to the culinary genius of the present, and promises a flavorful, soulful future.

SOUL FOOD

1

What Is Soul Food?

★ ★ ★ ★ ★

Circa June 2010, the Kingston-Persons, a typical middle-class African American family, sit down to eat a meal together as they regularly do. Marilyn, a very concerned maternal grandmother, has joined them. During the meal she announces, "I need to teach Lindsey [her thirteen-year-old granddaughter] how to make some real soul food." Kevin, Marilyn's tech-savvy, eleven-year-old grandson, blurts, "What's soul food?" Without missing a beat, Kevin's mother answers, "The number two cause of death of black men over forty!"[1] A laugh track kicks in, revealing that this is not your average family but a fictional family on a commercial for the now-cancelled Turner Broadcasting System sitcom *Are We There Yet?* I certainly perked up when I heard this commercial. After all, I was working on a soul food history at the time. "Dang!" I thought. "Is this where we are with soul food? On a show starring an African American family, presumably written by African Americans for a primarily African American audience, soul food is now a punch line?" A narrator then implored me not to miss the show's next episode and reminded me, "TBS. Very Funny." In this case, I wasn't so sure.

Why make such a big deal out of a TV commercial? It's not because I'm a black man over forty who likes soul food. The spot just felt a little too much like "black-on-black" crime. It seems a lot of African Americans are "hating on" soul food these days, and I hope to reverse that trend with this book. What a difference a generation makes. In the 1960s, soul food—defined for the moment as the traditional food of African Americans—burst into the American mainstream as the edible form of the emerging Black Is Beautiful and Black Power ethos. Once celebrated as a triumph over centuries of hard times, the cuisine has now fallen upon the same. And the worst part is that soul food's bad reputation is not merely contained within the black community.

In the mid-1990s, a *New York Times* reporter conducted a highly unscientific telephone survey of twenty-five people in Manhattan, asking all of them the same question: "What kind of food is worst for your health?" Behind "American fast food," "southern/soul food" was tied with Mexican for second place, with four responses each. When asked to elaborate, the respondents piled it on with statements like "all that grease and lard" or "southern fried everything." One person gave a half-compliment by saying, "soul food—most African American cooking . . . It's just delicious but awful for you."[2] If it weren't for caller ID technology and the prospect of arrest for making an obscene phone call, I would have conducted my own survey of random strangers. I have a sinking feeling I would garner similar results.

It's difficult to counter soul food's unhealthy image. First, the cuisine conjures up images of something excessively boiled, fried, sweetened, and topped off with a dash of hot sauce. Second, there's the high visibility of chronic diet-related disease amongst African Americans. Though the incidence of chronic disease is rising with several demographic groups in the United States, many think of soul food as "black people's food," and if that's what the cuisine is doing to those who primarily eat it, then "No thanks." Third, though they come at it from different angles, a number of black activists, community leaders, entertainers, nutritionists, and religious leaders have used their cultural cachet to criticize soul food, while few of the black community's tastemakers have risen to the cuisine's defense. Today, soul food may get an occasional culinary shout-out in a sermon here and a hip-hop lyric there, but the cuisine gets far less affection in black popular culture than it did fifty years ago. Collard greens get nowhere near the amount of airtime of another green leaf that is smoked more often than it's eaten. Finally, as a means to bolster their own superiority, segments of the white community have historically disparaged anything that African Americans eat. The net effect is soul food has become a toxic cultural asset inside the black community and a cuisine stigmatized from the outside.

This is a remarkable predicament, given that almost every other aspect of African American culture—clothing, dance, hairstyling, music, song, speech, and worship—has gone global. Yet, its signature food remains in the shadow. Elements of soul food cuisine like fried chicken, black-eyed peas, and cornbread have a global profile, but the African American associations with the food are obscured or have entirely gotten lost. Are there other explanations for this? Should we just settle with the idea that soul food is undesirable? Or is soul food unsung, and thus *unfamiliar*?

Soul food's invisibility on the global stage is only part of the story. For decades, a steady drumbeat of criticism against soul food has had consequences. In African American homes, private gatherings, and restaurants, innumerable "Big Daddies" and "Gran-mamas" are actively honoring the soul food tradition. Older African Americans are mystified that the perception of their traditional food has changed so quickly with the generations that follow them. "We've been eating this food for years, and now everyone says it will kill you" is the usual sentiment. Another consequence is economic. Across the country, legendary soul food restaurants are disappearing at an alarming pace. Restaurant closures are pronounced in the great cities that were beacons for African Americans who left the South in large droves during the twentieth century. Chicago alone has lost notable establishments like Army and Lou's (1945–2010), Gladys' Luncheonette (1946–2001), Izola's (1950–2011), and Soul Queen (1970–2009) within the last decade. The city would have lost Edna's (opened in 1966) had not some of its employees pooled their resources in 2011 to reopen the place as Ruby's. New York City lost Copeland's (1962–2007), and in Denver, M&D's Café, once my hometown's oldest soul food joint, closed its doors on New Year's Eve 2011 after thirty-four years in business.

Soul food restaurants are casualties of change. Their traditional customer base was drained as African Americans left their traditional neighborhoods for other parts of the city. What was once a convenient, local joint becomes a destination restaurant that few undertake the extra travel time to patronize. The economics of running a restaurant are challenging, even in the good times. During an economic downturn, these restaurants have little room to raise prices on a cuisine with such a strong reputation for being inexpensive. Also, working-class customers may opt for fast food rather than indulging in the relative luxury of eating at a restaurant. Other times, a soul food restaurant's problems are internal. The owner may simply want to move on, do something new, or enjoy retirement. More often than not, the owner's family members want nothing to do with the business. They view the restaurant as an albatross around their necks rather than as an heirloom. Tastes have changed as well. As diners look for healthier options, soul food is not at the top of their list . . . at least not without engendering some guilt.

Even the soul food innovators struggle. "Soul Daddy"—the "healthy soul food" concept that beat out stiff competition on NBC's 2011 reality television show *America's Next Great Restaurant*—lasted only a few months. This was despite having an entrepreneur's dream scenario of national exposure; start-up locations in Los Angeles, Minneapolis, and New York; private-equity financing; and the imprimatur of Chipotle founder Steve Ells, the Food Network's Chef Bobby Flay, Chef Lorena Garcia, and Bravo Network's Chef Curtis Stone. What gives?

This book endeavors to give soul food a very public makeover. I show the reasons soul food developed the way it did and why its current reputation is unfair. I tackle the vast subject of soul food by creating a representative soul food dinner and then taking a close-up look at each part of the meal. Not only do I investigate each food item's history; I also look at how food and culture intersect—something that scholars call "foodways."[3] Here, I'll explore foodways by asking, What are important items on the soul food menu? How does a food item get on the soul food plate? What does that item mean for African American culture and American culture?

This "anatomy of a meal" approach is controversial because inevitably something gets left off the plate. Once while speaking on a panel, I casually listed several foods I thought belonged on a representative soul food plate. I was caught off-guard when another author on the panel, an elderly black woman, interjected, "How *dare* you not mention neck bones!" Yes, soul food discussions can get heated, even when they're theoretical. With that episode in mind, let me point out that I've chosen these particular foods not to start a food fight, but merely because they are great vehicles to explain the forces that have sharply and subtly shaped soul food. My dinner meal includes the following: entrées (fried chicken, fried catfish, or chitlins); sides (black-eyed peas, greens, candied yams, and macaroni and cheese); cornbread to sop it up; hot sauce to spice it up; Kool-Aid to wash it down; and a sweet finish with a dessert plate of banana pudding, peach cobbler, pound cake, and sweet potato pie.

As much as I craved making it so, this book is not an all-you-can-eat buffet. Several iconic soul food items didn't make my list. You might wonder why fried pork chops, grits, okra, rice, sweet tea, and your other favorites are missing in action. I will not delve deeply into the biography of African American–inspired regional cuisines like the seafood-rich cooking of the Chesapeake Bay area, the famed Creole cooking of the Gulf South, or the Lowcountry cooking of coastal South Carolina and Georgia. I made these hard choices in order to discern whether or not soul food is a national cuisine. Therefore, I've put together what I think African Americans—more precisely, devoted soul foodies—are most likely to have for lunch or dinner, living in any part of the world and not just in the South.

To document the soul food story, I drew on my own lifetime experiences eating the cuisine at home, at gatherings, and at restaurants. To assess the current soul food scene, I spent a year visiting soul food restaurants around the country (150 in thirty-five different cities). Along the way, I posted photographs of my meals on my Facebook page. So many people reacted to my pictures with concern about my health during this project that I repeatedly had to assure them that I wasn't eating all of the food pictured. I quietly nicknamed that twelve-month period "my year of living dangerously." Still, they did have a point. Health concerns are integral to the current perception of soul food, and these concerns are addressed in this book.

I also went beyond my own experiences. I consulted a vast array of historical sources for this work: firsthand foodways accounts of the enslaved and formerly enslaved (called the FWP interviews, for the Federal Writers' Project interviews); written accounts from the slavers; and written observations of plantation visitors, newspapers, and nutritional studies. At times, pinning down soul food's origins has been as slippery as stewed okra. For most of their history, West African peoples have relied on oral traditions rather than the written word. Though the spirit of West African cuisine is certainly captured in these traditions, the exacting details of how things were done in the past can get lost. Not that the written word has been much better. Though some foreigners took the time to record their observations of West African foodways, we can never be too sure of their accuracy. I've had to sift through lapsed and false memories, misinformation ("fakelore"), and plain old bias.

I've also read a lot of cookbooks, several of which provide useful reference points for developments in African American cooking and American cooking. Hannah Glasse's cookbook (1747) anchors my thinking on what American colonists thought "British food" was in the eighteenth century. Amelia Simmons's cookbook (1796), as America's first, shows us how British food was translated for the colonists with American ingredients. Mrs. Randolph in Virginia (1828), Mrs. Bryan in Kentucky (1839), and Mrs. Rutledge in South Carolina (1846) define antebellum Big House cooking (performed by black cooks) in their respective regions. In addition, I've mined historical cookbooks written by Mrs. Malinda Russell (1866) and Mrs. Abby Fisher (1881). Though apparently written for a broad audience, these are the earliest known African American–authored cookbooks. A generation later, African American middle-class cooking gets a nod in Mrs. Hayes's cookbook (1912) and a couple of social-club compilations from Montana (1927) and New Jersey (1928). Freda DeKnight wrote the first "national" African American cookbook in 1948, and it is an important reference point for what foodways were like after black people left the South and settled in other areas. For the soul food era itself, I drew on many sources.

I've received a lot of unsolicited advice while working on this book. One of the funniest suggestions was "You should have a chapter titled 'How to Get Gran-mama to Give You Her Recipes.'" I instantly recognized the problem. I think it's safe to say that you might have a better chance of getting the nuclear weapons codes from the White House than prying some recipes from a soul food cook. Famed food writer M. F. K. Fisher tells of her own experience in trying to accomplish that task:

> I tried, a long time ago, to learn how our cook Bea made biscuits. She could not write or read, and smiled mockingly when I confessed that I had to copy down a recipe in order to remember it, but she let me stand beside her many times in the kitchen while her slender blue-black hands tossed together the biscuit mix. She always did it at the last minute, when several other things for the meal had reached their climaxes of preparation, so that it was always hard for me to separate them from the bowl I was watching. Every time, the ingredients were the same but in maddeningly different proportions; and every time, the biscuits were the same too: light, flaky but not crumbly, moist in the middle — as a cloud is moist, not a sponge. So I never learned, and Bea told my mother that I was not as bright as I looked to be.[4]

If it can happen to M. F. K. Fisher, it can happen to anyone. Fortunately, you'll be able to dive into the kitchen with a good selection of traditional, health-conscious, and contemporary recipes that I've gathered for you to use.

The late Edna Lewis also influenced these pages. She was the person food writers turned to when they wanted the best and last word on southern cooking. Ms. Lewis was quite emphatic that her style of cooking was not soul food. A *Southern Living* profile on her captured her perspective:

> Like her memories, her culinary convictions run deep. She shudders at the idea of "Soul Food" ("that's hard-times in Harlem — not true Southern food"), marshmallows atop sweet potatoes, and barbecue not cooked on a pit. And she scoffs at what some chefs are

doing with Southern food, such as serving grits with lemongrass gravy. "When I grew up, everyone had a garden, and we ate bountiful foods—vegetables, fruits, grains, beans, and more fish than meat. People didn't know any better than to be good cooks, and good food bonded us together." She pays tremendous respect to the seasons. "Nowadays you can get just about anything anytime—without its true taste, of course."[5]

Ms. Lewis serves as both my muse on southern cooking and a referee on the boundaries between soul food and southern food.

"Follow the people." That's the great advice I got in the early days of this project from Lolis Eric Elie, one of the writers for HBO's *Treme* series and an expert on African American foodways. How else can one truly understand the soul food story without chronicling the experience of its principal adherents? So we'll begin in West Africa and look at how with each significant migration a new iteration of African cooking developed in British North America. I've named these successive, and often overlapping, epochs. The Slave Food period (1619–1865) focuses on what enslaved West Africans, primarily field slaves, ate after making the transition from West Africa to British North America until Emancipation. The Southern Cooking period (1865–present) here means African Americans foodways within the rural South after Emancipation and before, during, and after the Great Migrations. The Down Home Cooking period (1890s–1970s) refers to the urban foodways of millions of African Americans who left the rural South during the Great Migrations. The Soul Food period (1950s–present) describes how traditional southern food is overtly merged with racial politics. Finally, in the conclusion, we'll track the Neo-Soul period (1990s–present) and see how soul food aesthetics have been reinterpreted or outright rejected.

Elie's advice also spurred me to give African American foodways a fresh perspective. Though the experience of West Africans was starkly different from that of many migrants to this country, we can still consider them a major immigrant group to the Americas. Is it possible that soul food could be framed as the descendant of a now invisible immigrant cuisine the same way we think of Chinese, Greek, Indian, Italian, or Mexican food? Jessica Harris's work reveals the culinary connections radiating from West Africa into all parts of the African diaspora as a result of the Atlantic slave trade. Yet, there has been little analysis of how the transplanted West African foodways, transformed by slavery, further changed as millions of African Americans left the rural South and forged new communities in other parts of the United States.

During his lifetime, Chef Louis Szathmary—a Hungarian immigrant, restaurant owner, and eventual chef laureate of Johnson and Wales University—was a keen observer of American cuisine and immigrant foodways.[6] Szathmary gives us some useful tools to evaluate how ethnic immigrant cuisines get "Americanized." Szathmary once posited "that all immigrants from all parts of the world arriving in the United States start to replace their everyday national dishes with their homeland's special holiday and festival dishes and Sunday meals. Germans in America don't eat daily German food, rather German Sunday fare. Similarly the French, Serbians, Polish, Spanish, and others in our country favor their special occasion meals."[7] He elaborated on his theory (I call it the Theory of Special Edibility) by listing factors that "influenced the change of festive or holiday foods into everyday dishes among the ethnic groups in America."[8]

The first factor was cost and availability of ingredients. Typically, the starches and vegetables from back home were either more expensive than or comparable to meats available in the United States. Often recently arrived immigrants to the United States couldn't get the staple vegetables they used back home, but the meats used for special occasion dishes were easily available and relatively inexpensive. The next factor is ethnic pride in making their cuisine's best dishes; as Szathmary says, "It is natural to want to look better in front of your neighbors than you actually are." Homesickness and nostalgia are also key factors. Szathmary elucidates: "These feelings tend to make you remember the highlights of your heritage, the best things that happened to you while in 'the old country.' Because as a rule, holidays are more memorable than workdays, pleasurable things would happen on them, and you remember them fondly." Thus, festive dishes were sometimes easier to make and, from another standpoint, served an emotional purpose for immigrants. We'll see if the factors Szathmary describes in relation to other ethnic groups in the United States, as well as his conclusions, apply to the African American experience.[9]

In terms of quoted language from oral and written sources, I've tried to keep faithful to how people spoke and wrote in their times. If you think spelling is strange in today's email and texting communications, try reading manuscripts printed before the twentieth century. If I used *sic* and parentheticals to explain every period spelling, this would be a much longer book. I use these devices only when explanation is absolutely necessary. When white writers use dialect to describe African American speech, I've kept that language rather than translating it because it shows you the writer's mindset—crucial to understanding the way soul food has been perceived. You'll also see the word "nigger" from time to time in these pages. I hate that word, and I don't use it in conversation—which puts me out of step with a lot of people who liberally use it, notably rappers and racists. However, I felt it necessary to quote people in their true voices to capture the tenor of the times. Language, particularly the use of that word, greatly illuminates how the speaker feels about the social status of African Americans and their food.

And therein lies the heart of the matter. Over time, the foods African Americans traditionally ate have had a more dynamic status than African Americans themselves. In other words, food has gone up and down the social ladder, but a disproportionate number of African Americans remained mired in the lower socioeconomic strata of U.S. society. For much of U.S. history, this was by design. Because of skin color, African Americans had a certain place in society with no prospect of upward social mobility. There were repercussions if anyone, white or black, did anything to change that situation. This status is what I describe when I use the term "racial caste system." Too often, food helped mark where African Americans belonged in the grand scheme of things. African Americans were "natural born cooks" relegated to preparing the best foods for whites while eating the worst foods themselves.

Soul food was a response to racial caste dictates as African Americans asserted their humanity. Food was one avenue to create identity, instill pride, and underscore a triumphal narrative. Those three ingredients cooked up a conventional wisdom of soul food that burst forth in the 1960s and endures to this day. In a 1970 newspaper interview, Hubert Maybell, proprietor of a soul food joint on the South Side of Chicago, effectively expressed the soul food ethos when he said,

> Traditionally, Southern Negroes took the cheaper cuts of the hog— ham hocks, shanks and pigs' feet, and things that white people threw away like greens and chitlings (hog intestines) and made a cuisine of them by cleaning and cooking them with skill and care. They did not call it soul then, but there was a kind of ritual significance to the food. When the church had a picnic or revival meeting,

people brought such dishes from their homes. . . . You have to remember that the cuisine was developed by people who lived in the kingdom of necessity. Soul food usually is gauged by the question, "Is it economical?"[10]

Except for an overt connection to slavery, all of soul food's dominant themes are there: the centrality of pork, the low social status of blacks, racial stigma, resourcefulness, ingenuity, and communal spirit. We'll watch how that conventional wisdom emerged and then test its accuracy. Most importantly, we'll ask what it means when soul food's reality doesn't match up with the conventional wisdom.

At the end of this book, I divine soul food's future, particularly in light of the strong health concerns associated with the cuisine. Please understand that I don't write this book as someone who resists change. We don't eat the same things in quite the same way we did 100 years ago, and that's part of what it means to have progress. But I do hope that through greater understanding about soul food—how and why it developed—the cuisine gets valued as a treasure, and we are not so quick to jettison it as cultural baggage.

At its core, this book is a love letter to past, present, and future African American cooks. The time has come for soul food cooks to take their rightful place in the pantheon of African American cultural performers. May they stand shoulder to shoulder with the athlete, the entertainer, the politician, the preacher, and the writer and receive the adulation they deserve.

West Africa

THE CULINARY SOURCE

The principal source of food for the majority of peoples inhabiting West Africa in the Middle Ages was, as it still is, agriculture—the cultivation of plants, particularly grain, starch-containing root crops, leguminous plants and vegetables. Food collecting (mainly the grain of wild grasses, and also of the fruit of wild trees), animal husbandry (including bee-keeping), hunting and fishing were also practiced to a large extent, providing, among other things, meat, milk and fish; nevertheless, the foods obtained by these means were far less significant than those obtained through cultivation. —Tadeusz Lewicki, *West African Food in the Middle Ages* (1974)

★ ★ ★ ★ ★

I didn't have my first memorable "African" meal until I was in my early twenties. I was living in Washington, D.C., and at the urging of some friends, we went to eat at an Ethiopian restaurant in Adams Morgan—D.C.'s funky, ethnic neighborhood. I was eager to try this new food and was very impressed when the waitress came by with what I thought were hot towels so that we might wipe our hands. As I was about to perform that task, the waitress admonished me by saying, "You eat with that, sir!" While giving my culture-savvy friends some cheap entertainment, I quickly educated myself on the proper use of the spongy bread Ethiopians call *injera*, which comes with the meal. I had eaten in other African restaurants (mainly Egyptian and Moroccan), but I had mentally categorized them as Middle Eastern. I realized that for me, African cuisine was a "blank plate." I've spent my time since learning more about African cooking. Africa's a big place, and soul food's true source lies in only part of it—West Africa.

West Africa, which I define as the band of countries on the continent's Atlantic coastline from Senegal in the north to Angola in the south, remains one of the most diverse places on earth. Food preferences do not respect nation-state boundaries and can vary tremendously from tribe

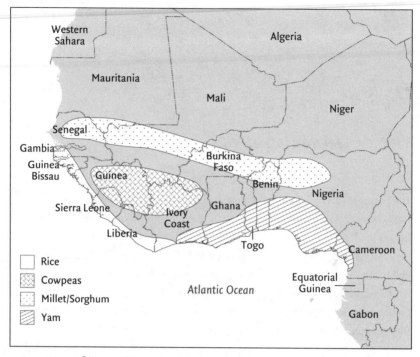

MAP 1 West African Culinary Carbohydrate Zones (adapted from Johnston, *Staple Food Economies*)

to tribe within a country. West African culinary history is challenging to trace, as West African cultures have historically relied on oral traditions to pass down practices and stories. Thus, we don't have any indigenous cookbooks written before European contact and colonization to consult. Much of what we know about precolonial West African food comes from the writings of medieval Arab traders to the region. Thanks to Arabic scholar Tadeusz Lewicki, this valuable source material has been translated into English.

Precolonial West Africans were primarily farmers who ate mostly vegetables, starches, and some meat—a pattern that persists to this day. Starches, particularly root crops, play a dominant role in the West African diet. West Africans can be very provincial about their starches, forming what I call culinary carbohydrate zones that feature rice, West African grains (millet and sorghum), or yams. Though these crops overlap in many areas, some retain more cultural value than others. The north—present-day Senegal, Gambia, and Sierra Leone into the western half of the Ivory Coast—is rice country. The native rice with a reddish hue (*Oryza glaberrima*) was cultivated in this area as early as 1500 B.C.[1] Millet and sorghum get top billing in a swath extending from present-day Senegal to upper Nigeria. The southernmost part of the region, now Benin, Ghana, and Nigeria, is dominated by root crops, particularly yams.[2] On top of, or alongside, the preferred starch, West African cooks added a substantial stew or sauce made up of vegetables, spices, and possibly fish or some other meat. That was a typical West African meal.

The West African larder changed dramatically when Western Europeans arrived during the 1400s. Europeans built forts at strategic points along the West African coastline to augment their nascent slaving empires. Europeans enslaved West Africans to build and work in the forts and, most germane to our purposes, had them maintain their gardens and cook their provisions. In these settlement kitchens, West African enslaved cooks were introduced to traditional Old World foods from Europe and Asia as well as exotic imports from the New World. Historian Alfred Crosby called the diffusion of the New World foods into the Old World, and vice versa, the Columbian Exchange. New World plants were so successfully integrated into Old World cuisines that it's hard to imagine those cultures without them. Can we excise the potato from Irish history? Can we imagine Thai food without fiery chile peppers? How about Italian food without tomatoes and maize for its signature marinara sauces and polenta? *Fuhgetaboutit!*

Because of the Atlantic slave trade, West Africa became an incubator for agricultural experimentation. Though few European crops succeeded in the region, the New World crops thrived. By trial and error, West African cooks learned how to cook the new ingredients, fit them into their meal structure (figured out which could be substituted for traditional ingredients), and determined what tasted good. West Africans incorporated an astonishing number of foreign foods into their larder and fell in love with three New World plants in particular: cassava, maize, and plantains. By the twilight of the eighteenth century, a British parliamentary committee on abolishing slavery reported, "The middle regions of Africa, from whence the persons called slaves are brought, appear by the testimony of witnesses, to abound in millet, pulse, Indian corn, wax, honey, palm oil, plantanes, yams, eddoes, potatoes, cocoa-nuts, cassada, pineapples, oranges, limes, grapes, the sugar cane, which grows wild, tobacco, peppers, ginger, cardamums [cardamom], cinnamon, equal to that of the East-Indies, (and some of it sold at a better price;) rice, superior to that of Carolina."[3] The collateral effects of the Atlantic slave trade made the West

African diet one of most cosmopolitan of its time, literally mixing the old with the new.

The apparent bounty of food onshore sharply contrasted with the limited food supply available to those doomed to slavery during the voyage across the Atlantic Ocean, also called the Middle Passage. The slave ship was a cruel microcosm of inhumanity. The captain ruled the ship, his crew of twenty, and hundreds of captives with a cold calculus: How much must be done to get the maximum number of people to the designated port of call with the least expense?[4] Depending on where they left West Africa and where the ship landed in British North America, the voyage could last from sixty to ninety-three days.[5] Under these circumstances, foods that lasted long without spoiling (too much) were preferred to feed the slaves during the hellish journey.[6]

At first, slavers tried to force-feed the enslaved a diet of European food. Of particular note was a nauseating mix of European horse beans with rotting meat that was called "slabber sauce." Too many slaves died, so slavers switched to feeding them more familiar foods (mainly their favorite starches) to boost survival rates.[7] The enslaved often got the same starch for the entire trip.[8] When slaves ate, every aspect of the meal was strictly regulated, mainly for fear of a possible rebellion. Since the captives were locked below in the ship's hold, coming up on deck to eat presented the enslaved with one of the few opportunities to take violent action. Slaves also rebelled by simply refusing to eat. Alexander Falconbridge, a slave ship surgeon and, later, an abolitionist, described the typical day for the enslaved during a 1788 voyage: "They are commonly fed twice a day, about eight o'clock in the morning and four in the afternoon. In most ships they are only fed with their *own food* once a day. Their food is served up to them in tins, about the size of a small water bucket. They are placed round these tubs and companies of ten to each tub, out of which they feed themselves with wooden spoons."[9]

Though a ship's crew often had a dedicated cook, the captain sometimes picked one of the captives to cook, probably hoping that someone familiar with African foods could make a palatable meal. As Marcus Rediker observes in his book *The Slave Ship*, "A substantial number of women seem to have been involved in food preparation. They performed what were likely familiar duties: they cleaned rice, pounded yams, and ground corn. Women also worked as cooks, in place of, or in some instances alongside, the ship's cook, to prepare food for the hundreds on board."[10] Black men were tapped for cooking duties as well, but not as often. Once the voyage ended, all of the captives transitioned to a more permanent hell of chattel slavery. George Rawick, a slavery scholar, writes eloquently of the West Africans' transition in *From Sundown to Sunup*: "Overnight they were transformed from merchants, or Arabic scholars, or craftsman, or peasant farmers, or cattle-tenders into American slaves. They ate what they were given, not what they wanted."[11]

The arithmetic of the Atlantic slave trade shocks the conscience. According to the latest estimates, approximately 12.5 million people were forcibly removed from West Africa and portions of Southeast Africa and subsequently transplanted in the Americas. Of those, nearly 2.5 million people died at some point during the Middle Passage. Approximately 380,000 West Africans were imported directly to British North America. We can add to that number another 50,000 or so who were first brought to the British Caribbean possessions for "seasoning" (a euphemism for arduous stints on sugar plantations) before arriving in the present-day United States. That means roughly 4 percent of the total Atlantic slave trade population came directly to the United States.[12]

The earliest documented cohort of enslaved Africans in British North America arrived in Jamestown, Virginia, in August 1619. Thus began the Slave Food period. Over roughly the next 200 years, more West Africans were forcibly imported into the colonies after failed attempts to use enslaved Native Americans and indentured blacks and whites to do the work that the masters in town and country required. This wasn't a steady, even process but one that happened in fits and spurts. Beginning with the macabre milestone in Virginia, as scholar Ira Berlin observes, "three distinct slave systems evolved: a Northern non-plantation system and two Southern plantation systems, one around [the] Chesapeake Bay and the other in the Carolina and Georgia low-country."[13]

The northern system of slavery in southern New England, Long Island, New York, and northern New Jersey focused on raising food and other commodities for export to the West Indies.[14] The early plantations in the Virginia colony raised tobacco and indigo crops. Rice was the lucrative crop grown along the coasts of the Carolinas, Georgia, and northern Florida. To Berlin's list, I add the coastal Gulf South area, particularly Louisiana, which had marked economic growth through rice culture and sugar refining. Last, there was the Black Belt, a stretch of land in the interior South from eastern Virginia and the Carolinas westward to eastern Texas, which served as slavery's last major destination before the Civil War, providing new land for planters whose indigo and tobacco crops had exhausted their prior landholdings and for upstart yeoman, or small-scale, farmers.

The interplay between diverse peoples (Native Americans, Europeans, and West Africans), soils, climates, larders, and culinary traditions led to the development of distinct cuisines within each slaving system. And those cuisines are still with us as subregional cuisines within southern cooking (see Map 2). The Chesapeake Bay area—where American chattel slavery began—earned well-deserved fame in the eighteenth and nineteenth centuries for its seafood-based cuisine and corn dishes. Its signature delicacies featured tasty preparations of blue crabs, oysters, terrapin, hominy, and a distinctive wheat bread called "beaten biscuits." Ultimately, the locals' appetite for their regional specialties proved too ravenous. The Chesapeake Bay's seafood resources were overexploited by the early twentieth century, and the region's cooks resorted to inventing "mock" versions of the old standby dishes as the area's estuarine animal populations recovered. Only now, almost a century later, is this regional cuisine making a comeback. Moving southward along the Carolina and Georgia coastlines, another seafood-based cuisine called Lowcountry cooking is noted for its versatile rice dishes (e.g., hoppin' John, okra pilau, and red rice). Many believe the region's iconic combination of "shrimp and grits" is due for a breakout like the "chicken and waffles" craze I discuss in Chapter 4.

Turning westward to the Lower Mississippi Valley, we come to two more familiar cuisines, Creole and Cajun. These cooking styles share many dishes, such as gumbo, the substantial meat and vegetable stew, and jambalaya, a rice-based mixture of meat and vegetables. Yet, Creole food is associated with sophisticated urban cooking while Cajun food has become synonymous with the country. As slave owners and upstart farmers moved from the coasts to the South's interior, what some call the Deep South or the Black Belt, their cuisine necessarily adjusted to new food supplies. Thus, the rice and seafood combinations of the coasts gave way to a diet dominated by corn and pork.

The migration and concentration of slaves in the Deep South was a pivotal moment in the soul food story. By 1860, the total African American population in the United States was 4,441,830, with approximately 4 million of that number still enslaved.[15] That same year, the South had a little more than 46,000 plantations. Of those, only 2,300 were the large, picturesque plantations that one now visits as a tourist. A "large" plantation was a landholding with more than twenty slaves, and its owners were

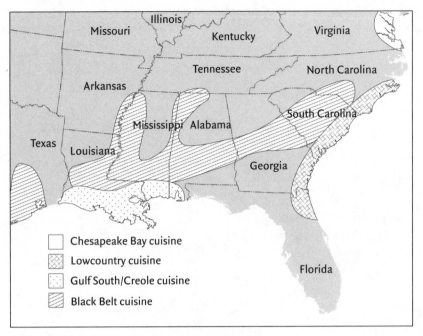

MAP 2 Culinary Zones of the American South, 1860

called planters. At the dawn of the Civil War, most slaves (62 percent) lived on large, cotton-growing plantations that occupied a broad swath of the Deep South. The rest of the enslaved lived and worked on farms of various sizes owned and operated by yeoman farmers, or in urban areas. Nicknamed the Black Belt for its dark soil, slavery's last stronghold extended from Virginia southward through the Carolinas, then turned west through Georgia, Alabama, Mississippi, Louisiana, Arkansas, and portions of eastern Texas (see Map 3).[16] If soul food had its genome sequenced, the Black Belt would have the highest DNA match. It had the highest concentration of African Americans in the United States until the mid-twentieth century. After Emancipation, the largest numbers of African Americans left the Black Belt for other parts of the country and took their cuisine with them.

In each successive, forced migration, the enslaved, black immigrants did what other immigrants do when they settle in a new place. They assessed their new environment, figured out how to adapt, and then began re-creating home as best they could. For a typical immigrant group, "home" also means the Old Country, a shared ancestral homeland. However, enslaved West Africans often didn't have a shared home, because slavers purposefully diversified slave cohorts, lumping people from dif-

MAP 3 The Black Belt, ca. 1938 (adapted from James S. Allen's *Negro Liberation* [New York: International Publishers, 1938], pamphlet 29)

ferent parts of West Africa together, thereby creating a clash of cultures. Planters often saw to it that their slaves lacked a shared language, thus making a rebellion difficult to organize. The efforts that slave owners put into gaining a sense of physical security also had implications for the food security of the enslaved.

So how did enslaved people re-create home through food? Though West Africans from different areas were used to eating different foods, particularly different starches, they shared a culinary framework—the "savory sauce/stew alongside or on top of a starch" meal structure. As the slaves built community, they reconciled their differing tastes in profound ways.

Just as they did with language and music, these diverse West Africans who were thrust together compromised on what they would keep and jettison from their own tribal culinary tradition and what they would accept and reject from other tribal culinary traditions. The slaves also tried to introduce their familiar West African crops into their personal gardens.

They also had to reconcile the use of their white masters' traditional foods from Europe and New World ingredients. Not all of these foods were unfamiliar, because several New World and European crops were introduced into West Africa during the Atlantic slave trade. Slaves already knew foods like chile peppers, rice, collard and turnip greens, maize, and sweet potatoes. For the New World foods they didn't know, the enslaved relied heavily on local Native Americans for guidance. From this vibrant process, an identifiable cuisine took shape. Yet the freedom to shape this cuisine only went as far as what the master permitted slaves to grow, procure, cook, and eat.

Despite the varied beginnings and influences of the Black Belt diet, a stereotype (often held by outside observers) of it coalesced. Southern food was "the 3 M's": meat (pork), meal (cornmeal), and molasses. Though the southern diet was much more varied in real life, this caricature contained some truth. Pork was widely valued in the South because pigs, often let loose to forage in the nearby woods surrounding a plantation, were the easiest to raise. Cornmeal was popular as corn grew easily throughout the colonies, especially in places where grains such as wheat and rice did not. Molasses, the by-product of the sugar-refining process, was a source of additional calories the planter could provide at little cost. These foods became staples of the slaving South, yet slaveholders rationed access to make supplies last throughout the year. The slaves were confronted with a paradox: They had much more food within reach than on the slave ships, yet the master regulated what, how much, and where they could eat. The struggle to get adequate food is one of slavery's leitmotifs that played out differently depending on three contexts: urban slavery; small-scale, yeoman farm slavery; and large-scale plantation slavery. There's much to tell about each of these slaving contexts, but I will just give the sense of a slave's typical day and how that affected what that slave ate.

Urban slaves were a sliver of the overall slave population; the North was industrializing, and slaves were not used for industrial labor. By contrast, the antebellum South was decidedly rural and agricultural, having only a few large cities.[17] There were two types of urban slaves: live-in and hired-out. Live-in slaves were usually women who worked as domestic servants.[18] Their masters often provided small rooms (10′×15′) that had no windows and little or no furniture.[19] Those who were hired out were engaged by a third party to do a certain scope of work that could last a day or months, depending on the task. The following describes the typical range of activity for urban slaves:

Well before dawn "reveille" called the slaves from their sleep. At five o'clock the drumroll or church bells sounded across the city, announcing the beginning of another day to the bondsmen. . . . Most of the womenfolk were domestics engaged in a constant round of household tasks. . . . Well-to-do masters with palatial homes and spacious grounds often had crews of servants, each member of which was carefully trained for a single responsibility—cooking, baking, washing, sewing, gardening, personal service, etc. but most commonly a few slaves cared for a modest middle-class estate and the whites who lived on it.[20]

In the urban environment, the confined space within the master's dwelling made it difficult to create social distance seen on the larger plantations, and slaves necessarily had more intimate contact with their masters, even to the point of sharing a common table.[21] As a result, dividing lines between the master's food and the slave's food were blurred. Charleston's Rev. Dr. James Henley Thornwell laments about the slaves' seeming omnipresence in white communities when he writes, "They are divided out among us and mingled up with us, and we with them, in a thousand ways." Thornwell adds, "They live with us—eating from the same storehouses, drinking from the same fountain, dwelling in the same enclosures."[22] Urban slaves had more autonomy over food transactions than their rural counterparts did. They had more food choices because running their master's errands, including food shopping, often connected them to and immersed them in a city's food networks.

Hired-out slaves were contracted out by their masters to corporations (particularly for mining and railroad operations), to city governments (for infrastructure work), and to individuals for specific tasks. The contracted wages went to the owner. Urban hired-out slaves had more in common with rural slaves in that their daily life was more regimented, their movement more regulated, and their food rationed out by those who hired them. Urban work, unfettered by the agricultural calendar, was more constant over the year. Still, urban slaves managed to get leisure time on the weekends, particularly Sundays. Slaves often could go to Sunday worship services, but they weren't allowed to linger long after service and had to disperse. Given the inherent flexibility of the daily work schedule, slaves managed to carve out opportunities to make some extra money on the side by doing tasks for others or selling food. The master turned a blind eye to his slave's money-making activity, knowing that it alleviated his own food expenses. With this income, slaves bought nice clothing, jewelry, and, too often, alcoholic beverages. Again, city elders tried to restrict such transactions but without much success. Rural slaves also had opportunities to make money in the city by selling produce, as we'll see in the chapters on fried chicken and greens. They, too, bought the finer things and couldn't wait to display their wealth in town during the biggest time of the year—the week between Christmas and New Year's Day. It was customary for slaveholders to let their slaves come to the city during this extended holiday.[23]

Like their urban counterparts, the slaves of yeoman farmers had a diet similar to that of their masters because they often lived in close proximity.[24] As Eugene Genovese writes in *Roll, Jordan, Roll*, "[On] farms of ten slaves or less ... the mistress or perhaps a female slave cooked for all at the same time and in the same way. Only segregation at the table drew a caste line."[25] Charles Sydnor writes in *Slavery in Mississippi* that "on small plantations or farms, one cook served for the master and the slaves. As this arrangement was once described, the negroes ate in the kitchen, the master in the dining room, with an open door between them and their food came 'right out of the same frying-pan.'"[26] Farmers usually had a common garden that everyone on the farm shared.[27] However, slaves on yeoman farms did not always have adequate food. A South Carolina commentator writes, "On small plantations, I have been several times told, the negroes sometimes do not have food enough; not so much from the penuriousness of the owner, as because he forgets or neglects to provide on time for them; because his arrangements are not systematic, or because, when from bad calculation, or no calculation, these stores run short, he has no money to replenish them."[28] In such situations, slaves went into survival mode and supplemented their food by foraging and hunting.

As much as social proximity and shared food marked urban and small-farm slavery, large-scale plantations were a different story. As Richard Wade elucidates in *Slavery in the Cities*, "The countryside provided enough room to give meaning to racial separation. The master could be physically quite removed from his blacks, though sharing the same plantation or farm. And together both were isolated from others."[29] If the enslaved didn't get the message, the plantation's feeding systems reinforced it. The ways that planters fed their slaves were as multitudinous as the planters themselves, but three general lines of plantation cooking developed. The black cooks in the planter's residence (often called the Big House) prepared the full range: European-style haute cuisine, high-end southern food using the finest ingredients, common fare, and Slave Food dishes adopted by whites. Aside from the Big House cook, a separate cook prepared communal meals for the field slaves. The third line of cooking involved the smaller family or individual meals slaves made in their own quarters. Big House cooking reinforced the caste system in a significant way: The master hoarded quality ingredients to make "prestige" foods—which were used only for his table—and limited access to these ingredients by the slaves. Thus, ham from the smokehouse, refined sugar, and processed wheat flour were usually off limits. Though these lines of cooking intersected, I'm primarily concerned with Slave Food prepared in the Big House and in the slave quarters.

In order to secure adequate yearlong food supplies for their labor force, planters carefully controlled the amount of staple food each slave and his or her family received. Masters usually kept a large garden and built a smokehouse to store meats, a granary for corn, a cellar for sweet potatoes, and a springhouse for fresh water supplies. Since there was no refrigeration, food was often kept cold in the cellar or in a nearby running spring. Weekly distributions from these storage units were called allowances, drawings, or rations. Rations were typically distributed once a week, usually on Saturday night when the workweek slowed. To emphasize their power, and their slaves' dependence, some planters personally distributed the rations with great fanfare.[30]

The 3 M's diet has often been computed as a weekly average ration of five pounds of corn, two pounds of pork, and a jug of molasses. The actual slave rations were more varied. In the Chesapeake Bay area and throughout the Black Belt, planters relied primarily on corn. In the Carolinas, Georgia, and Louisiana, planters doled out either corn or rice. Sweet potatoes were a popular substitute everywhere. According to one South Carolina planter, "The subsistence of the slaves consists, from March until August, of corn ground into grits, or meal, made into what is called hominy, or baked into cornbread. The other six months, they are fed upon the sweet potatoe. Meat, when given, is only by way of indulgence or favor."[31] During certain times of the year, planters in Florida and Georgia substituted sweet potatoes for corn as well.[32] In terms of meat, slaves were rationed beef, fish, and turtle meat, depending on the locale.

The rationing system was a lightning rod for attention from all directions. Planters knew that food was an important element of their near-hegemonic control over slave life. Invested in preserving the slave regime, planters shared advice on rations in the pages of specialty media like

DeBow's Review, Southern Agriculturalist, and Southern Planter. Much of the "advice" planters gave was self-serving bravado about what worked well on their plantations to increase productivity. If some planters were so concerned with the bottom line that they skimped on providing slave rations, they were apt to be scorned by their peers. A New York Times correspondent traveling through the South in 1853 writes, "If a man does not provide well for his slaves, it soon becomes known, he gets the name of a 'nigger-killer,' and loses the respect of the community."[33] Many southern state legislatures enacted minimum requirements for slave rations, mainly out of a sense of their own security. They knew that mass hunger amongst the slaves could ignite mass rebellion.

Abolitionists zeroed in on rations as a symbol of slavery's inhumanity. Antislavery publications used the 3 M's diet to show that slaves were not getting enough food, and that what they got was poor in quality. Planters retorted that even if the allegations were true, slaves were better off than other poor people around the world.

Perhaps the abolitionist critiques successfully got under southerners' skin, because some began arguing for reform of slave feeding systems in slavery's last decades. Some advocated for adequate food allotments and for introducing new foods to use as slave crops. Other writers pushed for granting slaves permission to grow their own food in private gardens rather than using a common garden for the entire plantation population. These private slave gardens were often called "provision grounds." As we'll see in the chapter on greens, the gardens proved controversial within the planter community.

The amount of time slaves could spend supplementing their diet depended heavily on their work schedule. It is often repeated that they worked from sunup to sundown, or from "see to can't see." Dr. Robert Collins, a planter from Macon, Georgia, prescribed a work schedule for slaves:

In the winter time, and in the sickly season of the year, all hands should take breakfast before leaving their houses. This they can do and get to work by sunrise, and stop no more until twelve o'clock; then rest one hour for dinner, then work until night. In the spring and summer, they should go to work at light and stop at eight o'clock for breakfast, then work until twelve o'clock and stop two hours for dinner, and work from two o'clock till night. All hands stop on Saturday at twelve o'clock, and take the afternoon for cleaning up their houses and clothes, so as to make a neat appearance on Sunday morning.[34]

If slaves didn't finish their work, they were frequently whipped. Some planters manipulated the availability of rations in order to incentivize work. In his "Directions to Overseer: June 4, 1863," William Minor, a Union loyalist planter near Natchez, Mississippi, cautioned his overseer that "when hands fail to work, rations must be stopped."[35]

Those fortunate enough to finish their tasks early had leisure time to do a number of things, including work on procuring and cooking food. Slaves supplemented their diet by fishing, foraging, gardening, and hunting as well as by cultivating provision grounds and raising livestock. Where there was an appropriate climate, the slaves raised foods they were familiar with in West Africa, often calling the plants by their West African names or a close approximation thereof. For example, the Gullahs of South Carolina used *bene*, the Bambara and Wolof word for sesame seeds, and *pinda*, the Kongo word for peanuts.[36] Livestock raised were primarily chickens and pigs, but there are numerous accounts of cows, goats, and sheep. When they had a surplus, and with the master's permission, slaves would sell to or trade with the master, poor whites, and Native Americans in the vicinity, and with itinerant traders passing through. Quite often, slaves had permission to travel to a nearby city and market their goods.

When it came to feeding their slaves, many planters centralized cooking operations and had food prepared by one experienced cook or a small team of cooks. Field slave cooks were often no longer productive workers because of old age or infirmity. Sometimes the master would supply food for the meals, but most often slaves would contribute some of their rations to communal meals while saving the rest for home use. All that the cook had at her disposal was wood to build a fire and a big iron pot that often did double duty as a wash pot after the meal was cooked. As Rawick describes, "Cooking was usually done outdoors or in a cooking shed; people sat out front of the cabins and talked and smoked; children played in front of the huts; young men and women courted whenever they could find privacy; gossip was exchanged while engaging in common chores outdoors. But this is hardly unusual. Most people, at most times and places, have lived that way."[37]

Weekday meals followed a predictable pattern. Breakfast was simple, typically some cornmeal mush or cornbread mixed up with buttermilk and served in a trough. Other times, for minimal interruption of the workday, cooks slopped the meal into a bucket that was carried out to the fields for the enslaved laborers to eat right on the spot. The big meal of the day was the noon meal. We call it "lunch" now, but in the eighteenth century it was "dinner." It was often a mixture of vegetables, milk, and bread also served in a trough. With trough feeding, it was paramount for the cook to prepare "thick" foods that could be eaten quickly with one's fingers or scooped up with something. Here, the West African tradition of thick starches and stews had been retained or passed down, so slave cooks were prepared to meet that challenge. In terms of dining accoutrements, it was very uncommon for slaves to have utensils, drinking containers, and plates. Planters had two big reasons not to provide utensils: They cost money and they were potential weapons. One former slave reported that "food was eaten either with the hands or sticks. I never saw a knife or spoon except in my master's house."[38] The enslaved improvised by using clam and mussel shells as spoons. Slaves who lacked cups got water by cupping their hands or drinking from a hollowed-out gourd (also a West African practice that reportedly improved the water's taste).[39]

After this noon meal, the slaves returned to the fields to work until sundown or when their task was finished. Then they returned to their cabins for another small meal that was typically called supper. One planter described it this way:

> They work in the field about eleven hours a day on average. Returning to the cabins, wood "ought to have been" carted for them—it is, commonly, perhaps—but if not, they then go to the wood and tote it for themselves. They then make a fire, a very great, blazing fire at this season, for the supply of fuel is unlimited, and cook their own supper, which will be a bit of bacon fried, often with eggs; Indian meal cake, baked in the spider (a cast-iron skillet with three iron legs) after the bacon to absorb the fat, and perhaps some sweet potatoes roasted in the ashes. Immediately after supper they go to sleep, often lying on the floor or a bench in preference to a bed. About 2 o'clock they very generally route up and cook and eat, or eat cold what they call their "mornin' bit," then sleep again till breakfast.[40]

Unless another communal meal was prepared, slaves cooked in their cabins. As one ex-slave remarked, "Generally there were no kitchens. Consequently, the cooking, if carried on at all in the cabin, was done in the big fireplace. They ate and slept in the same room."[41] Thus, cooking in slave cabins was limited to hearth cooking with only a spider for frying and a large pot for boiling. Unless a slave acquired a Dutch oven where hot coals could be placed on its top, baking was not an option in the cabins. This technological gap will resurface periodically in our story of soul food. All slaves technically had "leisure time" at the end of the day, but there were practical reasons why that time was not used to cook. One Virginia planter wrote, "But his love of indulgence or fatigue frequently induces him to fall asleep as soon as he reaches his cabin, and if he is unfortunate enough not to wake at midnight and cook his morning's meal (which indeed is a frequent habit with them), he is compelled to fast until his dinner hour the next day."[42] At times, the enslaved were just too tired to cook and eat.

Despite these constraints, slaves took opportunities to actively shape their diet and resist the master's hegemony. They pilfered from the master's food storage areas. They sneaked additional food out into the fields and cooked it when the overseer was not closely watching them. Some ex-slaves remember hearing a "popping" sound from eggs that exploded after they were left too long to cook in fires designed to clear land. Slaves who worked with grains wore oversized shoes to collect broken bits of grain to cook later in the cabin. Big House slaves got in on the act by sneaking leftovers from the master's kitchen to their loved ones. Daily life on the plantation, with respect to food, was certainly a cat-and-mouse game, and while the planter controlled access to food, slaves were proactive about improving their own nutrition.

The master's viselike grip on food was eased for special occasions. For slaves, a special occasion was any sustained break in the work schedule. This usually meant holidays and weekends from Saturday noon to Monday morning. On Saturday, the slaves fished and hunted, but the best feasting was usually reserved for Sunday. Though it was a scheduled rest day, slaves were still very busy. As one planter wrote in 1860,

> Sunday is the slave's own day, on all well-regulated plantations, except so much of it as their owner and require of them for washing and mending close, sharpening and repairing tools, and other necessary preparations for plantation work of the ensuing week, which must not be interrupted by these incidental avocations. . . . The Sabbath is the day for him to work for wages, cultivate his own patch, gather bottom of the market, market his chickens and his little crop of fruit and vegetables, and fit up or repair the rude comforts of his

own cabin. All this work of his own and his master's, crowded upon this single day, makes it a poor day of rest for the slave.[43]

On Sundays, slaves were allowed to prepare foods that involved prestige ingredients like whole milk, white sugar, white flour, and white cornmeal. With these ingredients and temporary access to an oven and baking equipment, black cooks made items like biscuits, rolls, cakes, cobblers, fried chicken, hams, pies, and spoonbread, which they could not do the rest of the week. Thus, in slavery, Sunday dinner was a time of some anticipation.

Sunday was also a day to worship for some. Planters felt uneasy about allowing slaves to worship for two reasons. First, a slave's conversion to Christianity could cause a range of problems from recognizing his or her own humanity to initiating manumission (emancipation) supported by state law. Second, any type of slave gathering, particularly one fueled by religious fervor, could lead to a rebellion. Consequently, planters and overseers were vigilant about slave gatherings and would disband them. If slaves wanted to worship, they had to do it in secret. Eventually, slave owners saw some utility to allowing instruction if it could be bent to suit their self-interest and to control slaves. Worship services for slaves usually meant a periodic dose of "Christianity-Lite." Typically, a white itinerant preacher or an empowered slave would preach a highly condensed sermon to the assembled slaves—obey your masters (Colossians 3:22) and don't steal (Exodus 20:15). Clearly, these sermons served the purpose of quashing any burgeoning sentiment to rebel against the existing order. Once the worship service was over, believers and nonbelievers alike gathered for a meal, so a strong association between religion, worship, and socializing grew.

The true plantation holidays were times for grand feasting. As planter James Battle Avirett explained, "The three great feasts on the plantation are Crismus, hog killin', and corn shuckin'."[44] These agricultural events provided the plantation with critical meat and grain supplies to last the entire year. Christmas was a weeklong celebration; as work was slow at that time of the year, planters allowed their slaves to rest from Christmas Day to New Year's Day. Christmas also had some buildup to it, especially in the Big House. Meats and a wide array of desserts were specially prepared. A Yule log, borrowed from English tradition, was burned to commemorate the occasion. In the slave cabins, excitement grew because it would soon be time to feast, travel to the city, and relax for a little while. The highest plantation holidays were in the fall and early winter. Blacks and whites on the large plantations usually had fairly separate food traditions, but those overlapped on Sundays, holidays, and other special occasions. Field slaves enjoyed Big House dishes or modest upgrades (using refined ingredients) of their own foods. The master and his family also gorged on presumed slave food, but such culinary convergences often get overlooked. In sum, after centuries under the yoke of a controlled diet, the cuisine of the enslaved became more Anglo-American in look, structure, and taste. West Africa remained influential, but it ceased to be the culinary source.

One of the most enduring explanations for why blacks and whites in the South have shared food traditions is that their eating patterns merged during the trauma of the Civil War. Andy Smith shows in *Starving the South* that the Union army's blockade successfully created widespread hunger in the region. Both the Union and Confederate armies began confiscating food supplies as they encountered plantations, thus exacerbating shortages. In southern cities, prices skyrocketed, in some part due to market forces, but also because of price-gouging by unscrupulous merchants. Southern cities were marred by frequent food riots.[45] Only out of sheer desperation and hunger would whites eat identifiably "black food."

A dramatic example of the Union army's successful blockade strategy (and exhibit A for the conventional wisdom on southern cooking's roots) was the capture of Vicksburg, Mississippi, in April 1863. By shutting off the flow of Confederate goods and materials, General Ulysses S. Grant struck a devastating blow to Confederate forces and to civilian eating habits. Isaac Stier, an ex-slave, recalls the hard times: "De hungriest I ever been was at de Siege o' Vicksburg. Dat was a time I'd lak to forgit. De folks et up all de cats an' dogs an' den went to devourin' de mules an' hosses. Even de wimmin an' little chillun' was a-starvin.' Dey stummicks was stickin' to dey backbones. Us Niggers was sufferin' so us took de sweaty hoss blankets an' soaked 'em in mudholes where de hosses tromped. Den us wrung 'em out in buckets an' drunk dat dirty water for pot-likker. It tasted kind salty an' was strength'nin,' lak weak soup."[46] In this desperate situation, the lines that separated black and white foodways dissolved. For a time, the vast majority of southerners ate poverty food.

3

From Southern to Soul

Before the Civil War the Southern white aristocracy literally ate higher off the hog than poor people. Their recipes were mostly British-inspired. Greens and fat back, pork ribs, chitterlings and black-eyed peas were poor people's food. But the devastation of the Civil War made food scarce. People ate what they could get, and that was mostly the foods blacks and poor whites had been living on for years. They soon came to realize how tasty these foods were, and now these dishes are part of the general cuisine. But as one black restaurateur put it, "When we eat it, they call it Soul Food; when white people eat it, they call it Southern cooking." —Marie Bianco, *Los Angeles Times*, 11 October 1984

★   ★   ★   ★   ★

What's the difference between soul food and southern food? I get that question a lot. Southern food author and writer Damon Lee Fowler once explained the difference to me this way: "Not all rectangles are squares, but all squares are rectangles." That's the conundrum. Both cuisines have so much in common that it's easy to equate the two, but there are enough distinctive elements to highlight considerable differences. Thinking of the two as shared cuisines was a gradual development. Before the Civil War, most Americans—the slave owners, the enslaved, abolitionists, poor whites, and cultural spectators—drew boundaries between what the slavers and the slaves ate in the South. To their minds, whites ate well in the Big House, and in the slave quarters, blacks ate a meager diet befitting a laboring class. As we have already learned, such thinking was a useful fiction. Prestige foods and stigmatized foods alike crossed racial and class lines in each direction. To those invested in maintaining the racial caste system of that time, the illusion that blacks and whites ate differently reinforced their sense of racial superiority.

It was impossible to maintain this illusion after the Civil War. The cumulative effect of war's human casualties, the cool efficiency of northern blockade strategies, and land seizures had made the South a very poor place. As Marie Bianco writes above, poverty food became the norm for almost everyone in the region regardless of class and race. In that historical moment, poverty food meant southern food for everyone. What often gets lost is just how widespread hunger was in the South still under the Civil War's shadow. Willis Cofer summed up the freedmen's plight: "After de War wuz over, dey jus' turned de slaves loose widout nothin'. Some stayed on wid Old Marster and wukked for a little money and dey rations."[1]

To avoid a humanitarian crisis, the federal government intervened. In March 1865, based on recommendations from the War Department, Congress established the Bureau of Refugees, Freedmen, and Abandoned Lands. Nicknamed the Freedmen's Bureau, the new entity was charged with "distributing clothing, food, and fuel to destitute freedmen and oversee[ing] 'all subjects' relating to their condition in the South."[2] The Freedmen's Bureau was given only a one-year federal charter and had to rely on the War Department for money and staffing. Still, several bureau offices were set up in southern states.[3] The bureau rationed out food supplies of pork, beef, flour, bread, cornmeal, beans, hominy, sugar, salt, pepper, and coffee to the starving masses.[4] Millions of blacks and whites received rations during those trying times.[5]

Government rations also gave freed slaves some leverage against the former plantation owners, now called landlords. Landlords used the promise of rations to induce chronically hungry laborers to work under onerous terms. Bureau representatives recognized this unequal bargaining power and often assisted laborers with negotiations, so that they would be adequately paid and fed. Government rations provided some security if laborers were unable to get work. Whites understood this as well and acted swiftly to remove that safety net by mounting a public relations campaign against rations. They argued vociferously that the government rations were a disincentive to work. By late August 1866, after mountains of unfavorable press and complaints from "prominent citizens" that "people are fed by the Bureau in idleness," O. O. Howard, major-general and commissioner of the Freedmen's Bureau, severely limited ration distributions to the sick and orphans.[6] The federal gravy train had left the station.

The rise and fall of Freedmen's Bureau rations portended what would happen to the status of African Americans in the South during the next decades. The Thirteenth Amendment to the Constitution (1865) abolished slavery, the Fourteenth Amendment (1868) guaranteed equal rights and protections, and the Fifteenth Amendment (1870) gave African Americans the right to vote. Blacks boldly asserted their new rights, yet white resistance soon blunted any progress made. The old economic, political, and social dynamics of the slave regime resurfaced after the 1876 presidential election; they coalesced in the late 1890s when racial segregation ("Jim Crow") became legally permissible. At the same time that whites were dismantling the ladder designed to help blacks improve their social condition, they used popular culture to reinforce caste position. One mode was to ingrain into the public consciousness that blacks were best suited for servitude. Food—growing it, cooking it, and eating it—proved an effective vehicle for redrawing caste lines. Elite southern whites wanted to get back to the ideal of eating higher-end foods dutifully prepared by blacks.

Food played a useful role in creating vicious caricatures of African Americans during the Southern Cooking era. Images of blacks eating fried chicken and watermelon were pervasive in white popular culture through newspaper articles, illustrations, and minstrel shows, which played to packed audiences nationwide. Since media outside the South were all too willing to transmit this racial propaganda around the country, it was part and parcel of our earliest national popular culture. Anyone who consumed such information in the late nineteenth century got the message that blacks are born cooks—thus, cooking jobs are best for them—and that they eat weird foods. Food was used to make black people the "other."

How did the black people who remained in the South respond to the stereotyping, and did it match up with reality? Unfortunately, little is written about what rural southern blacks ate during the 1870s and 1880s. What do exist are descriptions of the foods eaten during festive occasions. These foods weren't that much different from the prestige foods of the slavery era. What did change significantly was the context.

In the rural South, the very best food was showcased at Emancipation celebrations, holiday events, and black church gatherings. Of these, church gatherings were the most frequent and the most vital to community life. The black church was the undisputed center of social activity, and for those trying to live a moral life, there were few options.[7] Driving home this point a century later, Edna Lewis recalled, "The church was more of a social setting than it was for religious purposes."[8] Since church social functions featured the best foods, rural blacks gave those foods an elevated status. Such good times called for fried chicken, fried fish, cakes, sweet potato pies, red drinks, and watermelon. Whites often observed these conspicuous communal and public celebrations from afar and got grist for their mill of endless stereotyping.

The food news wasn't all bad. Black entrepreneurs continued to start and run food-related businesses with zeal. As in urban areas before Emancipation, as slavery scholar Ira Berlin reports, "the most common black enterprises were the small cook shops and groceries, which usually doubled as saloons and gambling houses where free Negroes, slaves, and occasionally whites gathered."[9] Formerly enslaved cooks tended to run small restaurants or became caterers or street vendors. Others went into various aspects of food retailing based on the particular expertise they had gained during slavery.[10] Since the caste lines in urban slavery had been dissolving for some time, urban blacks had appreciable opportunities to prosper. Entrepreneurs ate well, but the urban poor, like their counterparts in the countryside, struggled to get an adequate diet.

Blacks who continued to live in rural areas had few employment options other than getting an agricultural job. Southern whites might have lost the ability to use physical force to compel blacks to work, but they created a society with mechanisms that netted the same results. As late as 1946, white Mississippian Farris Craig summarized a demoralizing continuity from slavery to modern times: "You know, things in the south can't hardly be understood by any northerner. This is not so much different than in the slave days except now the Negroes get paid instead o' jus' bein' fed and given things. My sharecroppers are always a little in debt to me for things I give 'em and so I can keep 'em here to pay off their debts. It's a good thing to keep them on your place a little in debt to you. It keeps 'em more contented. It keeps 'em from runnin' away."[11] Any plantation landlord could easily have said the same in 1886, 1906, or 1926. The naked manipulation of labor arrangements and subsequently the laborer's food by the landlords created a weird social stasis that lasted all the way up to the Soul Food era.

There were three options for anyone who wanted to farm during the Southern Cooking era. One could be a landowner, a renter, or a sharecropper (giving the owner a share of crops in exchange for remaining on the land). Owners had legal title to their land; they raised livestock and gardened and thus faced the typical challenges in raising their crops. Owning land was uncommon for black farmers because racist whites created many barriers to ownership. To complete even the simplest land deal, one would have to approach a white landowner, ask for permission to make an offer on the land, and then make the offer with another white person to vouch for one's reputation. Even those with enough money to purchase at a premium could be refused. Whites knew that landownership meant independence, and that contravened the appropriate caste status for blacks in the Jim Crow South.

Regardless of race, landowners and their families had the best diets of all the agriculturalists. With proper planning, a black landowner's family could eat well, as we learn from Sara Brooks, an owner's daughter raised in Alabama:

> And when we're workin' in our field, my mother'd bring dinner to the field and we'd eat under the trees. She'd bring one big bucket of peas, and then in another bucket she'd have greens. We's always gonna have those peas and greens—be cabbage greens or collard greens—she's gonna boil a pot every day. And we'd always have cornbread. Then sometime she'd bring milk she'd maybe churned before dinner, and we had meat—big old hunk of boiled meat. . . . And then to top it off we'd always have some sweet. We'd have syrup bread, or we'd have a big old apple pie or some kinda pie or another—berry pie or peach pie.[12]

Throughout her memoir, Brooks mentions other foods like sweet potatoes, butter beans, turkey, guinea fowl, okra, and fish.

The next step down from owning was renting. My paternal grandfather, Samuel Miller, was a rent farmer in rural Arkansas, not too far from present-day Helena. "Mr. Sam," as many called him, began farming cotton in the 1920s and stayed with it until the mid-1960s. The renter's status and diet depended on the landlord's temperament. Fortunately, my grandfather worked for a fair-minded landlord. He paid a certain amount up front to farm the land annually and kept all the remaining proceeds from the harvest. All other expenses were left for my grandparents to manage—no small feat when you have thirteen children. From what my father, aunts, and uncles have told me, their foods and foodways were similar to those of owners; but sometimes their larder was adequate, and other times it wasn't.

Sharecropping, also called tenant farming, was a real snare, yet it was the most common situation for blacks who farmed. Sharecroppers ("croppers" or "tenants") came to the landlord with nothing; they relinquished a share of the crops produced and were highly dependent on the landlord for farming supplies. Croppers were doomed from the moment they had to get an advance from the landlord to pay for supplies. To add insult to injury, the landlord usually charged an additional 10 percent interest on the advance. Croppers felt the only way to get out from under their suddenly mounting debt was to cultivate as much of the cash crop they were assigned to grow and hope for the best.

Since croppers usually began the farming season in debt, they had a strong incentive to minimize any kitchen gardening and use all available land to grow the cash crop assigned to them by the landlord. Thus the cropper's family grew less of their own food, and they had to purchase food from other sources.[13] By design, the landlord usually ran a nearby store that supplied the croppers with food and other essentials. Croppers had to buy small amounts of food in cash—10 cents' worth of this, a nickel's worth of that—but most often they got credit, which was added to the mounting debt owed the landlord. Rarely did croppers come out ahead. Even when they did, the landlord would manufacture extra charges or reasons why they were still in debt. Thus, croppers typically entered the next growing season in debt, ready for the cycle to begin anew. As a result, croppers grew even more dependent on the store-bought food than on homegrown food.

Landlords rarely invested in giving their croppers updated cooking equipment, on the grounds that it was an unnecessary expense. As a result, rural black families were slow to get stoves and had to cook by boiling, frying, and roasting food in ashes. Just as in slavery times, cooking was done on a hearth or outside. Sara Brooks, who grew up in an owner's family in 1920s Alabama, remembers, "We didn't know about makin' *beef* roast or anything like that 'cause everything was boiled 'cause we didn't have no stove. So we used to cook on the hearth—my grandmother used to cook there."[14] Even as late as the 1960s, it was not unusual for a black rural residence to lack electricity, running water, and utensils.[15] Urban landlords treated their black tenants much the same way and did not provide electricity, gas, or running water in many cases.[16]

As a result of these constraints, croppers of both races developed a monotonous meal pattern. In his book *Human Geography of the South*, author Rupert Vance summarizes cropper foodways this way:

> For his noon meal in winter the board presents cornbread and that pork boiled with a vegetable, preferably potatoes, dried beans or cow peas, turnips, or turnip greens, collards or cabbage. Baked sweet potatoes also ranked fairly high, while boiled rice and canned tomatoes are less likely to be present. For beverage the tenant's first

choice is water, his second coffee, with milk a lagging third. If he desires a dessert, the syrup pitcher sits on the table the three meals through and possesses first call. During the garden season he has more green vegetables, but cornbread and boiled pork remain the universal staple. . . . This is a fair, and many will contend, a generous picture of the nutritional regimen of a third of the rural South. The vast majority of Negroes and many more white people than commonly realized live the year around on such a diet.[17]

Blacks and whites in similar circumstances were eating similar food, and usually not enough of it.

Chronically hungry blacks consistently relied on donated food (called "relief") from public and private sources. At first, plantation landlords were suspect about relief, thinking it would undermine work incentives. Once the landlords realized that donated food cut down their own expenses, they eased their opposition.[18] Relief was allocated in the South in such a way that landlords controlled the amounts and quality of food families would get. Surveys of relief distribution in the 1930s and 1940s show that, on average, rural whites tended to get more assistance in absolute terms than rural blacks. Whites in the North and South rationalized giving blacks less than adequate aid with the notion that blacks were adept at surviving on very little.[19] No doubt the notion was based on a reality— blacks called their own resourcefulness "making do." But the paltry aid— combined with systemic and economic factors—meant blacks were frequently stuck in a vicious cycle of getting barely enough food to survive but never enough to put them on the path to becoming self-sufficient.

Despite the hurdles, many blacks did manage to leave the South. This was not so easy to do in some instances, particularly if the plantation landlord was vindictive and wanted to maintain the status quo. Sometimes entire families left suddenly in the middle of the night to catch the landlord off guard. Other times, an individual would leave, establish a life in a new place, and then send for other family members. For several decades, emigration from rural areas happened slowly, with appreciable numbers moving to the North, the Midwest (commonly called "Exodusters"), the West, and urban areas within in the South. Still, the typical African American at the turn of the twentieth century was poor, rural, and working in agriculture. As author Douglas Blackmon notes in *Slavery by Another Name*, "In 1910, the vast majority, more than 93 percent, of the 10.2 million African Americans living in the United States continued to reside in the South. Nearly 60 percent of adult black men and nearly 50 percent of black women worked in farming."[20]

By 1970, that demographic profile had dramatically changed. During a six-decade period beginning in 1910, known as the "Great Migrations," millions of African Americans had moved to urban areas—primarily in the North and South—but to other parts of the country as well.[21] As Map 4 shows, three patterns held during the Great Migrations: Migrants from the western edge of the Black Belt, most notably Louisiana and Texas, populated much of the West Coast, particularly California. Those on the Atlantic seaboard headed for northern coastal cities like Washington, D.C., Philadelphia, New York City, and Boston. Those in the middle of the Black Belt (Mississippi, Alabama, and Georgia) settled in midwestern cities such as Chicago, Cleveland, Detroit, and Milwaukee. These massive migrations launched what I call the Down Home Cooking era.

Before the Great Migrations, the smaller number of black migrants who settled in urban areas during the 1890s actually tried to eat more like other Americans. Anthropologist Robert T. Dirks examined dietary studies conducted in Tuskegee, Alabama; Washington, D.C.; Philadelphia, Pennsylvania; and Franklin County, Virginia, around the turn of the twentieth century. The news flash here is that many foods associated with soul food were not initially the core diet of urban and rural blacks.[22] Dirks concludes in his study, "The relative absence of 'hog and hominy' on the urban side, thought to be a matter of trying to appear respectable, probably was as much a matter of cost and convenience. Fresh red meat in metropolitan areas could be purchased for about the same price as salted and smoked pork fat, and cornmeal was more expensive than flour."[23] In short, black migrants made their food choices based on rational economic decisions that could trump tradition.

During the Great Migrations, black migrants arrived in cities with tastes cultivated in the country. Depending on their economic circumstances, they were used to eating mostly vegetables (leafy greens, dried beans, sweet potatoes) particular to the South; varying amounts of salted or smoked pork; fish and chicken; corn-based dishes; maybe some wheat bread; a limited range of beverages (water, buttermilk, coffee, powdered soft drinks); and a few desserts. Much of the food was either boiled or fried. Unlike those of the generation before them, the tastes of the more recent migrants bent solidly toward familiar southern foods even when it didn't make economic sense. Jean Mayer, a professor of nutrition, wrote

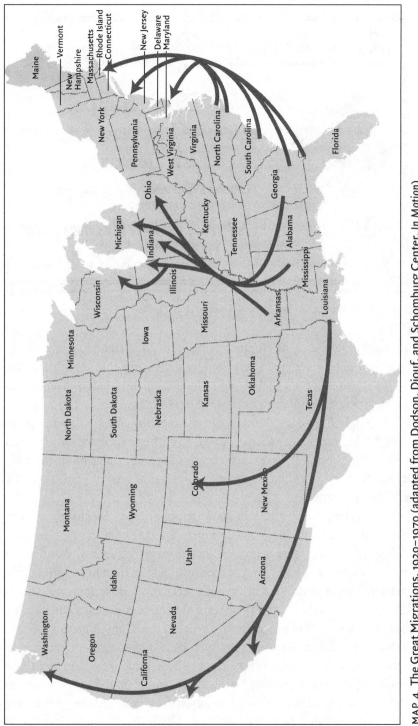

MAP 4 The Great Migrations, 1920–1970 (adapted from Dodson, Diouf, and Schomburg Center, In Motion)

Home Cooking Restaurant advertisement, 1910, Denver

in 1972, "Southern-born Negroes living in the North tend to retain Southern food habits, often at great inconvenience and cost."[24] Initially, the migrants couldn't get their familiar foods, but fortunately, black street vendors did sell southern favorites.[25] Street vending reached its apotheosis in places like 1930s Harlem, where passersby could hear a street cry called "The Harlem Menu" that laid out an entire week's menu of southern foods.[26] In providing these tasty, cheap, and recognizable foods (lovingly called "letters from home"), street vendors maintained cultural continuity for the migrants.

Eventually grocery stores in black neighborhoods adequately stocked southern foods, and black-run restaurants began showcasing the same. A few black restaurants in the new locales were "high class," but the vast majority were "low end." They had colorful names to indicate specialties, such as "ankle joint" (featuring pig's feet) and "whale stations" (fried-fish joints in Harlem), and there were also barbecue stands and chicken shacks. Though this was definitively the Down Home Cooking period, it took time for that name to stick. As black newspaper advertisements show, restaurant proprietors were apt to label their bill of fare "southern cooking" or "home cooking." Still, those monikers did evoke some regional sentiment. Migrants had to adjust from a place where life's pace was slow and isolating to the hustle and bustle of a crowded city with all of its distractions. Eateries offered an oasis—a place where you could get familiar food in a familiar setting—albeit in an alien locale. Getting some southern food into one's belly had to be a confidence builder and a cure for homesickness.

The black church, now in an urban setting, also met the food needs of the migrants in a number of ways. Churches provided emergency food supplies to migrants as they transitioned into getting a place to live and employment. Perhaps it was a peculiarity of the black community that its church went beyond donating lunch and launched food businesses. As early as 1917, Harlem's Metropolitan Baptist Church ran a butcher shop and a grocery store for the benefit of its congregation.[27] As in rural areas, church was a place for blacks to gather in the city, so naturally food and socializing blossomed together. Over the course of the Down Home Cooking era, church-affiliated restaurants literally fed (and grew) congregations around the country.

These public food options were important because the migrants had so many challenges to preparing food at home. Some simply didn't know how to cook for themselves and had to eat out. Excessive or irregular work hours for parents meant fewer sit-down family meals and a lot more improvised meals, snacking, and restaurant eating.[28] "The Promised Land" didn't live up to expectations. Jobs weren't as plentiful as migrants thought, and whites in the North were not as colorblind as believed. Speaking in 1971, Sababa Akil (formerly known as Willie Tolbert), summed up the feelings of many migrants that had come before him: "My whole family picked cotton until, when I was six or seven, we moved to the North—except it was still the South. I view the South as being, as Malcolm [X] says, 'Everything south of Canada.'"[29] Additionally, established blacks in the community pressured the new migrants to put aside their country ways, including country food. In a horrid replay of the rural South they had left, black migrants found themselves on the bottom of a different racial caste system—unemployed, underemployed, and ostracized—less in status than other recent arrivals to the cities, namely the Irish, the Eastern European Jews, and the Southern Italians. For them, city life "meant poor and cramped housing, meager kitchen facilities, cheap clothing, and little money to spend for food."[30]

As their ancestors did, the black migrants adapted to challenges set before them. Black migrants often lived in tenements once occupied by the initial waves of Eastern and Central European immigrants in the 1880s, 1890s, and 1900s. With the arrival of large numbers of black migrants, housing pressures were immense, so landlords reconfigured the tenement spaces to pack in as many people as possible. One expert noted, "City apartments with space at a premium are often built with little shelf and cupboard space."[31] This wasn't the good old rural South where black folks were used to keeping food in a smokehouse or putting it down a cool well, in a running stream, or under the house. Since there was little or no storage in urban apartments, food purchases were kept small. Tenement landlords also controlled the ability of families to cook when they devised a system called "kitchen privileges." Under this system, tenants paid extra to use a kitchen at certain times during the day or week.

Because of mounting concerns about living conditions and chronic hunger, Natalie Joffe, a nutritionist, did a pivotal government-backed study of black food habits in the early 1940s. Her work shows that "even in the North, where it is usual for refrigerators to be standard kitchen furnishings, many of the families have not access to them, for the payment for 'kitchen privileges' frequently includes only the use of the stove and sink."[32] In Chicago's heavily black "Bronzeville" neighborhood, "Kitchenettes are single rooms, rented furnished and without a lease. Sometimes a hot-plate is included for cooking, but often there are no cooking facilities despite the name. Hundreds of large apartment buildings have been cut up into kitchenettes to meet the routine housing shortage in the Black Belt."[33] Many skipped the kitchen privileges because they couldn't afford them. For those who did use kitchen privileges, utility costs were so high that they utilized cooking techniques that required less energy— quickly frying on high heat or simmering over long periods of time rather than roasting and baking. Thus, the boiling and frying culinary traditions carried over from the countryside and directly into urban slum kitchens.[34] Even when urban black cooks had better-equipped kitchens, a pattern of boiling most food during the weekdays and frying on the weekends persisted well into the Soul Food era.[35]

Some of the strategies to supplement food that blacks had developed in the rural South didn't translate well in new urban environments. Initially very few living in public housing had the space to plant a substantial garden; they couldn't hunt; foraging for pesticide-dusted greens and fishing in city waters for toxin-marinated fish were pretty bad ideas. It would be several decades before urban folks would clamor to raise chickens.[36] The primary caregiver often had to work outside the home to make ends meet. However, unlike in the South, blacks in the North working in private homes or restaurants could not bring home leftover food and feed it to their families (a practice called "toting" in the South, derived from an African word meaning "to carry"). Parents had to wait until their days off to make better meals for their families. As a consequence, urban black families increasingly relied on government and relief organizations for supplemental food.[37] Private individuals, charities, and churches distributed food to needy blacks from the earliest days that they arrived in the cities. Government assistance programs really didn't play a significant role until the Great Depression sparked a massive response to change the bleak economic conditions facing all Americans.

As the United States emerged from the Great Depression after World War II, African American social prospects were slowly progressing. Southern blacks began making civil rights gains in the 1950s, and the urban black middle class began to expand thanks to well-paying blue-collar jobs. These gains and other factors fed a racial consciousness that had not existed before, as well as a collective feeling that things, including food, were changing for the better. Formerly class-conscious blacks who had shunned "country food" no longer felt ashamed to eat that cuisine in public. As a 1960 *Philadelphia Tribune* article reported, "Some of Philly's most prominent lawyers, medics, politicians and businessmen eat regularly at Dell's Restaurant, an eatery which serves 'down home' food, which ten years ago was frowned upon by the masses of the so-called 'elite' Negro society. Now it's considered fashionable to eat 'down home' cooking."[38]

Those Philly diners, and others around the country, yearned to connect with their black brothers and sisters in the transforming South. Down home cooking, as a metaphor for the South, provided an opportunity to do so, even if an individual was not involved in the burgeoning civil rights movement. As black consciousness continued to rise, regional names like "southern" and "down home" for the traditional food of African Americans no longer sufficed. It needed a new name, one defined by black people, and that would be "soul food."

Conventional wisdom is that "soul food" was first coined in the 1960s as part of the Black Power movement, an adjunct of the civil rights movement, and then was quickly co-opted by America's mainstream media. That sequence of events is partly correct. The hidden history of the term "soul food" actually takes us back to the Elizabethan Age. William Shakespeare first joined the words together in his earliest play, *The Two Gentlemen of Verona*. The characters Julia and Lucetta are eyeing a hot guy named Proteus, and Julia says, "O, know'st thou not his looks are my soul's food? Pity the dearth that I have pinèd in, By longing for that food so long a time."[39]

Though Shakespeare uses "soul food" in a decidedly secular way, over the next 400 years, Europeans gave "soul food" a religious connotation. The term described ways to enrich one's spiritual life, to "feed one's soul," as it were, through hearing a sermon, saying your daily prayers, or studying scripture.[40] By the twentieth century, blacks also used "soul food" in the same way. In 1927, the Reverend Walter P. Stanley, an African American who was railing against corrupt preachers, told a black audience in Baltimore, "It is the minister who feeds the alley dwellers with soul food on Sunday while he takes the hard earned money they put in the collection plate and makes for the cool open spaces in a high powered automobile."[41]

A couple of decades after the good reverend's comments, soul food took a decidedly musical turn. In the 1940s, out of frustration, black jazz musicians began using "soul" in a secular sense. They were tired of whites' continued success at co-opting and cashing in on black art forms.[42] To stop that trend, black musicians took jazz to a place where they thought white artists were unable to go musically and mimic their sounds. That "place" was the sound and feel of the black church of the rural South. As one jazz commenter noted in a Down Beat magazine article, "The motivation, in my opinion, can be traced more to racialist feeling as Negroes than to the further development of jazz as art. It is as if they had the challenge at their white colleagues: 'Copy this if you can.' The Gospel feeling is indisputably theirs, and they know it."[43] These musicians started using the terms "soul" and "funky" to describe this new but old sound.

White record company executives, who saw the dollar signs in the term "soul," packaged it for white audiences, just as they had previously done with "race" records and "rhythm and blues." Both "funky" and "soul" quickly spilled out of the jazz subculture and spread throughout other aspects of black culture in the 1950s, including cuisine. "Funky" could have been the word that caught on, but "funky food" doesn't sound too appetizing. "Soul food" is the name that stuck. Not everyone was thrilled with the new term. The wealthier and more conservative elements of the black community, newspaper editors and columnists chief among them, saw the ubiquitous use of "soul" as merely a fad. They kept using "down home cooking" to describe the same foods that were newly christened "soul food." Thus, the two descriptive terms coexisted in black culture for some time. Others thought its use was profane because the usage was cheapening a word so strongly associated with church.

Though "soul" got attached to music first and food later, "soul food" evoked the black church just as well. Even by the time of the Soul Food era, rural and urban blacks still shared the black church as their main social center. As Joffe observed of both groups in the 1940s, "The most common pattern of community eating is the church supper, to which parishioners bring donations of food. These are occasions for pride in the display of one's skill as a cook and the women vie with each other for recognition. The Sunday dinner is another time for display and it is on this occasion that guests are most often invited to share a meal."[44] Hubert Maybell, the Chicago soul food restaurateur who gave us a good definition of soul food earlier, says of these church meals, "Everybody brought what they could afford. Nothing was charged for the food; it was a kind of sharing, and they called it 'feeding the soul.'"[45] By the late 1950s, "soul food" had transitioned from a mostly religious term in black culture to one that sat on the seam where religion, popular culture, and foodways intersected. Things became more complicated when racial politics got thrown into the mix in the 1960s.

On 1 February 1960, four black college students decided to challenge segregation by sitting down at the "whites only" lunch counter at the Woolworth's in Greensboro, North Carolina, and ordering—appropriately—apple pie. Following that bold move, a wave of successful sit-ins organized by college students happened throughout the South. A similar ripple effect had occurred in the 1940s when the Congress of Racial Equality (CORE) successfully utilized sit-ins to integrate restaurants throughout the North and the West.[46]

Sit-ins were a popular form of resistance with young activists, and their success snowballed into the formation of the Student Nonviolent Coordinating Committee (SNCC). SNCC was unique in that it contained a mix of black and white college students, most not from the South, who felt compelled to help foster racial progress in the South. Buoyed by the organization's success with sit-ins, SNCC leaders pivoted to registering black voters as their key initiative. The sit-ins received differing levels of white disapproval. Some places desegregated more easily than others. The sit-in victories were a great step forward, but going to a restaurant was still out of reach for the rural poor. The voter registration drives in the rural South, however, brought a torrent of opposition. Instead of taking important steps to change a culture, as the sit-ins did, increased political power derived from voter registration meant a possible change in the material condition of southern blacks.

In the early 1960s, Greenwood, Mississippi, was a hotbed for SNCC electoral activities, and it became a flashpoint of white resistance. White local government officials retaliated against SNCC's successful organizing in their communities by withdrawing from federal food assistance programs. They knew "that the surplus food was the only way many Negroes make it from cotton season to cotton season. If this is taken away from them, they have nothing at all."[47] SNCC workers responded to the sudden food shortage with a successful food drive that symbolized a turning point in local racial politics. SNCC's efforts buoyed the spirits of the rural blacks and linked food with politics. In the words of SNCC leader Bob Moses, the food collected was "food for those who want to be free," and being free meant registering to vote. Moses also argued that the food distribution helped SNCC gain "an image in the Negro community providing direct aid, not just 'agitation.'"[48] From that point, SNCC focused more on "how to put bread in people's stomachs."[49]

Yet race became increasingly salient for African Americans, and a focus on economic issues receded. "Something is happening to people in the Southern Negro community," remarked former SNCC leader and future congressman John Lewis in the spring of 1964. Lewis added, "There's been a radical change in our people since 1960; the way they dress, the music they listen to, their natural hairdos—all of them want to go to Africa. . . . I think people are searching for a sense of identity and they're finding it."[50] SNCC's next leader, a Trinidadian-born Howard University student named Stokely Carmichael (later Kwame Toure), gave the people what they wanted.

Stokely Carmichael became SNCC's chairman in May 1966 by riding a wave of black consciousness that led to expulsion of the organization's white workers and volunteers. Carmichael continued to push the envelope on crushing segregation even when others, including Rev. Martin Luther King Jr., had advised moderation. In 1966, Carmichael preferred a more "in-your-face" approach and began advocating for something he called "Black Power."[51] Carmichael was certainly not the first person to use this phrase, but he delivered the term with such great effect that he became its voice. When white America first heard the phrase, it lost its collective mind and questions abounded. What in God's name is Black Power? More importantly, how it is going to affect America's existing power structure?

After being coy for a considerable amount of time, the Carmichael-led SNCC finally laid out a Black Power philosophy in a position paper excerpted in an August 1966 New York Times article. In that paper, SNCC discussed food in a manner that changed the course of soul food history. "White people coming into the movement cannot relate to the black experience, cannot relate to the word 'black,' cannot relate to the 'nitty gritty,' cannot relate to the experience that brought such a word into being, cannot relate to chitterlings, hog's head cheese, pig feet, ham hocks, and cannot relate to slavery, because these things are not a part of their experience."[52] Though SNCC didn't use the exact words, they transformed the marketable, happy-go-lucky term "soul food" into edible Black Power.

Soul food was now a rallying cry for black solidarity. A cuisine 400 years in the making, melding African, European, and Native American influences, was now wholly black-owned. No matter where one lived, any black person could bond with another over this particular type of food. Many black entrepreneurs cashed in by writing cookbooks and opening restaurants showcasing the cuisine. Some stayed true to soul food's political roots. Black students protested to have soul food on the menus of high school and college cafeterias. Race pride was flying high, and this new attitude toward food achieved the same purpose that the jazz sound previously did.[53] It took food to a place where whites couldn't go—the black experience. The African Heritage Cookbook author Helen Mendes captured the soul food ethos when she wrote in 1971, "Soul food unites African-Americans not only with their people's history, but with their contemporary Black brothers and sisters around the world. Food is a symbol of love. Today, as never before, Blacks are learning to love their color and each other. It is appropriate that when they and their friends meet that they should share the symbol of this new-found love—Soul food."[54]

At first it worked, but the love feast didn't last long. Unwittingly, SNCC's definition, inspired by Carmichael, also planted the seeds for soul food's poor image. First, SNCC focused on the most hard-core poverty foods of the area where Carmichael organized—Black Belt Mississippi. Remember, Carmichael was not native to the region, and it's highly unlikely that local whites invited him over for dinner; so he didn't get a chance to see that they actually ate similar foods. In effect, SNCC's position paper cemented soul food with blackness, pork, and poverty in the public imagination. No doubt had SNCC presented a laundry list of foods from the region, they wouldn't have had the same impact. At least they could have mixed it up with some poultry, seafood, and vegetables! By equating Black Belt food with soul food, SNCC and early soul food boosters glossed over the rich and varied culinary traditions within the black community. The Chesapeake Bay, the Lowcountry, and the Lower Mississippi Valley cooking styles were all subverted to Black Belt cooking because that was the true poverty food. To outsiders, soul food became shorthand for all African American cooking.

The conscious effort to create, politicize, and racialize soul food runs against the typical immigrant food story. After all, that was the point. Americans tend to identify immigrant cuisines more by ethnicity, nationality, and race than by place. We use the terms "Chinese food" and "Italian food" instead of "Cantonese Province food" or "Southern Italy food." Depending upon the motive, ethnic food labels can benignly describe "the exotic things that group of people eats" or malignantly stigmatize the strange foods of foreigners. Yet, we can tell when immigrants, or at least their food, have been accepted by the majority culture—their food is no longer viewed as "ethnic." Bagels, hamburgers, hot dogs, and pizza, all once strongly identified as ethnic foods, are now fundamental components of the American menu. Where soul food diverged from other immigrant cuisines was in its explicit rejection of the white mainstream. Soul food's authenticity now lay in its outsider status, thus complicating the path for the broader acceptance of both the cuisine and the people who eat it.

Once soul food took hold as a concept, its dissenters within the black community were legion. Race-conscious blacks used soul food as a litmus test for blackness, which created a backlash from those who supposedly failed that test. The most enduring critiques were about the cuisine's consequences for bodily and psychological health. This was nothing new. As early as the 1920s, black doctors had exhorted readers to change their down home cooking diet.[55] Well into the 1970s, the chorus became stronger. Several alternative diets were advocated on the heels of soul food's debut. A slew of vegetarian soul food cookbooks presented menus based on African American food traditions minus the meat.

The other prominent critique focused on the supposed ridiculousness of celebrating this cuisine that descended from slave food. Black nationalists, including prominently the Nation of Islam, argue that eating soul food internalizes notions of white superiority that the master purposefully foisted upon the enslaved.[56] To this day, Nation of Islam sentiments and parlance season even the perceptions of blacks who aren't affiliated with the group. A telltale sign is when a black person calls pig's flesh "swine" instead of "pork." Class fissures also reasserted themselves within the black community. In addition to their earlier critiques of the term's faddishness and profanity, many upper-class blacks snubbed the cuisine as poor people's food.[57] Others were offended by the shallowness of the newfound connection to the poor. Black Panther activist Eldridge Cleaver, writing from California's Folsom prison in November 1965, blasted the view that the emergent cuisine is empowering: "You hear a lot of jazz about Soul Food. Take chitterlings: the ghetto blacks eat them from necessity while the black bourgeoisie has turned it into a mocking slogan. . . . The people in the ghetto want steaks. *Beef Steaks*. I wish I had the power to see to it that bourgeoisie really *did* have to make it on Soul Food. The emphasis on Soul Food is counter-revolutionary black bourgeois ideology."[58]

The white responses to soul food's apparent militancy were varied. Conservative whites fought against soul food's spread by refusing to serve it in restaurants, at high schools, and on college campuses, even in the face of protests. Most whites, especially those in the South, tended to react with a shrug. Soul food had no implications for their diet. At home and in restaurants, they continued to eat southern food, often made by a black cook, which was remarkably similar to the soul food that was supposedly outside their experience. White hipsters in urban areas continued their forays into black neighborhoods for soul food. Students at colleges where soul food was served experimented with the unfamiliar food during Black History Month, and teenagers of the era dove into fast food. Some whites saw an opportunity to make money. A congressional inquiry headed by U.S. Representative Henry S. Reuss of Milwaukee in 1968 found that grocers had huge (borderline obscene) markups on soul food items. When the findings were made public, Reuss's hometown newspaper, the *Milwaukee Star*, ran a headline screaming, "Chittlins Make Merchants Rich."[59] The cruel irony was that soul food—poverty food by definition—became too expensive for many poor blacks to afford.

White southern cooks also asserted their own race consciousness around food. Most significantly, media accounts of southern cooking whitewashed the cuisine by rarely mentioning the black cooks who greatly contributed to it (a circumstance that sadly continues to this day). Thus, an entire generation of black cooks became invisible. Cookbooks on Appalachian foods had been in print for some time, but the late 1960s and early 1970s saw a spike in "hillbilly" cookbooks. In terms of caricature and dialect, the cookbooks had a lot in company with the Mammy cookbooks of prior generations. About a decade later, in the late 1970s and 1980s, Louisianan Cajuns got a good run thanks in no small part to their televised ambassador, Justin Wilson. Ernest Matthew Mickler also made a splash with *White Trash Cooking* in 1986 and managed to take a few jabs at soul food. He wrote, "If you live in the South or have visited there lately, you know that the old White Trash tradition of cooking is still very much alive, especially in the country. This tradition of cooking is different from

'Soul Food.' White Trash food is not as highly seasoned. . . . It's also not as greasy and you don't cook it as long. . . . [It] has a great deal more variety."[60] Even white trash food had more to offer than soul food!

Meanwhile, back in the kitchen, black cooks continued to practice their craft. Some were conscious of the broader cultural and racial implications of making soul food; others were conscious of the past—an immediate past of honoring a type of cooking that had been passed down within their family. With this backdrop, let's now eat our way to the representative meal that's waiting for us on the table.

4

Fried Chicken & the Integration of Church & Plate

Legend says that the chicken is a holy bird, a gospel fowl. . . . These chicken worshippers say that in the spring time if a rooster sees a preacher coming he will warn all the chickens to hide and will declare war on the parson. I conclude that the chicken is an indispensable food in Virginia. Not for all the crisp fried chicken, it might even be baked and some Cavalier might broil this holy bird, but not me, No, sir, as a preacher, I would not think of approaching the chicken house after dark—unarmed.
—Anonymous African American Baptist preacher, ca. 1939, in Thomas, "Chicken"

★ ★ ★ ★ ★

I had never heard of "Gospel Bird," or the "Sunday cluck," for that matter, until I flipped through *Juba to Jive*, Clarence Major's dictionary of African American slang, in the mid-1990s. According to Major, the terms have been in southern usage since the 1930s. Both mean a "barnyard chicken, so called because in the south fried chicken was a favorite on Sunday, the Christian holy day, especially if the preacher was coming to dinner."[1] I could not help but laugh—only my people could invent these expressions. Intuitively, I got the punch line, but I wasn't really in on the joke. Though attending a black church has been a big part of my Sundays, I can't say the same for eating fried chicken. We were just as likely to have a beef roast. Suddenly faced with an existential crisis as to how authentically black my childhood in suburban Denver was, I had to speak with family. As it turned out, simply asking my southern-born-and-bred parents chilled me out.

Apparently I was born in the wrong place and the wrong time. For my parents, the Gospel Bird was a Sunday regular, carrying on a practice from the Slave Food period, rooted in West African religious belief. Over time, fried chicken became a culinary icon with strong religious connotations. Through the Down Home Cooking period, it was consciously linked in

African American culture to the preacher and to church social events in a process I call the integration of church and plate.

A caveat before we begin. For some—and not just those who aren't religious—what follows may be hard to swallow. A familiar practice for black preachers is to tease their audience about forgetting their roots. In that context, fried chicken is used as a symbol of a humble background or unpretentiousness. Now I myself would have had trouble believing this, had I not personally, and frequently, witnessed black preachers using fried chicken to illustrate their points. Seriously, do any clergy outside of the black church actually *preach* using fried chicken? While others may not invoke fried chicken with the same fervor, many people eat some form of chicken on their days of religious observance. French Christians got a lot of boiled chicken after King Henri IV (1553–1610) declared, "I desire that every worker in my kingdom shall be able to have a chicken in the pot on Sunday."[2] Raymond Sokolov, who has written extensively on Jewish foodways, once quipped, "A hundred million Sabbaths have begun on Friday nights throughout the Jewish universe with a roast chicken."[3] In the South, fried chicken gets the nod on Sundays, and this is a shared tradition for blacks and whites. In 1897, the *Atlanta Constitution* saw the connection and reported, with some perplexity, "Why fried chicken should invariably be the accompaniment for religious outings, such as campmeetings and Sunday School picnics, has never been explained."[4] And they were talking about *white people!* Knowing that southern whites share the tradition, it takes a lot of pluck to argue that fried chicken has been cooped up in the black church and, consequently, black culture.

Okay, I'll give you this: African Americans don't have full ownership of Sunday dinner and traditions featuring fried chicken, but they gave them a distinctive spin. Just as African American musicians drew on the rural southern church to make funky jazz and earthy blues, African American cooks went to the same cultural pantry to make fried chicken sacrosanct. Making fried chicken on Sunday evoked memories of the church supper that began as small gatherings during slavery but grew into major social events after Emancipation.

How did chickens get associated with black religion in the first place? Could it simply be that one of my West African ancestors bit into some glorious fried chicken and exclaimed, "My [insert your favorite deity], this is good!"? I had a moment like that after tasting a garlic-bits-studded bird prepared by the late, and legendary, Chef Austin Leslie of New Orleans. It was so good that I almost genuflected. When chickens were introduced into precolonial West Africa, several tribes considered them a sacred bird. However, chicken eating was not a uniform practice in the region, given the variety of religious beliefs and culinary traditions.

West Africans were not the only peoples who marveled when they came into contact with these creatures. Sometime between 7500 B.C.E. and 5000 B.C.E., people living in South and Southeast Asia also domesticated the jungle fowl (*Gallus domesticus*), ancestor of modern-day chickens.[5] The locals who first raised chickens considered them divine and highly valued the animals as instruments to predict the future.[6] Divination was so prized in the ancient world that some experts believe it was this trait, and not the chicken's value as food, that spurred humans to domesticate chickens in the first place.[7] And since they can't fly well, chickens began to be transported to other parts of the world by traders.

As merchants traveled along the westward trade routes, they introduced these strange, wondrous animals to potential customers. In order to close the deal, some traders talked about the chicken's fortune-telling prowess, some boasted about the thrill of cockfighting, and others advocated that chicken was just good eating. Whatever they said, it usually worked. As chickens crossed the Island of Rhodes to get to the other side of the Mediterranean, they were an instant hit with the Arabs, Greeks, Phoenicians, and Romans by at least 500 B.C.E. Because different cultures variably used chickens for food, entertainment, and religious purposes, a patchwork of chicken beliefs coexisted throughout Eurasia. When Arab traders introduced chickens to West Africa by 1000 C.E.,[8] their debut was nothing short of sensational.

Why were chickens so special in West Africa? Since antiquity, birds played a central role in several tribal mythologies, from stories of the earth's creation to explanations of their gods' actions. For some tribes, chicken was considered a taboo food, but many West Africans began integrating the newly arrived chicken into their bird-related folklore and religious systems in place of indigenous birds that previously served the same function. The Ashanti of Ghana developed a belief that a golden hen was a proxy for their god. The Yoruba of Nigeria believed that chickens were the god Odudwa's helpers in spreading life by scratching up the earth's surface, and possibly replaced pigeons in the original story.[9] Like their counterparts in South and Southeast Asia, West Africans valued chickens for spiritual purposes—as diviners and sacrificial animals—rather than for entertainment, as many Europeans did. As a result, native birds like guinea fowl, which previously had spiritual significance, were demoted.

Chickens arrived in West Africa when the region was urbanizing and once-isolated tribes were becoming more connected. Kevin MacDonald, an archaeologist specializing in West Africa, explains that "the chicken and other foreign goods entering the area would have found a society controlled by elites with wide trading networks. If they had arrived previously they may have been assimilated economically with little additional consequence, but they arrived at a time when West Africans were experiencing a greater degree of social self-awareness and inter-communication than ever before. . . . It was probably at this point that cocks acquired their widespread iconographic value as symbols of power and divinity."[10] With their irresistible combination of supernatural mystique and urban glitz, chickens became the "New Thing," making local birds so "yesterday."

As powerful cultural tastemakers, West African elites were in the best social position to actually possess chickens and manipulate chicken images in their architecture, art, and emblems. One of the most significant transitions was the increasing use of chickens instead of native birds during ritual sacrifice—a clear indication of the new bird's prestige. This symbolic shift also communicated to people with less status that the elite possessed access to divinity, power, wealth, and wisdom. The elites deftly gave themselves legitimacy by assigning special importance to the new animal, which they had an abundance of in their possession. Elites also proclaimed they could directly speak to the gods through these special creatures; so in a couple of smooth moves, elites managed to solidify their own powerful status.

We see how the chicken was used in the public spaces of some West African societies, but what about on the table? Specifically, was chicken fried in the West Africa of yore? The necessary preconditions for fried chicken were certainly present in the region: plenty of chickens, a strong tradition of frying foods in vegetable oils, and the development and use of iron cookware that can withstand the high heat of frying for prolonged periods of time. Yet we can't say for certain that fried chicken existed in precolonial West Africa; Arabic sources provide little commentary on chicken eating during the Middle Ages.[11] One of the few instances of chicken recorded during the Atlantic slave trade points to a chicken and rice dish served in Gambia in 1686, very much like it would be served today.[12] Though we lack convincing evidence of past practice, fried chicken is popular in contemporary West Africa. One expert on West African cooking observed that "there is a notion in Africa that even in the most impoverished households a good housewife will have at least one chicken, specially reared, in her backyard to prepare when an important guest visits the family unexpect-edly."[13] Otherwise, West African cooks these days resort to "stretching" the chicken by breaking it down into small pieces for use in a sauce, soup, or stew.[14]

While it's difficult to assert a clear African provenance for American-style fried chicken, some evidence points to Britain. The earliest written recipe that looks like the American-style preparation appeared in 1747 in Hannah Glasse's *The Art of Cookery Made Plain and Easy*.[15] The British cook-book was wildly popular in the American colonies during the eighteenth century, and American housewives who made the dish would have fol-lowed Glasse's recipe. In the nineteenth century, Americans began to assert their own way to make fried chicken, and two states laid claim to having the best method. Neither one was Kentucky. The first iconic southern-fried chicken recipe appeared in Mrs. Mary Randolph's *The Vir-ginia Housewife* (1824). Remarkably, fried chicken's basic formula has been pretty resilient in the nearly two centuries that have passed since Mrs. Ran-dolph's recipe was published. Edna Lewis, building on Mrs. Randolph, de-scribes Virginia fried chicken as floured pieces of chicken that were "fried in sweet, home-rendered lard, fresh-churned butter, and, in addition, we would put in a slice or two of smoked pork for flavor."[16] Other Virginia-style recipes call for bacon or ham. To use today's poker parlance, Virginia cooks loved to double-down on pork flavoring. The rival state and style was Maryland fried chicken. With this approach, chicken was battered and fried in shallow fat while the frying pan was covered, thus, the chicken steamed through. This style of chicken was traditionally served with gravy and waffles or corn fritters.[17] As fried chicken spread across the country, cooks riffed off these two basic versions of American-style fried chicken by varying the coating, the fat, the flavors, and the gravies served alongside.

Still, there have been two big changes in contemporary American fried chicken culture. First, many people started frying their chicken with vege-table oil instead of lard in the earlier twentieth century. This change was gradual, though, in African American circles, for Ruth Gaskins and Edna Lewis called for lard in the fried chicken recipes of their respective cook-books in 1968 and 1976. The other big change is that eating chicken no longer carries "outsider status," because Americans are eating a lot more of it these days. Mark Bittman writes in the *New York Times* in 2012, "This country goes through a lot of chickens: We raise and kill nearly eight bil-lion a year—about 40 percent of our meat consumption, compared with roughly 30 percent beef and 25 percent pork."[18] This is a remarkable change from a century ago, when beef and pork were by far the dominant proteins on American tables.

No one knows for sure how and when enslaved West Africans were first introduced to American-style fried chicken, but it probably happened in the Big House kitchens of some southern plantations. William Byrd II, Virginia's slave-owning governor, wrote about eating fried chicken in one of his 1709 diary entries, but no recipe is given. Undoubtedly, enslaved cooks fried the birds that Governor Byrd ate, building the black cook's reputation for making this particular dish. Virginia's enslaved cooks gained such wide fame for fried chicken in the colonial period that the combination of fried chicken and hot bread was nicknamed a "Virginia breakfast."[19] We could surmise that black cooks were so good at making fried chicken that they invented it at some point, but that's pure conjecture. But it's safe to say that, despite its obscure origins, a particular type of fried chicken developed in the American South, that many times enslaved African Americans were doing the cooking, and that *everyone* was doing the eating. Fried chicken belongs to all of us.

As enslaved West Africans formed a common culture in British North America, differing attitudes about chickens were reconciled. It was commonplace for slaves to raise their own chickens, often astonishing white observers with their success at doing so.[20] Chickens were an important part of the plantation economy. From their hens, slaves got a steady supply of eggs that could be sold to the master for money or bartered for goods from other slaves and poor whites who came to the plantation boundary fence to trade. Some slaves, often the aged or disabled, were given special privileges to sell chickens and eggs in nearby towns once they were no longer productive in the fields. On rare occasions, slaves earned enough money to buy their freedom and, if the master was willing, that of other slaves. With a rooster, the slaves got the necessary and natural partner to make more chickens and a reliable alarm clock. Plus, plantation cooks treated fried chicken as a seasonal specialty. Back then, chickens hatched in the spring (hence the term "spring chicken"), and cooks often waited until around their first birthday to cook them. These young chickens provided flavorful, tender meat when cooked. Older chickens were better for stewing. Even with all of those chickens available, the thought of killing and eating a chicken gave slaves pause, as it meant sacrificing a future income stream for the passing pleasure of a full stomach.

Once someone made the decision to prepare fried chicken, an elaborate preparation process ensued. The chicken must be selected (often a rooster instead of a lucrative hen); caught; killed (by wringing the neck until the head came off and the headless body ran around); plunged into scalding hot water to ease plucking the feathers; plucked; gutted; run over a fire to singe and remove the remaining pin feathers; and butchered into large pieces. At times, this hours-long process could get messy. Then the chicken was prepared according to recipe. A survey of slave narratives and interviews with former slaves shows that fried chicken rarely strayed from Mary Randolph's basic formula of floured chicken seasoned with salt and pepper and cooked in boiling lard. Finally, the chicken must be fried for fifteen to twenty minutes before it is thoroughly cooked and gloriously crunchy. Multiply this amount of work by several chickens, and one understands that traditional fried chicken takes a lot of time.

Fried chicken's long preparation time played a role in the gradual development of the Gospel Bird. Slaves, including the field cooks, had the most leisure time on weekends and holidays, which coincided with the observances of the Christian Sabbath and other days of religious importance. Slaves had varying levels of religiosity. Though all of them thought of the work stoppage as leisure time, only a segment associated it with religious observance. This irked masters and clergy alike, who believed that the Sabbath was not meant for partying. Early in the eighteenth century, Dr. Francis Le Jau, a minister in Goose Creek Parish, South Carolina, wrote that it "has been Customary among [the Negroes] to have their ffeasts [sic], dances, and merry Meetings upon the Lord's day."[21] At these frowned-upon "Negro feasts," dishes like fried chicken were invariably served and likely brought to mind good times rather than religion.

In the early decades of the nineteenth century, religiosity increased among whites across the country, as well as within slave communities. For the as-yet-unconverted, Sundays were still a day to catch up on personal chores, procure food, sell things at the market, and enjoy leisure activities. But for the increasingly religious slaves, Sunday activities meant a worship service with a communal meal afterward free of sinful entertainment but full of savory fried chicken. These communal meals invigorated the connection between fried chicken and religion.

The growing cohort of religious slaves set in motion the rise of another cultural icon—the black preacher. As planters relaxed their objections to slave religion, some took their slaves to church with them or allowed their slaves to worship on their own, provided they were supervised by a white preacher. In time, the white supervisors selected slaves with a gift for oratory to deliver the sermon, as long as it had a proslavery message.

In the plantation South, these were the first black preachers. Planters forbade unsupervised slave worship because such meetings could lead to a rebellion. In response, slaves employed a variety of tactics to conceal their worship services. Using his gifts of communication, coordinating sanctioned and covert worship services, and embodying God's representative, the black preacher gained significant status within the slave community.

That improved status conferred certain privileges on the black preacher—one being a steady diet of fried chicken. Somewhere along the line, perhaps remembering the past tributes to West African elites, slaves honored someone by feeding them fried chicken. The religious overtones of such edible "gifts" were emphatic for a black preacher within whom his congregants saw a direct link to God. Even the nonclergy could get in on the act, as Union soldiers could attest to during the Civil War. Scholars Jualynne Dodson and Cheryl Townsend Gilkes observe that "given enslaved women's and men's constraints in terms of their access to more adequate food supplies, serving of chicken may have been a way of honoring those who were part of the 'army of the Lord,' as the Union Army was termed by these African Americans."[22] Dodson and Gilkes also point out that escaped Union soldiers who were harbored by slaves complained about being fed too much chicken.

Though plenty of people ate fried chicken on Sundays, a stereotype emerged in the postbellum South during the nineteenth century that Sunday fried chicken was really meant for black preachers. There's a grain of truth to be pecked at here. Rural black preachers could be described in many ways, but "well paid" was not often one of them. Given their meager compensation, preachers looked forward to a nice after-church meal at the home of one of their congregants. For the reason described earlier, that meal often featured fried chicken. The seemingly benign custom of entertaining preachers for Sunday dinner gave rise to one the most traumatic collective memories for children raised in rural areas during the Southern Cooking era. I know because I heard it firsthand from my father.

My father grew up in a large family (he had twelve brothers and sisters) in rural Arkansas. My grandmother had developed a strong reputation as a cook, so the preacher was a frequent Sunday dinner guest at the Miller household. The obligatory fried chicken dinners meant bad news for both the chickens and the kids. My grandmother would dispatch one of the kids to get a chicken from the yard, to kill it by wringing its neck, and to start the preparations. My grandmother took over during the cooking phase, so everything was ready when the preacher arrived. Once the family was seated and grace was said, the preacher, as the honored guest, picked his preferred pieces of chicken (eventually nicknamed the "preacher's parts"), and then the remaining adults at the table got their pick. The kids would have to wait to eat until after the adults were done, *no matter how long it took and no matter how much they ate*. One of the few drawbacks to gloriously fried chicken is there's only so many pieces to go around. Not only did the kids shoulder the tough job of prepping the chicken, but many times chicken feet were all that was left for them to eat! They had no choice but to sop 'em up with some gravy.

This scene happened routinely in many black households across the rural South. Go ahead. Ask any African American over sixty who grew up in the rural South about those Sunday dinners with the preacher. You're going to hear a lot about fried chicken and longing, and perhaps a groan. Such a collective cultural experience had its good side and bad. On the bad, legions of hungry children quietly seethed as the preacher got preferential treatment. Many vowed that they would never do that to their own children. Some, like my father, lost a taste for chicken. They carried with them too many bad memories of wrung chicken necks and chicken feet–flavored breath. Understandably, the fried-chicken-and-preachers stereotype was a mild form of revenge. The stereotype mushroomed in black popular culture, inspiring songs, rich stories, and endless jokes. Country preachers were very aware of this stereotype, and some joined in on the fun. They really didn't have much to lose, because the expectation remained that when they were over for dinner, they better get some amazing fried chicken.

On a positive note, at least one person channeled his resentment over a childhood of eating chicken bones, feet, and necks into entrepreneurial success. In a 1985 newspaper interview, Harold Pierce—the self-proclaimed "Fried Chicken King"—of Harold's Chicken Shacks said, "When I was a child [in Midway, Alabama], the preacher came to our house and ate all of our chicken. I told my mother then, that when I got to be a big boy, I'd open up my own chicken place."[23] He did so in 1950 and ended up with much more. At the time of the interview, Pierce had thirty-eight stores in Chicago's predominantly African American neighborhoods that served up made-to-order "Chicago-style" fried chicken doused in hot sauce and resting on a bed of fries. Fortunately, some good things eventually did come to those who had to wait for their fried chicken.

Sunday fried chicken dinner in the rural South preserved and transmitted some important cultural values: reverence for God by observing the

Sabbath, respect for the preacher as God's representative, the feast as an acknowledgment of God's continued blessings, and the importance of family and community. As Ruth Gaskins, who lived her entire life in Alexandria, Virginia, writes in A Good Heart and a Light Hand cookbook, "Two or three times a year, the preacher came to dinner. No one had to remind us about our manners, because it was understood that if you ever wanted desserts again, you'd be extra careful that day."[24]

By the late 1800s, the black preacher stereotype was just one of several ways that all black people were yoked with chickens in white popular culture. Some of the enduring stereotypes date back to slavery, when whites made much of enslaved blacks stealing, selling, extraordinarily frying, and extensively eating chickens. At a time, blacks were depicted as being like chickens. In 1882, the New York Times ran an anonymous article saying, "The fact of the existence of this close affinity between colored men and chickens is so plain as to be impossible of denial, but its secret elusive. It is true that the negro and the chicken have many tastes in common. They are alike fond of gay colors, of singing at inopportune hours and in a way adapted to cast a gloom over the neighborhood, and of eating at all times and to an unlimited extent."[25] The purpose of all of this stereotyping was to underscore that the recently emancipated African Americans are still the "other."

The urban Sunday dinner tradition of the Down Home Cooking period certainly continued the integration of church and plate, but it differed from the rural tradition in two ways. First, it was less about the preacher coming over and more about gathering loved ones together. Urban preachers made fewer home visits than their rural counterparts, presumably because they were paid better and had larger congregations. Second, somewhat contrary to the prevailing stereotypes, urban and rural African Americans didn't eat that much fried chicken at home.[26] As Joffe notes, "Fried chicken is a 'company' dish and so is fricassee, but there are many who never have the opportunity to eat it, even on Sunday."[27] Unlike in the countryside, chickens were not readily available in the city; crowded tenement buildings didn't come with a poultry yard, and some lacked the necessary equipment to fry chicken. The newcomers had to look for fried chicken outside the home if they were going to get their fried chicken fix.

Street vendors were one option for fried chicken, and they did a brisk business selling this dish. A Boston newspaper swooned in 1908: "A choice delicacy of the curb lunch is fried chicken. It is the top liner too as to price, commanding double and in some instances triple the rate of the

Chicken and Waffles

African Americans feel a proprietary claim on chicken and waffles mainly because of its folkloric connection to Harlem, the longtime, unofficial cultural center of black America. An oft-repeated chicken-and-waffles creation story goes something like this: In Depression-era Harlem, jazz artists finished their gigs in the wee hours. Hungry for something to eat, musicians and club-goers alike went to a local restaurant run by Joe Wells. Since it was too late for dinner and too early for breakfast, Wells satisfied his customers by inventing fried chicken and waffles as a hybrid meal. Its popularity spread far and wide. A great story, but it's not true. This tasty combination is much older than the 1930s.

According to William Woys Weaver, a culinary historian, German settlers known as the Pennsylvania Dutch made chicken and waffles smothered in gravy a Sunday dinner dish during much of the nineteenth century.[1] The fried version was popular in the Big House kitchens of the antebellum South. By the early 1800s, a "Virginia Breakfast," featuring a combination of fried or baked meats with any sort of hot quick bread, was the gold standard of plantation hospitality. At these meals, fried chicken was a regular star, just as likely to be paired with a biscuit, cornbread, pancakes, or rolls as it was with a waffle. It was often enslaved African American cooks who made the Virginia Breakfast possible. After Emancipation, these same cooks frequently made chicken and waffles for social events in the black community, and also as professional cooks in elite hotels, resorts, and restaurants patronized by wealthy whites. Through their culinary talent, African American cooks effectively mainstreamed chicken and waffles by the early 1900s. Though the dish fell out of the mainstream a few decades later, chicken and waffles continued to thrive in African American homes and restaurants.

---

1 Author communication with Weaver.

more plebian edibles of the street. Colored men seem to have a monopoly on the fried chicken trade, as it is confined almost exclusively to them."[28] One finds similar accounts written for other urban areas, big and small, around the country. Fried chicken vendors catered to a very diverse clientele, including upper-class whites, and many street vendors prospered in this trade. African American–owned restaurants were another outlet for fried chicken, but these tended to be run-down, informal places. Sometimes black entrepreneurs ran illegal restaurants and flouted local law.[29] Black businesspeople have historically lacked the access to capital needed to establish and maintain a nice sit-down restaurant, and that problem remains to this day. Restaurants that were successful usually offered fried chicken as a Sunday dinner special. African American restaurants specializing primarily in fried chicken (known as "chicken shacks" or "chicken houses") begin to pop up in black neighborhoods in the 1920s and 1930s.

The black church itself became a welcoming place to get fried chicken. Sometimes it came as part of "free feeds" and other times during a church fundraiser. The most enduring memories of church suppers have come from their communal quality. Harlem's Mother African Methodist Episcopal Zion Church was profiled in the 1980s for its church supper tradition. Speaking of the church's longtime cook, Roland Baker, the *New York Times* wrote,

> Mr. Baker, who is 69 years old, represents a link in an unbroken tradition as old as the black church itself, a tradition that is observed by the congregations in most of Harlem's 350 churches: the communal Sunday dinner. The Rev. Calvin Butts, executive minister of Abyssinian Baptist Church, a block north of Mother Zion, says that the tradition "has a deep biblical as well as social and cultural meaning. It goes back to the early days of the church, back to slavery," he says. "It has to do with communion. Communion was a meal, a feast of love. It is a kind of extension of our Africanness."[30]

Though the Gospel Bird lost its overt connection to dinners with the preacher in the cityscape, the social aspect still proved vital.

The fried chicken dinners were so popular that churches gave them top billing at fundraisers and on their restaurant menus. Perhaps no one was better at mixing business, fried chicken, and religion than a fascinating character named Father Divine. Father Divine, aka Major Morgan J. Devine, aka George Baker, aka "God himself," arrived in Long Island, New

York, shortly after World War I. Divine quickly established a reputation for being a good preacher and leader by gaining converts with his message of God's divinity within each person, racial equality, and immediate prosperity. Father Divine's genius was to focus his church in the present, not on a futuristic afterlife, and address social conditions caused by the Depression. Divine's followers were starving for something new, and he gave it to them by calling on an old favorite for black preachers: fried chicken. A mainstream newspaper piece from the 1930s reads more like an ad than an article:

> Father Divine has something. It isn't the U.S. treasury. He hasn't congress in his hat and he doesn't collect taxes. There is a simple secret missing in the New Deal, by the communists and the Nazis, by social credit, Dr. Townsend and Upton Sinclair's classic. Father Divine is not dealing in futurities. When he says fried chicken he means fried chicken. It's in the pan. His promised land is not far off across the desert. Here's the gate and here it is. The country is wasting a lot of time on persons who promise and don't deliver. Father Divine is calling: "Come and get 'em while they're hot."[31]

Divine's followers opened up locations in various cities across the country during the 1930s and '40s. While dining at one of Divine's restaurants, you probably felt like you were in heaven. First of all, the restaurants were called "Heaven," so that helps. Also, the Heavens did double duty as dining and worship spaces. Third, the restaurants offered gargantuan meals that could be purchased for an amazing low price. And finally, all of the Heavens were fully integrated. Diners got a glimpse of a future America that seemed otherwise impossible at the time. Whatever their background, patrons were united by the "We specialize in fried chicken" sign that hung at every Heaven's gate, I mean, door.[32] The Heaven restaurants passed away soon after Divine died in 1965.

The other prominent fried-chicken-entrepreneur-pastor was Bishop Charles Manuel "Sweet Daddy" Grace, who founded the United House of Prayer for All People (UHOPFAP) in 1919. By the time of his death in 1960, Grace had garnered millions of followers. Many of Grace's churches started restaurants across the country, and several are still open for business. In 1986, *Washington Post* restaurant critic Phyllis C. Richman reviewed the United House of Prayer restaurant (now called Saints Paradise Café) in Washington, D.C., the way she would have done for any other restaurant (and the review was positive).[33] My personal favorite of this "chain" is Masada Kitchen, which is operated under the UHOPFAP Hudson Hill Mission in Savannah, Georgia. The day I visited, at the end of Masada's buffet line, past the wall full of the local accolades for "Savannah's best fried chicken," sat Saint Iretha Durham, who manages the restaurant.

While gospel music played in the background, a very welcoming Saint Durham told me about her interracial clientele who are beckoned by her award-winning fried chicken. She also told me about how the Devil was up to no good (my words, not hers), since several local chefs kept sending spies to ask questions about her fried chicken hoping to discern the magic formula.[34] Once I took a bite, I could taste the reason for all of the subterfuge. In my youth, I loved batter-fried chicken, not just for the taste, but for the audible entertainment it provided. I really wanted to hear that crunch! Now that I've put aside my childish ways, I favor the simple approach employed at Masada Kitchen. The fried chicken had a thin, papery crust seasoned with salt and pepper that clung to moist chicken meat without completely shattering after a bite. I know this is impossible, but the fried chicken seemed almost greaseless. Craig LaBan, restaurant critic for the *Philadelphia Inquirer*, described this phenomenon to me as "straight-ahead fried chicken" when we ate a similarly textured bird at Deborah's Kitchen in Philadelphia. I've applied that term to really good fried chicken ever since.

To date, these Divine- and Grace-inspired restaurants are the closest we've come to a national, African American–owned fried chicken chain. There are successful black-owned, regional chains like Ezell's (one of Oprah's favorites in Seattle), French's (Houston), The Golden Bird (Los Angeles), and Harold's (Chicago), but they remain regional favorites. There's certainly a hungry public clamoring for fried chicken, especially given the explosion of Asian-style and Latin American–style fried chicken places emerging in recent years. Even white-tablecloth restaurants are showcasing fried chicken. Black-owned chains are probably hamstrung by the lack of resources to expand nationally. In this context of persistent financial constraints, the church restaurant phenomenon makes even more sense. The church is one the few black institutions with enough resources to pool and to start up and operate businesses. Even with that possibility, an identifiably black, national fried chicken chain goes wanting.

Yet this vision almost came true. For a fleeting moment in the late 1960s to early 1970s, Mahalia Jackson (1911–72), the nation's greatest gospel

"Straight Ahead" fried chicken, Deborah's Kitchen, Philadelphia

singer, launched a national fried chicken chain. The marketing strategy was brilliant, given the racial tenor of the time. The company would have one fried chicken recipe sold by two independently operated chains, which separately targeted black and white consumers. Jackson would be the face of the black-oriented fried chicken chain, and the eccentric country-culture icon Minnie Pearl would sell the same fried chicken to whites. Since Jackson was a gospel star, the marketers hit the religious themes pretty hard. Perhaps a little too hard. Advertisements spoke of "Gloree-fried" chicken, how the spirit will move you into the restaurant, while you heard the mmm's and uh's of a church service in the background. According to one observer, the Jackson restaurants even looked like churches:

"The white brick, carry-out chicken stores look like highly stylized, modern churches, with their red roofs climbing to high-pointed peaks. Flying buttress wings, carrying signs shaped in the elongated oval of cathedral windows, flank the stores on either side."[35]

It was an ambitious endeavor, mixing Black Power, entrepreneurism, religion, soul food, and savvy marketing. The restaurants were envisioned to be black-owned, black-marketed, black-managed, and black-staffed. The menu featured a variety of fried chicken boxes and dinners, fish sandwiches, and sweet potato, apple, and peach fried pies.[36] The first restaurant opened in Chicago in 1968, with a second Chicago location by 1970. Additional outlets were planned for several other cities, and the new restaurants operated in combination with Gulf Oil service stations.[37] The only problem was the restaurant didn't attract enough followers. If there is a bigger gripe from black businessmen than the inability to get capital, it's the historic lack of support for black businesses by black people. Benjamin Hooks, the former NAACP leader, served as CEO for the nascent chicken chain. Looking back on the endeavor in 1993, he lamented its demise by saying, "It was supposed to be a place black people would go to. . . . But I still remember seeing them walk on past on the way to Colonel Sanders."[38] Within a few years of opening, the Mahalia Jackson fried chicken chain couldn't generate enough revenue, and it kicked the bucket. Though renamed, two orphans of the chicken chain remain open. One is Mayo's and Mahalia Jackson Fried Pies & Chicken in Nashville, Tennessee, and its slogan is "The Way Grandma Used to Cook." Jack Pirtle, formerly associated with Kentucky Fried Chicken (now KFC), took over the Mahalia Jackson location on Bellevue Street in Memphis.

Considering the meteoric rise and fall of the Mahalia Jackson fried chicken chain, Hooks's observation is telling. Here was the most well-financed public expression of the Gospel Bird concept during the late '60s/early '70s Soul Food era, but it lasted a fraction of the time that the Father Divine- and Daddy Grace–operated restaurants did during the Down Home Cooking period. Perhaps the biggest shift from one era to the next was desegregation. Mahalia Jackson was trying to win converts at a time when blacks had much more choice about where to eat. The 1950s saw the rise of fast food chicken places, which had cut heavily into the black restaurants' customer base by the time Jackson was trying to make her entrepreneurial mark. There's a saying in the black community that "the white man's water is colder." It speaks to the internalized belief that something offered by whites, even if identical to what blacks offer, will be superior.

Sign advertising Mayo's and Mahalia Jackson fried pies and chicken, Nashville

Certainly Hooks recognized that mentality was at play when his chain lost customers to Kentucky Fried Chicken. Another setback for Jackson's endeavor was that she launched her chain when the Gospel Bird, or the idea of it, was in transition.

The Gospel Bird concept thrived when people considered fried chicken the appropriate choice when they communed in religious settings or at family gatherings. Over time, fried chicken became a secular convenience food that could be eaten in any context; the symbolic bird no longer resonated in the same way. Had Mahalia Jackson's fried chicken chain been launched a generation earlier, that Gospel Bird may have taken flight. But, like me, Jackson's novel fried chicken chain was born at the wrong place and the wrong time.

Marta's Oven-Fried Chicken

Marta Wallace spent years perfecting this recipe because she wanted something lighter than chicken deep-fried in oil. I've been friends with Mrs. Wallace's daughter Anne since we were children. Mrs. Wallace used to volunteer in our high school's library, and one day I told her that she was beautiful, just like a southern belle. She graciously thanked me and then gently told me that she's from Utah. Perhaps she's from the southern part of Utah because this baked chicken gets close in taste to the southern fried favorite.

Makes 8 servings

> 8 chicken breast halves, preferably boneless with skin
> ½ cup (1 stick) butter or margarine, melted
> 1 cup all-purpose flour
> 1 teaspoon onion powder
> 1 heaping teaspoon garlic powder
> 1 heaping teaspoon lemon pepper
> 1 heaping teaspoon Lawry's Seasoned Salt

1 Preheat the oven to 400°F.
2 Rinse the chicken pieces under cold running water and pat them dry.
3 Pour the melted butter into a shallow baking dish large enough to hold the chicken in a single layer.
4 Mix the flour, onion powder, garlic power, lemon pepper, and seasoned salt in a large zip-top plastic bag. Working with one or two pieces of chicken at a time, add them to the bag, close it tightly, and gently shake to coat the chicken evenly in the flour mixture. Arrange the coated pieces skin-side down in the baking dish.
5 Bake the chicken for 15 minutes. Turn the pieces over and continue baking until the coating is golden brown and the chicken is cooked through, about 10 minutes more. An instant-read thermometer inserted into the thickest part of the meat should register 165°F. Drain the chicken on paper towels and serve warm, at room temperature, or chilled.

Corn Flake Fried Chicken and Cheddar Waffles

Fried chicken and waffles is a great playground for cooks. It's a chance to play off different flavors and textures. This version of chicken and waffles pairs very crunchy, slightly salty fried chicken with a tangy cheddar cheese waffle. I adapted this recipe from Hannah Sweets, a private chef who witnessed the rise of chicken and waffles in Aspen, Colorado, of all places.

Makes 4 to 6 servings

BRINE

½ cup kosher salt
¼ cup sugar
2 tablespoons black peppercorns
10 garlic cloves,
    peeled and crushed
2 bay leaves
1 cup buttermilk
2 cups water

CHICKEN

1 (3- to 4-pound) chicken,
    cut into 8 pieces
1¼ cups finely crushed corn flakes
2 cups all-purpose flour
1 tablespoon Old Bay Seasoning
1½ teaspoons poultry seasoning
¾ teaspoon dried thyme
¾ teaspoon granulated garlic
2 teaspoons dried parsley
5 teaspoons paprika
1 tablespoon kosher salt
2 cups buttermilk
6 garlic cloves, finely chopped
2 large eggs
Vegetable oil, for deep-frying

WAFFLES

4 cups all-purpose flour
1 teaspoon salt
1 tablespoon baking powder
¼ cup sugar
¼ teaspoon ground nutmeg
¼ teaspoon ground allspice
2 large eggs
3 cups milk
⅔ cup vegetable oil
¼ teaspoon vanilla extract
½ cup grated sharp
    white cheddar cheese
Maple or agave syrup, for serving

1 To brine the chicken: Mix the salt, sugar, peppercorns, garlic, bay leaves, buttermilk, and water in a very large bowl. Stir until the salt and sugar dissolve. Refrigerate until well chilled, at least 1 hour.

2 Submerge the chicken in the brine, cover, and refrigerate for 3 hours. Drain the chicken and discard the brine. Pat the chicken pieces dry and arrange them skin-side up in a single layer on a wire rack set inside a rimmed baking sheet. Cover lightly with plastic wrap and refrigerate overnight. Remove from the refrigerator, uncover, and let sit at room temperature for 30 minutes.

3 To fry the chicken: Mix the corn flakes, flour, Old Bay, poultry season-ing, thyme, granulated garlic, parsley, 1 tablespoon paprika, and salt in a large, shallow dish. Whisk together the buttermilk, chopped gar-lic, remaining paprika, and eggs in a large bowl.

4 Coat the chicken pieces with the corn flake mixture, dip them into the egg mixture, and then coat them again with the corn flake mixture. Arrange the coated pieces in a single layer on a platter that has been lightly dusted with flour, to rest while the oil heats.

5 Fill a deep fryer or a large, deep, cast-iron skillet with oil to a depth of 2 to 3 inches. (For safety, the oil should not fill the skillet more than halfway.) Heat the oil to 365°F on a deep-fat thermometer. Preheat the oven to 250°F. Set a wire rack inside a rimmed baking sheet lined with paper towels.

6 Cook the small pieces separately from the large pieces. Lower no more pieces of chicken than can float freely into the hot oil. Fry until the coating is brown and the meat is cooked through, about 12 min-utes for small pieces and about 17 minutes for large pieces, turning once midway. An instant-read thermometer inserted into the thick-est part of the meat (avoiding bone) should register 165°F. Reduce the heat if the coating darkens too quickly before the meat is done. Transfer the cooked pieces to drain on the prepared rack and place in the oven to stay warm until all of the chicken is fried and the waffles are ready to serve. Repeat with the remaining chicken, letting the oil return to 365°F between batches.

7 To make the waffles: Preheat a waffle iron. Set a wire rack inside a rimmed baking sheet.

8 Whisk together the flour, salt, baking powder, sugar, nutmeg, and all-spice in a large bowl. In another bowl, whisk together the eggs, milk, oil, and vanilla. Whisking constantly, pour the egg mixture into the flour mixture and stir until the batter is smooth. Stir in the cheese.

9 Bake the waffles according to the manufacturer's directions. Transfer each freshly cooked waffle to the rack. Keep them warm in the oven until all of the waffles are ready.

10 To serve: Divide the warm waffles among serving plates and top with warm chicken. Serve with maple syrup.

5

Catfish & Other Double Swimmers

Small fish should swim twice. Once in water, and once in oil.
—*Good Housekeeping Magazine*, January 1900

Then we had plenty of fish too, and Boss, I'se sure do likes fish. I had rather have
fish than all the other kinds of meat. Of course, negroes they all likes fish. When
you sees them that don't like fish they is something wrong with that negro.
—Louis Cain, Madisonville, Texas

★　★　★　★　★

"Tell my wife to fear God and cat-fish!" Those were the last words of a
man swallowed up by a huge catfish in Zora Neale Hurston's classic short
story collection *Mules and Men*.[1] More than a fish tale, the story serves as a
morality play: The protagonist mocks God by skipping church to fish on
the Sabbath and suffers the consequences. Hurston has given us a case
of art imitating life, and a useful hook for explaining the catfish's iconic
status in African American culture. Hurston grew up in Eatonville, an
all-black town in central Florida that's close to a lot of lakes. I like that
Hurston has linked catfish and sin in this story because catfish has had a
double life in the black community. On one hand, it's a favored fish that
shows a strong connection to West Africa. On the other hand, catfish is
often associated with sin. Some (Nation of Islam, Seventh-day Adventists)
consider it taboo to eat ("edible sin") because it's a bottom-feeding fish.
Caste-conscious whites considered it a "sin" to eat catfish because that's
what black people ate. At times, God-fearing people linked catfish with
depravity since it was often the choice entrée at raucous fish fries. On the
dinner plate, in perception, and at social gatherings, fried catfish has long
been the yang to the Gospel Bird's yin. Yet, the catfish's story is also one
of redemption. Catfish has done a lot to rehabilitate its image since the
Soul Food era began, and everyone loves a comeback. Like fried chicken,
catfish has broken into the American mainstream, losing its close (and

previously negative) association with blacks while maintaining a central place in the soul food repertoire. Looking at catfish history, we also witness a surprising continuity of West African foodways.

West Africans have been big fish eaters at least since medieval times.[2] While details of how precolonial West Africans fished and ate are scarce, written accounts have survived to show that fishing was not some sleepy pastime, but a thriving industry that fed local tribes on the coast and along interior rivers and that allowed these same tribes to provision and trade fish for goods with interior tribes and Europeans.[3] Nineteenth-century English adventurer Mary Kingsley provides fascinating detail on traditional fish customs in West Africa during the late 1800s,[4] revealing striking parallels to African American fishing and fish preferences. Kingsley documents West Africans using European techniques like the hook and line, poisoning water sources with herbs, and manufacturing traps and baskets to catch fish.[5] Kingsley also reports an interesting fishing method called "spearing": "It is carried on at night, a bright light being stuck in the bow of the canoe, and the spearer crouching, screens his eyes from the glare with a plantain leaf, and drops his long-hafted spear into the fish as they come up to look at the light. It is usually the big bream that are caught in this way out in the sea, and the carp upstream in fresh water."[6]

West Africans have traditionally preserved fish in a variety of ways. As early as 1678, Europeans gave written accounts of West Africans smoking fish.[7] Smoked fish was highly desired because of the unique flavor it imparted to a range of dishes, but West Africans would also salt and sun-dry fish.[8] As a modern example, the Mandingo and Wolof people in present-day Gambia prize dried and smoked herrings, tilapia, mud fish, and catfish for food.[9] Yes, you read that correctly. The Mississippi River is not the only home for catfish. West Africans—not just Gambians—are also familiar with a catfish species (*Crysichthys* spp.) and utilize this fish in their cooking. Once, I happened upon a West African grocery in Denver, Colorado, where I saw a barrel of dark, shriveled things that looked vaguely familiar. The clerk told me I was looking at smoked catfish imported from the Ivory Coast. He assured me that all types of West African immigrants in the area clamor for smoked catfish and wouldn't make a stew without it. The fact that there are catfish indigenous to West Africa evidences a notable continuity. West Africans (a significant number from Senegambia) first arrived in British North America in the eighteenth century. When they saw catfish, they would have instantly recognized it.[10]

West Africans came to the Americas with a very positive attitude toward fish. For centuries, it was a major part of their diet. They had honed ways to catch, prepare, and preserve fish over the ages, and they found similar fish in American waters. Western Europeans' take on fish, however, was at complete odds with that of West Africans. As Sandy Oliver explains in *Saltwater Foodways*, early white Americans carried a bad attitude about fish handed down from their ancestors: "For Northern Europeans and their New England descendants, fish-eating was associated with poverty and Roman Catholicism. At a time when wild food was not preferred fare, fish were undomesticated—so that didn't help. And significantly, fish was eaten and produced by people with whom many nineteenth century Yankees did not wish to identify."[11] Only social outsiders ate fish regularly, and in the eighteenth and nineteenth centuries, that meant African Americans, Native Americans, and poor whites. Whites with more status would certainly eat fish at times, but the activity didn't carry prestige.

Native American attitudes on fish, particularly catfish, were more in line with those of West Africans, and early European accounts attest to this. One of Hernando de Soto's men wrote about catfish in the Lower Mississippi Valley in the mid-1500s.[12] Robert Beverly's 1705 description of the Virginia Indians' practice of fishing with a spear and a torch strikingly parallels what Mary Kingsley wrote in the late 1800s about Africans.[13] In 1775, James Adair observed that in some southeastern tribes, hunters would catch catfish with their bare hands—a phenomenon that I had never heard of until I read Burkhard Bilger's *Noodling for Flatheads*.[14] Like West Africans, the Creek Indians have also poisoned waterways to catch large hauls of catfish for feasting.[15] Enslaved West Africans in British North America employed these and other techniques, some brought from across the Atlantic and others learned from Native Americans.

A distinctly African American approach to catching catfish was "muddying," and it survived from slavery well into the twentieth century. My father recalled muddying with a pitchfork, a hoe, and a tub while he grew up in rural Arkansas in the 1940s and 1950s. Boots were proper attire when muddying, as they protected you from leeches common in southern waters. Next, you find the spots of water without too much of a current. You disturb the water with your hoe. The fish come up to the surface because they can't breathe, and the snakes leave the water and head up the riverbank (added bonus). That's when you scoop the fish up! Dad recalled that the catch was mainly catfish and perch.[16]

With mastery of the methods described above, slaves were quite adept at fishing, and whites noticed. During the eighteenth century, money drove whites to capitalize on West African fishing expertise in two ways. First, there was a lot to be made by supplying a growing international market for fish, primarily for use in slave rations in the Caribbean Islands. Caribbean planters relied heavily on salted fish to feed their slaves and increasingly turned to importing fish, rather than harvesting and processing it locally. Accordingly, a thriving fishing industry sprang up along the East Coast with the express purpose of catching and salting fish and shipping it to the Caribbean Islands. Free and enslaved African Americans were an overwhelming part of the labor force that worked in every aspect of the fishing industry. Even as late as the 1970s, one scholar noted that "even now, generations after the end of slavery, professional Negro fishermen continue to be prevalent along the southeastern [U.S.] coast."[17] The overwhelming use of a black labor force in the fishing industry was the first conscious linking of fish to blackness, reinforcing fishing as a low-caste occupation in the South and the North.

Following the example of the Caribbean planters, southern planters realized they could save money by feeding their slaves fish. The use of fish as slave rations served as the second conscious linking of fish and blackness in the slaving South. Planters like Thomas Jefferson often found fish a cheaper alternative to other meats.[18] Other planters followed suit, and enslaved people fished on their own time to supplement their rations. Todd Savitt notes in his study of slavery, "Slaves also fished for their own meals in nearby streams, with or without the permission of overseer and master. Young boys not yet working full-time in the fields or the big house, and elderly 'retired' slaves, had the most opportunity to catch a little extra food for the family dinner."[19] Slaves also used leisure time to collect another important food source—shellfish. "'Us slaves lived off fish,' asserts Archie Booker, . . . '"Feed yo'selves," Old Marsa Tabb used to tell us. "You stealin' all my oysters anyway. Don't look fo' me to issue you no rations." '"[20] We also know that clams and mussels were consumed, based on the animal remains uncovered in archaeological excavations at coastal plantations in Florida and Georgia.[21] When planters miscalculated their slaves' food supplies, fish served as a vital stopgap during emergency food shortages. All of these trends deepened the ways whites associated fish with enslaved African Americans.

The FWP interviews also give us a window into African American practices related to fish. The former slaves extensively mention fish as a food source, specifically naming catfish (15 out of 198 informants) and perch (11).[22] When fish was preserved, it was dried, pickled, or smoked. The most vivid accounts in the FWP interviews describe fish being eaten fresh, and slaves cooked fresh catfish in a variety of ways. Clara Davis of Mobile, Alabama, recalls two examples from slavery "and the cat-fishing on the Alabama river, when the darkies would stretch a trot line completely across the river on a quiet night and then go the next morning in their boats for 'de catch', when 'dere wud be nine or ten an' sumtimes more catfish weighing nigh up to sixty an' seventy pounds.'" When asked how ex-slaves cooked the catfish, she replied, "'Well, honey, some niggers just skin dem an' fries de steak part, while odders cut dem up fine an' stews dem wid 'taters and tumatters an' seas'ning. Mah ma wud bake dem wid tumatter gravy an' sweet 'taters.'"[23] The frying and baking methods are certainly familiar to today's cooks, while the catfish stew, with its mixture of tomatoes and other vegetables, is reminiscent of West African cooking. The hardest part of cooking a catfish is removing the skin, which has to be pulled off. A typical practice for skinning a catfish was to nail the fish to a tree, make an incision in the flesh, and pull the skin off with pliers. Once they got past that part of the process, the cook and the eater would be rewarded with a good-tasting fish without a lot of bones.

It was a hit-or-miss proposition as to whether or not planters ate catfish in the Big House. Mrs. Randolph's *Virginia Housewife* gives a catfish curry recipe, and Mrs. Bryan's *Kentucky Housewife* gives a standard recipe for fried catfish. That's it. Some planters traded for catfish with their slaves, suggesting a lack of a stigma for the fish. Phillip Morgan notes in *Slave Counterpoint* that in 1760s South Carolina, prominent planter "Henry Ravnel frequently purchased corn, fowl, hogs, and catfish from his slaves. During this decade he recorded more than a hundred transactions with about twenty-five individuals."[24] Yet Anna Parkes recalls from slavery that catfish was used to emphasize racial caste distinctions: "Us had many fishes as us wanted. De big fine shads, and perch, and trouts; dem wuz de fishes de Jedge liked mos'. Catfishes won't counted fittin' to set on de Jedges table, but us Negroes was 'lowed to eat all of 'em us wanted."[25]

As the nineteenth century advanced, whites increasingly soured on the catfish and actively used it to stereotype blacks much the same way they did with fried chicken. As much as blacks were commonly called "chicken merchants" in the late 1700s, the "negro fisherman" and "negro fishmonger" became familiar references in nineteenth-century media and popular culture.[26] Whites also frequently commented on how much blacks liked to eat fish, especially catfish. In 1830, a visitor to a Charleston, South Carolina, plantation wrote, "During one of my usual visits to the country, about thirty miles from town, I was invited to accompany a party to the Major M's boat, down the Edisto river, for the purpose of drawing the seine, which generally, once a week, supplied the people of his plantation with an abundance of rock, trout, brim, and cat fish; the last of which the negroes are extremely fond of."[27] The sentiment that "catfish is for black people" was still strong even as late as the 1940s among blacks and whites. In 1949, a white itinerant gourmand went on a nationwide search for fried catfish, a gastronomical delight he feared might be extinct. "Again, in New Orleans, where the magnificent Mississippi flows, we put in an order for fried catfish, feeling certain it would be forthcoming, but the waiter replied: 'No, sah, we ain't got it; nobody but colored people eats catfish in Nawluns.'"[28]

The act of fishing itself was reinterpreted to confer on African Americans the traits of laziness, ignorance, and possession of a childlike mentality. One who held these views wrote in the late 1880s, "Laziness is the mother of patience and the godmother of the negro. Give Sambo a pole and line, a pocketful of worms or indisposed beef, a sunny nook along the river or on the wharf, and for the time being he will thank the good Lord for nothing else. . . . Sambo is a born fisherman."[29] The food stereotype finally comes into sharp relief when the undesired people are linked to the undesired food. In the late 1870s, a *Scientific American* contributor described catfish as "a disgusting creature, and yet with all their unattractive exteriors they are valued by any as a toothsome article of food, and by the negroes are considered a special delicacy."[30] Another writer, this one a *Forest and Stream* correspondent in the early 1880s, also laid out his catfish prejudice starkly: "The Southern large cats are coarse and nasty, and with few exceptions are only fit as nigger food." Yet the writer is willing to make an exception for catfish "from the fine cold water of our lakes[. W]hen rightly cooked, myself and all that have eaten of them, preferred [them] to all other of our fishes."[31]

A big challenge for the catfish's image was that the fish wallows in the mud. The English language has few positive references for mud. The *Oxford English Dictionary* lists several expressions that apply to what whites were doing with the catfish's reputation in the nineteenth century: dragging its name through the mud (to denigrate publicly); slinging mud at it (to make disparaging allegations or criticisms); and saying that catfish's name is mud (discredited, in disgrace or temporarily unpopular).[32] Yet these negative connotations are lost on the catfish, which is very much at home in the mud. That's where it lives and scavenges for food. Life in mud also gives its

Catfish sandwich, Johnson Street Fish House, Greenwood, Miss.

meat a distinct muddy taste, creating a sharp dividing line between those who preferred the taste and those who detested it. So while this catfish prejudice undoubtedly had an ugly racial tenor, it was also due in part to the fish's muddy taste, which turned off a lot of white consumers.

Joe Gray Taylor, a white southerner who extensively studied rural southern foodways, reminisces about eating fish during his own childhood: "We considered ourselves fortunate if we could bring home a string of catfish; and a river catfish of ten pounds or more, large enough to be cross-sectioned into steaks, was a delicacy indeed. When we bought fish, usually on Saturday, we had catfish if fresh, but otherwise a buffalo—a carplike member of the sucker family. A real racial difference in taste was to be noted concerning fish; Negroes preferred garfish and mudfish, varieties which the whites I knew would not eat."[33] Taylor's memory of his childhood during the earlier part of the twentieth century quickly disabuses us of the misperception that catfish was only eaten by blacks. He also reveals that catfish was not always what blacks preferred when all things were equal. At this moment, we should recall historical and contemporary descriptions of West African fish preferences. In different eras and parts of the region, mud fish were considered a delicacy. West Africans brought a

Buffalo Fish "Ribs," an Insider's Dish

Do you want to feel like a real insider at a soul food restaurant? Then ask for buffalo fish ribs. If you are not one of the restaurant's longtime customers, the person taking your order will probably ask you, "Do you know what it is?" Don't feel bad, it's not a race thing. I've gotten that response several times, and I'm black. Buffalo (Ictiobus spp.) is a large fish that always lives in the mud, and it tastes like catfish. Catfish lovers have long substituted buffalo when their favorite fish is not available. When a temporary catfish shortage hit Memphis in 1937, African Americans substituted buffalo fish.[1]

The only real downside to buffalo is that it is extremely bony, which limits its popularity outside soul food circles. Soul food cooks have gotten around that boniness by creating fish "ribs." Fish ribs are made from the larger bones closer to the fish's head. The ribs are breaded in cornmeal and fried just as the home cook would do with a whole catfish or fillet. I've had two memorable buffalo rib meals. The first was at Betty's Place in Indianola, Mississippi, not too far from the B. B. King Blues Museum. Miss Betty served up some meaty ribs that were crisp and hot, alongside green beans and meatless spaghetti. Imagine my surprise when I got a strikingly similar dish of piping hot ribs at the Catfish Corner in Seattle, Washington. I don't see fish ribs very often, but I'm so glad when I do.

---

1 "Catfish Eaters Sadly Admit Decline."

taste for mud fish with them and applied their flavoring practices to fish that they encountered in the New World. Taylor's recollection, bolstered by African American testimony, shows a continuing preference for muddy fish, among which catfish is the most well-known.

The catfish's muddy taste did not always cause a racial divide among consumers. As the Hartford Courant reported in 1901, Mississippi River catfish was caught and "shipped by express to Texas, Arkansas, Indian territory, Missouri, Colorado, Kansas, Utah, Nebraska and some as far as Idaho and Wyoming. . . . All over the West the Mississippi cat brings a good price as a table delicacy, and is served at the best restaurants and hotels."[34] Within a few decades, though, catfish had once again fallen out of favor with most whites. Some African Americans could also be fickle about cooking and eating catfish. Mrs. Russell gives a recipe for catfish fricassee in her 1866 cookbook, but there are no other catfish recipes in the known African American–authored cookbooks published before 1930. Catfish recipes resurface by the time A Date with a Dish was published in 1948 and have remained a prominent feature of African American cookbooks ever since.[35]

Though these upscale cookbooks seemed to have little regard for catfish, catfish eating was alive and well in both rural areas and cities. During the Down Home Cooking era, fish eating amongst African Americans was off the charts. A 1930s New York City food habits study indicated that "Negroes rank second in fish eating among the three groups who consume the greatest quantity of fish in the city. The other two are Italians and Jews."[36] The study went on to highlight regional distinctions, rather than class, as the basis for varied fish preferences: "Southern Negroes are fond of catfish, but the only cats that are marketed in New York are the bullheads; although a few sea-going cats are brought in by trawlers from Southern waters."[37] A similar dynamic was at play in Chicago. In 1953, the Chicago Defender asked, "If you were asked what group of people in Chicago consumes the greatest amount of fish per week, what would be your answer? Would you list them in this order? No. 1—the Jewish people; No. 2—communicants of the Roman Catholic Church; No. 3—the Chinese- or Japanese-Americans or No. 4—Negroes. If you would name anyone of the first three, you are mistaken because, in any given week, Negroes eat more fish than the other three combined."[38] Showing the full diversity of fish preferences, including catfish, the Defender went on to say, "What is true of Chicago and Manhattan is true of the rest of the country. Negroes are the no. 1 fish eaters of the nation."[39] Press accounts from that period confirm that during the Down Home Cooking period African Americans ate a lot of fish, particularly catfish, which not only puts them outside the American mainstream diet at that time but also challenges more recent stereotypes about what kind of meat is most common for blacks in the United States.

The Soul Food Era ushered in a boom in catfish farming as catfish became more popular with the general public. Small cotton farmers could no longer afford the mechanization required to remain competitive. Rather than abandon their fields, black and white cotton farmers alike opted to flood their cotton fields and start raising catfish. These farmers were "banking on research results showing that catfish thrive in crowded conditions and on the fact that catfish, having only back and rib bones are easy to gut, clean and ship."[40] Catfish seemed tailor-made for an industrial food system, and the results were dramatic. In 1970, catfish farmers raised 5.7 million pounds of catfish, and by the early 2000s, the yield was more than 630 million pounds, making catfish the largest farmed fish industry by far.[41] In the late 1980s, catfish appeared on the menu of white-tablecloth restaurants like Wolfgang Puck's Chinois on Main in Santa Monica, California, as it had almost a century before. Economically depressed parts of the South appeared to have found salvation through catfish.

Blacks and whites were also eating more catfish at home, primarily because it was cheap and catfish farmers had actually succeeded in removing the muddy flavor. The aquaculture farmers developed a grain feed that gave catfish a uniform flavor, taste, and texture.[42] And the feed floated on top of the water, so the catfish were forced to leave the muddy bottom and feed at the surface. Farmers thus changed the fish's eating habits, making it more attractive to a broader swath of Americans. The catfish's new, bland flavor also made it a good substitute for more expensive firm, delicate fish like sole, flounder, cod, sea bass, red snapper, and halibut.[43] For blacks, the catfish farming success story meant catfish was now available year-round in places where it wasn't always plentiful.

By the 1980s, more African American cookbooks reflected this market reality by including catfish recipes. "Firm, sweet and juicy catfish fillets," wrote the late Harlem restaurateur Sylvia Woods in her *Sylvia's Soul Food* cookbook, "are becoming more and more popular with home cooks. Now that they are being farmed commercially they are even easier to find."[44] The irony is that while farmers removed one of the qualities that appealed to African Americans specifically, they also made the catfish more widely available to black consumers outside the South.

The good times for catfish farming didn't last. International competition has been fierce in recent years, particularly from fish farmers in China and Vietnam.[45] Things have gotten so heated that the Catfish Farmers of America lobbied Congress to trademark the name "catfish" so American consumers won't be fooled by the presumably inferior foreign product. For the time being, Vietnamese catfish is currently marketed as "basa swai." International trade tensions have risen and so have the costs of catfish farming. Feed costs have soared so much in recent years that they eat up half of a typical farmer's operating costs.[46] The large catfish farming operations and catfish processors in the Mississippi Delta laid off thousands of workers in the 2000s. "It's unclear what can replace catfish as easily as catfish replaced cotton," observed the *New York Times* in 2008.[47] I've certainly seen the fallout in soul food restaurants where price increases have either made catfish ridiculously expensive or pushed it off the menu entirely. Outside the South, catfish can frequently cost more per pound than trout and salmon. I never would have expected that ten or fifteen years ago. In both restaurants and homes, African Americans are switching to cheaper fish, mainly to tilapia (another fish with relatives in West Africa) and whiting.

Though the price of catfish has wavered, its prestige in the African American community has not. Catfish is often the preferred fish for meals and big social occasions like the fish fry. The earliest accounts of fish fries in the American South often describe a bunch of white guys getting together on a riverbank to drink, tell stories, and shoot firearms while their slaves caught and cooked the fish.[48] African Americans developed their own fish fry tradition during slavery. Sometimes it was an impromptu feast, prepared while the fish was fresh—on the uncommon instance when they didn't have to share the catch with the master—and consumed by the riverbank. "Within a fifteen mile radius, there is seldom more than one fish fry a season . . . giving the dames, the damsels and the damsons ample time to get good and ready for the fun, fuss and fury," alliterated a journalist for *Canton's Weekly*.[49] Since a big haul of fish was needed fairly quickly, the preferred fishing method was to use a large net, or seine, rather than muddying or gigging. But as the Hurston story that opened this chapter indicates, the Sunday fishing taboo was so widely held that many fished and held their fish fries on Saturdays.[50]

After the Civil War, the fish fry as a social event really took off after it was conjoined with Emancipation and Fourth of July celebrations in the South. In the shadow of the Civil War, blacks celebrated the Fourth of July with more enthusiasm than whites. In fact, white newspapers like the *Atlanta Constitution* routinely warned their readership about the mass frolics that would take place on the holiday. The editorial board of the same newspapers never hesitated to caricature the accompanying fish fries as scenes where carefree blacks ate "fish 'n' braid" (fried fish with homemade bread) and drank red lemonade. In Georgia, the consumption of fish 'n' braid was as much a belittling stereotype as eating fried chicken and watermelon was elsewhere.

In the rural South, the fish fry was one of the few events where church folks were willing to look the other way when inappropriate behavior occurred. A 1918 newspaper article well-captured the relaxing of tensions between the saved and the unsaved:

> A fish fry is nothing more or less than an annual neighborhood get together, on the banks of some creek, lake or lagoon, that it may smack of fish, where saints and sinners, young and old can fraternize without the saints "giten churched" for associating with the ungodly. For, be it remembered, that it is strictly against the rules of the church for God's elect to sit in the seat with sinners or get in the way of the scornful (ungodly), but, on fish fry occasions, saints and sinners sit down together, walk and talk together, and, it sometimes happens, dance together, the saint not crossing his or her legs, which if not done, is not actual dancing.[51]

The *Canton's Weekly* article noted that African American fish fries became so known for ancillary activities like gossiping, drinking, and (gasp!) dancing, that they were sometimes held without any fish. No wonder the godly were nervous.

By the 1930s, fish fry organizers decided to drop all pretenses about the event as a wholesome activity. One woman in Mississippi decided to go straight for the money—and the sin—by offering whiskey at her fish fries.

> The southern Negro of the humbler type gets closer to heaven at a fish fry than anywhere else on earth. Whether the party is conducted in the backyard of a home or in one of the towns—with a red lantern on the gate by way of advertisement—or on the levee, as many are in Mississippi, the colored folk would gladly trade the promised marble palaces of the world beyond for this. In Mississippi river communities there is usually one cook justly famed up and down the levee for her fish fries, and she sometimes supplements her everyday wages by holding Saturday night fries. Connection with a bootlegger makes the venture even more profitable, and if she can get in on an all-night crap game she does right well. Saturday night is always chosen because it is pay day, and the feast is staged solely for profit, the cook having purchased some riverman's catfish with money furnished by the commissary and charged against her wages.[52]

At fish fries like this one, a diner could get hot fish and hushpuppies (deep-fried cornmeal balls) for 10 cents. Throw in another quarter and you could get a cheap whiskey presciently called "Stoop Down." Hot fish and whiskey proved to be an unfortunate combination at these fish fries, for newspapers reported numerous fights and the occasional murder. The tawdry activities cemented the fish fry's poor reputation.

Law enforcement officials were quite concerned about the violence and drinking and tried to prevent fish fries from happening in the first place. This was easier to do in cities rather than in the isolated countryside. In 1914, New Orleans officials, realizing they couldn't stamp out fish fries solely through on-the-street enforcement, tried to snuff them out with a targeted tax. As is often the case with attempts to regulate perceived sin, opposition was mobilized from unlikely sources in order to save the tradition. This time, a white Good Samaritan came forward to protect the interests of the largely African American fish fry operators. As a local newspaper reported,

> Barney McGovern, who dispenses nickels and dimes to the poor of the city, says if the Legislature passes the Earhart bill, providing an additional tax of 25 cents on permits for entertainments, fish fries, etc., it will be the finish of the fish fries. It now costs as much as 75 cents for the privilege of dispensing hot catfish under the sign of the red lantern, and to add another 25 cents may make the business a losing game. Saturday is the big day [for] fish fries, and usually there are a dozen smart darkies at the Mayor's parlor door to obtain permits for fish fries. The sign of the fish is a red light, or a Chinese lantern, hung over the door or gate, and hot catfish is the appetizing food that attracts the roustabout, trench digger, teamster or other laborer if his pockets are filled.[53]

The red lantern was either a repurposing of railroad lanterns or possibly a cultural borrowing from the Chinese who arrived in the South beginning in the 1870s.

Whether on a riverbank, a country road, or the window of an urban apartment, a red lantern was the universal sign advertising a fish fry during the Down Home Cooking era. In some cities, fish fries couldn't shake their sinful reputation, as this helpful "public service announcement" a *Pittsburgh Courier* columnist gave to his readers in 1957 indicates: "Word reaches the Column that weekend 'fish fries' and 'chitterling struts' will be investigated by the Police Department. They will be looking for the skin and crap games."[54] This was the fish fry at its lowest point, but there were

Buffalo fish ribs, Betty's Place, Indianola, Miss.

already some long-lasting trends in the black community during the Soul Food era that changed the way the fish fry was perceived. These trends involved the black church and black entrepreneurs.

Over time, urban black churches cleaned up the fish fry's reputation by presenting it as a wholesome event for their congregations that was more about socializing than carousing. The availability of cheap fish and relative ease of preparing and cooking it, as compared with barbecue or chitlins, made the fish fry a reliable church fundraiser. Budget-conscious black families also relied on fish for regular meals. As Ruth Gaskins wrote in her *Good Heart and a Light Hand* cookbook, "Because fish can be caught easily, it was and is a popular item in Negro kitchens. . . . We usually fry fish and it was always served with cider vinegar. A Friday fish dinner consists of fried fish, greens, cole slaw and cornbread."[55]

The fish fry experience was also replicated in restaurants. Just as African Americans found success selling fried chicken, black entrepreneurs did well running restaurants specializing in fried fish. It was often called "hot fish" because it was quickly eaten after being freshly fried in hot oil. In Atlanta during the early 1880s, hot fish was extremely popular. One reporter who ventured over to the black part of town wrote, "A little way down Ivy street the reporter encountered the odor of frying fish—an almost sure sign of a Negro lunch house. It is astonishing how these people take to lunch houses. There are hundreds of these little six by nine establishments over the city, or the whole stock in trade amounts to a boiled ham, the ever-present fried fish and bread to go along. These lunch houses are generally the essence of filth, but there are some that are quite decent. One in particular furnishes many white families with board."[56]

In Depression-era Harlem, hot fish places were known as "fried fish emporiums" or "whale stations." According to the *Philadelphia Tribune*, Greeks were displacing blacks in this industry.

Seems as though these fellows can take any kind of a cook-shop and make it pay: at any rate, they have in the past six months simply overrun the community with those poorly furnished, sanitary dumps, where for fifteen cents, a man, if his tastes are not to gaudy, may purchase a full complete meal of fried fish, fried potatoes, bread and coffee for the small sum of fifteen cents. . . . The Greeks stole this idea from some colored brethren over on the East Side. The latter are falling by the wayside, but the former are prospering on fried fish and fried potatoes at fifteen cents a throw.[57]

The Greek-run places served cod, haddock, mackerel, shrimp, and crabs— seafood supplied exclusively by their fellow Greek fishermen.[58] The black- and Greek-owned whale stations were tremendously popular during the Great Depression, when cheap meals did the trick.

While Greek-run places had their own seafood selections, the black-owned places lured customers by providing good ol' catfish. A 1933 *Washington Post* article on the Harlem restaurant scene observed,

A sign on a window, scrawled with whitewash, read: "Hot Fried Cat." Which could mean nothing in all the world, not even in New York, except catfish fried in corn meal. The wanderer inquired of a young Negro: "Tell me, is the catfish channel cat, mud cat or salt-water cat?"—there's a lot of difference. "How would I know," snapped the Negro boy, "I wasn't there when they caught it." But up from a corner came an older Negro, shuffling like a roustabout on a cotton steamer. "Hit's channel cat, cap'n," said he, "dey ship hit heah from Memphis. Now tell me, please, suh"—there was a yearning in his voice—"how's things around N'aw'lans?"[59]

In 1930s Chicago, a recent transplant from New Orleans reportedly told a local resident, "Catfish? Who sesso? Hit's the bes' eatin' fish you kin git anywhere. Don't keer where you go. There aint nothin' that tickle your palate like a chunk of channel cat fried crisp. Of co'se de snot cat good. Th' ole mud cat aint bad neither. I have eat pompano and buffalo fish and red snapper and a lot of others. But don't let nobody tell you any different. Catfish is the finest eatin' of all."[60] These glimpses into the '30s suggest that New Orleans natives were most wistful about catfish. But as mentioned earlier, catfish was special to many migrants who settled outside the South.

In the late 1970s, McDonald's picked up on this trend in its Filet-O-Fish sandwich advertisements that targeted the black community. A 1978 *Jet Magazine* advertisement carries the banner headline "HAVE A SATURDAY NIGHT FISH FRY AT MCDONALD'S ANY DAY." The advertisement includes a montage of collegial black diners grubbing on the sandwich. For further effect, the advertisement adds, "Good friends, family, food and fun is what a fish fry is all about. And good tasting fish makes it all come together."[61] Politicians have also gotten in on the act. U.S. Representative James Clyburn, the highest-ranking African American in Congress at the time of this book, has an annual fish fry (featuring whiting)—now an obligatory stop for anyone seeking votes in South Carolina, including presidential candidates.[62]

Hot fish places are still prevalent in black neighborhoods and are some of the few independently owned and black-run businesses left in those locales. Now, "hot" refers to both the serving temperature and the spice level. In an interesting parallel to black churches and fried chicken, Black Muslims do a brisk amount of business in the hot fish restaurant market, and they primarily serve whiting, since catfish is a prohibited food. At one point, their businesses became so lucrative that the Nation of Islam investigated creating a whiting farm in Peru to supply its many restaurants.[63] Most are combination fish market/restaurants where you can select your fish and they cook it to order on the spot. Increasingly, these urban fish joints are being run by immigrants who aren't black and do a brisk business catering to a largely black clientele, while black-run fish establishments struggle.

Given the current concerns about frying, ultimate salvation for hot fish places may lie in finding tantalizing ways to cook fish without baptizing them in grease. While I was eating my way through Los Angeles, I met a woman who has already seen the light—Georgette Powell, the owner of

Mel's Fish Shack. Powell is Mel's daughter, and she took over the business that her father started on a whim in 1982. Her father, a retired educator at Crenshaw High School, was going to open a Mexican restaurant when someone suggested doing a fish place instead. Mel changed course and put in a lot of work to get the fish shack up and running. Actually, Powell had planned to pursue a career in medicine at first. During her college days at the University of California at San Diego, she became politically active after some racial incidents on campus. Powell began to think about how business can help advance the black community. Seeing her father work so hard, she decided upon graduation to get involved in the family business.

Powell has used her business savvy to figure out creative ways for Mel's to help the surrounding community. Mel's has partnered with the county health department to host fairs and block parties at which community members get free health screenings, attend workshops on breast cancer, and even get a massage. The economy of late has tempered Powell's enthusiasm for these activities. "I'm in survival mode," she told me. Yet she has continued her activism by adding more healthy options to Mel's menu. The steamed-vegetable sides haven't gone over so well, but grilled fish and salads served with unique ginger vinaigrette (her brother-in-law's recipe) have been very popular. "I'm not doing it in response to customer requests. I understand the health disparities in our community, so I just wanted to be more conscientious and have grilled options," Powell emphasized.

All in all, the customers still clamor most for her fried shrimp, fried catfish, red snapper, and fillet of sole. "If I don't have one of those, they won't order anything else." I was more adventuresome, and I ordered a fish that I had never heard of: the sand dab. I got a nicely fried piece of fish that tasted as though it had just come out of the ocean. What I really enjoyed was the atmosphere, as Powell's regular customers wove me into their conversations and made me feel at home. Powell would tell me later that Mel's is trying to re-create the feel of a Friday night fish fry.[64] From my short time dining at Mel's, I would say, "Mission accomplished!"

Among the wide range of fish eaten by African Americans, the catfish—because it could be farmed and processed on a large scale—is the only identifiably southern fish that went national, though there was a trade-off in the process. Catfish lost its distinctive muddy flavor in order to go mainstream, but it remains the nostalgic fish of choice. Yet despite its declining presence in today's market because of the higher cost of farming and competition from other fish, it will take some time for the catfish to lose its hold on the soul foodie's imagination. What catfish has never lost is its communal feel, nurtured by generations of fish fries, by the riverside or in the home.

Nanticoke Catfish

Fried catfish is one of the easiest dishes to make as long as you have a well-seasoned coating and plenty of hot oil. This recipe from the Chesapeake Bay area was printed in a delightful publication titled *The Chesapeake Bay through Ebony Eyes*. "Nanticoke" is the name of a Native American tribe now in Delaware and the name of a river that flows through Delaware and Maryland. This dish is probably different from the fried catfish you've made before. There's flour in the dredge, there is egg batter (which makes it more similar to fish-and-chips-style fish), and it's pan-fried instead of deep-fried.

Makes 8 servings

1½ cups all-purpose flour
¼ cup cornmeal
1 tablespoon rubbed sage
1 tablespoon ground
   cayenne pepper, or to taste
1 teaspoon garlic powder
1 teaspoon onion powder
½ teaspoon ground nutmeg

1 teaspoon salt
1 teaspoon freshly ground
   black pepper
4 large eggs
8 catfish fillets
Vegetable oil, for pan-frying
Lemon wedges, for serving

1 Mix the flour, cornmeal, sage, cayenne, garlic powder, onion powder, nutmeg, salt, and pepper in a shallow bowl or pie plate. In another shallow bowl or pie plate, whisk the eggs until well beaten.
2 Rinse the fillets under cold running water and pat them dry.
3 Preheat the oven to 250°F. Set a wire rack inside a rimmed baking sheet lined with paper towels. Pour oil to a depth of ½ inch in a large, deep skillet. Heat the oil over medium-high heat until shimmering hot, but not smoking.
4 Dip the fillets into the eggs and let the excess drip off. Dredge them in the flour mixture and gently shake off the excess.

5 Working in batches to avoid overfilling the skillet, slip the fillets into the hot oil. Fry the fillets until the coating is crisp and golden brown and the fish is opaque in the center, turning once, about 4 minutes on each side. Transfer the cooked fillets to the wire rack and keep them warm in the oven until all of the fish is fried.

6 Serve hot with the lemon wedges.

Creole Broiled Catfish

Lisa Roy introduced me to this dish while we were dating. A concerned mother of three, she was always "trying to put a spin on a family favorite to make it healthier." This is always a huge favorite when I serve it to guests, so I've made a few changes and now it's part of my repertoire. Roy advises that when you buy catfish, it should already be "be-headed" (perhaps that's a Freudian slip about me?). If you don't like whole catfish, you may easily substitute catfish or tilapia fillets. This recipe has taught me two lessons: Sometimes the simplest things are the best, and if you're dating a good cook, always get a recipe before you break up!

Makes 4 servings

> 4 dressed whole catfish (12 to 16 ounces each)
>   or 8 fillets (6 to 8 ounces each)
> ¼ cup olive oil
> 1 tablespoon Lawry's Seasoned Pepper
> 1 tablespoon Lawry's Garlic Powder with Parsley
> 1 tablespoon Tabasco Seasoned Salt
>   *If you can't find the seasoned pepper, garlic powder with parsley, and Tabasco seasoned salt, you may substitute 3 tablespoons of your favorite Creole seasoning. My favorite is Black River Creole Seasoning from the Savory Spice Shop, Inc., in Denver, Colorado.*

1 Position a rack 5 inches below the heating element and preheat the broiler to high.

2 Rinse the fish under cold running water and pat them dry. Brush both sides with oil and arrange them in a single layer on a broiler pan lined with aluminum foil.

3 Mix together the seasoned pepper, garlic powder, and seasoned salt in a small bowl. Sprinkle half of the spice mixture over one side of the fish.

4 Broil for 5 minutes. Using a spatula, carefully turn the fish over. Sprinkle with the remaining spice mixture. Continue broiling until the fish is opaque in the center, 3 to 5 minutes more.

5 Serve immediately with sautéed vegetables and brown rice.

Catfish Curry

Fish curries were a popular Big House dish in the antebellum South. Both Martha Washington and Mrs. Randolph had recipes for this dish in their signature cookbooks. At some point, black cooks brought the dish into their kitchens. In 1939, Crosby Gaige's *New York World's Fair Cookbook* (from which this recipe is adapted) described catfish curry as "a favorite among the Negroes."

Makes 4 servings

2 pounds catfish fillets	2 tablespoons all-purpose flour
1 quart water	2 teaspoons curry powder
2 medium onions, finely chopped (about 4 cups)	2 tablespoons butter, at room temperature
Salt and ground black pepper, to taste	1 tablespoon chopped fresh parsley
	Boiled rice, for serving

1 Rinse the fillets under cold running water and cut them into 2-inch pieces. Place them in a medium saucepan and add the water, onions, salt, and pepper. Bring to a boil, reduce the heat, and simmer until the fish is tender, but not breaking apart, about 8 minutes. With a slotted spoon, transfer the fish to a serving platter and cover with foil to keep it warm. Boil the cooking liquid until it reduces to 1 cup, then keep it warm over low heat.

2 Combine the flour, curry, and butter in a small bowl. Mix with a fork or fingertips to form a smooth paste. Roll teaspoon-size bits of the paste into balls.

3 Return the cooking liquid to a simmer. While stirring slowly and continuously, drop the balls into the liquid one at a time, letting each one

dissolve before adding the next. Cook until the sauce returns just to a boil and thickens to the consistency of gravy, about 5 minutes. Check the seasoning.

4 Pour the gravy over the fish and boiled rice, sprinkle some parsley on top, and serve hot.

Chitlins

A LOVE STORY

"No way," said one young woman at the drive-through, when asked if she had ever had any chitlins. "I don't know what they are, but they're something nasty."
—Anonymous customer at Atlanta's "This Is It" Restaurant, 1998.

★   ★   ★   ★   ★

I'm a proud, but restrained, chitlin eater. I generally eat them only two times a year, on Thanksgiving and New Year's Day as part of family celebrations. Otherwise, chitlins are a rare treat for me. My first Thanksgiving alone was during my first year of college out in California. I couldn't afford to fly round-trip to Colorado just for the holiday weekend, so I stayed on campus. About a week out from Thanksgiving, it hit me—how and where was I going to get some chitlins? Could I possibly endure a Thanksgiving without them? I lamented my plight with John Towns, an older African American who was on my dorm's dining staff. If I attempt to capture the sequence of emotions on his face, I'd say at first he was tremendously surprised that I ate chitlins, then gave me a "he's one of us" look, and finally sympathized with my situation. The Wednesday before Thanksgiving, there was a knock on my door. I opened it, and amazingly, there was John, with his distinctive silver Afro, holding a plate of chitlins, wrapped up and ready to eat! "Have a great Thanksgiving, Adrian!" he said, and merrily went on his way. Given the circumstances, that was the best plate of chitlins that I've ever had.

Chitlins—pigs' intestines—are by far the most controversial item in our soul food meal. I don't know anyone who's on the fence about chitlins. You either hate them or you love them. There's not even agreement on how to spell the word "chitlins." Some throw in an extra t, while others liberally add apostrophes. What people on both sides seem to agree on is that chitlins are stigmatized (for reasons we'll explore in a moment) within black culture. Even the people who eat chitlins tend to admit as much with a whisper. Yet sharing, identity, and communion are the stuff of which chitlins are made. In African American food culture, chitlins are about connection to community, family, friends, complete strangers, and foreigners around the world.

The grievances against chitlins are pretty straightforward. First of all, chitlins are pigs' intestines. Who would willingly eat that? Second is the belief that whites gave us chitlins because they didn't want them. This makes chitlins worse than leftovers, for at least whites at one point ate the food that would become leftovers. Thus, eating chitlins implies that blacks are internalizing white notions of superiority by relishing white folks' trash. Third, as a pork product, chitlins are taboo in several religions, most notably Judaism and Islam. Black Jews and Black Muslims disdain them. The fourth, a widely shared criticism, is that chitlins have a hygiene problem. They have a very distinctive smell when raw, while cooking, and when cooked. For some the smell is a perfume; for others it's just too funky. To love chitlins is to know them.

Reflexively snubbing chitlins seems odd to me, given the current popularity of "nose to tail cooking." The *New York Times* celebrated the face of this trend, Fergus Henderson, as "a London-based chef who inspired the cheeks and bellies on New York menus." The same article notes that Henderson "cooks every conceivable part of every conceivable animal: grilled calf's heart, rolled pig's spleen, a terrine of duck neck, four versions of lamb's brain, critters' feet, bellies, cheeks, tongues, intestines, bladders, kidneys, lungs—even a sheep's windpipe for his version of haggis." Henderson adds, "Basically, it's just common sense to use all the parts of an animal—and it's courteous to the animal."[1] Looking at Henderson's list, I scratched my head and wondered why New York chefs and reporters never took the A train up to Harlem, where black cooks have been very courteous to chickens, cows, and pigs for decades. It's ironic, but nonetheless historically appropriate, that an English cook is the current face of internal organ cookery. Chitlins, as we Americans understand them, trace their roots to rural England and France, not to the plantations of the South.

This tale begins with deer hunting. The English fell in love with eating innards several centuries ago, and much of it had to do with the aristocratic sport of chasing deer. For the British, the deer's internal organs were a high-end dish: "The term 'umbles' came to refer to the edible offal and lights of animals, usually deer or boar. . . . The parts mainly referred to are

Thanksgiving Crock-Pot of chitlins at the Miller residence

the soft organs of the animal including those referred to today as offal—heart, liver, kidneys—but they also include sweetbreads, spleen and lungs (the lights or the pluck). . . . The term 'umbles' seems mainly attached to deer. . . . Hunting deer was always considered as an aristocratic pastime, especially in the medieval period when it was reserved to royalty and the aristocracy."[2] The umbles were a key ingredient of "humble pie," and Raymond Sokolov clarifies, "If you want to find humble pie, you look in a book and see that it has nothing to do with humility. It is a pie composed of all manner of meats, from hare to bacon, and sometimes fruit."[3] The English and French relished the deer's internal organs until the internal organs of cows and pigs made an acceptable substitute.

As late as the eighteenth century, beef and pork intestines were a high-end food featured in British cookbooks. Hannah Glasse includes a beef chitterlings recipe in her iconic cookbook.[4] Glasse's recipe is a clear relative of the French chitterling sausages now called andouillettes, which is likely what Glasse refers to when she tells her English readers a similar dish is made with pork. Glasse informs her readers that the beef version is a substitute for hog chitterlings during the summer months. The winter hog killing, a feature of rural English life, was transplanted to the South as soon as the settlers could raise a large number of pigs—in the Virginia colony by 1627 and in the Maryland colony by the mid-1630s.[5]

Since pork was the meat most consumed in the antebellum South, a hog killing was a momentous occasion on the plantation. As Constance Fuller McIntyre reminisced in 1902, "In the ante-bellum days the planters would kill as many as seventy to a hundred head of hogs at a time, and then negroes from neighboring plantations would come in and help. Now they seldom kill more than fifteen or twenty at a time, and it does not pay to keep any but stock hogs longer than one year." Many slaves remembered how the hog killing was a Herculean task. Joseph Holmes recalled of his enslaved childhood in Virginia, "Now you axed about hog-killin' time? Dat was de time of times. For weeks de mens would haul wood an' big rocks, an' pile 'em together as high as dis house, an' den have several piles, lak dat 'roun' a big hole in de groun' what had been filled wid water. Den jus' a little atter midnight, de boss would blow de ole hawn, an' all de mens would git up an' git in dem big pens. Den dey would set dat pile of wood on fire an' den start knockin' dem hogs in de haid."[6] Henry Rountree of North Carolina spoke of how his master would have to call for additional help to get all of the work done. "In de col' winter time when we'd have hog killin's we'd invite de neighbors case dar wus a hundred er two hog ter kill 'fore we quit. Yes, mam, dem wus de days when folkses, white an' black, worked together."[7]

The untold story of chitlins is not only that blacks and whites worked together to do the butchering that created chitlins, but also that both groups enjoyed chitlins, even though they ate them separately. In some Big Houses, masters ate chitlins and were exacting as to how they wanted their chitlins prepared. In her book *The Plantation Mistress*, Catherine Clinton recounts one particularly acute chitlin confrontation between a slave and her mistress: "When she was little more than four years old, Lucy McCullough listened to her mistress 'scold my mammy 'bout de sorry way mammy done clean de chitlins.' She had never heard anyone berate her mother before. In turn, she drew herself up and rebuked her mistress, 'Doan you know Mammy is boss ef dis hyar kitchen. You can't come a fussin' in hyar.' Lucy's mother grabbed a switch 'en gin ticklin' my laigs.' 'Miss Millie' laughed. Only her intervention saved little Lucy from a serious whipping."[8] Constance Fuller McIntyre added these memories of how whites feasted after the event, "Very numerous are the dishes which appear on the table in hog-killing time. . . . Most farmers seem very fond of chitterlings which they call 'Highland oysters,' but the smell of them is more than enough for most people."[9]

The FWP interviews with former slaves give further evidence that whites enjoyed chitlins. Chitlins had enough prestige in the Big House that Willis Woodson of Texas remembers his mother auditioned for a cook's position by proving she could make chitlins. "Maw didn't work in de field. She say she done been hurt when she got a whippin' when she ain't growed, and her back ain't good no more. Old Miss say, 'Eva, you come in de kitchen and make some chittlin's, and iffen you cooks good, you can work in my kitchen.' Maw, she make dem chittlin's and dey's damn good, so she gits to cook den."[10] Claiborne Moss further cements proof of the interracial bond over chitlins when he reminisces about a visit to his plantation by Confederate army major general Joseph Wheeler's unit during the Civil War: "When Wheeler's cavalry came through they didn't take nothing—nothing but what they et. I heard a fellow say, 'you got anything to eat?' My mother said, 'I ain't got nothin' but some chitlins.' He said, 'Gimme some of those; I love chitlins.' Mother gave 'em to me to carry to him. I didn't get half way to him before the rest of the men grabbed me and took 'em away from me and et 'em up. The man that asked for them didn't get a one."[11] "I love chitlins." That came from the white soldier—not Moss's mother!

Despite the fact that many whites appreciated and ate chitlins, there's currently a strong consensus that there is a racial divide with respect to eating them. A lot of this thinking can be traced to how slaves described meat being divided after a hog killing. In *What the Slaves Ate*, Herbert Covey and Dwight Eisnach quote a Mr. Norris who recalls how racial caste notions were reinforced through food during slavery: "An' 'bout our eatens . . . When we killed hogs, the white folks got all the good part, least they thought that, and we got the neck bones an' ears, an' snoots, an' tails, an' feet, an' the intrails [entrails]; what they called the chitlings. The white folks didn't eat any of that stuff, 'till the last years, when hard times begin to hit 'em and they seen how we fared, now you can't get to the counters to get them things 'for the whites."[12]

Norris's last sentence is telling. Though whites supposedly shunned chitlins during slavery, Norris believed that was no longer the case when he was interviewed in the 1930s. An anonymous *America Eats* essay titled "We Refreshes Our Hog Meat with Corn Pone," written around the time of Norris's interview, corroborates his observation. "But love for chitterlings in the South is by no means confined to Negroes, or to the humbler strata of Whites. . . . And Memphis, New Orleans, Atlanta, and Mobile, and other southern cities all have 'chitterlings cafes.' "[13] Here, the writer bears witness to extensive chitlin eating by whites, at least around the time of the Great Depression. "Chitlin struts" were what southern blacks and whites called the occasions where massive amounts of chitlins were consumed while people drank, sang, and danced in addition to eating.[14] How does one square these observations with the current perception that only blacks eat chitlins? For both blacks and whites, only in the past half-century has eating chitlins gained a racial stigma with whites and a class stigma with blacks. Before then, chitlins were for everyone who had a taste for them.

Unlike in British and French cookbooks, chitlins recipes are notably absent from the nineteenth-century cookbooks authored by southern tastemakers of both races. Mrs. Bryan, Mrs. Dull, Mrs. Fisher, Mrs. Hayes, Mrs. Randolph, Mrs. Russell, and Mrs. Rutledge don't feel the need to give us a chitlins recipe, either because the dish was too uncouth or because the dish was too familiar to warrant notice. The earliest printed recipe that I could find in an African American–authored cookbook comes from A Date with A Dish (1948). Notably, the cookbook's author, Freda DeKnight, gives her readers recipes for boiled and fried "chitterlings" without the anecdotes and comments that she provides to introduce other recipes.[15]

As the hard times of the Great Depression came to an end, racial caste considerations about eating chitlins resurfaced. Chitlin eating among whites went private or entirely underground, while blacks continued to eat chitlins publicly. Walk into a working-class southern restaurant today that has a predominantly white clientele and you won't find chitlins on the menu—a sharp distinction from soul food restaurant menus. Even today, if white people are eating chitlins, it's done at home, out of sight from the neighbors.

However, once a year, all of the caste, class, and race considerations that come with chitlins get thrown out the window. That's at the annual Chitlin Strut in Salley, South Carolina, where chitlins get a very public display of affection in this predominantly white town of 600 people. It started off as a fundraising idea in 1966 and has grown into a huge event attracting as many as 30,000 visitors. According to the *Chicago Defender*, a White House aide attended the 1975 Salley Chitlin Strut and returned to Washington, D.C., with a five-pound box of frozen raw chitlins. History is silent on what happened with those chitlins, but I'd wager that the longtime black employees at the White House handled them with aplomb.[16]

Now that chitlins have fallen mostly out of favor with whites, what explains their continuing appeal with African Americans? For African Americans, chitlins are more than just a food. Particularly during the Down Home Cooking era, chitlins reminded southern migrants of how good times were had at hog killings in the rural South. Rural blacks came together for those hog killings, performed the work, then shared in the rewards.

Janet Driskell Turner, a sharecropper's daughter, provides a detailed hog killing description in her book *Through the Back Door: Memoirs of a Sharecropper's Daughter Who Learned to Read as a Great-Grandmother* (1985). In it, we get an African American perspective of the event that's often glossed over in the slave narratives and interviews. Turner was born in 1920 and grew up in rural Georgia, southeast of Atlanta. "I come from a family of 12 children. We were sharecroppers. Not much money, just a little schooling," Turner writes. "I went through ninth grade and still couldn't read good. We worked from sunup till sundown. Trying to live by white man's rules, that's how it was in the South. We were told what to say, where to sit, where to eat and where to drink. The struggle was hard. With God's help, we survived."[17]

Turner is blunt about her home life: "People didn't have good homes to live in. The house I grew up in . . . was in bad condition—floors and walls with cracks, a loft half without a ceiling, one window with no glass in, fireplace in every room, two lamps that burned kerosene, and water from the spring. It was heated with wood and it was cold in the winter." She also gives us a glimpse into her family's cooking space: "The kitchen sat in a building separate from the house. It had a stove, but no refrigeration. We cooled things by hanging them in the well or putting them in the spring. There were ice boxes, but we had ice only on some weekends because you could only get it in a little town called Eatonton, about 12 miles away from our house."[18]

Turner's description clues us into why hog killings happened in the late fall and winter. Because sharecropper dwellings lacked refrigeration, hog killings took place when the weather was cold enough to keep the butchered meat from spoiling, or being swarmed by insects, during the time it would take to kill hogs and process the meat. Thus, these events were often held during the months that end with an r—October, November, or December—and chitlins had the seasonality commonly associated with oysters. Hog killings for a single family were significantly scaled down as compared with what happened on plantations. Only a small number of hogs were needed to meet the family's food needs. As Turner describes it, the hogs were penned until they were fat enough, then men performed all of the prep work for butchering: building a fire, boiling water to remove the pig's hair, killing the pig, hanging it up by its back legs, and slitting its neck to drain the blood.[19] Depending on the number of pigs to be butchered, a farmer might call on neighbors to help out. Neighboring farmers would coordinate their hog killings to avoid overlap and to maximize the amount of available help. Those who assisted rarely got paid hard cash, but they got fresh meat and offal to take with them. That was payment enough. This egalitarian and coordinated exchange of food for work is an important part of the ethos that enveloped the hog killing. All benefited from being good neighbors.

The next phase was to immerse the pig's body in scalding water to remove its hair. Many written accounts describe how the hog's body would be a gleaming white color after the scalding. The pig's extremities were removed next. With the inside hollowed out, the pig was butchered and processed, and specific preservation techniques were applied to different cuts of meat. Some meat, like the hams, was seasoned and sent to the smokehouse. Other parts, like the pork belly, were salted (yielding the ubiquitous "salt pork"). Some intestines were set aside for making seasoned sausages and sent to the smokehouse later.[20]

Then came time for the chitlins. As Turner describes it, "We took the pig's intestines and squeezed the filth out of them. Then, we cleaned them in warm water until they were white. Mom used to soak them overnight. The next day, we had to scrape them and get everything out. The scraping makes them as thin as the plastic wrap everyone uses today. We cut the intestines into pieces about two feet long. These are called chitlins."[21] Croppers usually had no way to refrigerate chitlins, so they had to be prepared relatively quickly. The transience of chitlins goes a long way to explaining why they became an African American feast food. Chicken could be eaten year-around (though it was preferred in the spring) and catfish could be caught and preserved — but neither was possible with chitlins. There was a very small window of time to relish chitlins, heightening anticipation for the dish. In addition, it's really hard work to make chitlins. I'm a witness after receiving two chitlin-cleaning tutorials — one from my Aunt Joyce Halsey a few years back and one from my brother Duran Lloyd. It takes at least a couple of hours to get through the average ten-pound pail of chitlins. When one sees the yield at the end, one wonders what it was all for — the aching back, the prune-textured fingers, and a dulled sense of smell. As with any satisfying love story, chitlins demand sacrifice.

Given all the fuss, why on earth would anyone want chitlins? In *Onje Fun Orisa* (*Food for the Gods*), a study of Yoruba religious practices in New World foodways, Gary Edwards and John Mason challenge us to consider that slaves may have wanted chitlins for spiritual reasons:

> A myth about the eating of chitterlings is that chitterlings were the only part of the pig that the Master did not want, and that the slaves ate it because there was nothing else to eat. However studies have shown that the slave masters not only gave the slaves chitterlings, but gave the slaves slab of bacon and other parts of the pig as well. In West Africa, although pig's intestines were not eaten, the intestines of other animals were [definitely] eaten (the Hausa even eat the intestines of the chicken), and a small portion is traditionally given to the gods as an offering. In Africa the children received the intestines, and other parts of the innards are eaten (the heart symbolizes strength, the liver is good for the blood, and etc.). Many of the culinary habits have survived until this day. Black people still eat all parts of the chicken, pork and all parts of the fish, just as for example, fish heads, wing tips and chicken feet are considered a delicacy in Africa.[22]

Edwards and Mason describe a ritual hierarchy wherein the intestines of four-legged animals were accorded an *ache* (godly essence or spiritual force), while those of two-legged animals were not.[23] Thus, for the enslaved adhering to Yoruba religious beliefs, a pig's intestines had greater spiritual value than those of a chicken. Edwards and Mason also illuminate the possibility that eating animal innards and extremities is another foodways signature of the West African diaspora and not solely an imposition by white people. We must take into account that slaves could have freely chosen chitlins because they were a spiritually significant food. For many, reconsidering chitlins a sacred food is definitely going to take some getting used to.

During the Southern Cooking era, some African Americans abandoned chitlins while others carried on the tradition. In rural areas, chitlins remained a post–hog killing treat or the centerpiece of a church fundraiser. In urban areas, blacks got chitlins from meat processors who were just going to throw them away. Either the processor gave away the chitlins or blacks would later retrieve chitlins from the trash themselves. Suddenly, black migrants in urban areas had year-round access to chitlins without having to do any of the hard work associated with a hog killing. This was an unexpected thrill for transplanted black southerners who used chitlins to cure their homesickness.

It wasn't so much the love of money but the absolute need for it that spurred rural blacks to transplant the chitlin strut fundraiser to the city. Those free chitlins were vital—and literally kept African Americans in their homes. Urban blacks creatively morphed the rural chitlin strut tradition into the urban rent party, a means to raise much-needed funds among friends. The sheer numbers of migrants who descended on cities in a short period of time created immense pressure on available housing. The combination of restrictions on where blacks could live, white flight from those designated neighborhoods, and opportunistic landlords led to skyrocketing rents. Newly arrived migrants to places like New York City met this challenge by transforming the chitlin strut for the urban environment. Frank Byrd, who wrote extensively about Harlem for the FWP, explains: "Harlemites soon discovered that meeting these doubled, and sometimes tripled, rents was not so easy. . . . Someone evidently got the idea of having a few friends in as paying party guests a few days before the landlord's scheduled monthly visit. It was a happy, timely thought. . . . Thus was the Harlem rent-party born."[24]

While explaining to its readers how to party like it's 1939, the *Cleveland Plaindealer* felt it necessary to give a history of the Harlem rent party: "The land lady, the housewife, and the buffet flat ladies took great pains and pleasure to invite all of her friends to come over and bring their friends Sattidy nite for a little fun. There was music for dancing, plenty of homemade wine, bath tub gin and bootleg likker to drink, at ten cents a glass; and abundance of pigs feet, chitterlings, potato salad, cabbage slaw, hot sauce and pickles. Usually a 25 cents admission was charged at the door to keep out the floaters. The proceeds went to pay the rent, electric and gas bills, and possibly an installment on the furniture and radio."[25] Though the circumstances were different, the hog killing and the rent party shared a core dynamic: Neighbors gathered together to help someone in need, and good times were fueled by great southern food.

The lure of cheap food, good music, and hard liquor proved irresistible for many on the Saturday nights when the rent parties were usually held. This was convenient timing for working-class blacks because Saturday was their payday, and Sunday was a day off.[26] Even whites living outside of Harlem couldn't resist the rent party's siren song and went "slumming."

In 1932, the *Atlanta Daily World* took note and ran a headline saying, "Rent Parties in Harlem Attract White Patrons."[27] Rent parties also became magnets for vice. Since drugs and prostitutes were often on the "secret menu," law enforcement began to raid the rent parties regularly. Given this bad publicity, rent parties gradually faded out, though the black press hints at rent party comebacks in the 1940s and 1950s. For those who preferred to eat their chitlins in a less raucous environment, urban restaurants featured chitlins as a specialty. As early as 1910, someone walking along Chicago's State Street could see a sign like this: "Come To Our Great Opening. Fine Delicatessen at No. — Prairie Ave. Pig's Feet, Chitterlings, Pig Tails, Hog's Head, Hominy, Souse, and Watermelon in Season. You don't Have to go to State Street Any More For What You Want."[28] After seeing shop after shop selling chitlins, one mystified visitor to Harlem surmised in 1928, "Their savory odor is their chief lure to those who like them."[29]

One would expect the smell to be a big factor that kept chitlin-cooking to a minimum in private homes. Why tip off your neighbors that you have country ways? Well, the opposite was the case. An *America Eats* series essay reveals that chitlin events were actually quite popular among middle-class blacks during the winter: "These [chitlin] suppers, held usually in private homes, often are for the purpose of raising money for church affairs, promoting clubs and societies, providing funds for charities. Equally often, however, they are simply get-togethers for purely social purpose."[30] Though more sedate than Harlem rent parties, these chitlin suppers also accomplished the twin tasks of raising money and fostering community. Still, hosts were mindful of what could get out of hand if the wrong "element" arrived. When William Johnson hosted a Chicago "chidlins supper" in 1908, he advertised the event with a notice imploring guests to "bring along your appetite, also your pocketbook. God loves a cheerful spender." Johnson also emphasized that he wanted a classy affair and admonished readers to "leave your razors at home." In a follow-up interview for the newspaper, Johnson confided, "I boil de chidlins half a day . . . an' season dem up to suit de taste. De Irish can have dier corned beef an' cabbage an' de Germans deir sauer kraut and spareribs, but give a colored person chidlins. Jest a little bit of cold slaw of de side of de plate, an' you've got a dish fit fer a king."[31]

Necessarily, I think, a lot of folklore developed about masking the smell. Most people will tell you if you clean chitlins well, they won't stink. That pretty much leads you to the "plastic-wrap-looking-chitlins" school of thought that we got earlier from Janet Turner, our sharecropper, and my brother Duran. With this approach, you pretty much remove everything that's considered "the rough part" of chitlins. The downside for some is that by removing the fatty, rough part instead of trying to clean it, the dish can lose flavor. Others advise adding a halved raw potato to the pot to soak up the grease and, consequently, the smell. Another trick is to boil vinegar right alongside the chitlins as they cook. This works well for anything that smells bad while it's cooking. An isolated few will instruct you to throw them in the washing machine and use the gentle cycle, but I haven't tried that. Science may have come to the rescue. Based on initial studies, a team of Japanese scientists concludes that cilantro leaves (*Coriandrum sativum*) — frequently used in Asian and Latin cuisines — "exhibited a strong deodorizing effect against porcine internal organs."[32] Unscientifically speaking, cilantro takes the "stank" out of chitlins!

By the beginning of the Soul Food era, whites had left chitlins behind as they moved up the economic ladder. Even in cookbooks aimed at poor whites, a chitlins recipe sighting is less likely in current times. Ernest Mickler's *White Trash Cooking* (1986) and Janis Owens's *Cracker Kitchen* (2009) have no chitlins recipes, even among all the funky dishes those odes to poor white cooking contain. On the other hand, *Boilin' 'n' Bakin' in Boogar Hollow* (1971) and *Cookin' in Rebel Country* (1972), cookbooks authored by whites a few decades prior, do.[33] Over lunch at Atlanta's Busy Bee Café, I discussed the matter of what poor whites and blacks ate with Jim Auchmutey, a former *Atlanta Journal-Constitution* food writer and a white southerner. Auchmutey grew up in Atlanta and has extended family in northern Georgia. He told me, with Owens's book in mind, "Cracker food is soul food. My people ate chitlins a couple of generations back."[34] I think a number of white southerners can lay claim to the same heritage, but they have clearly moved on.

For blacks, the current and future state of chitlins is much more in flux. A large number of blacks eschew chitlins for the reasons mentioned earlier, but plenty still chew on chitlins. Chitlins are widely available in fresh and frozen forms in major grocery stores across the country all year long. Though the hog killing custom no longer applies to current circumstances, many blacks save their chitlin eating for the winter months, the time of year chitlins were traditionally available. In stores that have a predominantly black clientele, chitlins are usually on sale from Thanksgiving through New Year's Day in recognition of this tradition. Otherwise, chitlins are pricey during the rest of the year, thus undermining their reputa-

Lema's World Famous Chitlins

KNOXVILLE, TENNESSEE

After taking a wrong turn during a rainstorm in Knoxville, Tennessee, and getting a little lost, I pulled into a fire station parking lot to turn around, but coincidentally, a fire truck was pulling out at that exact moment. So I had to wait. What I thought was coincidence I now know was fate. While waiting, I saw a sign that said, "Lema's World Famous Chittlins." Thinking it was a joke, I drove over to the place to investigate. Once inside, I was introduced to a world that I never knew existed, a place where a chitlins-only restaurant could exist and thrive.

Robert Bennett and his sister have run this place since the 1980s, and the restaurant has a very limited schedule. It's open on Fridays and Saturdays from October to April. I was there on a Thursday, yet fate had shown its hand again, as the only reason the place was open was the constant rain. "People want chitlins when it's bad weather," Bennett told me. "I figured I would come down, turn on the lights and start selling chitlins." Sure enough, customers started to trickle in.

Oddly, Lema's doesn't have that distinctive chitlin aroma even when Bennett is cooking a batch. I told him as much, and he quipped without missing a beat, "I took the stink out of the [insert colorful substitute for "chitlins" here]." Lema's sells generous portions of chitlins (ranging from a half-pound to two and a half pounds) with sides of coleslaw and spaghetti.

Lema's has also made me a believer in chitlins' motivating power. A cancer patient strolled in during my visit. One week before, he couldn't swallow anything because of his chemotherapy regimen. He vowed to himself that once he got well, he was going to get some chitlins, and get them he did.

Sign at Lema's World Famous Chittlins, Knoxville

tion as a poverty food. For those who do carry on the chitlins tradition, it's become more about collegiality rather than marking class boundaries. As a shrinking population, we chitlin eaters have to stick together.

Chitlins are often presented as a divisive force within soul food, but the dish has done a lot to bring people together. A well-known black proverb is "Know who makes your chitlins," the idea being that someone who cares about you, the diner, is going to take the time to thoroughly clean those chitlins so that you won't get sickened. Through this added assurance, family, friendship, and kinship bonds are emphatically reinforced in the sharing of this food. There's also the famous "Chitlin Circuit," which cultural critic Mark Anthony Neal describes as a "loose network of black nightclubs, juke joints, and after-hours clubs [that] was invaluable for the creation of common aesthetic and cultural sensibilities among the African American diaspora."[35] Here, chitlins symbolically represent the literal connection of disparate entertainment venues where black culture thrived relatively free of white interference. Longtime musician Isaac "Sax" Kari explains why the circuit got its name. "Chitlins to black people were like caviar to Europeans. It's played out now, but it was a delicacy. The average chitlin' dinner was a dollar. You could go to one place and buy supper, drinks, and see an orchestra perform."[36] Black artists like Jimi Hendrix, Millie Jackson, B. B. King, and Lou Rawls performed a range of musical genres on the circuit, all realizing that they were paying dues and hoping to make it big. Though many of the circuit's spots were rough-and-tumble, there were several classy venues, like Harlem's Apollo Theater, Chicago's Regal Theater, and the Royal Peacock in Atlanta.

When black musicians who grew up in isolated parts of the rural South hit the Chitlin Circuit and experienced city life, they must have thought that they were being transported to another world. Little did they know that chitlins actually do connect them with a larger world. When someone sups on chitlins, they commune with the English, the French, Native Americans, the Argentines (*chinchulines*), and the Ecuadorans (*tripa mishqui*).[37] Every Easter, the Greeks eat a traditional sheep's intestines dish called "Resurrection Pie." Koreans grub on grilled beef or pork intestines in a dish called *gop chang*. Many African Americans may be surprised to learn this, but there is indeed an international brother- and sisterhood of guts eaters. It took a particular band of brothers, the African American troops, to find this out.

After serving in World War II, some black veterans opted to live abroad in voluntary exile in Europe rather than return home to live in the persistently racist environment of the United States. Many gravitated to France, which seemed like a paradise. Numerous letters from black soldiers and dispatches from black newspaper correspondents described the basic liberties available to black expatriates in Paris. Another desirable thing available in Paris for blacks and whites was chitlins.

Leroy Haynes of Clinton, Kentucky, took full advantage of all that France had to offer. The former All-American football player at Morehouse College and World War II army veteran found a wife, began an acting career, and opened up a southern-style restaurant in Paris in 1949. The restaurant would make him America's unofficial ambassador to France for down home cooking and, later, for soul food. His calling card was chitlins. One newspaper reporter wrote in 1966,

"Chitterlings," it says on the menu. "Fatback and Greens. Panfried sausage." Harlem? South Side Chicago? No, this is Paris, where Leroy Haynes, a fiftyish ex-GI is doing rather well, thank you, as the proprietor of Chez Haynes (3 Rue Clauzel, Paris 9) France's only American Negro restaurant. . . . "It was only a little place, with room for about 30 people," he says. "But for the first year or so we'd have settled for 15. Business was real bad. Then the word started getting around among Negro GI's stationed in France that my place had food like mother use dto [sic] make."[38]

As we now know, the French knew something about chitlins, so it was no small thing when the French film superstar Brigitte Bardot proclaimed that Haynes's chitlins were *formidable*.[39]

In its heyday, Haynes's restaurant had a reputation that spanned the continent. A description from one visitor reveals the ways in which American blacks began to participate in French society. Writing in 1955, a *Chicago Defender* correspondent said, "I soon found out that this was not just a restaurant; it was a gathering place for many of the 'brethren' who for one reason or another happened to be in Paris. GI's from all over Europe manage to find their way here, and so do their French girl friends. Stars of stage and screen should also be included, because I've seen them there. . . . It's a sort of 'Information Center' about activities of Negroes in Europe; and the pattern changes every hour with the customers going and coming."[40]

In its last years, Haynes's restaurant continued to offer chitlins, staying true to its founder's roots by featuring the one item that attracted Americans and French alike. Haynes died in 1986, and his third wife and widow kept the restaurant running until it finally closed in 2009.[41] I was a student in Paris in 1990, but I knew nothing of Haynes's place. I would have been elated to experience something that reminded me of home more deeply than the Golden Arches. *C'est la vie.*

Europe was not the only place where soul food thrived. Some African American veterans opted to stay in Asia during the military conflicts of the 1950s and 1960s, and some even opened up soul food joints. No surprise, these places often featured chitlins. In April 1973, Bob Adams, an air force staff sergeant (E5) stationed at Yokota Air Force Base in Japan, wanted to make some chitlins. He remembers chitlins were available at the base's commissary in two U.S. brands, Swift and Hormel, with one in a red pail and the other in a yellow pail. Though Adams can't recall which one he chose, he remembers that one brand had the reputation for being "cleaner," so he purchased that one.[42] Actually, Adams could have gotten his chitlins from local sources. Asian food cultures have much of the same culinary vocabulary as soul food: fiery hot condiments, fish, leafy greens, rice, sweet potatoes, and funky parts of chickens, cows, and pigs—all are on the menu along with chitlins.

From the 1960s until the late 1980s, following the Vietnam War, soul food joints run by black military veterans were popping up all over Asia. In April 1970, air force master sergeant Allen A. Rious opened up the BP Club on the outskirts of Yokohama, Japan. The entire time the club was in business, there was controversy about whether the BP stood for "Beautiful People" as Rious claimed, or "Black Power" as the Japanese cops suspected. The BP Club welcomed lots of famous visitors. Muhammad Ali stopped by after he fought Mac Foster in Tokyo on 1 April 1972.[43] Soul food spots also popped up in Bangkok, Thailand, like Jack's American Star Bar Bangkok (which was fictionally depicted as a restaurant called Soul Brothers in the 2007 film *American Gangster*).[44] The soul food business was so good even the locals got in on the act and opened up restaurants that catered to black servicemen. Army sergeant Leon A. Casey recalled visiting a restaurant near the Tan Son Nhut Air Force Base in Vietnam in the early 1970s. He dined on chitlins, black-eyed peas, collards, and a Vietnamese version of cornbread, all washed down with a local beer while Lou Rawls crooned from a record player. As he left, the Cambodian owner implored him to tell all of his GI buddies about the place.[45]

The L&M Guest House, located on Coathang Street in the heart of Saigon (now Ho Chi Minh City) quickly established itself as Vietnam's most popular soul food restaurant. In a familiar pattern, Andrew Mitchell, a former merchant marine steward and New Yorker, opened up the L&M after he fell in love with a Vietnamese woman and settled in Saigon in 1966. A *Washington Post* correspondent visited the L&M in 1967 and described the scene: "Except for the petite Vietnamese woman who glided silently by putting plates of fragrant barbequed spareribs or steaming platters of chitterlings on the huge table in the middle of the room, everybody in the place was Negro." The correspondent added that on that day, L&M's "'Menu Pour Le Jour' features Kansas City Wrinkles, Bar-B-Q Ribs, Fried Brook Trout, Fried Chicken, butter beans, rice with gravy, greens."[46] Once again, chitlins were a star attraction, and Mitchell explained emphatically in a newspaper interview why chitlins were such a big draw: "'Sometimes I buy 180 pounds of chitterlings [Kansas City Wrinkles] a week, pigs feet, hog maws—they're easy to get over here because the Vietnamese eat them too. . . . A lot of the fellows over here get a little lonely' Mitch said. 'And when you're down and out and thinking about home there ain't nothing like some chitterlings, potato salad and greens to make you feel better.'"[47] Homesick GIs frequently redefined the places they ended up in to make them like home. The Khanh Hoi neighborhood immediately surrounding the L&M Guest House was called "Soulsville," and darker-skinned Asian women were called "Soul sisters." On the flip side, Vietnamese people often called black soldiers "souls." If you were a good lover, Vietnamese women might call you a "soul one."[48]

Regardless of where these soul food joints took root, the restaurant experience was about getting together with the other brothers. In a *New York Times* interview on why he frequented the Saigon soul food places, one black soldier said, "Look, you've proven your point when you go out and work and soldier with Chuck all day. It's like you went to the Crusades and now you're back relaxing around the Round Table—ain't no need bringing the dragon home with you."[49] The soul food restaurants became a place where black soldiers could "get away from 'the man'" and "luxuriate in blackness" or "get the black view."[50]

In the past, chitlins have been put in such a negative light that it's hard to believe that something good could come from them. Yet, in every phase of African American history, chitlins have been about connection. During slavery, preparing chitlins was a way to connect to other slaves, particularly those who held Yoruba beliefs. In the Southern Cooking era, hog killings were about connecting to people in your immediate community. In the Down Home Cooking era, chitlins became a way to connect with urban neighbors in need and with whites who enjoyed the dish. The black GI experience abroad during the Soul Food era shows that chitlins continued to connect people with one another in difficult circumstances and reveals that African Americans share food traditions with both Europeans and Asians. Today, chitlins link a shrinking, and passionate, group of African Americans who are holding onto tradition simply because they love the taste of chitlins. In all of these contexts, chitlins consistently evoke thoughts of camaraderie and home.

Chitlins Duran

Chitlins need a lot of attention and plenty of time if you're going to properly clean them. I got my best chitlins-cleaning lesson standing at my brother Duran's side. Duran's so adept at it that he's taught many others. His chitlins wind up being velvety, less greasy, and less smelly. If you don't want to do the arduous task of cleaning chitlins, you may take your chances with the precleaned chitlins products now available in grocery stores. My experience is that "precleaned" on a package of chitlins is more of an aspirational statement than a reality. Make sure that you do a close inspection before you throw your chitlins in a pot. In all likelihood, you probably will still have to clean them.

Makes 12 servings

20 pounds fresh or thawed chitlins, cut into 6-inch lengths
1 large onion, coarsely chopped
4 garlic cloves, chopped
¼ cup crushed red pepper flakes
Hot sauce, coleslaw, and meatless spaghetti, for serving

1 Bring a very large pot of water to a boil. Drain the chitlins and transfer them into the boiling water and let cook for 5 minutes. This step helps kill germs and does not interfere with cleaning the chitlins.

2 Drain the chitlins in a colander, pour them into a clean sink or very large bowl, and cover them with fresh, cold water. (If the chitlins came in buckets, use one of them to hold the parts that will be discarded.) Refill the large pot with cold water to hold the chitlins after they are cleaned.

3 To clean each strip of chitlins, use your fingers to separate the thin, transparent membrane from the rough part. (This is like pulling the top piece of tape from double-sided tape.) Rinse the membrane under cold running water until it is free of debris and dirty fat, but leave any clean fat. Drop the cleaned part into the pot and discard the rest.

4 Drain the pot of cleaned chitlins and cover them with fresh cold water. Repeat the draining and rinsing process until the water is no longer cloudy.

5 Bring to a simmer over medium-low heat. Simmer for 1 hour. Drain the chitlins, return them to the pot, and cover with fresh water. Simmer for 1 hour. Drain the chitlins, return them to the pot, and cover with fresh water. Add the onion, garlic, and pepper flakes. Simmer until the chitlins are very tender and a little shiny from the grease, about 2 hours more. They will look like long, gray-brown thick noodles.

6 Remove the chitlins from the pot with tongs and divide among serving plates. Serve hot with hot sauce, coleslaw, and spaghetti with a meatless tomato sauce.

Deep-Fried Chitlins

The most soulful way to eat chitlins is to stew them, but a lot of people fry them up as well. These will remind you of other crisp, porcine treats like pork rinds or snoots. The other plus is that you don't get the smell. Well, not as much. This recipe is courtesy of Chef Joe Randall of the Savannah Cooking School in Georgia.

Makes 4 servings

> 2 large eggs
> 2 cups milk
> ¼ cup cornstarch
> 3 cups all-purpose flour
> 2 teaspoons salt
> 1 teaspoon freshly ground black pepper
> Peanut oil, for deep-frying
> 5 pounds cooked chitlins (see Chitlins Duran, above), drained
> Hot sauce, for serving

1 In a medium bowl, whisk together the eggs and milk. In another large bowl, whisk together the cornstarch, flour, salt, and pepper.
2 Fill a deep fryer or large, deep, cast-iron skillet no more than one-third full with peanut oil. Heat the oil until it is shimmering hot.
3 Working in batches, dip the chitlins into the egg mixture. Let the excess drip off and then coat them lightly and evenly in the cornstarch mixture.
4 Lower the coated chitlins into the hot oil, adding no more than can float freely, and cook until golden brown, turning once, 2 to 3 minutes per side. Drain well on paper towels.
5 Serve hot with the hot sauce.

7

Black-Eyed Peas

WHAT'S LUCK GOT TO DO WITH IT?

Do you want good luck for New Year's? Then try the recipes given for dried black-eyed peas. If you shun them on the market shelves or never heard of them before, just try cooking them as suggested. They are a real New Year's tradition in the South. Cooked with a tasty hog's head, pigtails, salt pork, ham or bacon, they make a fine dish; not only on New Year's but any day you desire a hearty and delicious nourishing dish. In the summer and early fall when fresh black-eyed peas are in season, add them regularly to your vegetable list. — Freda DeKnight, *A Date with a Dish* (1948)

★   ★   ★   ★   ★

In 2006, I got the scintillating idea to spread some holiday cheer and share a longtime soul food custom. With some items donated by Glory Foods, I organized a New Year's Day feed at a local shelter for distressed families in Denver. The shelter's culinary staff helped put together a meal featuring black-eyed peas for good luck and greens for money in the upcoming year. Who could appreciate the sentiment more, I thought, than families in distress? Well, I wasn't mentally and emotionally prepared for what happened next. As people moved through the serving line, upon spotting the black-eyed peas and receiving my exuberant explanation of the tradition, some were ecstatic, some were anguished, and most gave me a "Whatever, dude" look. One would have thought that I was trying to serve them chitlin tartare.

At that moment, I couldn't help but think of the late comedian Rodney Dangerfield. Dangerfield built a successful career on the fact that he couldn't "get no respect at all." The same could be said of the black-eyed pea 364 days out of the year. But on New Year's Day, the plebian pea takes on magical qualities, beckoning millions of black and white southerners (and people with a southern heritage) across the country with a promise: "Eat me, and I will bring you good fortune." I got to wondering how and why a onetime slave food gets such a star turn with so many on that one particular day. As I learned the black-eyed peas story, I realized that I was thinking about the wrong celebrity. In a surprising historical twist, black-eyed peas are a rare example in which enslaved African Americans used a familiar West African food to consciously reinterpret an old European superstition and then presented it to white southerners as something they invented. In short, black-eyed peas are the closest thing soul foodies have to a "reverse Elvis."

Before we delve into the history, let's sort out what a black-eyed pea actually is. Food expert Ronni Lundy provides a good definition of black-eyed peas (*Vigna unguiculata*) in her book *Butter Beans to Blackberries*: "'Crowder peas' is the generic name given to a number of these small legumes which are actually beans, not peas. The name refers to how closely the edible beans grow in the pod, and technically may be crowder, semicrowder, or noncrowder peas, although those distinctions are ignored by folks who are talking about supper and not horticulture. Black eyed peas are the most well-known crowders."[1] For the past few centuries, black-eyed peas were also called calavances, cornfield peas, cowpeas, and field peas. Though imprecise, when the sources I cite use one of these other terms, you should think black-eyed peas.

Black-eyed peas are native to Africa, where they have been a popular food at least since the Middle Ages. Black-eyed peas are believed to have been first domesticated near Africa's Lake Chad in what is presently northeastern Nigeria and northern Cameroon.[2] Lewicki states that there are "numerous references in the medieval Arabic authors to the cultivation and consumption of kidney beans or cowpeas in various areas of West Africa."[3] Through trade routes, black-eyed peas spread in all directions, showing up on tables throughout Europe (served by the ancient Greeks and Romans, in particular) and in India.[4] As a favored crop for West Africans, the peas were used to provision slave ships and were introduced into the New World in areas where slavery thrived.[5]

Europe's colonial and slaving rivals were largely responsible for bringing black-eyed peas to North America. Anthropologist Mark Wagner observes, "The Spanish are believed to have introduced the plant into Florida before 1700 and the French are believed to have introduced it into Louisiana in the early eighteenth century. It is reported in North Carolina by 1714, in Virginia by 1775, and in Rhode Island by 1773. The reference to the plant in Rhode Island is contained in the manifest of the slaver *Cleopatra*. Its manifest states that 'Two Hogshead black ey'd peas' were loaded

Black-eyed peas, Red Rooster Restaurant, Harlem

as supplies for the voyage to Africa."[6] Wagner further notes that Native Americans loved black-eyed peas and planted them extensively—so much so that some mistakenly believed this food was native to the Americas. Though black-eyed peas abounded, not everyone wanted to eat them. One influential detractor was Amelia Simmons, the U.S.'s first cookbook author. Using the synonym "calivanse," Simmons wrote in *American Cookery* (1796), "Calivanse, are run out, a small yellow bush, a black speck or eye, are tough and tasteless, and little worthy in cookery, and scarcely bear exportation."[7] Exporters apparently didn't take Simmons's advice, because ships were regularly arriving from the South and the Caribbean to trade and sell black-eyed peas in major ports like New York City.[8]

Simmons's sentiment was part and parcel of a long-running, twofold bias that some Europeans had against beans. The main gripe was spiritual. As one folklore expert wrote, "In Northern Europe and England, beans were associated with this demotic, rowdy, peoples' time at the year's end and beginning. . . . In ancient Greece and Rome, splitting beans was used as a charm to ward off witches and ghosts. According to Pliny the Elder in his *Historia Naturalis*, beans were thought to contain the souls of the dead. Because of these associations, beans were shunned by the rich and powerful and considered taboo by the priests of Rome and Egypt."[9] Aside from supernatural concerns, beans have traditionally been seen as "poor people's food" in Western Europe, and immigrants from that continent brought that sentiment to North America.

In the antebellum South, "poor people's food" typically meant slave food. As Aliza Green writes in Beans,

> In the United States, black beans were first raised in the Gulf Coast areas near Mexico, where they were an important food in the diet of local slaves. Because many people associated these beans with slave food and didn't like the fact that they stained every food cooked with them in inky color, black beans were not well received at first. The name "black turtle Bean" seems to have resulted from a marketing effort by a 19th-century seed company that tried to popularize them by selling them as "turtle beans," suitable to add to or use as a substitute for turtle soup was that considered the utmost in luxury foods.[10]

Planters cultivated a number of beans for their slaves, including Congo peas, goober peas, cream peas, crowder peas, lady peas, lima beans, purple hull peas, southern checker peas, and whippoorwill peas, to name a few. Yet none of those beans surpassed the black-eyed pea's reputation for feeding slaves and animals.

George Simmons remembers from his time in bondage in Alabama that "Massa Jaynes . . . He gives us plenty to eat and lots of cornbread and black-eye' peas and plenty of hawg meat and sich."[11] Notable planters like George Washington and Thomas Jefferson experimented with growing black-eyed peas. Jefferson was so pleased with the results that he once wrote, "I have also received . . . all the good kinds of field pea from England, but I count a great deal more on our southern cow-pea. . . . It is very productive, excellent food for man and beast."[12] A planter in the late 1840s added, "As there is no vegetable of which Negroes are more fond of it than of the common field pea, it is well to save enough of them in the fall to have them frequently during the spring and summer. They are very nutritious; and if cooked perfectly done, and well seasoned with red pepper, are quite healthy."[13] The positive reports on black-eyed peas were mainly from the South, where planters, yeoman farmers, slaves, poor whites, and Native Americans all ate black-eyed peas.

In the North, the black-eyed pea really couldn't get out from under the navy bean's shadow. American Cookery magazine advocated in 1914 that "black-eyed peas are better flavored than beans, and cost about the same, yet grocers in the north say they sell but a few black-eyed peas in comparison with the amount of white beans sold, and that when sales are made of these peas they are generally to negroes."[14] By World War I, constant food shortages spurred the federal government to become a black-eyed pea booster. The U.S. Department of Agriculture published pamphlets and disseminated recipes touting the use of cowpeas as a substitute food. Northerners weren't going for it, and the black-eyed pea stayed primarily a regional (in the American South) and ethnic (with African Americans) specialty.

Before we can get to how black-eyed peas became magical, we have to understand how black-eyed pea cooking changed from colonial West Africa to contemporary America. West Africans have a number of traditional ways to prepare black-eyed peas. Black-eyed peas could be cooked whole and mixed in with other ingredients in soups and stews. Black-eyed peas were also ground into a dry flour, or they were made into a wet paste to deep-fry in balls or steam in leaves like a tamale. Today in West Africa, black-eyed peas are a popular food for young children.[15] When cooking for adults, West African cooks prefer black-eyed peas that "stick together as a 'mushy whole.' This is preferred to cooked cowpeas that remain separate and display 'grainy' characteristics."[16] At least among modern West African cooks, there's a decided preference for a mushy preparation.

On slave ships, black-eyed peas were typically stewed, but we don't have adequate descriptions of how grainy or mushy those stews were. Fortunately, Mrs. Randolph describes in her *Virginia Housewife* cookbook how black-eyed peas were made in the Big House. The recipe for "Field peas" actually outlines three different ways to cook black-eyed peas. Part of the recipe instructs, "Have them young and newly gathered, shell and boil them tender; pour then in a colander to drain; put some lard in a frying pan; when it boils, mash the peas, and fry them in a cake of a light brown; put it in the dish with the crust uppermost—garnish with thin bits of fried bacon." Mrs. Randolph's second suggested preparation is that black-eyed peas "are also very nice when fried whole, so that each pea is distinct from the other; but they must be boiled less and fried with great care." Lastly, she suggests that "plain boiling is a very common way of dressing them."[17] Of the three recipes, the first "mashed" one from Mrs. Randolph merits our attention. Except the very "Virginia-like" addition of bacon, the mashed black-eyed pea cake evokes the current West African preference for black-eyed pea dishes that stick together.

The preference for mushy black-eyed peas continued past the Slave Food era into the Southern Cooking era. The *Housekeeping in Old Virginia* cookbook (1879) has a mashed black-eyed pea recipe that explicitly linked the dish to blackness for its white audience. The "Resipee for Cukin Kon-Feel Pees" attributed to a Mozis Addums was very popular and widely copied by other cookbook authors of the time:

> Gether your pees 'bout sun-down. The folrin day, 'bout leven o'clock, gowge out your pees with your thum nale, like gowgin out a man's eye-ball at a kote house. Rense your pees, parbile them, then fry 'em with som several slices uv streek, middlin, incouragin uv the gravy to seep out and intermarry with your pees. When modritly brown, but not scorch, empty into a dish. Mash 'em gently with a spune, mix with raw tomaters sprinkled with a little brown shugar and the immortal dish ar quite ready. Eat a hepe. Eat mo and mo. It is good for your general helth uv mind and body. It fattens you up, makes you sassy, goes throo and throo your very soul. But, why don't you eat? Eat on. By Jings. Eat. *Stop!* Never, while thar is a pee in the dish. *Mozis Addums.*[18]

Once one gets past the dialogue, one sees that Mr. Addums's recipe captures soul food's narrative arc. He suggests fresh peas, marries them with pork fat, mashes it all up, adds something sweet, pairs it with another vegetable, and throws in the term "soul" for good measure. Though mashed black-eyed peas were associated first with Africanness and later with blackness, the dish was eventually associated with Virginia cooks of all backgrounds. *America Eats* writers said in their 1940s survey of Virginia cuisine, "In regard to black-eyed peas the eternal question is whether to mash or not to mash."[19]

Outside Virginia, the "grainy," "non-mashed" black-eyed pea preparations are much more common. Most of these grainy dishes were simple stews of black-eyed peas with some pork—a direct descendant of the British "pease pottages" that were cooked with other beans. Sometimes other ingredients were thrown in the pot, as is the case with South Carolina's famous dish, "Hoppin' John." In 1950, an American Dialect publication defined Hoppin' John as "rice and cowpeas cooked together, usually with a piece of bacon or a hambone or some other sort of pork." As for the dish's name, the same source theorized that it was "probably from *pois à*

How Did Hoppin' John Get Its Name?

Let's investigate possible origins for the quirky name "Hoppin' John." One theory is that a physically challenged black street vendor named John peddled the dish on the streets of Charleston as he hopped along. Another theory is that the wife of a man named John was cooking the dish for dinner, and when he peeked into the kitchen, she invited him to sit down and eat, saying, "Hop in, John." A lesser-known theory is that children had to hop around the table and sing a tune before they could eat.[1] Culinary historian Karen Hess, in her superbly annotated reprint of *The Carolina Rice Kitchen*, wove a very interesting theory that "hoppin' John" is an approximation of *bahatta kachang*—a name evidencing the Arabic roots of the dish, since bean and rice dishes are also prevalent in the Middle East.[2] In England, "Hopping John" was the name of a laborer's breakfast consisting of hot, skimmed milk poured over bread.[3] In 1830, "Hopping John" was also the name of a half-brandy and half-cider drink sugared to taste.[4]

There's another possibility. *Pois à pigeon*, the French name for pigeon peas, when said quickly sounds a lot like "hoppin' John." In the years leading up to and immediately after the Haitian Revolution, many white planters fled the French colony and established themselves in South Carolina. These French émigrés and their slaves likely brought the dish with them and shared it with their English neighbors. Eventually, *pois à pigeon* was Anglicized as "Hoppin' John."

---

1 Covey and Eisnach, *What the Slaves Ate*, 84.
2 Hess, *Carolina Rice Kitchen*, 100.
3 "Old English Farm Fare."
4 "Counterpart Cousins," 26.

pigeon of Jamaica, although other derivations have been proposed."[20] *Pois à pigeon* (*Cajanus cajan*), or pigeon peas, are small, beige, speckled beans native to West Africa. Slaves introduced the plant into the Caribbean during the slave trade.[21] The combination of rice and beans is common throughout the West African diaspora. Thus, Hoppin' John is the South Carolina cousin to New Orleans's red beans and rice, Jamaica's peas and rice, Puerto Rico's *arroz con gandules*, and Cuba's *moros y cristianos*.[22] A dish identical to Hoppin' John appears in the New Orleans *Picayune's Creole Cook Book* (1901), but there it's called *jambalaya au congri*.[23] Traveler accounts from the Old South show that Hoppin' John crossed caste lines and was enjoyed by the enslaved, poor whites, and the wealthy alike.[24]

When contemporary West African cooks make black-eyed peas with rice together, they have some pretty strong opinions about which peas to use. Once again, our West African nutrition experts instruct, "When cooking cowpeas with rice, colour is also important and a red or golden brown variety that does not 'bleed' its colour is preferred. The red or brown varieties are also the most popular for stews because they usually exhibit binding qualities rather than 'grainy' characteristics."[25] Two centuries earlier, Mrs. Rutledge certainly agreed that red peas (with black eyes) were essential to the recipe for Hoppin' John she includes in *The Carolina Housewife*.[26] Fast-forward to the twentieth century, and red peas were the standard choice for making Hoppin' John in the United States. Writing in the late 1920s, a *Washington Post* food writer explained the proper way to make Hoppin' John to her readers: "It seems there are several varieties of these [peas], but I am sure now that none but the red ones should be used in combination with rice—twice as many beans as rice—and hoppin' John. . . . Great emphasis is placed on the fact that the red, not white peas—I should call them beans—shall be used, and that the dish must be of a dark reddish color."[27] By the time American writers and cooks started dictating the use of red peas, the reason for doing so was apparently lost. Using red peas was a matter of tradition.

Tradition had to be tossed aside, because it wasn't always easy to get these particular red peas outside of the Carolinas. Black-eyed peas, a readily available substitute, sprang back into the picture. As Karen Hess shows in *The Carolina Rice Kitchen*, a definite parochialism about peas existed in South Carolina.

> In any specific district the inhabitants will insist that there is only
> one proper pea for hoppin' John, the one that is used there, with

its own name. But there must have been a number of varieties of *V. unguiculata* in use in the Lowcountry, although it does seem that the red or black peas were traditionally favored. While closely related, all those peas are surprisingly different in flavor and other characteristics. In practice people in any given corner of the South *know* which pea to use, and as far as the rest of the country is concerned, black-eye peas are generally the most easily available.[28]

Convenience, that was the key. Dried black-eyed peas were available to more consumers around the country and thus were a ready substitute for red peas. Over time, the black-eyed peas substitution was so smooth and successful that, today, South Carolina cooks no longer insist that red peas be used in the dish.

Black-eyed peas, and consequently, Hoppin' John, made their way out of the South and across the country largely for two reasons: Black migrants wanted black-eyed peas wherever they settled, and dried black-eyed peas were well suited for industrial shipping to distant locales. In the 1920s, one fan touted dried black-eyed peas by writing, "In this form it bears transportation well and is comparable in its nutritious quality to other dried beans, such as navy beans, kidney beans and lima beans."[29] This market-friendly quality aided the spread of black-eyed peas outside the South. Well into the Down Home Cooking period, black-eyed peas were in high demand. The *Broad Ax*, a black newspaper published in Salt Lake City, reported in 1904, "Mrs. Marshall Drish, 4613 Dearborn street, received a small bag of black eyed peas from one of her lady friends who came from behind the sun down In Tennessee; with the request that she should cook and eat them all on New Year's day; If she did so she would have plenty of money all the year round. We are not in a position to state whether Mrs. Drish followed her friend's advice or not."[30] Decades later, a 1930s consumer survey of Harlem showed that "of legumes the black-eyed pea or cow pea which is really a bean is the heaviest seller."[31] For southern-born-and-bred blacks who had migrated and wanted to re-create home in a new locale, black-eyed peas were the overwhelming, and most convenient, choice for a New Year's Day meal and most other meals during the rest of the year.

For believers, eating black-eyed peas on New Year's Day carried the promise of either good luck or more money in the new year. Dulcina Baker Martin of Winchester, Kentucky, recalling her life under slavery, falls squarely in the first category: "Folks uster b'lieve dat cookin' certain things on New Year's Day en certain other days of de year ud bring good luck. Dey uster cook black eyed peas er dry beans fer New Years Day, en some folks cooked kraut."[32] In the late 1960s, another person spoke for the alternative view in a *New York Amsterdam News* article: "In Harlem and Chicago's South Side, they say that 'Eating peas is just for coins. Collard and other greens bring folding money. And pig, all parts of the pig, will make you healthy, wealthy and sharp.'"[33]

Because of these superstitions, black-eyed peas became a special occasion food for the enslaved even though they were regularly eaten on the plantation. Black-eyed peas even inspired poetry. Della Fountain from Oklahoma recalls, "Mother always say, 'If you visit on New Year's, you'll visit all de year.' We always had black-eyed peas and hog jowl for New Year's dinner, for it brought good luck."[34] And Harriet Collins of Texas remembers this refrain:

> Dose black-eyed peas is lucky,
> When et on New Year's Day:
> You'll allus have sweet 'taters
> And possum come your way.[35]

The prospect of having a constant supply of delicacies like sweet potatoes and possum available year-round was incentive enough to indulge in the superstition. New Year's Day was also an important day on the plantation. That's when planters made annual contracts for hiring out slaves for the year or decided who was going to be sold. The enslaved surely hoped for good luck on this date, namely that their families would not be broken up through a slave sale. In West Africa, black-eyed peas have no folkloric connection with money, but they have long been associated with good luck.

Eyes have significant folkloric meaning in contemporary West African belief systems. The "evil eye" and its power to wreak havoc on daily life are of such concern to many West Africans that they seek constant protection from its effect. Some West Africans believe that wearing something that contains an eye, or something that resembles an eye, will provide protection. While studying how West Africans utilized plants in the late 1930s, J. M. Dalziel observed that in northern Nigeria, black-colored plant seeds were used to suggest "the pupil of the eye, and they are therefore an ingredient in charms to ensure invisibility [from evil spirits]."[36] Within this worldview, it's not so much that black-eyed peas gave a person good luck, but that they thwarted bad luck.

Though we don't have much historic information on beliefs about black-eyed peas during the Atlantic slave trade, West Africans have many contemporary beliefs about black-eyed peas. On Good Friday, a cowpea-and-coconut-custard combination called *frejon* is a traditional meal in parts of West Africa.[37] A dish called *ewa-Ibeji* (known colloquially as Beans for Twins) was originally cooked with oil and only for ailing twin children, but now it is ceremonially prepared for even healthy twins.[38] The most widely shared and folkloric cowpea preparation in the African diaspora is *akara* (cowpea fritters fried in palm oil). In many West African countries, this is traditionally served at funerals or large gatherings.[39] Another expert pointed out, "The Yoruba people of West Africa make ground black-eyed peas into fritters fit for the traditional goddess of the wind, *Oya*. Called *acara*, it is a filling snack sold by street vendors in Nigeria."[40] The *acara* and *akara* show that even fried black-eyed pea preparations, reminiscent of the Virginia-style black-eyed pea cakes, can have a spiritual element.

This is why the demise of the Virginia-style, mashed black-eyed pea cake and the increased popularity of grainy preparations like Hoppin' John are so important to the story. When cooks make mashed black-eyed pea dishes, the "eyes" of the peas are either minimized or disappear entirely because the outer skin is altered or removed. The only time we hear of black-eyed peas being linked with good luck are when they are prepared as a grainy whole. When it comes to making black-eyed peas magical, the "eyes" have it.

Ken Albala, in *Beans: A History*, clarifies how the current spiritual elements concerning black-eyed peas are rooted back in the time of the Atlantic slave trade.

Among the Yoruba black-eyed peas are one of the principal ingredients used to feed the gods or Orishas, who protect the community. This religion was carried to the New World where it took various forms such as Candomble in Brazil and Santeria in the Caribbean. There too the Orishas are fed with their favorite foods. Obatala, for example, prefers yams, rice flour paste, corn meal dumplings and black-eyed peas. Yemaya, the mother of the Orishas, also eats black-eyed peas, watermelon and fried pork rinds, while Oxun prefers them in savory dishes with shrimp and palm oil. The specifics of each sacrifice differ among various forms of worship, but black-eyed peas are one of the most important, traditional foods these discriminating gods demand.[41]

These primarily Caribbean and South American examples leave questions about how this practice of "feeding the gods" became associated with eating something for good luck or prosperity in British North America. We do know that West African religious systems existed in the region, but there is not much early documentation of how or whether such worship was integrated into slave life. Information that eventually surfaces in the nineteenth century is slanted heavily toward sensational accounts of voodoo practice in Louisiana and a random assortment of conjuring practices and superstition.

Despite the lack of documented proof, some have put forward theories to explain the eating-black-eyed-peas-brings-good-luck belief. Charles Mangam, in his article "The Magic of the Black-eyed Pea," suggests fertility as the basis of the belief:

> Many people in the South will say that the black-eyed pea is some-how related to fertility, because it grows in a tangle of almost rank profusion. Here it may be like a multitude of other good luck charms. The twin subjects of good-luck and fertility are hard to separate once and for all. Good luck has always been within the province of the deities of fertility. . . . Black-eyed peas belong apparently to this class of amulets. Carrying one or other of them around as a charm, ha-bitually, would be too awkward, of course, but eating them annually for the sake of good luck is no more unreasonable than, say, eating hot cross buns at Easter. A naked girl walking through a garden at midnight was once regarded as a way of destroying the caterpillars that feed on young cabbages. Eating black-eyed peas once a year is another good way of doing such things, and it is much, much less embarrassing. A ceremony of this quiet kind, to millions and millions of up-to-date people, is only a genteel fertility rite.[42]

Mangam's proposition that black-eyed peas are as good as any symbolic amulet and much more convenient than some rituals make sense, but the question remains: Why must black-eyed peas be eaten on 1 January?

Celebrating New Year's Day on 1 January is a European practice that has an interesting past. In ancient Rome, the new year was marked on 1 March with a festival for Mars including all of the requisite feasting. Julius Caesar, fancying the god Janus more than Mars, moved the new year celebration to the first day of Janus's namesake month, January. He also made it a day of fasting. Not everyone bought into Caesar's bold move, and much of Europe followed at least two different calendars, creating all kinds of errors in timekeeping. Our modern calendar began with a 1750 Act of Parliament. With the creation of a special day came special traditions, and one that the British brought with them to their colonies was particularly important—the superstition of the first-footer.[43] "The first person to set foot over the threshold on New Year's morning must in most districts be dark-haired or dark-complexioned; he or she is then a bringer of good luck. Sometimes the first-footer brings a present of coal and bread, symbolizing a wish that the house shall never be short of fuel or food in the coming year."[44] Reinforcing this was the idea that whatever happened on that first day—whether good or bad—would happen for the rest of the year. The first-footer tradition was clearly on the mind of some of the enslaved. Recall that Della Fountain remembered her mother saying, "If you visit on New Year's, you'll visit all de year." This recasting of the first-footer tradition by African Americans gets us closer to understanding the superstition's origins.

Journalist Sue Hubbell attempted to put it all together in a comprehensive article she wrote for *Smithsonian* magazine in the early 1990s.

Traditions in various cultures call for eating foods on New Year's Day that began small and swell as they cook. In parts of northern Europe, for instance, groates, fragments of broken grain, were cooked to fluffiness and became a part of New Year's fare. How interesting, how fortuitous, how magical it must've seemed to the white Carolinian cooks to discover the black-eyed pea that their slaves knew. Here was a bean that came in many shades, ranging from copper-colored to red, but always with its own pair of black eyes, to fit in with their belief that a dark man with black eyes should be the first through the door on the year's first day.[45]

Noticeably, Hubbell gives credit to the "white Carolinian cooks" for minting the tradition by linking black-eyed peas with the first-footer tradition. It would be a plausible interpretation of what happened except for one thing—whites throughout the South fully attributed the creation of the New Year's Day tradition to black cooks.

Southern whites consistently framed the New Year's Day tradition of eating black-eyed peas as a curiosity of slave culture that carried over into contemporary black culture, erasing the fact that it was a widely shared southern custom until the twentieth century. W. M. Rowland, in a 1913 agricultural bulletin promoting black-eyed pea farming, wrote, "My negro cook, and thousands of other negro cooks, have been brought up to believe that if you want good luck, eat cow peas on New Year's day, and though my eating of cow peas is by no means limited to New Year's day, as long as I have a negro cook I have never failed to be reminded that they must be ready for eating on January the first."[46] In 1936, a *Washington Post* article said, "Hopping John is supposed to have a magic power to produce good fortune for the New Year if one eats it on the last day of the old. Of course, it is a superstition, originating, no doubt, with a colored and taught to young citizens by Mammy with much embellishment until it has become one of the cherished customs of all."[47] That same year, the *Baton Rouge Advocate* reported, "Many, especially negroes, believe that black-eyed peas possess a good luck charm when eaten on New Year's Day. The recipe calls for a dry hunk of salt meat in some sections, in others a hambone, and in some parts of the country the peas must be cooked with liberal quantities of rice."[48] Three years later in 1939, an *Atlanta Constitution* article said, "It's an old custom. In the cotton field cabins everybody knows the charm works because mammy has handed down to mammy the secret. Now the white folks are learning about it."[49] However, what the formerly enslaved African Americans remember backs up a different idea: that folklore around black-eyed peas was borrowed from English sources, melded with West African beliefs, and circulated within the black community—until it was adopted by southern whites.

There's only one slight problem with that theory. We may be overlooking an important folkloric contribution from another part of Europe. In 1905, the *Boston Herald* described a scene in which some stage actors gathered after a performance to ring in the new year. Without mentioning anything about the South, the article stated,

Following an old German custom, Miss [Lillian] Kemble had a table spread with the various foods that mean money and prosperity for the new year. The story goes in Germany that if the clock strikes out the old year and announces the new, you should eat heartily of lentils, pork, white cabbage and potato dumplings so the new year would bring you good luck and an abundance of money. Lentils mean gold; dumpling, the big round silver dollars, the white cabbage, greenbacks. The significance of eating pork is that the pig is the only animal that roots ahead for his food—therefore he signifies progress.[50]

Eating Black-Eyed Peas on New Year's Day for Luck Is Custom in the South

African American cook shares a New Year's Day tradition (reprinted with permission of *The Dallas Morning News*)

My jaw dropped upon reading this article, for it is a perfect analogue to the New Year's Day meal my family has traditionally had: black-eyed peas instead of lentils, chitlins instead of pork, greens instead of white cabbage, and candied yams as the starch instead of potato dumplings. The South had its share of German immigrants who were slaveholders in the antebellum period. Their influence on southern cooking is quite pronounced among the breads (waffles), cold salads (coleslaw and potato salad), hot dumpling stews, and pork dishes, just to give a few examples. Some enslaved African Americans, then, likely made a traditional New Year's Day meal for their German masters similar to the one described at the actors' dinner in Boston. No doubt they borrowed the folklore, gave it an African American spin by substituting in their own foods, and passed it along from the Big House to slave cabins.

Today, black-eyed peas have special meaning in the black community because of the New Year's Day eating tradition, and because black migrants took the tradition (and a taste for black-eyed peas) out of the South and planted it wherever they settled. Blacks carried on a mostly European tradition even after European Americans had abandoned it. At the same time that blacks were using black-eyed peas as a vehicle to syncretize certain West African and European beliefs, black-eyed peas necessarily lost some of their Africanness. Black cooks moved further from making mushy black-eyed preparations to various iterations in which the individual beans remained soft but separate. While the cultural importance of this bean remained, its overt spiritual connotations faded, but they weren't lost on the West African descendants. Inspired by European superstition, black cooks found an inventive way to bring the magic back to black-eyed peas.

Black-Eyed Peas

This is one of the first recipes that I got from my mother, Johnetta Miller. Though this is a recipe for black-eyed peas, this is my standard approach for making any vegetable in "soul food style." If you want to give this recipe a "Hoppin' John" feel, make some rice separately, mix together, and eat.

Makes 8 servings

> 1 pound dried black-eyed or other field peas
> 1 smoked ham hock or smoked turkey wing (about 8 ounces)
> 1 medium onion, chopped
> Crushed red pepper flakes, to taste
> Salt, to taste

1 Rinse the peas and pick through them to discard any small stones or broken peas. Pour the peas into a large saucepan and cover with cold water by 2 inches. Bring them to a boil and cook for 5 minutes. Remove the pot from the heat, cover, and let stand for 1 hour. (Alternatively, place the peas in a large bowl, cover with cold water, and let stand at room temperature overnight.)

2 Meanwhile, make a stock by placing the ham hock or turkey wing in another large saucepan. Cover with water by 2 inches. Bring to a boil, reduce the heat, and simmer until the stock is flavorful, about 1 hour. Remove the hock or wing.

3 Drain the soaking liquid from the peas and add them to the stock. Make sure the peas are submerged. Stir in the onion and pepper flakes.

4 Simmer until the peas are nearly tender, about 30 minutes. Season with salt and continue simmering until the peas are tender and well seasoned, about 10 minutes more.

5 Serve the peas warm.

6 If desired, you may pull meat off the ham hock or turkey wing and add it to the dish before serving.

Purple Hull Peas

This versatile yet rustic recipe comes from Hardette Harris, a private chef from Minden, Louisiana. Chef Harris recalls, "I think my first memory of purple hull peas didn't come from eating them but from shelling them. If you are from the rural South, you may have shelled bushels of peas at some point in your life. Shelling peas on a daily basis was a common as making your bed. As kids we were assigned a minimum of one bushel apiece to shell. Ahh, the memories of a southern childhood; sitting on the porch shelling peas, bushel after bushel . . . all day long!" Purple hull peas are a variety of field pea. If unavailable in your area, you may substitute black-eyed, cream, or crowder peas. If you can't find purple hull peas at your local grocery store, try a farmers' market or roadside stand. A pot of peas makes a wonderful main dish when served with cornbread, yellow onion slices, tomato slices, and a couple dashes of pepper sauce or apple cider vinegar.

Makes 8 servings

> 2 large smoked ham hocks (about 1 pound)
> 3 large smoked pork neck bones (about 1 pound)
> 5 ounces thinly sliced salt pork
> 10 to 12 cups water
> 8 cups shelled fresh purple hull or other field peas (about 2 pounds)
> 1 small yellow onion, sliced
> 2 fresh whole okra pods
> ¼ teaspoon seasoned salt, or to taste
> ¼ teaspoon garlic powder
> ½ teaspoon ground black pepper

1 Rinse the ham hocks, neck bones, and salt pork. Place them in a large pot and cover with water. Bring just to a boil, reduce the heat, and simmer for 1 hour. Skim away any foam from the surface. Taste the cooking liquid. If it is too salty, discard 1 cup at a time and replace it with fresh hot water until the flavor is adjusted to your taste. If the liquid is bland, continue simmering to concentrate the flavors. Remove the solids.

2 Return the cooking liquid to a simmer. Stir in the peas, onion, okra, seasoned salt, garlic powder, and pepper. Cover and simmer until the peas are tender, but not falling apart, 45 to 60 minutes. (The fresher the peas, the more quickly they cook.) Check the seasoning and serve hot.

3 If desired, you may pull meat off the ham hocks and add it to the dish before serving.

How Did Macaroni & Cheese Get So Black?

The popularity of macaroni and cheese never seems to wane.
This dish is always in high favor, particularly for church suppers,
PTA get-togethers and other group luncheons and dinners.
—*Chicago Defender*, 27 October 1956

[Macaroni and cheese] is a traditional Sunday or holiday dish at
all of our family gatherings, especially during Christmas times.
—Kathy Starr, *The Soul of Southern Cooking* (2001)

★　★　★　★　★

Shortly before Thanksgiving 2011, former secretary of state Condoleezza
Rice sat down for an interview with *700 Club* television show cohost Kristi
Watts. The two African American women discussed a lot of things, but
given the pending holiday, they talked about food. Watts asked Secretary
Rice, "What's that one thing at Thanksgiving you just have to have?" Rice
responded, "It's mac 'n' cheese," and the two went on to have a terrific
"girlfriend moment" over the iconic food. Back in the studio, when tele-
vangelist Pat Robertson, the show's other host, joined Watts for a follow-
up on the Rice interview, he was clearly intrigued by one aspect of that
conversation. "What is this 'mac and cheese'?" Robertson asked. "Is that a
black thing?" A surprised Watts answered, "It is a black thing, Pat!" As part
of her spirited defense of the dish, Watts added, "Listen! And you guys! The
world needs to get on board with macaroni and cheese. Seriously, I just—
Christmas and Thanksgiving, we have to have macaroni and cheese, and
it just trips me out that you [Robertson] just don't." Robertson ended the
segment by saying, "I don't, and I have never!"[1] Robertson's answer was

pretty bewildering to me, but not for what you think are the obvious reasons. Robertson grew up in Lexington, Virginia, and I thought all southerners were well acquainted with macaroni and cheese.

Nevertheless, Robertson raised an interesting question. Here's the answer: Yes, mac 'n' cheese is "a black thing." More like rotini than elbow macaroni, the history of this dish goes through so many twists and turns that the ethnic identity of this purely Italian food gets lost. Over two centuries, macaroni and cheese became "mac 'n' cheese," a soul food favorite, because African American cooks have been called on to make the dish in wealthy and poverty-stricken kitchens alike. For soul food cooks, mac 'n' cheese had multiple identities as rich people's food, a special occasion food, a convenient comfort food, a meal-stretcher, and a poverty food. In addition, mac 'n' cheese is part of a larger, ongoing noodle craze that African Americans have had.

At first, I wasn't going to include mac 'n' cheese in my representative meal. I thought it was so universally embraced that it would be difficult to give it an African American angle. When I shared my planned omission with some of my black friends, I was roundly criticized. When confronted with threats of getting "slapped upside my head," I reacted the way any friendship-valuing culinary historian would: I caved, and I'm glad I did.

Looking at traditional West African foodways, mac 'n' cheese is an unlikely soul food classic. Nothing like macaroni and cheese existed in West Africa before the Europeans arrived.[2] They had neither macaroni nor cheese.[3] Originally, macaroni was a generic name for any pasta, but over time it became linked to a specific type of pasta noodle.[4] Enslaved African Americans first encountered cheese, though infrequently, on the other side of the Atlantic. The antebellum South didn't have a strong dairying tradition, so cheese was often purchased at stores in the city and brought back to the plantation as a special treat on Christmas and July Fourth. Though they are no longer considered a special treat, save for buttermilk, cheese and other dairy products have never been a large part of the African American diet.

For much of its early history, macaroni and cheese was a dish eaten by the European elite. That's right. The dish so common in school cafeterias and middle-class and lower-class dinner tables across America was rich people's food. As this recipe from the influential *Forme of Cury* cookbook (ca. 1390) shows, cheese was wedded with macaroni by the Middle Ages:

Macrows: take and make a thin foil of dough, and carve it in pieces, and cast them on boiling water, and seeth it well. Take cheese, and grate it and butter cast beneath and above . . . and serve forth.[5]

The *Forme of Cury* was the "go-to" cookbook for Europe's royal kitchens, including those of England's King Richard II and Queen Elizabeth I. Macaroni and cheese gradually moved out of the palace to Europe's aristocratic homes, where the dish was enjoyed well into the eighteenth century. America's own upper crust—eager to ape the Continental lifestyle—followed suit when macaroni and cheese arrived in the United States.

If one person could be a poster child for this trend, it's Thomas Jefferson. Jefferson often gets credit for single-handedly introducing macaroni and cheese to Americans. Jefferson developed a macaroni mania while he served as the U.S. minister to France from 1784 to 1789. At the end of this diplomatic stint, Jefferson took great pains to have a macaroni-making machine sent from Naples to his Philadelphia residence.[6] The eventual soul food connection here is that enslaved black cooks were the ones preparing macaroni and cheese for their masters. In Jefferson's case, the task initially fell on James Hemings, Jefferson's enslaved African American *chef de cuisine* and the older brother of Sally Hemings (Jefferson's enslaved sister-in-law and paramour). During his tenure as minister to France, Jefferson brought James Hemings to Paris with him and financed his extensive training in classical French cooking techniques. Once his three-year education ended, Chef Hemings ran Jefferson's kitchens while the statesman lived in both Paris and Philadelphia. Hemings's version of macaroni and cheese had more cream than the *Forme of Cury* recipe above, showing a pronounced French influence. Jefferson clearly reaped immediate benefits from Hemings's culinary education.

Chef Hemings yearned for liberty while in Philadelphia and asked Jefferson to free him. Jefferson agreed, provided Hemings teach another one of Jefferson's slaves how to cook like him. Hemings ended his servitude in 1796. The primary task for making Jefferson's food (including macaroni and cheese) then fell upon Hemings's younger brother Peter and two enslaved women, Edith Fossett and Frances Hern, all of whom cooked at Monticello, Jefferson's main residence in Virginia. When Jefferson was inaugurated as president, he brought Fossett and Hern to Washington, D.C., where they were the assistant cooks to the head White House chef, a Frenchman named Honoré Julien. Jefferson thought so highly of macaroni that he served it at a small dinner party he held at the White House on 5 February 1802. One of the guests that night, the Reverend Mannaseh Cutler, was not a fan. Cutler later wrote that the dish was "not very agreeable."[7] Luckily, Fossett and Hern never had a *Top Chef* moment where Jefferson asked them to "pack their knives and go." They remained with Jefferson in the White House until he finished his second term as president, returned with him to Monticello, and continued preparing his meals, including more macaroni and cheese, until his death.

Was Jefferson the first to serve macaroni and cheese in the United States? Probably not. Macaroni and cheese was already an extravagant, trendy side dish on wealthy English tables well before Jefferson served it at his dinner parties in the United States. *The Experienced English House-keeper* (1769), another British cookbook that was popular in the American colonies, had a macaroni and cheese recipe. For the American cook, the main hurdle to making the dish was getting its expensive ingredients. Both macaroni and Parmigiano-Reggiano (aka Parmesan) cheese were primarily made in Italy, and discriminating hosts only wanted the real thing served on their tables. By the dawn of the nineteenth century, British and American entrepreneurs had set their sights on making macaroni and cheese more affordable, and initially they had the most success with cheese.

British cooks had begun substituting Parmesan with their own cheddar, a local cheese since the 1500s, and American cooks often followed suit. According to culinary historian Rachel Laudan, substituting cheddar for Parmesan made sense because "a good, traditional British cheddar has a lot in common with traditional Parmesan: both have a granular texture, deep flavor, and a sandy color (it was much later that cheddar took on the rubbery texture and deep orange hue of today's supermarket offering) and grating best brings out their sharp flavors." This was a good solution for the British, but not so for Americans, who would still have to import the cheese from England instead of Italy. Cheddar became inexpensive once Americans started making their own version of it. Cheddar production was much higher in the North than in the South. The "industry" began as a patchwork of small dairy farms, but by 1851, the first cheddar factory on American soil opened outside Rome, New York. The results were stunning. By 1862, England got more cheddar from the United States than from anywhere else.[8]

Though cheddar became more plentiful in the mid-nineteenth century, American cookbooks didn't necessarily reflect that changed circumstance.

Macaroni and cheese recipes tended to just list "cheese" as an ingredient, which meant any local cheese could be used and typically that was cheddar. When a recipe in an American cookbook specifically called for Parmesan, according to food historian Anne Mendelson, the recipe was from "a cook who insisted on every ingredient really coming up to snuff."[9] What was slow coming up to snuff were the American attempts to replicate Italian macaroni. Authentic macaroni's key ingredient is durum wheat, which was hard to grow in the United States. The macaroni made with different wheat that ultimately was sold to consumers got mixed reviews. The *National Cookery Book* (1876) warned cooks in its macaroni and cheese recipe that "American macaroni takes longer to boil than the Italian."[10]

Pasta problems aside, southerners made macaroni and cheese in two main ways. Once again, we look to Virginia, which had a casserole method epitomized by this "Maccaroni Pudding" recipe from *The Virginia Housewife*:

> "Maccaroni Pudding" Simmer half a pound of macaroni in plenty of water, with a table-spoonful of salt, till tender, but not broke — strain it, beat five yelks [yolks], two whites of eggs, half a pint of cream — mince white meat and boiled ham very fine, add three spoonsful of grated cheese, pepper and salt; mix these with the macaroni, butter the mould, put it in, and steam it in a pan of boiling water for an hour — serve with rich gravy.[11]

This is a richer version of an already rich dish. It's got cheese, cream, eggs, pasta, and meat. Because it is vague on what type of cheese to use, the dish could have been made with cheddar or Parmesan.

The Carolina Housewife shows the other popular way the dish was made in the antebellum South — macaroni with a cheese sauce. Mrs. Rutledge instructed the cook this way:

> To Dress Macaroni A La Sauce Blanche. Take a quarter of a pound of macaroni, boil it in water, in which there must be a little salt. When the macaroni is done, the water must be drained from it, and the saucepan kept covered; roll two table-spoonfuls of butter in a little flour; take a pint of milk, and half a pint of cream; add the butter and the flour to the milk, and set it on the fire, until it becomes thick. This sauce ought to be stirred the whole time it is boiling, and always in the same direction. Grate a quarter of a pound of parmesan cheese;

butter the pan in which the macaroni is to be baked, and put in first, a layer of macaroni, then one of grated cheese, then some sauce, and so on until the dish is filled; the last layer must be of cheese, and the sauce with which the macaroni is to be well covered. Ten minutes will bake it in a quick oven. *Italian Receipt*.[12]

This is another macaroni and cheese in high style, but for different reasons. Mrs. Rutledge's recipe is extravagant because of the copious amounts of Parmesan cheese used despite the increasing availability of cheddar cheese. For good measure, she also emphasizes that the recipe is authentically Italian.

From these recipes, we know that enslaved African American cooks were making different types of macaroni and cheese in Big House kitchens. Unfortunately, we have little account of black cooks preparing the dish in their own homes. We also don't know if Big House cooks made macaroni and cheese for field slaves on special occasions. It seems likely, since so many other Big House dishes crossed castle lines on holidays, but no one bothered documenting it. After Emancipation, former slaves formed the bulk of the population that would migrate to the larger cities around the country. It was in these urban spaces that they encountered Italian immigrants and learned about their food traditions. Those who didn't get their first taste of macaroni on the plantation got it in the city.

Most Italian immigrants to the United States were from Italy's southern region, and they must have been amazed when they saw how many Americans were eating macaroni. Back home in southern Italy, macaroni dishes, particularly those made with fresh pasta, were still rich people's food, as they had been since the Middle Ages. Among the southern Italians, the poor used their wheat to make basic breads, and the well-to-do used their wheat to make macaroni.[13] If the poor got macaroni, it was the result of an act of charity. Sometimes a wealthy person living in the countryside displayed some benevolent hospitality by hosting a feast for the rural poor that included macaroni. The urban poor would even hang around the *maccaronaro*, Naples's macaroni street vendors, hoping someone would take pity on them and give them some macaroni.[14]

Southern Italian immigrants carried macaroni's elevated status with them when they arrived in the United States. As they began to prosper, they ate more of it than they used to in the homeland. Hasia Diner explains what macaroni meant to Italian immigrants in her book *Hungering for America*:

In all the places they settled in America, they built families, communities, and ethnic practices out of a set of iconic foods and dishes. None mattered as much as macaroni. A food of affluence for the southern Italian, and it embodied Italian food culture for the masses in America. In Italian American communities, small and big alike, entrepreneurs operated macaroni factories. In the early years of the migration, macaroni was prepared in tenement sweatshops by family labor, and "then sold up and down" the streets of the neighborhood. Larger macaroni factories "symbolized in brick and stone a recognition that the ethnic colonies had moved from a transitory mentality to a more permanent status."[15]

After successive decades of heavy immigration, Italian Americans were concentrated mainly along the eastern seaboard from Massachusetts to Pennsylvania. By 1930, more than a million Italians had settled in New York City, and Philadelphia was a distant second with 182,368 Italians.[16]

Once in the United States, the divergent foodways of southern Italians coalesced into "Italian American food." Though blacks and Italians may not have lived in the same neighborhoods, they were often shoehorned into the same sections of cities because of their low-caste status. For reasons I won't get into here, Italian immigrants were not considered "white" by nineteenth-century standards. Becoming white would only happen after several decades of assimilation.[17] Living in close proximity to one another gave both groups ample time to learn about each other's cultures and foods, including macaroni and cheese.

Though it makes sense to focus on how the black/Italian dynamic in the North fostered a macaroni and cheese culture, we shouldn't forget how something similar happened in the South. Italians have long had a presence in that region, particularly in New Orleans. As Chef John Folse writes in his extensive Encyclopedia of Cajun & Creole Cuisine, "Since New Orleans' founding in 1718, Italian immigrants were part of the populace. By 1850, New Orleans' Italian population numbered 915, which was larger than that of any city in the United States, even New York, which was home to just 833 Italians."[18] Those numbers appreciably increased after Emancipation.

In the early 1880s, Louisiana's sugar planters, hoping they could eliminate the need for black workers, actively recruited Sicilian labor. Blacks were asserting their bargaining power for better wages and work conditions and had become a more unreliable labor supply to their previous masters.[19] Chef Folse adds, "By 1902, Italian immigrants rapidly replaced

Negro labor in the sugar fields."[20] In order to acculturate and meet the food needs of their Sicilian laborers, planters made sure that "plantation stores stocked boxes of spaghetti, macaroni, cheese, olives and sardines. Often, the Italians made their own macaroni and dried it in the sun."[21] The blacks who remained on the plantation frequented these same plantation stores—the only grocery options in the vicinity—and may have learned about macaroni and cheese there as well.

Some Italians didn't stick with plantation work and moved to the southern cities. Some, like their counterparts up north, started making macaroni. These macaroni ventures were so successful that, by 1901, *The Picayune Creole Cook Book* boasted,

> Macaroni is a general article of food in New Orleans among the rich and the poor. It is very cheap, and is a most excellent dish. We have in New Orleans large Macaroni factories, where not only Macaroni is made by the Italians themselves, but the twin sisters of Macaroni, Spaghetti and Vermicelli, are also manufactured fresh daily. While there is no city in the United States in which Macaroni is cooked in real Italian style but New Orleans, which has long been a favored point of migration for the sons of sunny Italy, the Creole cooks have modified and improved upon the Italian methods, so that Macaroni a la Creole is just as famous a dish as Macaroni *a l'Italienne*, and by many considered far superior.[22]

If this description is accurate, New Orleans's significant black population would have had easy access to macaroni and cheese. Added proof: Lena Richard, a well-known black caterer in New Orleans who opened up a cooking school in 1937, included a macaroni and cheese recipe in her *New Orleans Cook Book* (1939).[23]

The dawn of the twentieth century saw American home economists pitching macaroni and cheese as a perfect food for the working classes. In 1902, Mrs. Sarah Rorer, a noted American culinary expert, wrote, "Macaroni and cheese forms an almost typical food. It is the bread and meat of the Italian laborer; even hard at work he finds it a satisfying and perfect diet. . . . Until within the past few years, macaroni was prepared as a luxury only for the tables of the very rich. Even now it is sparingly used throughout the country by the American laboring classes. There is no reason, considering the price, and the ease with which it is prepared, why it should not enter extensively into the food of all our people. It is nutritious, palatable, slightly and much more easily prepared than many of our everyday dishes."[24] Mrs. Rorer went on to lament that the one thing holding macaroni and cheese back was that so many cooks didn't prepare it well.

Though perhaps not the intended audience, African Americans of all classes got Mrs. Rorer's message. In the first few decades of the twentieth century, African Americans embraced macaroni and cheese and other Italian foods. All kinds of macaroni (and spaghetti) recipes were consistently appearing in cookbooks aimed at African American audiences. The earliest printed recipe in an African American cookbook is for a macaroni croquette with cheese sauce in the *Kentucky Cook Book* (1912).[25] A decade and a half later, the *Montana Federation of Negro Women's Clubs Cook Book* (1927) had recipes for chicken spaghetti, macaroni and roast steak, spaghetti loaf, and macaroni loaf, and two recipes for Italian spaghetti.[26] By the 1930s, restaurants called "spaghetti houses" were all over Harlem and patronized by blacks. Harlemites could easily get macaroni in their own backyard, thanks to the Harlem Macaroni Co. factory that operated on 239 E. 108th Street through the 1930s.[27] By the early 1940s, the *New York Amsterdam News* reported that "Italian cooking plays a most important factor in Harlem life, not only on the account of the tremendous Italian population in the community, but also because that particular cuisine appeals to so many Negroes."[28] Natalie Joffe, in her 1940s study of African American food habits, wrote, "In Northern urban situations certain 'white' kinds of food have been incorporated in the eating pattern both in and outside of the home. To go to an Italian or Chinese restaurant, to eat spaghetti or chow mein, is a form of celebration."[29] What happened in Harlem with these foods didn't stay in Harlem. Italian food took off in black neighborhoods around the country.

Macaroni and cheese had many faces by the 1930s. Though its stature as rich people's food had fallen, it was still an ethnic dish relished mainly by Italian Americans, African Americans, and middle-class whites. How macaroni and cheese finally reached the masses is intertwined with the company that most comes to mind when one thinks of the dish these days—Kraft. Based in Chicago, by 1930 Kraft had come up with "a practical method for processing cheese and canning it so that it would keep." Building on this innovation, Kraft developed Velveeta, an inexpensive processed cheese spread, and it was an immediate hit during the Great Depression. A 1976 newspaper article highlighted that Kraft's last and most important contribution to macaroni and cheese lore came in 1936, when the company "ushered in the age of convenience meals with its macaroni and cheese dinner, a Depression favorite that could be made into a meal for four in nine minutes. A box sold for 19 cents and today, 40 years later Kraftco notes, the price is only 10 cents more and is still the largest selling packaged dinner in the world."[30] Almost forty years since that article was published, Kraft still holds a dominant position in the macaroni and cheese market.

Food rationing policy implemented during World War II also played an important role. As Jane Holt, the New York Times food editor, wrote in 1943, "No account of processed food, especially those that are suitable for main dishes, is complete without a mention of Kraft 'dinners.' . . . The other [besides spaghetti], likewise speedily assembled, is a macaroni and cheese combination that is good 'as is' or can be varied endlessly by mixing it with cooked meat or chicken, by adding mushrooms, chopped bacon, green pepper or pimento. Either 'dinner' serves four, takes one ration point in red stamps and is sold at most chain and independent stores throughout the city at a modest price."[31] Five years later, the African American–centric A Date with a Dish cookbook informed its readers, "For economical tasty meals, there's nothing quite like macaroni, spaghetti or noodles served in different styles to suit various tastes. If cooked properly, they are worthy of your culinary efforts, from a side dish to a main course."[32] Finally, ease of preparation, economy, and versatility due to added ingredients made macaroni and cheese irresistible to millions of middle-class homemakers of various backgrounds.

During the Down Home Cooking period, two different lines of cooking macaroni and cheese developed in African American households. Many families made a quick version of this dish several times during the week by using commercially prepared mixes and dinner kits. The richer version with fresh eggs and/or milk that evoked the dish's glorious past was made on the weekends. One dietary study of blacks in Charleston, South Carolina, from the late 1950s states, "Regardless of the meat dish, macaroni baked with milk, cheese and eggs is a traditional dish of the area for Sunday dinners, and it was served in most of the older families of average or better means."[33]

Macaroni and cheese took longer to catch on in rural areas. During the late 1920s, a home economist named Dorothy Dickins studied the food habits of rural Mississippians and found that "most African American women had never tasted macaroni and cheese and few cooked it for their families because they complained that it was too 'starchy and gummy.'"[34] When Dickins revisited the area's food habits again between 1936 and

The Chinese Noodle Connection

At the same time that African Americans were eating up Italian noodle dishes, Chinese noodles were equally popular. Much like Italians, Chinese immigrants had low social status when they arrived, settled in the big northern cities, and were recruited by southern planters to replace black workers in the second half of the nineteenth century.[1] Chinese immigrants in the South soured on plantation work, and many transitioned to running grocery stores, a legacy that exists to this day. In the big cities, Chinese immigrants operated restaurants by the 1890s, and blacks were regular customers. In 1891, an adventurous diner reported, "I went into a Chinese restaurant the other evening . . . and was considerably amused to have large beer and spaghetti offered me, and to notice that the patrons of the place seemed to be chiefly negroes. Evidently the Chinese are all things to all men."[2]

By the 1930s, Chinese noodle dishes appeared in black cookbooks and were served in Harlem's and Chicago's hot night spots.[3] Blacks so loved noodles that some of the earliest civil rights lawsuits filed against eating establishments targeted Asian-run noodle joints that drew the color line as early as 1907.[4] Noodles still thrive in black culture today; for example, *ya ka mein* radiates its culinary influence from New Orleans—where it's also known as "ghetto pho, low-rent lo mein, and . . . Seventh Ward ramen"—to the Midwest and the West Coast.[5]

---

1 Folse, *Encyclopedia of Cajun*, 106.
2 "Phases of City Life."
3 *To Work and Serve the Home*, 15–16; "Tavern Topics," 18 April 1942; "What the Cats Do."
4 Greaves, "Negroes Ask Civil Rights"; Bolden, "Majority of Chinese Restaurants."
5 Edge, "Seventh Ward Ramen," 45.

Mac 'n' cheese tray, Bethlehem Bistro, Chattanooga

1948, she concluded that black sharecropping families were purchasing more of the dish's constituent parts—cheddar cheese, macaroni, and spaghetti—than comparable white families.[35] African Americans were also purchasing more evaporated milk during this same period. Evaporated milk was a fancy upgrade for rural blacks and gave rise to a third class of macaroni and cheese recipes that one finds in working-class cookbooks like Starr's *Soul of Southern Cooking* and Mickler's *White Trash Cooking*. By the 1980s, Starr indicated that in the Mississippi Delta, macaroni and cheese was a "traditional Sunday or holiday dish at all of our family gatherings, especially during the Christmas times."[36] Just as they did in the cities, blacks and whites developed a united taste for macaroni and cheese in the rural South.

Back in the cities, African Americans were still enthusiastic about macaroni and cheese, but the appeals from home economists to use the dish were getting more class-conscious. A *New Journal and Guide* article from 1950 captures the tenor of the times:

> The secret behind the young homemaker's success lies in making good use of thrifty foods. Macaroni, spaghetti and noodles can be an excellent help to the bride as they have long been for her mother and more experienced sisters. The protein content of these foods helps to satisfy hearty appetites and their bland flavor makes them the perfect companions to all sorts of meats, seafoods, vegetables and fruit. So they can act as extenders for small amounts of more ex-

pensive foods. When we think of macaroni we immediately think of the universal favorite among casserole dishes, macaroni and cheese. Although it is as delicious as it is, with a nippy cheese sauce holding the chewy macaroni together, it's a good idea to vary this main dish in a variety of ways.[37]

Here, macaroni and cheese is presented as a potential side dish or entrée. The article's commonsense advice also minimizes macaroni's association with cheese and proposes combinations with other ingredients instead. One consequence of making macaroni and cheese an "everydish" is that it is no longer a special treat. By the dawn of the Soul Food era, macaroni and cheese was transitioning into "mac 'n' cheese"—a reliable, filling meal for low-income blacks.

The low-class status of mac 'n' cheese congealed out of the best of intentions. American industry had become so good at making macaroni and cheese products that there was simply too much of it around. The federal government and private organizations acquired these surpluses, which were often donated to the poor. In 1930, the *New York Amsterdam News* reported that "the Harlem [Relief and Employment] committee's baskets will contain one chicken, fresh string beans, sweet potatoes, macaroni and cheese, bread, butter, fresh fruit, tea, sugar, canned milk and probably a pie. The supplies will feed a family of six. Only the neediest families will be considered."[38] In the South, mac 'n' cheese, even as a charity food, got caught up in racial politics. An Urban League study of relief in southern cities in 1933 found that unemployed African Americans received packages labeled "colored," which had less food than those designated for their white counterparts, and they were also given no macaroni and cheese.[39] From the late 1940s on, millions of poor children across the nation ate mac 'n' cheese as part of the School Lunch Program. President Johnson launched an extensive collection of welfare programs in the mid-1960s that he hoped would create the Great Society. Mac 'n' cheese— using surplus processed cheese or "government cheese," as it was popularly called—was the Great Society's national dish. Government cheese may not have been of the highest quality, but it could certainly be used for that one dish. After centuries as a high-end dish, mac 'n' cheese was now "poor people's food."

Mac 'n' cheese as poverty food persisted well into the Soul Food era. In 1966, several black-owned radio stations commissioned a marketing study of their predominantly black audiences in order to lure advertisers:

The progress of the Negro people was said to be best reflected in such product categories as butter, waxed paper, household cleaners, cream deodorants, baby foods and drugs. But the report went on to say that the inequities of the American society continued to be reflected in lower Negro ownership of convenience goods, including some frozen products and the more expensive versions of old products such as spray starch and self-polishing floor wax. The report points out that the previous patterns of Negro living standard continue to show up in product categories such as oleomargarine, flour, spaghetti and macaroni, which it terms the common denominator of a low-income society, regardless of race.[40]

In other words, macaroni marked the African American's lack of economic progress.

These words ring somewhat true even today. Mac 'n' cheese remains a reliable favorite for millions of people, particularly working parents with kids. Mac 'n' cheese mixes are on the shelves of grocery stores with an upscale clientele as well as the dollar stores that are so prevalent now in poor neighborhoods. In many instances, mac 'n' cheese is returning to its aristocratic roots as chefs play around by adding ingredients like lobster—a riff on what housewives were doing with the dish in the 1950s. For most people, though, mac 'n' cheese is just pure comfort food, something that reminds them of their childhood or home. Whether or not it was made from a box doesn't seem to matter.

It took more than thoughts of home to give African Americans a special affinity for macaroni and cheese. Macaroni and cheese bolstered the enslaved black cook's reputation in elite kitchens. Lots of black people fell in love with macaroni and cheese after they were introduced to it by their Italian neighbors in northern cities and on southern plantations. Macaroni and cheese was on the short list of foods that generated anticipation, whether one was going out to a welcoming restaurant or having Sunday dinner at home. It then became a survival food during lean times. After Emancipation, African Americans chose this foreign, European food and elevated its status within the black community. Today mac 'n' cheese can be considered a "black thing" because African Americans adopted the dish so successfully that its ethnic origins were completely forgotten. In other words, it was the first major ethnic dish African Americans assimilated into their diet before the larger American public did. That makes it ours, and that's *amore!*

Mac 'n' Cheese

For sticklers, this is a recipe for macaroni with cheese sauce, rather than one for a mac 'n' cheese casserole. It is a favorite when I make soul food for my friends. I make a white sauce and then add cheese. I use Tillamook cheddar cheese, but any cheese that easily melts should do the trick. Watch your butter roux carefully so that it doesn't burn before you add your milk to create the white sauce.

Makes 8 servings

> 1 1/2 cups macaroni (8 ounces)
> 1/4 cup (1/2 stick) butter
> 1/4 cup all-purpose flour
> 2 cups whole milk, warmed
> 1 teaspoon salt
> 1 1/2 cups grated sharp cheddar cheese (6 ounces), divided

1 Preheat the oven to 350°F. Lightly grease a 1 1/2-quart baking dish.
2 Cook the macaroni al dente according to the package directions. Drain in a colander and set aside.
3 Melt the butter in a medium saucepan over medium-high heat. Sprinkle the flour over the butter and whisk until smooth. Cook, whisking, for 3 minutes. Do not let the flour darken.
4 Whisk in the milk and salt. Cook, stirring, until the sauce comes just to a boil and thickens enough to coat the back of the spoon. Remove the pan from the heat, add 1 cup of the cheese, and stir until smooth. Stir in the macaroni.
5 Scrape the mixture into the prepared dish. Sprinkle the remaining 1/2 cup of cheese over the top. Bake until the cheese melts and the macaroni mixture bubbles around the edge, about 15 minutes. Let sit for 5 minutes before serving warm.

Nyesha Arrington's Mac and Cheese

Chef Nyesha Arrington seemed to be everywhere at once when she first came to my attention. I watched her win the executive chef position at Wilshire Restaurant in Santa Monica after a one-on-one competition on the Food Network's 2011 reality show *Chef Hunter*. Then, a few months later, she had a great run on Bravo TV's *Top Chef: Texas*. When we got to talking about mac 'n' cheese while I interviewed her for this book, I asked her if she was in a sharing mood (in order to get the recipe), and fortunately she said "Yes."

Makes 10 servings

1 pound elbow macaroni
3 ½ tablespoons butter, divided
1 medium yellow onion, sliced
3 tablespoons all-purpose flour
2 ¼ cups whole milk,
    plus more as needed, warmed
1 teaspoon salt
⅛ teaspoon ground white pepper
Pinch of freshly grated nutmeg
3 ½ cups coarsely grated Cantal,
    Gruyère, or sharp white cheddar
    cheese, divided (1 pound)

2 tablespoons chopped
    fresh parsley
1 tablespoon finely chopped
    fresh rosemary
1 tablespoon chopped fresh thyme
2 cups fresh white bread crumbs
2 tablespoons melted butter

1 Preheat the oven to 350°F. Butter a 2 ½-quart casserole dish.
2 Cook the macaroni al dente according to the package directions. Drain in a colander and set aside.
3 Melt 1 tablespoon of the butter in a medium skillet over medium-high heat. Add the onion and cook, stirring often, until very soft and golden brown, about 12 minutes. Set aside.
4 Melt the remaining 2 ½ tablespoons of butter in a large saucepan over medium heat.
5 Add the flour and cook, stirring constantly, until the mixture is pale yellow and frothy, about 2 minutes. Do not allow it to brown. Slowly whisk in the warm milk and continue to whisk until the sauce comes to a boil and thickens enough to coat the back of a spoon, 2 to 3 minutes. Season with the salt, pepper, and nutmeg. Reduce the heat to very low, add 3 cups of the cheese, and stir until the cheese melts and

the sauce is smooth. The sauce should be the consistency of pancake batter, so thin the sauce with a little milk if necessary.

6 Stir in the macaroni, onions, parsley, rosemary, and thyme. Pour into the prepared baking dish. Sprinkle the remaining ½ cup of cheese over the top.

7 In a small bowl, toss the bread crumbs with the melted butter and sprinkle over the casserole.

8 Bake until the casserole is warmed through and the top is lightly browned, about 30 minutes. Let sit for 10 minutes before serving warm.

Classic Macaroni and Cheese

This recipe proves you don't have to give up your favorite dishes to eat heart-healthy meals. Here's a lower-fat version of a true classic. You still get the creaminess that you've come to expect from macaroni and cheese without all of the fat. This recipe is courtesy of the National Heart, Lung, and Blood Institute's *Heart Healthy Home Cooking African American Style* recipe collection.

Serves 8

2 cups macaroni
2 cups onion, chopped
2 cups evaporated fat-free milk
1 medium egg, beaten
¼ teaspoon black pepper
1¼ cups low-fat cheddar cheese, finely shredded
Nonstick cooking spray, as needed

1 Cook macaroni according to directions—but do not add salt to the cooking water. Drain and set aside. Spray casserole dish with nonstick cooking spray. Preheat oven to 350°F. Lightly spray saucepan with nonstick cooking spray. Add onions to the saucepan and sauté for about 3 minutes.

2 In another bowl, combine macaroni, onions, and the rest of the ingredients and mix thoroughly. Transfer mixture into casserole dish. Bake for 25 minutes or until bubbly. Let stand for 10 minutes before serving.

9

Sometimes, I Feel Like Motherless Greens

"[We] had all the vegetables they wanted; [we] grew them in the gardens, . . ." [Henry Brown said. He] seemed so proud of his garden, with its broad view across the Ashley River, showing his black walnut, pear and persimmon trees, grape vines and roses, that the writer said, "Henry, you know that a poet has said that we are nearer to God in the garden than anywhere else on earth." "Well, ma'am, you see," [Brown] replied, with a winning smile, "that's where God put us in the first place." — Interview of Henry Brown, Charleston, S.C., ca. 1939

★   ★   ★   ★   ★

"Sometimes, I feel like a motherless child," is the classic line from an old Negro spiritual. It beautifully captures the sense of alienation, loneliness, and contradiction that has permeated the African American experience. By the 1930s, sharecroppers, in an interesting turn of phrase, were using a similar expression to describe food. To them, "motherless greens" were greens (edible plant leaves) prepared without any pork, implying perhaps that without the meat, those poor greens lacked a solid anchor.[1] There was a time when motherless greens were anathema to a soul food menu, but no longer. Though greens are extremely popular at soul food restaurants and in soul food homes, pork is not always invited to the party.[2] During my national soul food tour, so many waitstaff in soul food restaurants proudly told me that their establishment is "pork-free" or "vegan" with such pride that it finally hit me that soul food is well into transition. Even while in the Deep South, I was left to wonder, can a brother get some pork with my greens these days? More than any other aspect of our representative meal, greens track the major trends in African American cooking.

Look in a pot of simmering greens and you'll know exactly how the cook feels about soul food. A traditionalist gets fresh greens and cooks with some form of pork; the pragmatist lives in the moment and uses whatever is available—fresh, canned, or frozen greens; the reformer flavors greens with leaner meats like chicken, fish, smoked turkey, or a meat broth; and the progressive goes completely without meat. As tempted as I may be, I don't use the term "radical" for the latter group, for I don't think they're crazy. In fact, I'll show later that there is a method to their apparent madness. Much of the soul food story since the early 1960s has been about weaning African Americans from their "dependence" on pork flavors.

Although a large number of greens are eaten in the American South, the short list of familiar soul food greens includes cabbage (*Brassica oleracea*), collards (*Brassica oleracea v. acephela*), kale (*Brassica oleracea v. acephela*), mustard greens (*Brassica nigra* and *Brassica alba*), and turnip greens (*Brassica rapa* or *Brassica campestris*). From now on, when I refer to "greens," I mean the edible leaves of these five plants. Greens all belong to the same botanical genus, *Brassica*; thus they are closely related. They are hardy plants and are easy to grow because they adapt to several climates.[3] The early Greek and Roman farmers grew greens, and the Romans eventually brought them to the British Isles.[4] Once again, the nomenclature gets quite confusing, which makes it hard to track a specific plant's history. Cabbage, collards, and kale were often used interchangeably in the old historical sources in Europe.[5] "Coleworts" was an old term applied to both collards and kale. However, the two greens are distinguishable in the supermarket (collards tend to be flat, while kale looks curly), and they do taste different when cooked (I find kale has a sharper flavor).[6]

Believe it or not, cooking greens with pork is old-school European cooking. We do know that the Romans, as early as 2,000 years ago, were making greens pretty soulfully, boiling them with a piece of pork. The Roman poet Ovid includes a story in his epic *Metamorphoses* (8 C.E.) about Baucis and Philemon that makes mention of greens. The poor peasant couple was visited by two traveling strangers and didn't think twice about inviting them in, heading out to the garden, stripping some collard greens, pulling down some smoked pork ("a chine of bacon") from the fireplace, and boiling it all in a pot of water until it was ready to eat. The poor couple was quite embarrassed to serve such a meager "company dish," but it was the thought that counted. Their dinner guests turn out to be none other than the Roman deities Jupiter and his son Mercury (Zeus and Hermes are the Greek counterparts) in disguise. Because they have been hospitable to the apparent vagabonds—while their neighbors were not—Baucis and Philemon are spared from a devastating flood that destroys their town. Proof that collards with smoked pork saved lives and was food for the gods over 2,000 years ago.

By the time this culinary combination reached Britain, it was called "bacon and greens," which shows the meat had more social value since it was listed first. Greens may have had less prestige, but they were a critical part of the British diet because they, especially cabbage, were among the few vegetables available during the winter. One expert notes, "For nearly a thousand years, kale and collards were the main winter vegetables in England."[7] Thus, cabbages were important to survival. Even as a survival food, bacon and greens gained some status. The dish was mentioned in Elizabeth Moxon's *English Housewifery* (ca. 1752) as a recommended side dish for a first course of "boil'd fowls," "a dish of Scotch collops," and "minc'd Pyes or Pudding."[8]

Boiled greens were a fairly standard food for laborers and the poor, who often ate it as one of several ingredients thrown into a one-pot meal simply called "pottage." Writing in 1542, Andrew Boorde, a British cookbook author, defined pottage as "made of the liquor [broth] in which the flesh is sodden [cooked] in, with putting-to chopped herbs, and oatmeal and salt."[9] Make no mistake, though, pottage's starring attraction was the cereal, not the vegetables. Whether it was oatmeal, wheat, or barley, the cereal made the pottage filling for those who ate it. Pottage was so popular locally that Boorde exclaimed that "pottage is not so much used in all of Christendom as it is used in England."[10] Around the same time Boorde wrote these words, class differences were developing as to how the English ate greens.

As the seventeenth century progressed, wealthy Brits were increasingly eating more raw plant leaves as salads.[11] And as C. Anne Wilson, a historian on British foodways, observes, boiled leaves in pottage were consumed in different ways depending on class. "For the nobility the vegetables or herbs, duly chopped up, were boiled in good meat or fish broth or sometimes in broth along with beef, for the peasant family the pottage would often had been entirely vegetarian. And whereas the well-to-do had separately prepared meat or fish dishes to eat alongside their vegetable pottages, the peasant family, when a little bacon or salt cod or herring was available to them, would have put it straight into the pot to be cooked with the herbs or roots."[12] Thus, regularly having meat in one's pottage was a sign of wealth. Another sign of wealth in greens eating was access to a technological development of the sixteenth century: the fork. With the fork, there were far more possibilities; the wealthy could enjoy a wider range of discrete, definable foods on a plate. Everyone else was still stuck eating an amalgamation of ingredients in pies, pottages, and puddings—foods that could be eaten with fingers, handheld, or slurped from the side of a bowl. As we look at the place of greens in West African foodways, we must remember that all classes of the British ate greens, but having greens without a decently sized piece of meat and eating them with one's fingers indicated low social status.

West Africans are serious about their edible green leaves and have a long tradition of combining plant leaves and proteins to make a boiled meal. Unlike Europeans, West Africans have long considered edible green leaves a vital part of their meals, not just as a filler or famine food. As Judith Carney writes, "A signature ingredient of the foodways of Africa and the diaspora is greens. Perhaps no other cooking traditions feature them so prominently."[13] In Ghana alone, at least forty-seven kinds of green leaves are considered edible and are used in cooking.[14] Greens typically show up as a key ingredient in the stews and sauces that are most popular in the region. Perhaps the best example is the famed "palaver sauce" of Ghana, Liberia, and Sierra Leone—a hearty mixture of leafy greens, meat, and other vegetables all boiled together.[15] Traditionally, West African cooks use very little meat and water when cooking their edible green leaves. When meat is used, small pieces of dried, salted, or smoked fish are a popular choice. Meat is not the centerpiece of a typical meal but thought of more as a seasoning. Other types of meat like beef, goat, poultry, and wild animals, called "bush meat," are luxury foods that could fall into the pot, but pork is an unlikely choice. Pork was not traditionally widely available, and even if it were, the region's large Muslim population would consider it taboo to eat.[16]

West African cooks employ several culinary strategies when they make dishes with edible green leaves. Carney notes, "Greens generally impart a bitter taste to food, a trait much emphasized in Africa-based cuisines. . . . The centrality of greens to the food culture of sub-Saharan Africa cannot be understated."[17] One of the green leaves most extensively used in cooking in Nigeria is the aptly named "bitter leaf" (*Vernonia amygdalina*). Aside from their desired bitterness, green leaves give dishes an appropriate texture, what some West Africans describe as "mouth feel." Okra has a similar effect; when boiled, it has a mucilaginous property that both thickens a sauce or stew and makes it slippery on the tongue. Though this quality is highly prized in West Africa, boiled okra has gotten mixed reviews from U.S. diners who don't care for its sliminess. When not using okra, West

Africans use baobab tree leaves.[18] West African cooks also wrap leaves around particular foods to protect and flavor them during cooking processes (such as baking, boiling, or steaming), even though the leaf itself is not consumed. Latino cooks use a similar technique in preparing tamales, which are wrapped in corn husks and steamed.[19]

During the Atlantic slave trade, West Europeans brought their greens with them to West Africa and the New World. Turnips (and turnip greens) and kale were reportedly growing at Elmina (in present-day Ghana) as early as 1572. Collards and turnips were grown in Mali as early as the 1600s. Cabbages were being farmed on the Gold Coast by at least 1669.[20] Because of such accounts, some mistakenly believe that the *Brassica* greens originated in West Africa, but they were introduced by Europeans.[21] In the New World, greens flourished because British, French, and Spanish settlers planted greens throughout their North American colonies during the sixteenth and seventeenth centuries.[22] So when enslaved West Africans arrived, they would have found colonial gardens replete with familiar plants. In addition, European settlers and enslaved Africans learned about using local plants for food from the Native Americans, who also used edible leafy greens extensively.[23]

Eventually, southerners developed some class distinctions regarding which greens were eaten and how. Judging by southern media outlets and elite southern cookbooks, cabbage, mustard greens, turnip greens, and spinach (*Spinacia oleracea*) were the few greens worthy of Big House tables, and collards were deemed low class.[24] Greens preferences varied wildly within the South, so it's difficult to settle on hard and fast rules about social acceptability for greens. As the formerly enslaved William H. Harrison recalls, "I took Martha Jane, Easter Ann, Jane Daniel, my young mistresses and their mother's sisters, Emma and Laura, to parties and dances all the time. We went to Asheville, North Carolina, to a big party. While they was having fine victuals after the dance they sent me out a plate of turnip greens and turnips, fat meat and corn bread. I took it and set it down. When Miss Martha Jane got in sight I took her to our carriage. She said 'Empty it to the dogs,' and give me one dollar and fifty cents and told me to go town and buy my supper. I was treated as kin folk. I et and drunk same as they had use to."[25] Apparently, even though the author of *The Virginia Housewife*, Mrs. Randolph, included turnip greens in her cookbook for the Big House, Miss Martha Jane thought of them as dog food. Again, of all the greens, collards were the ones that were uniformly associated with low status, meaning for slaves and poor whites.

For the enslaved, greens were a major part of the plantation diet because they supplemented rations. Planters gave their slaves a great deal of autonomy over how they got their greens, and slaves did it primarily in three ways: grew them on a patch of ground near or next to a slave cabin (often called a "provision ground"); procured them from a communal garden provided by the master; or foraged for wild edible plants during the little leisure time available.[26] When cooking greens, slaves employed techniques similar to those used by their West African forebears. They ate what was in season, using greens as flavoring agents for food, as ingredients for one-pot meals, as medicine, as protective wrappers during cooking, and to prepare teas.[27] It was during communal mealtimes in the morning and at noon that the enslaved often ate greens out of one big pot.

First-generation West African cooks in North America had to make adjustments in how they prepared edible plants. The first was to find edible plant leaves that would give an acceptable level of bitterness and the mouth feel I described earlier. It's no coincidence that soul food greens are also bitter. For subsequent generations, bitterness became less valued. Many a cook will tell you that greens are better to eat after the first frost has hit them and made them sweeter. Ezra Adams of Columbia, South Carolina, echoes this belief when he recalls from slavery days, "If you want to know what I thinks is the best vittles, I's gwine to be obliged to omit (admit) dat it is cabbage sprouts in de spring, and it is collard greens after the frost has struck them."[28] Second, they had to season their greens differently, mainly with pickled, salted, or smoked pork rather than dried, salted, or smoked fish. As we learned in the catfish chapter, fish was plentiful during slave life either as rations or as supplemental food. Yet we see few references to fish being used to season pots of greens. An easy African aftertaste could have come through, but it didn't.

Two distinct ways of eating greens developed in the plantation South with respect to solid food versus liquid nourishment. General Jefferson Davis Nunn, still a small child at the time of Emancipation, remembered that "for dinner, us had pot-licker, but no meat. De grownups would have de greens."[29] Pot licker (more commonly spelled "pot likker") is the seasoned broth that remains after greens have been cooked in a good quantity of water with meat and additional spices. Today, nutritionists argue that this is the best part of a greens dish because the broth contains all of the vitamins and nutrients that leached out of the greens during the stewing process. Abram Sells shows us that "potlicker" was a term that could be applied to any vegetable broth, not just greens. "They fed all us nigger chillen in a big trough made out'n wood, maybe more a wood tray, dug out'n soft timber like magnolia or cypress. They put it under a tree in the shade in the summer time and gave each chile a wood spoon, then mix all the food up in the trough and us goes to eatin'. Mos' the food was pot-licker, jes' common old potlicker; turnip greens and the juice, Irish 'taters and the juice, cabbages and peas and beans, jes' anything what make pot-licker. All us git round like so many li'l pigs and then us dish in with our wood spoon till it all gone."[30] Though Sells describes a childhood memory, poor adults, white and black, pretty much ate the same way. Clearly, planters were economizing by feeding children pot likker. Giving some people solid food and others just liquid food and feeding from a trough re-inforced the caste position of all slaves. Planters ate some greens, but be-cause greens were part of the shared "pottage" regularly made by slaves on their own initiative, eating greens was strongly associated with blackness.

Greens are an appropriate metaphor for how the enslaved asserted their autonomy because they often did so through gardening. Southern whites took pride in their gardens and were quick to let others know. The *Charleston Mercury* editorialized in 1855, "The people of the South have a great advantage over the Northern and Middle States, in having good fall and winter gardens, yet few seem to appreciate the fact that they can have them."[31] While planters were fine with whites having gardens, they were increasingly concerned about the prodigious gardening slaves were doing. Georgia Telfair testifies to the prowess of the enslaved at gardening vegetables: "Us always kep' a good gyarden full of beans, corn, onions, peas n' taters an' dey warn't nobody could beat us at raisin' lots of greens, 'specially turnips and colla'd greens."[32] Slaves that were allowed to garden took full advantage of the small privilege. They grew so much surplus produce that they regularly sold it to or exchanged it for other goods with poor whites in the vicinity of the plantation or in a nearby city.

Beth Fowkes Tobin, in her study of Jamaican plantation foodways in the nineteenth century, tells of a similar dynamic, and some of her conclusions apply to the situation in the antebellum South. Tobin notes that by displaying such expertise in gardening, the enslaved challenged planters' "beliefs about Africans' inability to manage themselves." Tobin explains that "the abundance of provision grounds and markets presented planters with a contradiction that threatened the logic of their ideological justification for slavery."[33] The way Jamaican slaves formed an informal economy consistently undermined the planters' ability to control their slaves' material conditions. In the nineteenth century, American planters grew very

Soul Food Greens

Soul food greens are just some of the greens African Americans have traditionally eaten, particularly in the South. Here's a short list of some of the greens that have been mentioned as regulars on African American tables since the Down Home Cooking era.[1]

Beet greens	Cress	Mustard	Sweet potato
Broccoli rabe	Dandelion	Pepper grass	Turnip
Burdock	Dock	Poke	Watercress
Cabbage	Kale	Sheep cress	Wild lettuce
Chard	Lamb's quarter	Sourdock	Wintercress
Collard greens	Milkweed	Spinach	

---

1 "'Green' Greens"; "Greens in Our History"; Hughes, "Mail Me Some More Kinds of Greens"; Fambro, "Mess o' Greens."

concerned about how much the slaves were growing crops and asserting their independence. However, differences of opinion emerged on how to handle the "problem."

In 1830, the *Southern Agriculturalist and Register of Rural Affairs* recommended that planters establish a central plantation garden, "a large garden . . . placed under the superintendence of one intelligent Negro." This publication also recommended that "every slave be compelled to work a certain number of hours, each week in it, under the direction of the head gardener. Perhaps it would not require an average of more than a half, or at most an hour's work from each hand, per day, and increased comfort not only of himself, but of his family, would surely compensate him."[34] Many planters felt that recommendation was unworkable, and they continued to let their slaves have their own small gardens, knowing the enslaved cultivated them extensively during their leisure time. As one planter commented, "It is next to impossible to keep them from working their crops on Sabbath. They labor of nights when they should be at rest."[35] This shows beyond a doubt how important their gardens were to the enslaved.

As noted earlier, the slaves were making some "green" (money) by sell-ing their greens. This greens-fueled semi-independence was more than some American planters could stomach. One planter put forward a per-verse logic to insist that allowing slaves to harvest their own crops was bad.

> The first bad effect I mention, from allowing slaves to make crops for market, is this — it *opens a strong temptation to theft*. The privilege of making a crop, with many of them, is a privilege to make a *good crop*; and if they can't make it, or do not make it on the lands allotted them, it's a part of the religion of many of them to take it out the master's gin house or corn crib, or his neighbors. . . . A privilege to work in their patches until 9 or 10 o'clock at night is often construed into a privilege to visit a neighbor's hen house or pig yard; or perhaps to get a mule and take a turn of corn to some market and barter it for a jug of whiskey, or something of little value.[36]

To limit slave gardening, some planters prohibited gardens outright (though this was infrequent), and some made themselves the exclusive purchasers of their slaves' crops. Others discouraged whites from trans-acting business with their slaves and sought retribution against those who did. Despite efforts to clamp down on the practice, so much business was being done that planters eventually turned a blind eye to the practice, and an informal slave economy thrived until slavery's end. In this sense, greens functioned the same way that chickens operated in the slave economy. Slaves were also good at raising, selling, or trading chickens for other goods and money. Masters soon realized that they could do little to con-trol that practice as well.

With all of that effort during slavery to carve out relative independence through gardening, changes in the rural southern economy set in mo-tion after Emancipation reduced gardening over time. In rural America, sharecropping blacks grew less of their own food because the landlord gave incentives to use available ground to grow cash crops. Thus blacks depended more upon food supplies from the plantation store. For those who did plant gardens, as a dietary study of rural Alabama in 1897 found, greens were an important means for blacks to vary their diet, and they were cooked with bacon "to make it rich."[37] By the time of the Down Home Cooking era, gardening was rarer. Describing a black community in south-ern Illinois during the early 1940s, one commentator put his finger on the issue this way: "For some, the transition to the city was so disruptive that African American migrants became dependent . . . on store bought food. By comparison with that of the whites, the total gardening tends to be slight. The care of the growing plants is considerably more casual. This all leads to the inevitable suggestion that the Negroes, on the whole, are less dependent upon their gardens and more dependent upon the local stores."[38] For completely different reasons, urban blacks and black croppers gardened much less or stopped altogether.[39] This trend endured. In 1972, a nutritionist wrote that few black residents in Los Angeles garden, but when they do, "greens are the main vegetable grown."[40]

The decline in gardening didn't necessarily mean that fewer fresh greens were eaten. Rural southerners resorted to an age-old practice: foraging. "In addition to the garden source of foods, the [rural] Negroes have recourse to various wild foods. The regularity with which they gather various types of berries makes these very similar to agricultural products in their reliability in the diet. Wild plants which are regularly collected in the appropriate seasons include grapes, poke, elderberry, wild mustard, strawberries, dewberries, blackberries, broom sage, berry briar, and various docks."[41] And urban blacks who remained in the South did not have to forage as much and frequently continued gardening, but these gardens tended to be small.

In urban areas, entrepreneurs responded to the increasing customer demand for fresh greens. Take these newspaper accounts of black life in Harlem and Chicago during the Down Home Cooking era. The *New York Amsterdam News* reported that Harlemites were fond of kale, cabbage, collards, and turnip and mustard greens, cooked with some sort of pork.[42] In 1928, the *Chicago Daily Defender* reported that with the arrival of twenty-nine carloads of mustard greens, "the Negro has brought his diet to Chicago, and he has no superior judge as a judge of good food."[43] The same article noted that there was little demand for these greens outside black neighborhoods.

The increased availability of greens happened in other cities as well as in Chicago and Harlem. Evoking the old British name for the traditional dish (but with the greens listed first), Joffe wrote in the 1940s, "'Greens and bacon' or salt pork is a most characteristic and popular dish. The leaves of turnips, mustard, kale and cabbage, or the whole collard plant, are set to stew with a piece of fat meat. The dish requires little attention and can be left on the fire to be eaten by anyone who gets hungry. In Northern cities, often spinach is eaten so combined, but it is felt that spinach is not so tasty prepared this way as are the other greens. In recent years, in New York, broccoli has been coming into favor, for it responds well to the panning method."[44] Greens fit well into the new urban reality of varying work schedules that often thwarted a family's attempts to have set times to eat together. The reference to the "panning method" reflects nascent efforts by home economists to move the Down Home Cooking method of preparing greens (with plenty of water) toward the European practice of using little water and no seasoning meat. In short, home economists were trying to take the soul out of greens.

The earliest voices on this subject were European culinary experts like Hannah Glasse who were comfortable with cooking vegetables with a lot of water. But Glasse was not so thrilled with using seasoning meat. In her 1747 cookbook, Glasse advised cooks to "Boil all your Greens in a Copper Sauce-pan by themselves with a great Quantity of Water. Boil no Meat with them, for that discolours them."[45] A century later, American culinary experts were divided on Glasse's advice. It appears this practice was followed in the Big House kitchens where The Virginia Housewife and The Carolina Housewife were used. Mrs. Randolph and Mrs. Rutledge don't call for meat in their boiled greens preparations, though Mrs. Randolph does allow that turnip tops are "still better boiled with bacon in the Virginia style."[46] The Kentucky Housewife is squarely at odds with Glasse, for Mrs. Bryan consistently requires meat when preparing greens.

Having discouraged the practice of using seasoning meat with vegetable preparations, English culinary experts then trained their sights on pot likker, arguing that using a lot of water to make vegetables is wasteful and that steaming was a preferred method.[47] American culinary experts were not quite ready to transition to steaming. In 1844, Eliza Leslie advocated that vegetables should be completely drained and free of any liquid when served.[48] Sarah J. Hale, a very influential home economist, echoed Glasse's sentiment when she wrote in 1857 that vegetables should be boiled alone.[49] In 1879, Juliet Corson offered a compromise by writing, "When vegetables are cooked for use with salt meat, the meat should first be cooked and taken from the pot liquor, and the vegetables boiled in the latter."[50] We don't get a definitive word from early African American cookbooks as Mrs. Russell, Mrs. Fisher, and Mrs. Hayes included neither greens recipes nor pot likker recipes. From the sources we do have, it appears African Americans continued to eat their greens with pot likker and pork.

During the Down Home Cooking era, African American cooking experts started advocating for a change in the ways greens were made. In 1948, DeKnight's *A Date with a Dish* strongly admonished readers to "always use as little water as possible when cooking greens."[51] As an exclamation point, she makes no mention of pot likker at all. Clearly DeKnight thinks of pot likker as a wasteful product. In 1951, the *New York Amsterdam News* weighed in on the subject with "Since most of the nutrients will dissolve in water, the less liquid the better. Succulent greens like spinach contain their own 'juice' so just drop them in a cold pan with only the moisture clinging to the leaves and a little salt to start them off. . . . Someone cooking less juicy greens such as kale, turnip and mustard greens and collards may need as much as an inch of boiling salted water. Or if you want the seasoning of ham or corned beef, use a little of the stock. It doesn't take an ocean to give the flavor."[52] Urban-based home economists tried to change the way urban blacks prepared greens. It appears that the tried-and-true way of overboiling this particular food seemed unsophisticated.

African American food experts also tried to bend the African American palate toward the Anglo-American practice of eating raw greens. This was not easily achieved, as Joffe observed in the early 1940s: "On the whole, Negroes do not like 'raw' foods, and eat few salads and not much fruit."[53] Still, the *Chicago Defender* tried to persuade its readers in 1951 to come over to the raw side. "Spinach is becoming more plentiful now, and it can serve salad purposes. When you buy spinach, look for large fresh appearing leaves that have a good green color, and avoid those that are wilted or have started to turn yellow. Endive, escarole, and chicory are three other greens to keep in mind when shopping for salad ingredients now."[54] Salad consumption may have increased, but despite the advocacy, boiled preparations remain the primary way that African Americans eat their greens.

The way African Americans traditionally cook their greens is sharply distinguished from the method of West Africans by the use of pork—whether it is bacon, bacon drippings, hock, or salt pork. As soul foodies become more health conscious, the use of pork has become the biggest liability. Personally I bounce back and forth between being a greens traditionalist and a greens reformer. Sometimes I make my greens with ham hocks; other times I use smoked turkey parts. Once during a culinary presentation, I told an audience that I found smoked turkey to be just as flavorful as pork. Someone in the audience shouted back to me, "What's wrong with the pigs in Colorado?" I couldn't help but laugh, but I suspect that many home cooks who still take the time to make their own greens are making similar adjustments. In most soul food restaurants across the country, even in the Deep South, pork is no longer the default seasoning for vegetables. A soul food place is much more likely to serve greens and other vegetables with smoked turkey or in chicken broth, or by using a heavier hand with herbs and spices. Those are the best-case scenarios. It's with great sadness that I must inform you that quite a few places have cut out the pork but aren't doing much else to season their greens. I think they're relying on us to make up the difference with a dash of hot sauce or vinegar.

Why are soul food restaurants going whole hog to serve greens without pork?[55] The short answer is they hope to make more money. Without pork, or any meat at all, some soul food restaurateurs figure that they can attract a wider range of customers: the health conscious, the vegans, the vegetarians, and anyone who considers it taboo to eat pork. This is a no-brainer for soul food joints in places like Philadelphia, Pennsylvania, where a large Black Muslim population can easily dictate the market. The restaurant industry is challenging even in the best of times; thus it makes economic sense for a restaurant to attract all of the customers it can.

I hope more restaurateurs will embrace Imar Hutchins's approach at the Florida Avenue Grill in Washington, D.C., where pork is not an either/or proposition. Hutchins, a vegetarian who previously operated the wildly successful Delights of the Garden restaurants in the 1990s before going to Yale Law School, opted not to "green" the grill's menu when he purchased the business in 2005. "I didn't get rid of anything on the menu, but I supplemented it with the things that I like. That way, no one could get mad," Hutchins told me. Hutchins also told me that it was good business sense. "Blacks are disproportionately vegetarian when compared to the overall population." That was news to me. I won't give away Hutchins's clever compromise (at his request), but he's figured out an ingenious way to prepare pork-infused dishes and vegetarian delights in the same kitchen without comprising the integrity of either one.

When I ate at a restaurant, I always asked how the greens were made. If they didn't use pork, I followed up and asked why. Though most soul food restaurateurs told me they were trying to expand their customer base, a significant number added that they were responding to the health crisis in the black community. The proprietors hoped that "motherless" greens could give birth to a change in their customers' eating habits while still honoring the soul food tradition.

In the past couple of decades, a wider variety and quantity of greens have become available through a mix of technological change, a return to gardening, and increasing demand from recent African immigrants for particular types of greens. Technology has certainly made eating greens more convenient for both home and restaurant cooks. With frozen, pre-washed, and packaged greens now available in the grocery store, the arduous task of cleaning greens has been eliminated.

I've cleaned fresh greens, and I can tell you that it is *work*. One has to strip the leaves from the stalk, carefully pick through the greens, and rinse in several waters to remove all of the dirt and the "extra meat" (my mother's euphemism for bugs) that may be clinging to the leaves. If you want a nice shortcut, Sharon Hunt, in her *Bread from Heaven* cookbook (1992), suggests using a washing machine and putting the greens on the "gentle cycle."[56] That's a trick that I have yet to try. After all of that washing, one cuts up the greens or tears them into smaller pieces before putting them into the pot with the other ingredients. Knowing all of the hard work that goes into making greens from scratch, my spirit is always buoyed when I step into a place like Bully's Soul Food in Jackson, Mississippi. In Bully's, there's a table just off the main dining room that frequently has piles of fresh greens on it—ready to be cleaned, chopped, and cooked. Here's a quick warning for anyone planning to cook frozen, precut greens. The small, uniform, industrial cut is a dead giveaway to soul food aficionados that the greens were once in the frozen food section. If you don't mind the possible scorn, then frozen greens with the right amount of seasoning will get the job done. Plus, you shouldn't have to worry about finding any bugs.

Of the technological advances with greens, canned greens seem to bug soul foodies the most. I find the strong criticism interesting because critics seem to forget or overlook the strong "canning" traditions within the rural South—and that glass containers were used for storage. Greens were certainly among the foods that were canned. Canning at home has nearly vanished since the Down Home Cooking period ended, and soul food cooks opted for fresh, frozen, or packaged greens.

One entrepreneur saw a market opportunity with the lack of canned greens, and Glory Foods was launched in 1989 precisely to fill that vacuum. According to the company's website, its late founder, Bill Williams, talked to friends about "the number of hours and care that went into cooking a savory pot of collard greens and how no African American family celebration is complete without them. How great it would be to have truly authentic canned collard greens, Williams thought. After extensive research, Williams and his partners realized that preseasoned, canned collard greens were not available anywhere."[57] They've been popular ever since.

The greens table at Bully's Soul Food, Jackson, Miss.

As Michael Moore, Glory Foods's chairman of the board, shared, "Collard greens put Glory on the map because now you don't have to cook and clean collards, and they're already seasoned. Glory offers the convenience of getting 'soul food in a can.'" Though the black-owned Glory Foods has had a traditionally African American market, Moore tells me that the company now sells to a larger group that enjoys Glory's particular flavor profile. "White folks talk about Glory with as much passion as our core market." After launching the canned products, Glory now provides fresh and frozen food products as well, and Moore adds that its "all natural" product line is one of the fastest growing.[58] I was somewhat skeptical of Moore's assertion about white people's passion for Glory greens until I picked up *The Cracker Kitchen*, Janis Owens's ode to poor white cooking. Owens writes, "If you're crunched for time, Glory Mixed Greens (sold in a can) are about as close to homemade as you can get. You don't have to mess with picking and sorting and degritting, just heat and add a little crushed red pepper and you're done."[59]

Even as technology has made more greens more convenient, more people are getting their greens the old-fashioned way—by gardening. Leading the way is the black church, which has made gardening a health ministry. Through pilot projects, and particularly through growing greens, they attempt to increase access to fresh food and to build community inside and outside the church. Two projects in the Mississippi Delta have shown real promise.

The Growing Together project began in 2009 with funding from the Centers for Disease Control and technical assistance from the Delta Health Alliance and the Mississippi Health Department's Delta Health Collaborative. Growing Together sought to raise health consciousness in the region and reverse the alarming rise in chronic disease by starting a church gardens project. As Ryan Betz of the Delta Health Collaborative, who was heavily involved with the project, explains, "Churches remain a strong institution in the South, and we wanted to focus on African Americans." When approached, many black pastors jumped at the opportunity. Betz added, "A lot of pastors felt a duty and responsibility to preach a healthy diet, and could quote scripture to support that. It was also something for kids to get involved in, to give them a chance to take care of something."[60]

Herman Sullivan, a member at Shiloh Seventh-day Adventist Church in Greenwood, Mississippi, discovered after his church joined the project that gardening was also a way to bridge generation gaps and foster fellowship between the church congregation and the surrounding community. Edna Lewis once said, "When you're living in the city you don't see how things grow and under what conditions they grow."[61] Sullivan's experience at Shiloh shows that even people in small towns have lost that connection with nature, especially young people. When interviewed on the subject, Sullivan says, "We got a group [of young people] called the Pathfinders. They're something like the Boy Scouts and the Girl Scouts. We bring those guys out and let them help out doing the ground preparation, some of the planting, and they were surprised. They thought everything come from the grocery store. They didn't know you could grow greens out of the ground, so we got some Styrofoam cups and gave them all some watermelon seeds and, you know, let them participate and, and have some firsthand experience."[62]

Once the gardening program was under way, Shiloh members delivered fresh produce to the elderly who couldn't get around easily. In the same interview, Sullivan gives a poignant example of just what a bag of greens could mean to someone: "Yeah, Miss [Mary Lena] Broom, she lives around the corner and I . . . she been knowing me all my life. Me and her son grew up together. Her son is deceased now but . . . she's about ninety-two, ninety-three and she . . . she got those greens. She . . . she's just crying man. . . . People that haven't had greens in so long that can't get out and move around. . . . It's a good feeling to—for those people to see the peoples' faces light up." Forty churches had planted gardens by the time the Growing Together program ended in 2011, and there were plenty more hoping to get grant money to start a garden. The word from Betz is that many churches, like Shiloh, are keeping their gardens going even though the seed funding has run out. Many more people in the Delta are eating better because of the program, watching their health indicators more closely, and therefore living healthier lives.

Benita Conwell of Mound Bayou, Mississippi, is leading another noteworthy effort. Conwell is affiliated with Women in Agriculture and with the Southern Rural Black Women's Initiative for Economic and Social Justice. These organizations are helping poor women in the region break a cycle of dependency by teaching them skills that could lead to employment or running their own small business. As Mound Bayou is one of the earliest and continuously operating African American communities in America, it's no surprise that forward-thinking practices are emerging there. Conwell got her start with a sweet potato growers' cooperative in the 1980s while running Robert's Meat Market (named after her late father) at the same time. Ever the entrepreneur, Conwell noticed that aside from the sweet potato vines and tubers used for replanting, growers threw away the rest of the crop. She started thinking about ways to use what was thrown away.

Somehow, a person (Conwell won't reveal his identity) who ran a produce market in Houston, Texas, found out about Conwell's sweet potato operation and reached out to her hoping they could solve a mutual problem. He needed someone to supply large amounts of sweet potato greens to his growing customer base—West African immigrants. West Africans were not too keen on sweet potatoes themselves but have loved the greens since the plant was introduced in their homeland in the seventeenth century. Conwell and her Houston connection have a promising venture under way, and like the church garden project, her business is getting young people involved during the summer and connecting people back to the land.

Conwell hopes to expand the sweet potato greens market beyond African immigrant consumers.[63] If African Americans begin eating sweet potato greens in large numbers, Dr. George Washington Carver's spirit will rejoice. Dr. Carver pushed these greens in 1941: "The young, tender vines and leaves of the sweet potato are especially rich and palatable when cooked like spinach. They are equally good mixed in boiled with other greens."[64] Expanding the sweet potato greens market could reap a two-fold harvest: Farmers would utilize a renewable resource that currently gets thrown away. The increased demand for the produce would help poor women in the Mississippi Delta break free from a cycle of dependency caused by poverty and poor diet.

Greens still have primacy in soul food circles. They are often the first answer that people give when asked to name a soul food. Though most of these associations are now lost, African Americans have a vague idea that West Africans eat a lot of greens, so there is some connection to a shared culinary past. Okra and black-eyed peas, which have a stronger connection to West Africa, have no such luck. Speaking of luck, greens also represent money on the traditional New Year's Day plate. They're also a steady companion for almost any meal, from barbecue to Thanksgiving dinner. I'm not surprised that greens are so ubiquitous. Greens have been there in every phase of the African American experience and they are the one of the few foods that haven't been rejected with increased demand for healthy foods. The future certainly looks bright for dark, leafy greens.

Johnetta's Mixed Greens

This is my favorite thing to make in the soul food genre. I didn't grow up eating collards. My mother usually made a combination of mustard and turnip greens. Turnip greens seemed to be the popular option for greens as I traveled through Tennessee. I love the peppery aroma that mustard greens give off while they're cooking. I've lately been using smoked turkey parts to season my greens because they give good flavor with less fat. Yet, every once in awhile, I go retro and put on a pot of greens with some ham hocks.

Makes 8 servings

2 smoked ham hocks or smoked turkey wings, or 1 leg (1 pound)
1½ pounds turnip greens
1½ pounds mustard greens
1 tablespoon granulated garlic or 2 minced garlic cloves
1 medium onion, chopped

Pinch of crushed red pepper flakes
Pinch of baking soda
Pinch of sugar
Pinch of salt

1 Rinse the hocks, wings, or leg, place them in a large pot, and cover with water. Bring to a boil and cook until the meat is tender and the cooking liquid is flavorful, 20 to 30 minutes. Discard the hocks, wings, or leg or, reserve the meat, cut it up, and mix into the greens for serving.

2 Meanwhile, remove and discard the tough stems from the greens. Cut or tear the leaves into large, bite-sized pieces. Fill a clean sink or very large bowl with cold water. Add the leaves and gently swish them in the water to remove any dirt or grit. Lift the leaves out of the water and add them to the hot stock, stirring gently until they wilt and are submerged.

3 Stir in the onion, pepper flakes, baking soda, sugar, and salt.

4 Simmer until the greens are tender, about 30 minutes. Check the seasoning and serve hot.

Sweet Potato Greens Spoonbread

Chef Ann Cashion and I served together on the Southern Foodways Alliance board, and she is currently the executive chef at Johnny's Half Shell Restaurant in Washington, D.C. Ann and I were on a Southern Foodways Alliance field trip to the Mississippi Delta when I first heard of sweet potato greens. She developed this recipe, which gives an interesting spin to a very soulful combination of greens and cornbread. If you've made spoonbread before, this version creates a very soft custard. If you can't find sweet potato greens at a farmers' market or Asian grocer in your area, baby spinach and stemmed chard are good substitutes.

Makes 8 to 12 servings

10 ounces sweet potato leaves
with 1- to 2-inch stems
¼ cup olive or vegetable oil
1 cup red onion, thinly sliced
3 cups whole milk

⅔ cup stoneground
white cornmeal
1 teaspoon sugar
2 teaspoons salt
2 teaspoons baking powder

½ cup heavy cream
1 cup (2 sticks) butter
4 eggs

Dash of Tabasco or other
hot pepper sauce (optional)

1 Preheat the oven to 375°F. Butter a 9-by-2-inch round cake pan. Line the bottom with a round of parchment paper and butter the paper. The spoonbread bakes in a water bath, so have ready a large baking pan that can hold the prepared cake pan.

2 Bring a large pot of salted water to a boil over high heat. Have ready a large bowl of ice water. Stir the greens into the boiling water. As soon as the water returns to a boil, use a small sieve or slotted spoon to transfer the leaves into the ice water. Drain in a colander. Pick up small handfuls, squeeze them as dry as possible, and then coarsely chop them. Fluff them with your fingers to separate the pieces.

3 Heat the oil in a large skillet over medium heat. Add the onions and let them cook, stirring occasionally, until they are soft, about 8 minutes. Add the greens into the skillet and stir to mix well. Season the mixture with salt and pepper and set aside.

4 Combine the milk, cream, and butter in a large saucepan. Cook over low heat until the butter melts.

5 Whisk the eggs in a large bowl. Whisk in the cornmeal, sugar, salt, baking powder, and Tabasco, if using.

6 Whisking constantly, add the warm milk mixture to the cornmeal mixture in a slow, steady stream. Pour this back into the saucepan and cook over medium heat, stirring constantly with a heatproof spatula until the mixture thickens enough to coat the spatula, about 3 minutes. Do not let the mixture boil. Remove the pan from the heat.

7 Drain any accumulated liquid from the greens mixture. Pour about one-fourth of the hot cornmeal mixture into the greens mixture and mix well. Scrape into the prepared cake pan.

8 Scrape the rest of the cornmeal mixture into the pan. Smooth the top.

9 Set the cake pan in the large pan. Pour very hot tap water into the large pan until the water comes halfway up the side of the cake pan.

10 Bake until the spoonbread is set, about 45 minutes. Let it rest in the hot water bath for 10 minutes and then remove it from the water.

11 Place a large serving plate over the cake pan. Hold them together firmly, flip them over to release the spoonbread, and remove the pan. Cut the warm spoonbread into wedges and serve at once.

Candied Yams

WEST AFRICAN IN NAME, BUT NOT IN TASTE

As a food for human consumption, the sweet potato has been, and always will be, held in very high esteem and its popularity will increase in this direction as we learn more about its many possibilities. There is an idea prevalent that anybody can cook sweet potatoes. There is a very great mistake, and the many, many dishes of illy cooked potatoes that are placed before me as I travel over the South prompt me to believe that these recipes will be of value. —George Washington Carver

Quand patate tchuite, faut mange li.
(When the sweet potato is cooked, it must be eaten.)
—Louisiana Creole proverb

★ ★ ★ ★ ★

Benita Conwell's revelation to me about sweet potato greens opened up a window on West African history I previously had not known. I knew Europeans introduced sweet potatoes into West Africa during the Atlantic slave trade. It turns out West Africans loved the greens but were blasé about the root itself. Conwell thinks both parts of the plant should be loved. In the 1980s, she figured out she could make more money farming sweet potatoes than with what she calls "row crops" like greens and beans. Sweet potatoes are not native to the Mississippi Delta (whites introduced them into the area centuries ago), but the area's soil and climate make it a great place to grow sweet potatoes. Conwell also swears that the region's soil makes sweet potatoes sweeter. When we considered the proverb above, Conwell told me about two popular ways that sweet potatoes get cooked and eaten. Conwell said the most nutritious and natural way to make sweet potatoes is to bake them plain. Conwell added that people also "love to yam it up," which she described as putting precooked sliced sweet potatoes in a skillet, adding butter and sugar, and then cooking the sweet potatoes until the sugar caramelizes.[1] This is the beloved "candied yam" side dish that unites Thanksgiving Day tables across America. Like black-eyed peas on New Year's Day, once that special day is over, yams typically spend the rest of the year as a soul food/southern specialty. The root gets its "yam" name from a West African staple, but that's where the similarities end. How African Americans prepare candied yams is the legacy of fancy European recipes for carrots, not a contemporary adaptation of the way West Africans prepare true yams. When soul foodies "yam it up," they're standard-bearers for upper-class English and French cooking, not West African cooking.

First, let's discuss the name. What we call a "yam" in the United States is really a sweet potato, and the sweet potato has been an edible ball of confusion in the English language for several centuries. Though both are root crops, the sweet potato (*Ipomoea batata*) and the potato (*Solanum tuberosum*) are two completely different plants. Sweet potatoes originated in Peru, and "archaeological evidence gives a date of *at least* 2000 B.C.E. for the presence of the domesticated sweet potato in the New World, while suggesting a possible domesticated form as early as 8000 B.C.E."[2] The indigenous people in northwestern South America and the Latin American tropics knew the difference between the plants and used distinct names, calling sweet potatoes "batata" and potatoes "papas." European explorers brought batatas and papas with them on their return trips back home during the 1500s, but they kept calling both plants potatoes, using only the adjective "sweet" to distinguish the two. Another layer of confusion was added when someone started calling sweet potatoes "yams."

West Africans may have started the yam talk when they first encountered sweet potatoes in the sixteenth century. African Americans were certainly doing so by the nineteenth century. Several West African languages have words that sound like "yam" that describe the edible root or act as a verb meaning "to eat." When Lorenzo Dow Turner studied the Gullah language of South Carolina blacks in the mid-twentieth century, he noted *nam* and *yam* as African word survivals that respectively mean "to eat, to eat up" and "sweet potato."[3] So a sweet potato is neither a potato nor a true yam, but it gets called a yam in the United States.

No one knows for sure exactly when or how this happened, but we definitely know that it's a case of identity theft by the sweet potato.[4] True yams are the roots of a wide variety of tropical plants belonging to the genus *Dioscorea* that have been cultivated as early as 6000 B.C.E.[5] West African cooking author Ellen Gibson Wilson points out that yams are "the staple of many people in West Africa, [and] this tuber comes in 59 varieties of which five are eaten the most: Chinese, trifoliate, water or winged, white and yellow."[6] West African cooks have developed traditional ways to cook particular yams based on their unique properties. Some yams are better roasted, while some are better fried. The most popular way to cook most yams is to boil them and prepare "pounded yam," also known as *foo-foo* or *fufu*. With this dish, the yam is boiled and then pounded with a pestle and mortar until it's an elastic mass. The mass is then shaped into a loaf or individual balls to be scooped up with the diner's fingers and eaten with a savory sauce or stew.[7] If you've never seen a West African eat this way, it's an impressive sight to behold. Notably absent from West African cooking are past and present recipes or accounts of sweet yam dishes. Overall, nothing like the candied yam or a sweet potato existed in precolonial West African foodways. For West Africans, the idea of sugaring vegetables is nonsensical.

Since this terminology can get very confusing, from now on, I'll use "true yam" to describe the tropical root food from West Africa, "sweet potatoes" for the edible tubers from South America, and "yam" to mean a particular type of deep, orange-fleshed sweet potato. I know the latter perpetuates a historical error, but that's a sacrifice that I'll have to make.

A lot of people around the world eat true yams, but West Africans are distinguished by the central role this particular food plays in their diet and culture. One expert wrote, "The dominant role of root crops and plantains as staple foods in western tropical Africa is unusual. In Ireland and Germany, European countries noted for their high consumption of potatoes, root crops represent only about one-fourth to one-third as many calories as cereals. . . . In East Africa roots and tubers are far less important than in West Africa and the Congo."[8] The true yam's home territory in West Africa extends from the Ivory Coast in the north all the way south to Cameroon, with the highest concentration of cultivation in Nigeria. Nigerians, especially the Ibo (also spelled "Igbo"), hold true yams in high esteem. Dr. Bede Nwoye Okigbo, a Nigerian researcher, notes that "the yam is unquestionably the 'central' or key crop of the Ibos. . . . Among the peoples of West Africa none is so devoted to the cultivation of yams as the Ibos."[9]

The Ibo attach strong cultural meaning to the true yam because they believe true yams have a divine origin.

An old Igbo myth says that during a severe famine Igbo (from whom the tribe takes its name) was told that he must sacrifice his son,

Ahiajoku, and his daughter, Ada, in order to save his other children. After they were killed, their flesh was cut into pieces and buried in several different mounts. A few days later, yam sprouted from the flesh of Ahiajoku, while cocoyams sprouted from the flesh of Ada. Igbo and his other children survived the famine by eating them. The spirit of Ahiajoku became the God of Yam. . . . The yam is symbolic of a human being who was sacrificed so that other humans might survive.[10]

At the time of the Atlantic slave trade, the true yam's dietary and cultural status in West Africa was challenged by the introduction of New World crops. The true yam's main rivals during the colonial period were plantains, maize, and sweet potatoes, with each affecting yam culture in different ways. The Portuguese introduced maize during the sixteenth century, though scholars have debated a prior introduction into the region as early as the eleventh century.

West African farmers quickly adopted maize for food. Aside from its higher growth yields and nutritional value, maize was a popular crop because farmers could grow it the same way they grew their traditional crops. Jacques Miege, an agricultural historian of West Africa, argues that "maize was so readily adopted in the 'yam culture' of the eastern Guinea Coast in part because it lends itself to planting in hills in a manner similar to the culture of yams. Maize apparently has gained ground as a staple food mainly at the expense of yams and sorghum."[11] In the areas where yams were important, the West African elites ("Big Men") gained status through yam farming and the number of yams they possessed—signs of wealth. Maize's increasing popularity, however, was destabilizing the established order, as upstarts successful at growing the New World crop began to gain more wealth and status. Still, rather than abandon yams for maize, the Big Men did more to enhance the true yam's cultural value.[12]

Even if the New World plants were a popular substitute on the dinner table, they couldn't compete with true yams in terms of cultural meaning. Accordingly, true yam festivals proliferated in the eighteenth and nineteenth centuries as the Big Men fended off their rivals and consolidated their power. Today, the new true yam festival continues in Nigeria:

It usually takes place around the end of June, and it is considered taboo to eat the newly harvested YAM for this date. The high priest sacrifices a goat and pours its blood over a symbol representing the god of the harvest. Then the carcass is cooked and a soup is made from it, while the yams are boiled and pounded to make *foofoo*. After the priest has prayed for a better harvest in the coming year, he declares the feast open by eating the pounded yam and the soup. Then everyone joins in, and there was dancing, drinking, and merrymaking. After the festival is over, it is permissible for anyone in the community to eat the new yam.[13]

The Big Men's gambit on cultural reinforcement worked. "West African yams remained the most esteemed forest crop in the Atlantic era (and still are today), and forest communities celebrated the end of the West African true yam harvest as their major annual celebration."[14] As further evidence of the importance of the true yam, the celebration migrated to various parts of the New World as the Jonkonnu festival, where it took on different forms in Jamaica, the Carolinas, and Georgia.[15]

Europeans also valued true yams because they worked well as slave ship provisions. As Mark Wagner notes,

West African yams were among the earliest of the African cultigens to arrive in the Americas. . . . Yams were attractive to European slavers primarily because they could be obtained in enormous quantities all along the West African coast. Also, cultural food preferences of the African slaves sometimes precluded the use of any type of food other than yams. In 1701, an officer on the Don Carlos declared that a ship that takes in five hundred slaves must provide above a hundred thousand yams. . . . The slaves there [the Guinea Coast] being of such a constitution that no other food will keep them: Indian corn, beans, and mandioca disagreeing with their stomach so they sicken and die apace.[16]

On some voyages, yams also nourished the slave ship's white crew as well.[17] Wagner adds that true yams spoiled quickly, so they were often eaten while the slave ship was still off the West African coastline, during the early part of the Middle Passage.[18]

Because true yams spoiled quickly, European slavers looked for a substitute. They tried sweet potatoes, but they also spoiled quickly.[19] Though sweet potatoes were discounted as a slave food, free West Africans tried them, but the new food, which they called "European or white man's yam," never got major status.[20] Ellen Gibson Wilson wrote in the early 1970s that "in parts of West Africa, [sweet potatoes are] regarded as pig food. Some people grow sweet potatoes as a 'fooling crop,' an extra that need not be taken seriously. Smaller and more perishable than true yams, sweet potatoes are valued much more for their leaves."[21] Poor sweet potato. You know it's not going well for the sweet potato if a West African thinks it's not a suitable root to eat. Given the sweet potato's limited use as a slave ship food, and the West Africans' legendary preference for true yams and long-standing indifference to sweet potatoes, it's unlikely that this particular food played an important role in West African cuisine during the Atlantic slave trade era.

If West Africans were lukewarm to sweet potatoes, sixteenth-century Europeans were red hot for the exotic import from the Americas. According to historian A. Hyatt Verrill, the sweet potato logged a lot of miles during its Western European tour. "Long before the conquest of Peru, the sweet potatoes had been carried back to Spain. From Spain they were introduced to Italy, from Italy they travelled to Belgium, thence to Vienna, from Vienna into Germany and from Germany they found their way to England years before the first white potatoes were brought home by Sir John Hawkins in 1565."[22] England's upper classes had one of the loudest cheering sections in the sweet potato's fan club. The same historical account notes, "Oddly enough the English people took kindly to the sweet potatoes from the very first, although it took them two hundred years to accept the white potatoes as fit for human consumption. But the sweet potatoes were not the food of the masses by any means; in fact they were considered such a rare and expensive delicacy that only royalty and the very wealthy could afford to eat them, and in 1619 they cost two shillings to half a crown per pound which in those days was almost equivalent to their weight in gold."[23]

By the time of the Atlantic slave trade, sweet potatoes were already a feature of high-end English cooking, and they were typically prepared the same way the English prepared one of their own root crops—the carrot (Daucus carota). It's not so far-fetched that someone, particularly a cook, would think of sweet potatoes and carrots as kindred spirits. When Christopher Columbus first laid eyes on a sweet potato, he thought carrots. He wrote in the log of his 1492 voyage that sweet potatoes were "like great carrots that they grow and plant in all these countries and it is their living and they make bread of it and it has the flavor proper to chestnuts."[24] Both carrots and sweet potatoes come in a range of colors, though orange has become the preferred color for each. Both foods were also known as aphrodisiacs, and most importantly, both are sweet when cooked.[25] An expert on carrot history looked at the staple in many cuisines: "Carrots lent themselves to stews and soups but also to sweeter treatments. Dishes were also conceived that capitalized on the flavor of what many experts dub the second sweetest vegetable. . . . The English made puddings enriched with carrots. Hannah Glasse . . . offered a recipe for carrot custard in puff pastry."[26]

Europeans, particularly the Spanish, valued the sweet potato's sweetness, which is why the new food quickly found its way into European dishes whose structure and spicing were identical to those of traditional carrot preparations.[27] By the eighteenth century, sweet potatoes merited their own recipes in Hannah Glasse's cookbook. For example, one of Glasse's potato pudding recipes was renamed "yam pudding" and reprinted in Richard Briggs's English Art of Cookery, published in 1788.[28] This recipe tips us off to the fact that sweet potatoes, true yams, and yams were being confused in name on the Continent as well.

Since home cooks in the American colonies often used English cookbooks and both plants were growing in the colonies from an early date, they prepared interchangeable carrot and sweet potato recipes. Phillip Morgan states in his study of early slavery in the Maryland and Virginia colonies, "A little bit before he left South Carolina [in the early 1700s], Mark Catesby noted the introduction of a new variety of yam, 'a welcome improvement among the Negroes,' since they were 'delighted with all their African food, particularly this, which a great part of Africa subsists on.'"[29] Catesby, an English naturalist, had observed some early gardening experiments by the enslaved Africans. Intriguingly, Catesby suggests that the enslaved were growing true yams in a temperate South Carolina climate. However, foodways scholar Judith Carney acknowledges that true yam cultivation was very successful in the Caribbean, but "climate prevented the crop from thriving on the North American mainland, despite the efforts of the enslaved to establish the yam as a foodstaple."[30] Indeed, Catesby himself notes the low yields and the fact that true yams would not grow north of the Carolinas.[31] Thus, when Thomas Glover, an Englishman in Virginia, comments that in the early days of the colony, "Their Gardens have . . . Carrets, Potatoes, and Yams," he's really talking about sweet potatoes.[32]

There are few examples written down before the Civil War of slaves using "yams" when they meant "sweet potatoes." Jeptha Choice remembers of slavery in Texas, "We was fed good and had lots of beef and hawg meat and wild game. Possum and sweet yams is mighty good. You parboil

Possum 'n' Taters

THE MOST FAMOUS DISH PROBABLY UNKNOWN TO YOU

Were this history written 100 years ago, roasted possum with sweet potatoes (aka, possum 'n' taters) would have been featured as the pièce de résistance of a supper. That's what a North Carolina newspaper called it in 1900. According to the available slave testimony, possums were for eating, but the most thrills came from hunting possums. Possums are wily animals that inspired a great deal of folklore. They gave impressive chase to slaves who hunted them during their leisure hours, mostly at night. Possums can also feign death, and there are several stories about possums disappearing several hours after being caught.

When it came to cooking possum, the standard method was to bake it with sweet potatoes. Some commentators have described the dish as a substitution of the English roast with white potatoes. The possum was typically seasoned with red pepper, and it is said to taste like pork. The sweet potatoes were enriched by cooking in the possum's gravy. Possum 'n' taters was not restricted to the slave cabin. Slave masters and U.S. presidents (William Taft and Franklin Delano Roosevelt) salivated for the dish. In 1950, possum 'n' taters made its debut in high society when *Gourmet* included a recipe for the dish in an article about cooking game.

Today, possum is eaten on occasion in rural areas. As a result of severe restrictions on supplying wild game to restaurants, possum has slowly declined as a regular food. Even so, possum recipes have been included in soul food and southern cookbooks well into the late 1980s and early 1990s. Ernest Mickler's *White Trash Cooking* (1986) and Sheila Ferguson's *Soul Food: Classic Cuisine from the Deep South* (1994) are just two examples.

the possum about half done and put him in a skewer pan and put him in a hot oven and just 'fore he is done you puts the yams in the pan and sugar on 'em. That's a feast."[33] Despite this Choice example, slaves usually called sweet potatoes "taters," which was the old English-language nickname for potatoes.

Whatever they were called, sweet potatoes were an integral part of plantation foodways, and poor whites ate them as well. Southern planters were effusive about the benefits of using the sweet potato crops for slave food. William Summer, a South Carolina planter, wrote in 1845, "Such is the partiality of the plantation negroes for potatoes, as an article of food, that as soon as the season for digging arrives, they prefer an allowance of root to any of the cereal grains."[34] A year later, another planter wrote, "To my negroes I give one-half of the usual allowance of meal, in potatoes; and this they greatly prefer to all meal. I couldn't do without the sweet potato crop."[35] This partiality for sweet potatoes could be read in a couple of ways. Perhaps sweet potatoes just tasted better than maize. Another possibility is that the enslaved were clamoring for sweet potatoes because they were the closest thing they could get to their beloved true yams of their long-vanished homeland.

Sweet potatoes were a critical survival food during the winter, and southern planters and slaves alike knew that sweet potatoes had to be stored properly if they were to last the entire season. Many slaves and sharecroppers talked about constructing and maintaining sweet potato "banks." Sara Brooks, in her sharecropping memoir of the 1930s, wrote,

You know, sweet potatoes grows in the ground somethin' like a carrot, but they're on a vine. . . . My father'd dig a big round hole in the ground. Then you get some straw from the woods—pine straw—and you'd line the bank with this pine straw. Then you put the potatoes on the straw. Then you would take corn stalks—we cut the corn stalks—and stay in the stocks all the way around these potatoes like teepee. And then you would put boards over that—labor boards overlapping that it wouldn't rain in the bank—and they left a place would be a door where you could move it back and get potatoes out of it. . . . So the potatoes'll stay in there and stay dry all winter, and we just ate potatoes out of the tater bank. We'd have a lot of 'em—we had five, six, and sometime seven or more tater banks. They'd be right behind the house outside of the palins. And then we'd have this rail fence laid that the hogs couldn't get into them.[36]

Storing sweet potatoes this way was also called "curing," and some planters swore that curing actually sweetened the sweet potatoes.[37]

Recall the Igbo creation myth about true yams and its central theme of survival. Sharecroppers, though they were not conscious of the Igbo myth, did consider their true yams to be an important survival food. The following excerpt from nutrition researcher Natalie Joffe's study of African American food habits in the 1940s summarizes one Mississippi tenant farmer's experience:

> Although the majority of tenants and owners plant spring gardens, they store no vegetables for later use. The crop of sweet potatoes which is gathered in the fall is an exception. It is kept in a corncrib if the tenant is fortunate to have one, otherwise it is stored under or inside his cabin. If the potatoes do not rot, they constitute the tenant's chief guaranty of security against starvation during the winter, and are regarded by tenants as exactly similar to the urban worker's store of wages — except that the potatoes are surer. At the time when sweet potatoes are dug, there is considerable rivalry among tenants with regard to the size of their crops, and great pride and happiness on the part of those who harvest a large crop. In a year of low incomes from cotton, such as 1934, tenants speak of their store of sweet potatoes in terms which make it clear that they regard this store as life itself. A man's sweet potatoes are his banked resources, his protection against starvation and destitution until advances begin in the spring.[38]

A "survival food" is often considered undesirable, something that is only eaten during hard times. For sharecroppers, the opposite was true with sweet potatoes. Farmers spoke of them with an almost spiritual reverence. The fact that the sweet potato got African Americans through hard times enhanced its culture value, and we see that elevated status in the way sweet potatoes were cooked by African Americans during slavery and after Emancipation.

In Big Houses and slave cabins, roasting was a popular way to cook sweet potatoes. William Summer wrote in 1845, "To the negro, the potatoe is a blessing; for, to the known improvidence and carelessness of this race, it is particularly adapted, as it requires no culinary skill to make it both edible and palatable, simple roasting in the ashes being the best preparation the cook can give them."[39] The Virginia Housewife (1828) has a "sweet potatoes broiled" recipe.[40] The Kentucky Housewife (1839) mentions using a

"Spanish potato" in its "baked sweet potatoes" and "broiled sweet potatoes" recipes. "The Spanish potatoes are considered the finest," Mrs. Bryan writes, "and next to them the red permudas, the white and yellow potatoes are not so admired."[41] "Spanish potato" was a common nickname for sweet potatoes since the sixteenth century, when the Spanish got credit for introducing the food in Europe. The Carolina Housewife advises its readers, "Among the various ways of dressing sweet potatoes, that which appears the most generally preferred, is to bake them twice. . . . This way of baking twice, makes them more candied."[42]

Now it's time to unravel another layer of confusion caused by the use of the term "candied." Some in the South, like Mrs. Rutledge, applied the term "candied" to sweet potatoes that had been roasted plain rather than baked in a sweet, syrupy sauce. It's the latter cooking method that soul foodies and southerners think of when someone says "candied yams." What's the source of the sweet syrup method, and how did that become known as "candied"? Three possible answers all point to a French connection.

In one scenario, enslaved sugar workers created candied sweet potatoes as an impromptu snack. A traveler's account from the early 1800s to a French island colony in the Antilles records workers' practices: "The negro's who make sugar do not fail to throw their potatoes in the sirup pot, where they let them cook for a half hour. They make a delicious meal for the negroes."[43] Unfortunately, there are no such similar accounts from sugar plantations in French Louisiana to confirm that sugar slaves did the same thing in the United States. There are descriptions of sugar slaves on Louisiana plantations drinking hot sugar syrup during the refining process, but no mention of dipping a sweet potato in that syrup.[44] Most importantly, we don't know if the enslaved got the hot syrup idea from their French masters.

Another possibility is that classically trained French chef émigrés to America came up with the idea. One South Carolina newspaper asserted in 1887 that "the candied sweet potato is a Philadelphia confection. It is nothing but sweet potatoes carefully boiled and quartered and then candied in boiling syrup, but it is said to be dainty and tender and of delicious flavor."[45] During the eighteenth and nineteenth centuries, Philadelphia was a fashionable, trendsetting city and had long been a magnet for French chefs. The earliest French cookbook published in the United States was The French Cook, published in Philadelphia in 1828. Author Louis Eustache Ude wrote, "Carrots are like turnips, to supply the scarcity of vegetables at a time of the year, when vegetables are dear and scarce."[46] Ude's first carrot recipe, "Carrots à la d'Orleans," involves stewing a few young carrots "with a lump of sugar and a little broth" and is a possible predecessor to candied sweet potatoes. The French chefs applied one traditional preparation of a familiar root, the carrot, to the newer root, the sweet potato.

A third scenario gives credit to a particular group of French immigrants. The author of a 1937 *Better Homes and Gardens* article on "plantation" sweet potatoes wrote, "With the coming of Hugenot refugees [to Charleston, South Carolina] from France, sweet potatoes got a real break. It never takes a Frenchman long to discover foods with such possibilities as sweet potatoes."[47] Planters often paid to have their enslaved cooks learn the latest developments in French cuisine. If candying vegetables was a hot trend at all, the Big House cooks would have certainly been familiar with it, since they were the ones doing the cooking. Of the three possibilities, the French chef's adaptation theory seems the most probable.

Southern cooks generally prepared sweet potato side dishes in one of three ways, as one *New-York Tribune* writer reported to his northern audience in 1896:

> The uses of two vegetables, rice and sweet potatoes, give an insight into salient points of Southern cooking. The sweet potato is used throughout the South, and every day in the winter the Southern dinner table contains this succulent root. The Northerner expatiates upon the various fashions of preparing Irish potatoes, but after they are all told the sweet potato goes on developing its infinite possibilities. Beginning with their natural condition, one finds them roasted in their jackets in ashes; next comes the fried sweet potato, cut in thick, lengthwise slices and browned in boiling lard. Then follows a dish more elaborate: The potatoes are boiled and sliced, put in a pan with sugar, butter, bits of lemon and spices, a glass of water, and baked a delicate brown.[48]

The last example is obviously an interpretation of candied sweet potatoes. Poor rural blacks lacked stoves to make the new style of candied yams and continued to cook in their fireplaces or on outdoor fires. If a cook were fortunate enough to possess a cast-iron Dutch oven, he or she could get the job done. Otherwise, the "old school" candied yam—the roasted sweet potato—was prepared.

Though sweet potatoes were common down south, up north they had long been a luxury item enjoyed by the wealthy.[49] That changed in the later nineteenth century when northern farmers in several states, most notably New Jersey, began farming sweet potatoes on a large scale.[50] During this time a sharp geographical line was drawn on desirable sweet potato characteristics. Northerners and southerners had strong notions about a sweet potato's proper moisture, sweetness, and texture, and color served as a turnkey for these desired traits. A sweet potato industry pamphlet published in 1918 summarized the differences of opinion for farmers thinking of going into the business:

> If a grower wishes to supply the Northern market he should select a potato that has a light colored flesh and is dry and mealy when cooked. To the average Northern family the ideal potato is the Irish potato. The nearer the sweet potato approaches the Irish potato in texture and flavor, the more salable it will be in the Northern market. . . . In the South the demand is different. To the average Southern family a potato with a rich, yellow flesh and a very sweet flavor is preferred. A potato that has a candied appearance after baking, as though it has been dipped in cane sirup, is ideal for the Southern market. The Jersey Yellow or Yellow Nansemond, Triumph and Red Jersey are typical of the dry mealy varieties belonging to the first class. The Pumpkin yam, Providence, Nancy Hall, Porto Rico Yam and Golden Beauty represent the yellow, moist, sweet varieties that are popular in the Southern markets.[51]

The North/South consumer preferences are still present but not as strong as they were in the past. It's not unusual to spot two different types of sweet potatoes displayed side by side, with the lighter-skinned and off-whitish-fleshed variety called "sweet potatoes" and the darker-skinned, orange-fleshed variety called "yams." Noteworthy is the pamphlet's reference to the southerner's preference for the roasted sweet potato that looked like it was dipped in sweet syrup after baking—not that it actually was. Southern cooks like Mrs. Rutledge wanted that visual effect, and they only got it with sweet potatoes that had a higher concentration of natural sugars.

Some are probably surprised to see the sweet potato industry trumpet yellow yams instead of orange-fleshed ones. Yellow-fleshed yams were incredibly popular a few decades into the twentieth century. Even within

A box of sweet potatoes
ready for action, the Country
Platter, Cleveland, Miss.

African American culture, the "Georgia yellow yam" got the most accolades and pop culture references of any vegetable other than corn. The
Georgia yellow yam also got some national and then international exposure because of war. In our chitlins discussion we learned that a significant
number of black troops served in World War I, and in one instance, black
and white troops teamed up to get more yellow yams. As the *Los Angeles
Times* reported in 1918, "From the negro and white southern soldiers, who
are serving in France, came the cry for yellow yams."[52]

At the time, Congressman Frank Park represented Georgia's Second
Congressional District, where a lot of yellow yams were farmed. Being a
dutiful representative, Park persuaded the army's quartermaster general
(with the help of another Georgian, President Woodrow Wilson) to make
yellow yams an official army food.[53] Coincidentally, army food scientists
found that candying and compressing the yellow yams into cans gave the
food a long shelf life "without losing any of their original nutritious and
appetizing qualities."[54] In short order, soldiers who endured boot camps
in the South, survived World War I, and returned home had become am-
bassadors of the yellow yam.[55] The yellow yam was all set to take off na-

tionally, but it never really happened. Within a decade after the war, the yellow yam was already going out of style.

In whatever shape and color, sweet potatoes were a totemic food to rural and urban blacks at the turn of the twentieth century. As Robert Dirks observed, "Curiously, the sweet potato alone found a home everywhere. More than side meat and corn bread, it occupied an important place from the cotton lands of the Black Belt to the slums of Philadelphia. Sweet potato's popularity was obscured somewhat by its seasonality. For example, from an annual perspective, it appeared to be a secondary item in the Tuskegee diet. Nevertheless, when fall and winter arrived, it became a primary food."[56] Rural blacks retained a strong affinity for sweet potatoes well into the twentieth century, even when such loyalty didn't make economic sense. Dorothy Dickins found in 1948 that black families in rural Mississippi purchased as many sweet potatoes as they did Irish potatoes, even though the Irish ones were cheaper.[57] The fact that black families went for sweet potatoes even when the choice wasn't cost effective further evidences their strong affinity for that particular vegetable.

It's no surprise that after rural blacks migrated out of the South, big cities became hot spots for sweet potato eating. Roasted sweet potatoes were extremely popular, perhaps more so than candied yams. There were several reasons for this, one being convenience. Roasted sweet potatoes were an early version of fast food—quickly prepared, cheap, nutritious, and delicious. "Besides that," said one street vendor of the time, "it's too much trouble to the average man or woman to be bothered with cooking things like that when they can be bought so cheap. That's the way we keep in business. We sell our yams so cheap that it don't pay for the people to cook them at home. The extra trouble is worth the few extra cents they'd have to pay for enough for a good meal."[58] Roasted sweet potatoes also helped working parents satisfy their child's hunger pangs between meals. Natalie Joffe noted in her early 1940s nutrition study that "the older child may get money to buy food after school or for his lunch. With this money he is apt to purchase hot dogs, soda pop, ice cream, or even sweet potatoes, which are hawked on the streets of Harlem."[59]

Roasted sweet potatoes were also popular because they were easier on the budget. As an essay on Harlem life in the 1930s elucidates: "The vendors were almost unanimous in their explanation of the reason why so many people prefer buying their yams in the market in preference to preparing them at home. It was pointed out that in order to keep their gas bills down to normal, many of these women who might enjoy cooking their own yams refrain from doing so for reasons of economy."[60] Belonging to a chronically poor people, budget-conscious black cooks took advantage of every opportunity to save.

Because utility costs discouraged the long cooking times that come with baking and boiling, urban black cooks utilized sweet potato recipes that could be prepared faster and on top of the stove. In the *Montana Federation of Negro Women's Clubs Cook Book* (1927), Mrs. W. E. Royster of Billings offers a stovetop recipe:

Candied Sweet Potatoes — Wash, pare and cut into slices lengthwise, sprinkle with a little salt and put in frying pan one or two rounding tablespoons of butter and lay the potatoes in and stir them so they will all be coated with the butter. Then sprinkle them with 2 cups of brown sugar, cover closely and cook very slowly, stirring them as they brown until all take on that yellow, glossy look of candy.[61]

Tellingly, Mrs. Royster ends her recipe by saying, "This is the way they cook them in the South, and they use a heavy iron frying pan to cook them in." In addition, there are two pertinent recipes in *To Work and Serve the Home* (1928), the New Jersey State Federation of Colored Women's Clubs cookbook. Mary Goodwin gives a recipe for "Candied Sweets" that calls for boiling them "slowly uncovered until a syrup is formed and potatoes are soft and clear." Ida E. Brown's "Braised Sweet Potatoes" recipe places all of the ingredients "into a frying pan." These candied sweet potato recipes show how African American cooks transitioned from open-fire cooking with a Dutch oven to cooking in a contained, indoor space using a stove and a frying pan. The transition that has yet to be explained is how African Americans came to prefer yams over other sweet potato varieties. Unfortunately, there's no clear answer as to how this happened, but we have clues as to when it happened.

Many African Americans in the North and the South, particularly women, worked as domestic servants in wealthy and middle-class white households. A yam preference may have developed in these kitchens. Harriet Ross Colquitt wrote in *The Savannah Cookbook* (1929), "In the North 'sweet potato' is apt to be a more inclusive term, than as it is used by Southern cooks who make a distinction between yams and sweet potatoes. Charleston housewives specify the yam whenever they can get it — a luscious, orange-colored tuber, much more exotic looking than the light, yellow sweet potato, with its mealy texture. All recipes are applicable to either type of potato, but more liquid is usually required in cooking the dry, mealy kind."[62] It's unclear here if Colquitt is contrasting the orange yam with the yellow yam previously discussed or to what I've earlier described as the sweet potatoes preferred in the North.

The end result is that discriminating southern cooks wanted orange yams as early as the 1920s. Now the race was on to get these yams to the consumer. Scientists had been conscientiously trying to improve sweet potatoes, and their experiments created tubers that ranged from yellow to "salmon-colored." Though more and more people like Harriet Colquitt wanted the orange yams, no one had developed one that could be successfully farmed on a large scale. That changed in the early 1930s when Dr. Julian Miller at Louisiana State University developed a variety (the Unit 1 Puerto Rico yam) that increased yields, resisted disease, and had double the vitamin A content.[63] Georgia, a longtime producer of yellow yams—and the world's largest—soon lost its sweet potato supremacy as other states ramped up their efforts to grow the now more familiar orange yams. In short order, yellow yams went from being a cultural icon to only having a following—albeit cultlike—in certain pockets of the South, such as northern Mississippi, where it is still appreciated by old-timers. If you're curious, try to track down the Nancy Hall sweet potato variety. Some heirloom crop farmers are trying to bring this sweet potato variety back, and it will get you closest to the yellow yam of yesterday.

During the Down Home Cooking era, black cooks used yellow-fleshed and orange-fleshed yams interchangeably until orange became the de rigueur color for yams. In a parallel to the yellow yam craze of World War I, World War II helped catapult the orange yam to prominence. Clementine Paddleford explained the circumstances in her nationally syndicated newspaper food column in 1946: "That red yam of the moist sweet flesh grown in the deep South goes traveling this autumn into major markets of the nation. It's the only 'sweet' potato to date to achieve national distribution. Several years before the war, Louisiana growers got together on a statewide program to push yam production and to improve the potato's size and shape." The Louisiana sweet potato growers' association marketed the red-skinned, orange-fleshed sweet potatoes as yams and sent them around the country. "Then came the war, bringing nutritional glory to the red potato. So mighty in vitamins—the yam was chosen by the Army for dehydration when it set out to find the six most desirable foods to nourish our fighting men."[64] When Paddleford calls the potato "red," she refers to the yam's skin, not its flesh, which was orange.

The marketing effort to popularize the red-skinned, orange-fleshed yams worked, at least with black consumers. In *A Date with a Dish* (1948), DeKnight shares how her great-grandmother explained the difference between a yam and a sweet potato to her: "The original yam, she told me, was brought over from Africa. As for the sweet 'taters, well, they're sort of 'country cousins' to the yam. 'T'aint nowhere as sweet and juicy,' she said." DeKnight then emphasizes that "the color of the potato makes a difference." Referring to the skin color, Sharon Hunt writes in her *Bread from Heaven* (1992) cookbook, "A pumpkin-colored potato that has a higher sugar content is most often preferred. However, a red-colored sweet potato is used."[65] The red-skinned sweet potatoes have gained a stronger reputation for being sweeter; thus, they are the definitive yam for soul food cooking. The Beauregard, Garnet, and Jewel varieties are the yams you'll most likely see in the produce section.

Sweet potato production dropped dramatically after World War II, but now production levels are rising again. Sweet potatoes started making a comeback in the mid-1990s when mainstream restaurants began presenting sweet potatoes as a new comfort food. Sweet potatoes began showing up in baked goods, hashes, and soups.[66] Today, sweet potatoes are increasingly showing up as fries or tater tots on restaurant menus. Sometime in the 2000s, sweet potatoes became a health food, according to Charles Walker of the U.S. Sweet Potato Council. He was in true advocate form when he sent me an email declaring, "SWEET POTATO NUTRITION is the big, big story, and that seems to be part of why there has been a large increase in interest, in production and in consumption of sweet potatoes over the past 6 to 8 years."[67] Centuries after black and white southerners figured it out, the broader American public is now catching on to the fact that the sweet potato is a "superfood."

Candied Yams

Here's an unusual way to make candied yams that will still leave you satisfied. Instead of putting spices in the sweet sauce, you put them in the boiling liquid. This recipe calls for peeling the sweet potatoes first, but many
prefer to boil the sweet potatoes in their jackets and then peel them when
they are cool enough to handle. I recommend the Beauregard, Garnet, and
Jewel "yam" varieties for this dish.

Makes 4 to 6 servings

1½ to 2 pounds small sweet potatoes
¼ teaspoon ground cinnamon
¼ teaspoon ground nutmeg
½ cup (1 stick) butter
½ cup firmly packed dark brown sugar

1 Peel the sweet potatoes and cut them into large wedges. Place the
   potatoes, cinnamon, and nutmeg in a large saucepan and cover with
   water. Bring to a boil, reduce the heat, and simmer until the potatoes are tender when pierced with the tip of a knife, 20 to 30 minutes.
   Drain them well.
2 In the same saucepan, melt the butter and brown sugar over medium-
   low heat, stirring until smooth. Add the sweet potatoes and stir to
   coat. Cook over medium heat until the potatoes are warm and the
   sauce bubbles, about 3 minutes. Serve warm.

Momma Cherri's Candied Carrots

I first heard of Charita "Momma Cherri" Jones while watching an episode of Gordon Ramsay's *Kitchen Nightmares* that aired in June 2005. Jones grew up in a Philadelphia suburb and moved to England when she married a Brit. In 2001, she opened up Momma Cherri's Soul Food Shack—the only soul food restaurant in the United Kingdom. In her cookbook, Jones introduces this recipe by writing that soul food "tends to be a combination of sweet and savoury. It's not unusual to find a vegetable smothered in a candied sauce."

Makes 6 to 8 servings

> 2 pounds carrots
> ½ cup (1 stick) butter or margarine
> ½ cup firmly packed brown sugar
> ¼ teaspoon salt
> 1 teaspoon ground cinnamon
> 1 teaspoon pure vanilla extract
> Finely grated zest and juice of 1 orange

1 Preheat the oven to 350°F.
2 Peel the carrots and cut them into ½-inch-thick rounds. Place them in a small saucepan and cover with water. Bring to a boil, reduce the heat, and simmer until crisp-tender, about 2 minutes. Drain and then spread them into a shallow baking dish.
3 Melt the butter and brown sugar in the same saucepan over medium-high heat, stirring until smooth. Stir in the salt, cinnamon, vanilla, orange zest, and orange juice. Cook, stirring, until the sauce begins to thicken and bubble, 5 minutes. Pour the sauce over the carrots and stir gently to coat.
4 Bake until the carrots are tender, stirring occasionally, about 30 minutes. Let sit for 5 minutes before serving warm.

11

Cornbread

DROP IT LIKE IT'S HOT BREAD!

The North thinks it knows how to make corn bread, but this is gross superstition.
Perhaps no bread in the world is quite as good as Southern corn bread, and perhaps
no bread in the world is quite so bad as the Northern imitation of it. —Mark Twain

★ ★ ★ ★ ★

Cornbread can be one of the more hotly contested topics within southern food. Perhaps not as intense as barbecue, but it's up there. Like barbecue, cornbread has geographic fault lines that are summed up in an article from *Cook's Illustrated*: "Typical Southern cornbread contains more cornmeal than flour and no sweetener at all, and it is baked in a skillet to make sure the exterior is well browned and crisp. The texture is crumbly, making a thin cornbread the ideal partner to saucy dishes. By contrast, a typical Northern cornbread is made with more flour than cornmeal and a fair amount of sweetener. Because it is cooked in a baking pan, the exterior is very pale. The texture is cakey, making this thick cornbread ideal for breakfast or a snack."[1]

Elite white southerners have done much to stoke the fires about cornbread, dabbing their cornbread with as many rules as they would butter. To many southerners of all stripes, these rules seem ridiculous because making cornbread was purely local—whatever kind and color of corn grew nearby, that's what you used. True cornbread, the southern purists say, is made with white cornmeal and savory (no sugar at all) and is served hot. They also insist that "cornbread" is spelled as one word. In these pages, I follow their directive. As much as these rules drew a bright line between southern and northern cornbreads, soul food cooks straddle the line. Soul food cornbread can be yellow, white, hot, lukewarm, or cold. But it's always sweet. The puzzle is how could African Americans, recognized by legions of white southerners as the standard-bearers of cornbread cookery, so brazenly flout the rules? Black cooks fluidly define corn-bread because their racial caste position has demanded it. Blacks have often lacked regular access to ingredients and cooking equipment that enable the luxury of making cornbread one preferred way, all of the time.

Native Americans developed the first rules for using and growing corn, since it's an indigenous crop in the Americas. Maize was growing in Mexico at least 5,000 years ago, and the crop spread throughout the hemisphere, including the Caribbean, where Europeans first encountered the plant. The Aztecs who first cultivated the crop called it tlaolli, but it got other names as it spread through the Americas. When Columbus encountered the indigenous people of present-day Dominican Republic, they called the crop mahis plant, which eventually became maiz in Spanish and "maize" in English.[2] In the United States, we call maize "corn" because that was a ge-neric term the English settlers had for any grain. Bran, maize, oats, rice, rye, and wheat could all be called corn. At first, the settlers called maize "Indian corn" to distinguish it from the other grains, but eventually "corn" became the name for maize.[3]

Though there has been some debate about this, scholars generally agree the Portuguese introduced corn into West Africa during the sixteenth cen-tury. West African cooks readily embraced the imported crop. Recounting how thoroughly corn has entrenched itself in the region's contemporary diet, Raymond Sokolov wrote in 1991, "Corn has also become a staple in West Africa. Before Columbus, the staple African grain was millet and the other main starch source was the true yam, served most often as a porridge or mush. Today cassava and maize round out the West African starch diet, and they are most often boiled to resemble millet or yam mush. The Afri-canization is so complete that one even finds a fermented corn flour por-ridge completely analogous to a fermented millet porridge."[4] West Afri-can farmers and cooks experimented with the new crop for several years before they integrated it into their cuisine. By the twentieth century, sev-eral varieties of corn were grown in West Africa, and the locals held some cornmeal varieties in high esteem.[5] Today, in Ghana and Nigeria, white cornmeal is the key ingredient of kenkey, a sour dumpling that is a popular accompaniment for fried fish.[6]

Europeans had different feelings about corn. Rather than embracing corn's bread-making potential, Europeans living in West Africa forced slaves to grow wheat and cooks to make wheat breads. This isn't sur-prising, since Europeans had long favored white wheat breads over their darker-colored traditional breads made from barley, oats, and rye. The wheat experiment quickly proved impractical in a tropical climate, so they resorted to making European-style breads with West African grains and corn as wheat substitutes.[7] Europeans used these hybrid breads, especially cornbread, to provision slave ships heading to the Americas. Daniel Usner, a historian of slavery in the Lower Mississippi Valley writes, "People in the Upper Guinea region of West Africa, where a vast majority of Louisiana's African slaves originated in the 18th century, were generally more familiar with maize than were their European contemporaries." Usner continues, "This previous knowledge of cultivating and cooking maize helped slaves adapt to American Indian horticulture and provides a reason for the persistence of distinct features from the Indian diet in southern foodways."[8] What Usner says of Louisiana's slave population applied equally to other enslaved groups in the South.

The earliest European accounts of corn agriculture in the South show that the indigenous American tribes grew several types of corn, sometimes intending a specific culinary use, such as for hominy or bread.[9] Observing Native Americans in eighteenth-century Virginia, Robert Beverly described four types of cultivated corn—two ripening early and two ripening late in the year. The late-ripening type, Beverly wrote, "has a larger Grain, as if it had never come to Perfection; and this they call She-Corn. This is esteem'd by the Planters, as the best for Increase, and is universally chosen by them for planting." The She-Corn was "what the Indians call flour corn."[10] Elsewhere in the Mississippi Delta region, the Choctaw were growing "three principal varieties of corn: the little corn of the nature of popcorn, which was first to mature; the flint or hominy corn, the kernels of which were hard and smooth and were of various colors—white, yellow, red, and blue; and the flour or dent corn with corrugated kernels. Bread was made oftenest of the flour corn; it was the most valued and it seems to have been the time of its maturity which determined the occurrence of the green corn dance."[11] Thus, the Choctaw of the Mississippi Valley in addition to the Virginia tribes were also exacting about which corn should be used for bread.

Native Americans taught the Europeans and the enslaved Africans how to make bread using corn. Lucien Carr, a Native American foodways expert, summarized their bread-making as follows:

> The Indians made several kinds of bread of their corn, or failing this, of chestnuts, beans, acorns, sweet potatoes or any other suitable ma-

terial that they could get. This involved an entirely different process of cooking, and the fact that some of this bread, as for instance, the ash-cake, johnny-cake and the pone, still finds favor with us, is proof of the success that attended their efforts. In preparing these dishes, the ripe corn was pounded to a fine meal, which was duly sifted, and having been made into a rough dough with water or, as [James] Adair suggests, with bear oil, it was covered with leaves and baked in the ashes, or on broad stones or "broad earthen bottoms" placed over a fire. In baking loaves, and the same account will apply to pones, they make a strong fire and when it is burned down to coals, they carefully rake them off to each side, and sweep away the remaining ashes; then they put their well kneaded bread loaf, first steeped in hot water, over the hearth and an earthen basin above it, with the embers and coals atop. This method of baking is as clean and efficacious as if done in any oven, and the loaf cooked in this manner is said to be firm and very white.[12]

According to its originators, cornbread could be mixed with other savory ingredients, was to be eaten while hot, and had a white appearance. Southern rules about cornbread were clearly taken from the earliest days of contact between Native Americans and Europeans, and they were lessons that kept on giving during lean times. But when things got better, Europeans quickly put aside cornbread for the wheat breads they coveted more.

Europeans strove hard to establish wheat and make wheat breads once they settled in British North America. As food historian Karen Hess observed, "At the very beginning, maize was the chief crop, but as the country became more sedentary, wheat forged ahead. By 1796, La Rochefoucauld notes 'Wheat, as has already been observed, is the chief object of cultivation in this country.'"[13] Wheat (*Triticum aestivum*, syn. *T. vulgare*) was grown in the North and the South, but the enslaved had limited access to wheat, getting small portions on weekends and special occasions, if at all. Anna Miller drives this point home when she recalls of slavery in Texas, "White flour, we don' know what dat tastes like. Jus know what it looks like."[14] As one nineteenth-century southerner put it, "The favorite food of the cotton-field hand, the food he cannot live without, the strengthening bread made from corn meal, has its expressive name, 'John Constant.' Wheaten bread, a rare treat to the field hand, is 'Billy Seldom.'"[15] In the early Virginia and Maryland colonies, a planter observed, "[Indian corn] is the chiefest Diett they have in the cuntrey espeshally where there are great ffamilies of Negroos."[16] Though everyone on the plantation ate corn to some extent, being black meant being heavily dependent on corn over wheat, on cooking and eating certain types of cornmeal, and on making certain types of cornbread.

Being black also meant doing the lion's share of work on the large plantation to grow corn. Slaves planted and harvested the crops, and the biggest agricultural event next to the hog killing was the cornshucking. A successful cornshucking was critical to having enough grain supplies to last the entire year. As folklorist Roger Abrahams indicates in *Singing the Master*:

> In the early fall, the corn was cut on the stalk and gathered into shocks awaiting the end of the harvest. In the South, the corn would be brought in after the other crops were harvested, and a shucking would occur sometime between November and mid-December. . . . The event was commonly held at night, so pine knots were also gathered in abundance to light the occasion, and to provide warmth as well, should the night be chilly. . . . As the corn heap grew in the yard near the pens, anticipation grew that a shucking might be held soon. . . . Whoever initiated the idea, the master was responsible for sending out the "news" of the oncoming event in some form. . . . Before the arrival, the heap of corn was divided. Sometimes this was done simply by making two mounds, or dividing the one in half. . . . But more commonly the mass of ears was divided by a long fence rail or pole laid down the center. . . . After the division, two teams were chosen which would then contend for a prize.[17]

Cornshuckings happened in the North as well, and as Abrahams states, these events were still strongly identified with slaves.[18]

In an FWP interview, John Van Hook recalled how during slavery the cornshuckings thrived on rivalries lubricated with hard liquor:

> Oh—oo-h! Everybody had cornshuckings. The man designated to act as the general would stick a peacock tail feather in his hat and call all the men together to give his orders. He would stand in the center of the corn pile, start the singing, and keep lively things for them. Now and then he would pass around the jug. They sang a great deal during cornshuckings, but I have forgotten the words to those songs. Great

excitement was expressed whenever a man found a red ear of corn, for that counted for 20 points, a speckled ear was 10 points and a blue ear 5 points, toward a special extra big swig of liquor whenever a person had as many as 100 points.[19]

In a similar interview, Charley Hurt revealed what the red ear meant: "I can't 'member dem songs, 'cause I'm not much for singin'. One go like dis: 'Pull de husk, break de ear; Whoa, I's got de red ear here.' When you finds de ear, dat 'titles you to de prize, like kissin' de gal or de drink of brandy or somethin'. Dey not 'nough red ears to suit us."[20]

As the formerly enslaved Preston Klein of Alabama reported, these cornshuckings could be so successful that "sometimes dey was so much corn it would stay on de ground 'twell it rotted."[21] After the work was completed, an impromptu celebration would take place for the winning team, and that often included hoisting the master on their shoulders and carrying him back to the Big House. At that point, the real party was on. Van Hook reported that "after the work was finished they had a big feast spread on long tables in the yard, and dram flowed plentiful, then they played ball, tussled, ran races, and did anything they knew how to amuse themselves."[22] Willis Cofer of Athens, Georgia, adds, "It wouldn't be so long before all de wuk wuz done and dey would call us to supper. Dere wuz barbecue and chickens, jus' a plenty for all de Niggers, and corn bread made lak reg'lar light bread and sho' enough light bread too, and lots of 'tato pies and all sorts of good things."[23]

Cornshuckings remained an important part of rural black life well after slavery ended. Abrahams informs us that "David Barrow, reporting in the 1880s, indicated that in fact the slaves had valued the shuckings sufficiently that they maintained the tradition under the condition of freedom. He pointed out that they were still taking place among the black freemen farmers in his area of southwest Georgia. . . . The great number of small farmers who have sprung up in the South since the war necessitates mutual aid in larger undertakings."[24] In short, they had to give to get. The same was true throughout the Black Belt, for cornshuckings happened wherever corn was grown. Cornshuckings took on the same community feel as hog killings, because the tasks and subsequent celebration made people feel like real neighbors.

Once the cornshucking was over, the enslaved were doled out their corn rations steadily over the course of a year until the next cornshucking was needed. On the smaller plantations, corn was distributed for the slaves to grind themselves. One traveler commenting on Maryland plantations wrote,

> The servants and negroes after they have worn themselves down the whole day, and gone home to rest, have yet to grind and pound the grain, which is generally maize, for their masters and all their families as well as themselves, and all the negroes, to eat. . . . As to articles of food, the only bread they have is that made of Turkish wheat or maize, and that is miserable. . . . The corn, when it is to be used for men, has to be first soaked, before it is ground or pounded, because the grains being large and very hard, cannot be broken under the small stones of their light hand-mills; and then it is left so coarse that it must be sifted. They take the finest for bread, and the other for different kinds of groats, which when it is cooked, is called *sapaen* or *homma*.[25]

Homma meant "hominy," which was a soupy corn preparation similar to grits. Unlike planters, yeoman farmers didn't have enough slaves to do the massive amount of work required for corn grinding, so the yeoman farmer and his family often had to complete cornshucking and corn-grinding tasks themselves.[26]

On the large plantations, massive amounts of corn were sent to commercial millers to be converted into cornmeal that would be rationed out through the year. For cornbread epicures in the antebellum South, the type of milling process made a huge difference to the cornmeal's quality. As one planter in the late 1840s observed, "The most important differences in the bread are owing less to different modes of cooking, than to the grinding of the meal. Common water-mills, with large and slow running stones, furnish the best meal, which in common parlance is a 'round meal.'"[27] Water-milled cornmeal quickly earned a reputation for being essential to an excellent cornbread. During slavery, both the Big House and slave cabin cooks were supplied with water-ground cornmeal, but the cornmeal's color and quality could vary based on racial caste considerations. If there was an opportunity, the master rationed to his slaves what he believed to be of poorer quality.

The color of cornmeal rations for the enslaved made abolitionists see red. Abolitionists were constantly looking for any angle that would give them a solid argument against slavery. Slave rations were a focal point for abolitionists who argued that slaves were woefully malnourished. Planters countered that the slaves were well fed, especially when compared with laborers and the poor in other countries. Cornmeal eventually became a proxy for nutritional adequacy. Framing the issue in 1839, an abolitionist periodical stated, "The northern reader must bear in mind, that the corn furnished to the slaves at the south, is almost invariably the white gourd seed corn, and that a quart of this kind of corn weighs five or six ounces less than a quart of the 'flint corn,' the kind generally raised in the northern and eastern states; consequently a peck of the corn generally given to the slaves, would be only equivalent to a fraction more than 6 quarts and a pint of the corn commonly raised in the New England States, New York, [and] New Jersey."[28]

White northerners thought yellow cornmeal was superior for human food and that white cornmeal's best purpose was for animal feed. White southerners felt the opposite. These sentiments died hard, for as late as 1909, the bewildered editors of Georgia's *Macon Telegraph* felt the need to comment: "The preference of Northerners for yellow cornmeal and their contemptuous attitude toward superior white cornmeal as good only for chicken feed are as incomprehensible to the average southerner as the preference of the Esquimaux [Eskimo] for rancid meat."[29] It's difficult to say whether the preference for yellow corn in the North is a result of slavery politics or is simply a matter of taste. Whatever the reason, the respective color prejudices still linger.

Well into the twentieth century, how one procured one's cornmeal reflected one's status. Blacks in the rural South carried their corn to a nearby mill for grinding. Sharecropper Sara Brooks describes her experience in rural Alabama: "You shells the corn until you get a bag of corn big as you want to take to the mill, and when you take it to the mill you can tell the man, 'I want cornmeal and I want grits.' Then you get a bag of grits and a bag of cornmeal. They put the grits inside of the cornmeal in a smaller sack."[30] For some, going to the rural mill brought some shame because it meant one was too poor to purchase cornmeal at a store. Izola White, who operated Izola's Family Dining for fifty years in Chicago's South Side, was interviewed as part of a 2008 oral history project: "Well, when you're in the South and you don't have no money, you get the corn and you take it to the gin, and they ground it up and make it into yellow cornmeal. That's what we had. I never liked it from that day on."[31] Those bad memories stuck with White so much that she only used white cornmeal in her restaurant for fifty years until it closed in 2011.

Whatever color it was, cornmeal was the primary ingredient of the primary bread that nourished millions of black people in the plantation South. What follows is an overview of the various cornbreads developed in the antebellum period. Separately, each cornbread's ingredients and method of preparation implicate how racial caste considerations affected daily cooking and feasting.

In the antebellum South, cornbread was not a static concept. As the Soul Food Cornbread Family Stalk illustrates, a wide variety of cornbreads were made with varying degrees of sophistication. Cornbread was ideal sustenance for the slave regime because corn was easy to grow and easy to cook, and whites often used that to reinforce the racist attitude that black slaves had limited intelligence:

> The only difficulty in making bread of Indian Corn, is in the simplicity and ease of the process; which indeed is so simple as to be successfully practiced by every ignorant negro woman in Virginia, and, indeed, by almost every child, and by every male laborer, when at work away from home. So easy is the task, and so slight the danger of failure, that few mistresses of families have found it necessary, for the purpose of instructing their servants, to learn and practice themselves, or to watch the ordinary process of bread making. So palatable is this food, and so universal the preference for it, that every laborer would choose to prepare and bake his own corn bread, and eat it fresh and warm, rather than to use cold and older bread.[32]

Many slaves did not always get to "choose" to have warm cornbread. Slave testimony shows that their typical evening meal (also called "supper") included a cold piece of leftover cornbread from the midday meal. At the end of a long day, many slaves opted to forgo building a fire to reheat food, so they could eat and get on with doing chores, gardening, and other tasks before going to sleep.

When the enslaved made their own cornbreads, the popular choice was ash cake, also known as ash pone, the basic bread of the Native Americans in the South. We have already described the process to make ash cake, but in a 1846 New York Express article, an anonymous southerner explicitly linked ash cakes with blackness: "'Ash pone,' is the usual mode in which our negroes prepare bread in the fire places of their own houses; and by laborers when cooking in the field, or hunters when lodging in the forest. . . . The 'ash pone' that is the most palatable of all plain is corn bread.

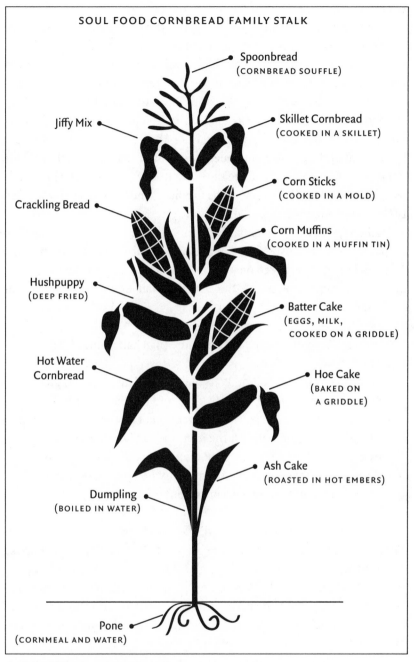

SOUL FOOD CORNBREAD FAMILY STALK

Spoonbread
(CORNBREAD SOUFFLE)

Jiffy Mix

Skillet Cornbread
(COOKED IN A SKILLET)

Corn Sticks
(COOKED IN A MOLD)

Crackling Bread

Corn Muffins
(COOKED IN A MUFFIN TIN)

Hushpuppy
(DEEP FRIED)

Batter Cake
(EGGS, MILK,
COOKED ON A GRIDDLE)

Hot Water
Cornbread

Hoe Cake
(BAKED ON
A GRIDDLE)

Ash Cake
(ROASTED IN HOT EMBERS)

Dumpling
(BOILED IN WATER)

Pone
(CORNMEAL AND WATER)

Soul Food Cornbread Family Stalk

But it requires more time and trouble; and for this reason, as well as for the rude preparation, it is rarely used except by those who enjoy but few conveniences for cooking; other than a large fire and plenty of fuel."[33] Clearly, the sentiment was that making ash cake was beneath most whites, but it was a suitable way for blacks to make cornbread. Former slave John Van Hook of Georgia nostalgically described how ash cakes were made during slavery: "Cornbread dough was made into little pones and placed on the hot rocks close to the fire to dry out a little, then hot ashes were raked out to the front of the fireplace and piled over the ash cakes. When thoroughly done they were taken out and the ashes washed off; they were just like cake to us children then."[34] Take away the fireplace, and the process is identical to the Native American method.

In the Big House, a much larger, well-equipped fireplace was used to prepare cornbread. Instead of being placed in the ashes of a live fire, the cornmeal dough was baked on a flat metal surface called a "hoe," thus acquiring the name "hoe cake." The same *New York Express* writer described hoe cakes:

> The dough is shaped into cakes not more than half an inch thick, and laid upon a fit iron plate, (usually an old weeding hoe,) previously well heated, but not so hot as to burn or "blister" the dough. The cakes remain uncovered while baking, and of course the fire is applied only below the "hoe." When a very thin crust has been formed on the dough in contact with the iron, the cake is separated from it by a knife, and turned. — Ten minutes will usually be enough for the baking. These cakes, especially, are best when just baked, and hot, and lose much of their fine flavor [when] cold and stale.

The writer then described cornbread's "everywhere" status in the South. "The principal, if not the only dinner bread, at almost every country house in Virginia, is in one or both of the above forms. It is thus used in preference to wheaten bread, for economy. And this preference, from taste, is general among the rich and luxurious, as well as with those to whom greater cheapness would be sufficient ground for choosing. It is in our towns only, or by persons bred in towns, that wheaten bread is used, or is preferred for dinner."[35] Socially speaking, cornbread was raised from the ashes, and the hoe cake became an acceptable alternative to wheat bread.

There is some disagreement over how the hoe cake got its name. As we

Hot water cornbread, Sands Soul Diner, Nashville

now know, a hoe was a metal cooking surface used in Big House kitchens. We also know that we call a particular gardening tool a hoe. This shared name caused many to believe that slaves cooked the bread on their hoes while taking a break from field work. That theory made perfect sense to me until I came across Rod Cofield's essay on hoe cakes in *Food History News*. Cofield clarifies that "some food historians use ex-slave narratives as proof that hoe cakes were cooked on a hoe. . . . Though these narratives say how the hoe [cake] got its name, the narrators do not give any examples of the cakes actually being cooked on a hoe; they are always cooked in a skillet, on a brick or rock, or in/on another cooking implement."[36] We don't know who started the "field slave cooks hoe cake on hoe" story, but it seems to be a nineteenth-century equivalent of the "Al Gore said he invented the Internet" myth that persists today. Despite any facts to the contrary, once the initial erroneous story started circulating in public, it became accepted fact.

The enslaved also prepared steamed and boiled cornbreads. Charlie Richardson of Warrensburg, Missouri, recalled, "This here hoe cake was plain old white corn meal battered with salt and water. No grease. Not much grease, jest 'nough to keep it from stickin'. This here hoe cake was fried, jest like flap-jacks, only it were not. Not flap-jacks I mean. When we didn't have hoe cake we had ask cake. Same as hoe cake only it was biled. Made of corn meal, salt and water and a whole shuck, with the end tied with a string."[37] Richardson's account is significant in two ways. First, he gives the only explicit mention in the FWP interviews of a black cook using white cornmeal. Second, though he calls it "ask cake," probably meaning ash cake, the wrapping and tying with a string shows that he's describing a tamale. The Mississippi Delta has a strong tamale tradition, and its tamale is made with cornmeal coarser than what you would find in a traditional Mexican tamale.

Before I read Richardson's interview, I thought it likely that Mexican agricultural workers brought tamales with them while doing seasonal agricultural work in the American South during the latter half of the nineteenth and early part of the twentieth centuries. Richardson's memory, if accurate, means the tamale entered the African American foodways not only outside the Mississippi Delta, but also at a time before significant Mexican immigration to that area. The enslaved most likely borrowed tamales from local Native Americans who were making something similar, and they eventually wound up in the Delta. By the 1920s, black street vendors were hawking tamales in Chicago, Los Angeles, New York City, and San Francisco, and tamale references surfaced in black popular culture. Most famously, bluesman Robert Johnson sang about tamale vendors (and women) in his 1936 song, "They're Red Hot."

Take that same tamale, remove the protective wrapping, add some folklore, drop it in boiling fat instead of boiling water, and you've got a hushpuppy. Its fanciful name comes from this story: "Years ago, it's said, the Negroes in Tallahassee used to gather on warm fall evenings for sugar cane grinding. After their work of grinding cane and boiling down to use was completed, they would cook themselves a savory snack over the big outdoor fire. Around the edge of the circle, their hounds would gather with much sniffing of the air and many whines of hunger. To quiet them, the Negroes would stop eating fried fish and corn pones for a minute, tear off a piece of the bread, and toss it to the dogs with the admonition 'Hush, puppy!'"[38] As hushpuppies (also spelled "hush puppies") became more popular with whites, the legend about their name grew popular as well— so much so that whites whitewashed the story by removing blacks and retelling it in any number of contexts, but it usually has a food created accidentally while camping out in the woods. Though antebellum recipes for hushpuppies are extremely rare, cooks have developed a subset of rules for this fried cornbread. Hushpuppies today must have some chopped onion and parsley, and if one wants to live on the edge of popular opinion, perhaps some corn kernels. Hushpuppies were also known in other parts of the South by different names, such as "Three Finger Bread" (a description of the finger imprint left by the cook shaping the raw dough), "wampus" in Florida, "red devils" in Georgia, and "red horse bread" (named after the Red Horse fish [*Moxostoma carinatum*] with which it was often paired) in South Carolina.[39] Hushpuppies could also be made with yellow or white cornmeal. In the South, hushpuppies are sometimes a special occasion dish in the sense that they are most associated with barbecues and fish fries.

Now we enter the class of cornbreads made for festive occasions, when the enslaved had access to more luxurious ingredients and a self-contained oven or large fireplace. That is, these cornbreads were uncommon for the field slaves. They often got their names based on the principal ingredients used. For instance, Mrs. Malinda Russell's 1866 cookbook has one cornbread recipe and it's a "green" cornbread. The entire recipe is "Three dozen ears of corn, grated, one egg, milk, a little salt."[40] That's all of the instruction the cook gets. The author expects her readers to be familiar with how to make this particular cornbread. "Green corn," the name given to corn harvested while it's still milky, is a sharp contrast to dried cornmeal. Thus Russell's recipe was probably very custardlike. When eggs and milk were added, cornbread was usually called "batter bread" or "egg bread." Other times, a cornbread could be named after the cooking equipment used. Thus one finds references to "spider cornbread" when a batter bread is cooked in a spider, a cast-iron skillet with three raised legs for placing in a hearth. If the cook used its legless relative, the batter bread was called "skillet cornbread."

Crackling bread was a purely seasonal and prized cornbread for the enslaved. In 1888, the *Augusta Chronicle* described it as a kind of cornbread "much liked by the negroes . . . [and] made by mixing fragments of pork cracklings."[41] Cracklings are tiny, crisp bits of rendered lard that were made at hog killings when lard was a plentiful by-product of the work. The highest form of cornbread artistry was spoonbread, which the late chef Bill Neal described in his *Southern Cooking* as "an elegant soufflé."[42]

Cornbread soufflé involves such an intricate process (e.g., separating eggs and beating the egg whites) that spoonbread was certainly made in Big House kitchens and not in the slave cabins. After Emancipation, more black cooks became skilled at making spoonbread, and it became more commonplace in African American cookbooks.

Besides corn, the one thing that binds all soul food cornbreads together is sugar. That's where authenticity crumbles for southern cornbread purists. As one southern commentator boldly declared in the *Saturday Evening Post* during the 1930s, "The introduction of sugar into it was a rank form of barbarism, the kind that makes a man of the old corn bread school tremble with rage, and yet sugared corn bread is served in nearly every restaurant in the country."[43] Slaves welcomed sweetness with their cornbread. Unlike their masters, slaves did not eat composed desserts at the end of their meals. Someone came up with the idea of combining elements of the slave rations, putting some molasses (slaves nicknamed molasses "long sweetin") on their cornbread, and this became a regular dessert. In a letter to the *New-York Tribune* in 1861, a Weldon, North Carolina, resident described this phenomenon: "A stiff bread, compounded of white corn-meal and water, and taken hot from the ashes is eaten with complete contentment, and with no complaint at the absence of butter. The negro munches his with molasses, his peculiar and undisputed luxury, of which he is usually allowed a quart per week."[44]

After Emancipation, black cooks transitioned from using sweeteners as a condiment and began incorporating them directly into the cornbread as an ingredient. A *Good Housekeeping* magazine article in the 1890s described an African American cook named "Aunt Chloe" who moistened her cornbread with a "half cupful of molasses."[45] In contrast, none of Abby Fisher's cornbread recipes calls for sugar, though one recipe calls for "sweet milk," an old name for whole milk.[46] By 1912, Mrs. Hayes's cornbread recipe called for a tablespoon of sugar, and the "Indian meal bread" recipe required half a cup of molasses.[47] Black cooks exhibited flexibility by making sweetened bread when cooking for other blacks and then pivoting to make unsweetened cornbread for whites.

Why did black cooks also feel the need to doctor up their cornbread with sugar? The answer brings us back to the cornmeal's color. Wealthy white southerners consistently held white cornmeal in high esteem, not only because of the archetypal white color, but mainly because they believed it tasted better than yellow cornmeal. In 1892, one southerner rhapsodized in a newspaper article, "The Western or Northern corn—white or yellow— will not make the smooth, sweet meal of the Southern white corn. . . . I can tell you what it was like: it was very white between the crusts, very moist, very light, with the peculiar sweetness of sweet green corn, and really more like sweet green-corn cake—where the corn is grated from the cob before it is boiled—than anything else I have ever tasted."[48] White corn tasted better because of its natural sweetness. If one was making bread with high-quality, white cornmeal, adding sugar was redundant.

Yellow cornmeal use meant low status, which meant blacks and poor whites. African Americans internalized the inferiority of yellow cornmeal as well. "In the south, the region of the best corn meal dishes in the world, the colored cook holds yellow meal in utter contempt, fit only for 'chicken feed,' always replying when asked about it, 'I makes my co'n braid yellow with aigs,'" reported one newspaper in 1901.[49] Even when they were within the same economic class as whites, blacks showed a stronger preference for white cornmeal. In her study of rural Mississippi eating habits, Dorothy Dickins found that during a white cornmeal shortage in the early 1940s, black families, unlike white families, made less cornbread when only yellow cornmeal was available.[50] A researcher in the 1980s found that Louisiana blacks retained a strong consumer preference for white cornmeal.[51]

Blacks may have preferred white cornmeal because it tasted better and had higher prestige, but in many instances they simply couldn't grow it, couldn't afford to buy it, or lived in a place where it wasn't available. By the late 1800s, industrial millers favored yellow corn, and in short order, yellow cornmeal increasingly crowded white cornmeal out of the consumer market. In 1913, the *Salt Lake City Telegram* assessed the situation:

Corn breads of various kinds are known [in] all parts of this country, but it is the flaky, white cornmeal, ground in the old fashioned water power mill which is the basis of the corn breads so long the delight of epicureans in the south. It is being replaced in the cities by other breads, not so much because it is no longer recognized as an excellent food, but because modern conditions are such that good cornmeal is not so easy to obtain. The speed at which the modern roller process mills are operated produce more heat and therefore extract more oil from the meal than did the water wheel process. The water ground cornmeal is, therefore, different in its chemical composition and distinctly different in taste. It is also more perishable, as the oil becomes more rancid and in a few weeks causes the meal to lose flavor. Good meal must be freshly ground.[52]

With the profound industrial changes, yellow cornmeal, perceived by some as of poorer quality, was far more available. In 1921, the *Columbus Ledger* informed its readers that the industrially milled cornmeal was "convenient for use, for it keeps well and is suitable for making corn breads which contain baking powder or eggs, or in which the corn meal is combined with wheat. For some sorts of cooking it requires softening by scalding."[53] The rise of industrial milling coincided with the migrations that typified the Down Home Cooking era. As migrants settled in places outside the South, the poorer yellow cornmeal was the only cornmeal that they could get. Ingenious black cooks had to doctor up the yellow cornmeal, and adding sugar was an obvious and practical way to recapture the taste of home evoked by memories of white cornmeal's natural sweetness. Unlike their counterparts in rural Mississippi, urban cooks decided that sweetened yellow cornbread was better than no cornbread at all.

White cornmeal's waning influence and availability sparked a wave of nostalgia. Southern whites who actively participated in this nostalgia tended to link blacks to yellow cornmeal and cornbread and also blamed blacks and Yankees for the spread of yellow cornbreads. On the relatively late date of 1948, one wistful southerner wrote, "Northerners, however, prefer the yellow meal. These preferences have their roots in the civil war. Northern soldiers on the drives into the South learn to make cornbread from the field Negroes, who often were cooks for the Union forces. They use the yellow meal and when the boys in blue went back home they showed their women folks how to do it."[54]

Southern whites also deplored when blacks bucked established norms and ate wheat bread. In an 1898 excerpt from the *Richmond Dispatch*, one writer spewed, "Now the darkies eschew [cornbread] where wheat bread is to be obtained, and upon the tables of thousands of southern and western whites it never appears at all, while others continue to use it only for dinner. . . . The high-toned colored damsels who are turned out by our public schools are not the adepts that our old Aunt Dinahs and Aunt Peggys were."[55] Nearly two decades later, another white southerner wrote in 1915, "In the south there is a tradition that the negroes began to lose their strength and ambition for work when they began to eat 'wheat flour bread' instead of that made from cornmeal."[56] Wheat bread had become a metaphor for unwanted black progress. Robert Dirks's dietary studies of blacks at the turn of the twentieth century show that they did eat more wheat bread than before because it was now cheaper to purchase wheat flour and premade bread.[57] Even with the increase in wheat bread consumption, cornbread remained "the staff of black life" well into in the Soul Food era.

By the 1940s, black families were eating cornbread and wheat bread, but bread-making in general was often constrained by the equipment available. Joffe points out, "Corn bread and biscuits are . . . direct descendent[s] of the old 'hoe cake,' which was baked in the fireplace. Since many of the older houses in the rural South lack proper stoves, these pan-baked breads are most important. Where there is no stove, hoe cakes or breads put into covered iron pots can be baked in the embers, and where there is no oven they may be baked on top of the stove."[58] This study overlooks "hot water cornbread," essentially a hoe cake made with yellow cornmeal that was scalded with hot water to bind it and then fried in a skillet in shallow oil.

It's tempting to think of cornbread as a complete sideshow to a meal, but rural black cooks made cornbread a central part of meal planning. In 1940s rural Mississippi, black cooks determined first if they could make cornbread. If "yes," then they added boiled vegetables like greens, lima beans, cowpeas, and string beans.[59] If "no," they skipped serving those particular vegetables. I was puzzled by this strong preference, but it got me to thinking about pot likker. All of the vegetables above made a good broth or pot likker. For at least a century, southerners of all backgrounds liked to mix their cornbread with these wet foods. One reason this was popular was that it made certain foods easier to eat with one's fingers. I've been told that both black and white elderly southerners still practice this utensil-free way of eating. Mixing cornbread with food wasn't limited to eating. Lots of black and white southerners like to pour a glass of cold buttermilk, crumble in some cornbread, and then drink the mixture with great satisfaction.

This topic actually came up during a southern food talk that I gave in Chattanooga, Tennessee. During the question-and-answer time, a white guy in his fifties or sixties asked me why I didn't mention cornbread in buttermilk. I explained that the drink was certainly outside of my own experience, and I never saw it listed on a restaurant menu. I further speculated that it was something people only did in their homes and was a fading practice. After double-checking that he imbibed this drink himself, I added with some trepidation, "Sir, I don't know you, but you're definitely country!" Much to my relief, the audience erupted with laughter, and so did he.

When the enslaved got bread, it was overwhelmingly made with cornmeal. Wheat bread carried too much prestige to be regularly rationed to them, so they got it on special occasions. That's why the enslaved nicknamed cornmeal "Johnny Constant" and wheat "Billy Seldom." Creating a cornmeal vs. wheat divide wasn't enough. Elites claimed white cornmeal for themselves, and yellow cornmeal was appropriate for everyone else. As hard as wealthy whites tried to maintain these culinary barriers, African Americans and poor whites routinely crossed them. They ate whatever corn grew locally, and that often included white corn. That changed when industrial practices made yellow cornmeal more plentiful.

Rather than holding on to one definition of how cornbread should be made, black cooks adapted how they made cornbread based on changing (and improving) economic circumstances, the available ingredients, and the cooking equipment used. The ash cake baptized in fire begat the hoe cake sizzling on a griddle, which begat hot-water cornbread fried in a skillet, which begat egg-and-milk-enhanced cornbread or one made from a commercially prepared mix and baked on a stovetop or in the oven. All the while, black cooks varied the type of cornmeal used. In Freda DeKnight's *Date with a Dish*, cooks had a complete mishmash of thirteen cornbread recipes at their disposal, some calling for white cornmeal, others for yellow cornmeal, and one for both! Except for one very lonely recipe for corn sticks, all of the recipes have some amount of sugar.[60] Other African American cookbooks showed the same tendency until the past couple of decades, and now yellow cornmeal recipes predominate. One thing that rarely varied, showing soul food's only rule, is that all of these cornbreads had some sugar. Yes, these cornbreads were sweet, but they would never be mistaken for cake.

Cornbread and Pot Likker as National Discourse

Southern whites were also enthusiastic about combining cornbread with pot likker, but there was some difference of opinion as to whether or not one should dunk cornbread in pot likker and then eat it, or if the cornbread should be crumbled up in the pot likker and the mixture consumed like a drink. This eternal (and internal) debate within the South got national attention in the early 1930s when U.S. Senator Huey Long of Louisiana fiercely advocated for dunking cornbread in pot likker. Lots of politicians from around the country weighed in, including then–New York governor Franklin Delano Roosevelt. Roosevelt spent many vacations in Warm Springs, Georgia, to get treatment for his polio, and this, he believed, gave him some credibility on the subject. Roosevelt quipped, "Because I am at least an adopted Georgian I am deeply stirred by the great controversy. . . . In order to avoid serious differences, I suggest referring the whole subject to the platform committee of the next Democratic National Convention. I doubt the wisdom of seeking to have the national committee pass on this great question when they meet shortly in Washington. In the meantime, I am hoping the New York State Legislature will soon adjourn in order that I may return to Georgia for my own pot likker and cornpone. I must admit I crumble mine."[1] From what I can tell, Roosevelt was in good company with many African Americans who did the same.

---

1 "Cornpone Factions."

Hot Water Cornbread

This is the contemporary version of the hoecake. My mother would make hot water cornbread upon occasion. She acknowledges that others don't add sugar and egg, but "that's how I make it." Really, that's all that I need to hear. I'm not going to argue with my mother.

Makes two dozen 3-inch cakes

1 cup cornmeal
1 cup all-purpose flour
1 tablespoon baking powder
½ teaspoon sugar
1½ teaspoons salt

1 large egg
1½ to 2 cups boiling water
1 tablespoon oil,
    plus more as needed

1. Whisk together the cornmeal, flour, baking powder, sugar, and salt in a large bowl. Whisk in the egg. Whisking constantly, add enough boiling water in a slow, steady stream to make a thick batter that holds its shape on a spoon.
2. Heat the oil until it shimmers in a large skillet over medium-high heat.
3. Working in batches, drop the batter by heaping tablespoonsful into the hot oil. Use the back of the spoon to gently spread the batter into 3-inch rounds. Cook until the cakes are golden brown on the bottom, flip them over, and continue to cook until the other side is golden brown, about 2 minutes on each side. Add more oil between batches as needed. Serve hot.

Minnie Utsey's "Never Fail" Cornbread

Minnie Utsey was one of my many "second mothers" in my home church. She was always very encouraging and interested in my soul food history project. Unfortunately, she's already gone on to Glory, so she didn't get to see this book. I honor her loving memory with this cornbread that lives up to its title.

Makes 8 servings

1 cup all-purpose flour
¼ cup sugar
4 teaspoons baking powder
¾ teaspoon salt
1¼ cups coarse yellow cornmeal
2 large eggs
1 cup milk
¼ cup vegetable shortening, melted and cooled

1 Preheat the oven to 425°F. Grease an 8-inch square baking pan.
2 Sift together the flour, sugar, baking powder, and salt into a large bowl. Whisk in the cornmeal. In a small bowl, whisk together the eggs, milk, and shortening until smooth. Pour the egg mixture into the flour mixture and stir until smooth. Pour the batter into the prepared baking pan.
3 Bake until firm and the top is golden brown, 20 to 25 minutes. Serve hot.

Hot Sauce

THE BEST MEDICINE EVER?

PEPPER

One of the most useful vegetables in hygiene is red pepper. Especially in warm countries it has been considered invaluable as a stimulant and auxiliary in digestion. Among
the French and Spanish races it is used in, the largest quantities, and they invariably
enjoy most excellent health. Of late, particularly since the cholera visited our State,
our planters have begun to discover the advantages of this vegetable, and mingle large
quantities of it with the food of their negroes. Considerable attention has been drawn
to the selection and cultivation of the best kinds of pepper. Among those who have
appreciated the importance of this vegetable is that admirable planter and exceedingly practical gentleman, Col. Maunsel White, the proprietor of "Deer Range," commonly known as the model sugar plantation. Col. White has introduced the celebrated
tobacco (sic) red pepper, the very strongest of all peppers, of which he has cultivated
a large quantity with the view of supplying his neighbors, and diffusing it through the
State.

The tobacco (sic) pepper yields a small red pod less than an inch in length, and
longitudinal in shape. It is exceedingly hot, and a small quantity of it is sufficient to
season a large dish of any food. Owing to its oleaginous character, Col. White found it
impossible to preserve it by drying; but by pouring strong vinegar on it after boiling,
he has made a sauce or pepper decoction of it, which possesses in a concentrated form
all the qualities of the vegetable. A single drop of this sauce will flavor a whole plate of
soup or other food. The use of a decoction like this, particularly in preparing the food
for laboring persons, would be found exceedingly beneficial in a relaxing climate like
this. Col. White has not had a single case of cholera among his large gang of negroes
since that disease appeared in the South. He attributes this to the free use of this vegetable agent.—*Southern Planter*, August 1850, excerpted from the *Daily True Delta* of New
Orleans, 26 January 1850 (courtesy of ProQuest LLC)

★ ★ ★ ★ ★

To get into the right frame of mind for thinking about hot sauce, it helps to play the musical prologue to any one of Barry White's songs. My personal choice would be "I'm Gonna Love You Just a Little More, Baby." Hot sauce is about seduction, and African Americans fell hard for hot sauce long ago. Judging by the hot sauce display at a typical soul food restaurant, one would think the love affair involved multiple partners. There tend to be at least two sauces available, many times different brands of the same type of sauce. But these displays are really about monogamy. Once a soul foodie falls in love with a particular hot sauce brand, they're mated for life. By having a customer's likely hot sauce favorite on hand, a restaurant is merely hedging its bets.

How did Louisiana-style hot sauce become the beloved condiment for soulful chow? The answer lies in part with the enslaved population on the Deer Range Plantation near antebellum New Orleans, and in part with the marketing genius of a white dude in a colonel suit. No, not the fried chicken guy, but the man referenced in this chapter's opening article—Col. Maunsel White. In 1850, Colonel White used an innovative hot sauce to end a health crisis among his slaves, and by telling anyone who would listen, he shined a big spotlight on the way slaves used chillis.[1] After you've played all of that Barry White, here's the cold shower: Hot sauce was medicine, and had been for some time before it became a condiment. Once it became a condiment, African Americans made hot sauce their most popular, and enduring, choice. Before we get to the ingenuity of Colonel White and the Deer Range Plantation slaves, we need to get our facts straight on hot sauce and chillis.

A "hot sauce" in the United States is a condiment that adds flavor to prepared food.[2] As Dave DeWitt and Nancy Gerlach of *Chile Pepper* magazine clarify,

It is important to differentiate among hot sauces, picante sauces, and salsas. Generally speaking, hot sauces are made with chiles and water or vinegar, plus herbs, spices and occasionally fruits and vegetables. The ingredients are sometimes cooked, but always liquefied, and the hot sauces are usually more thin than thick in consistency. Picante sauces are processed (and often crushed or cooked) combinations of chiles, tomatoes, and onions, and are much thicker than hot sauces. Salsas are thicker still, and consist of discernible chunks of chiles and vegetables or fruits mixed together but not crushed or cooked.[3]

The "hot" in "hot sauce" has a surprisingly long history. The *Oxford English Dictionary* (OED) defines "hot" as an adjective: "Of a food, drink, spice, etc.: having a taste or smell characterized by a burning sensation; pungently spicy; acrid, biting. Also of a taste or smell (occas. in figurative contexts)."[4] The *OED* also approximates that the earliest use of the word "hot" was around 1200 A.D. The food-related meanings of the word "hot" are a shout out to Galen, a second-century Greek physician whose theory of physiology dominated European medical thought and practice in the Middle Ages. In the Galenic system, everything has, in varying degrees, inherent qualities of cold, dryness, heat, and moisture. Illness could be traced to having one of the elements out of balance in relation to the other three. Thus, if a person had a "cold" illness, a cure would be something that generated heat and brought the person back into balance. This is likely why pepper sauces are the traditional condiment for seafood dishes, since seafood, coming from cold water, is considered a cold food. Hot sauce is also known as "pepper sauce" in English, a term that dates back to at least 1648.[5]

Louisiana-style hot sauces have a pretty consistent DNA: cayenne or Tabasco chilli (giving the sauce a reddish-orange color), garlic, vinegar, salt, and spices. This basic recipe stands in sharp contrast to Caribbean or West African hot sauces. Those hot sauces tend to be thicker, have hotter chillis (like datil or habanero), may contain fruit, and can be a variety of colors. I've had meals in West African restaurants where I didn't get a bottled sauce at all. Instead, I got a small plate with a dollop of an intensely hot chilli puree. In addition, there are liquid hot sauces in contemporary West Africa. As one newspaper reported in 1966, "AFRICA'S 'CATSUP' is a hot sauce, made with red peppers in West Africa and with curry in East Africa where the Indian influence is greatest."[6]

A hot sauce's starring attraction is a chilli, which is the pungent fruit of plants belonging to the genus *Capsicum*. Though they are often called peppers, chile peppers, hot peppers, and red peppers, chillis are not a pepper. "Pepper" properly refers to the berries of *Piper nigrum*, a plant native to Asia. That's the pepper that Americans are used to shaking on our food. As we've seen with corn, greens, and sweet potatoes, this particular misnomer can be traced to the Europeans who first visited the chilli's native habitat. One of Columbus's primary reasons for setting sail in 1492 was to find new trade routes so that Spain could get pepper without interference from rivals. Whenever Europeans first experienced chillis, rather than using the native term, they called them peppers because chillis most

The Chilli's Rush Explained

Physiologically, we get the "hot" in hot sauce when our mouths react with capsaicin—a chemical compound that is chilli's active ingredient. As chilli expert Tom Hudgins explains, "Capsaicin is an alkaloid which produces the following effect: the sensation of heat created by capsaicin is caused by an irritation of the trigeminal cells, which are pain receptors located in the mouth, nose and stomach. They release substance P, a chemical messenger that tells the brain about pain or skin inflammation." The brain then releases endorphins to soothe the irritation, creating a "warm" sensation. Hudgins adds, "Repeated consumption of chile peppers confuses the substance P receptors, which is the reason people eventually build up a tolerance to capsaicin and can eat hotter and hotter foods."[1]

Capsaicin levels in chillis are measured in Scoville units. Here's how some familiar chillis score:[2]

CHILLI VARIETY	SCOVILLE UNITS
Bell pepper	0–600
Paprika	0–2,500
Jalapeño	2,500–10,000
Cayenne	30,000–50,000
Tabasco	30,000–50,000
Habanero	80,000–150,000

A word from the wise: Capsaicin is not water soluble, so chasing chilli-drenched food with several glasses of cold water won't work. Ari Weinzweig of Zingerman's Deli in Ann Arbor, Michigan, gave me a very helpful suggestion—drink buttermilk. I did just that after taking a big bite of Zingerman's rendition of Nashville-style "hot chicken," and it worked!

---

1 Hudgins, "Hot Sauces," 124.
2 Adapted from a chart in McGee, *On Food and Cooking*, 421.

resembled the spicy berries they already knew. According to food historian Clifford Wright, "Today, there are five cultivated species [of chillis] and some twenty wild ones. *Capsicum annuum*, native to either South America or Mexico and the most widely cultivated and economically important species, includes nearly all the varieties of hot and mild chiles sold in the United States. All of the others, *C. frutescens, C. chinense, C. baccatum*, and *C. pubescens* are native to South America."[7] For the soul food story, we're primarily concerned with two types of chillis: cayenne chilli (*Capsicum annum*) and the Tabasco chilli (*Capsicum frutescens* var. *tabasco*).

Before chillis arrived, West Africans spiced their food with several native and introduced piquant spices, namely true black pepper, cardamom, ginger, nutmeg, and the melegueta pepper (also known as "grains of paradise").[8] All of these spices have chemical compounds that create an effect similar to that of capsaicin but pack far less punch. Europeans tended to group these all together. In 1791, a British publication called cayenne chilli "a species of ginger, cardamoms, wild nutmegs and cinnamon."[9] A heavy use of those warming spices meant that the West African palate was already "hardwired" to appreciate the taste and heightened piquancy of chillis when they were introduced to the region in the 1500s and 1600s by European traders returning from the Americas.[10] Aztecs, Incas, and Mayans across the Americas traditionally used chillis to treat a variety of ailments.[11] Often the peppers were merely mixed in with some food or liquid that was to be consumed as part of a typical meal.

West Africans embraced chillis, using them in a prototypical hot sauce to season traditional foods, as well as for remedies. As one early-seventeenth-century observer noted, West Africans boiled guinea pepper with pressed cassava juice (utilizing another New World plant) to a make "an excellent and wholesome sauce."[12] Of all the chillis, cayenne seems to have earned the earliest reputation as a medicine in the Old World of Europe and Africa. As late as 1797, cayenne pepper was a popular rheumatism cure in parts of West Africa.[13] West Africa's native melegueta pepper (the berry kind and not a chilli) was used to provision slave ships early in the Atlantic slave trade. As Wagner observes, "References to melegueta peppers on slave ships are common[,] one of the earliest being [an] account of the English slaver *Hannibal* [that] traded for melegueta peppers along what was known as the 'Grain' or 'Malaguette' coast in West Africa in 1693."[14] The reason given by the ship's captain for buying this pepper was "to give it to our Negroes in their messes to keep them from the flux and dry belly-ach, which they are incident to."[15] The slavers used melegueta pepper as a preventive medicine first and a condiment second. Chillis eventually replaced melegueta peppers on slave ships because they were inexpensive and stored well in a dried form.

When enslaved West Africans arrived in the Americas, they encountered indigenous chilli-eating traditions and preparations like the ones Christopher Columbus observed in 1493.[16] One of the earliest culinary lessons the West Africans learned was how to make hot sauce. In the Jamaica colony, circa 1700, one traveler observed that cayenne chilli "is the most commonly planted of any of the *Capsicums*, and used extremely by Indians and Blacks. It is very often pickled by cutting off the largest part next the stalk, and clearing it of seed, and putting into pickle of vinegar and salt. The Indians and Negroes make it the corrective for all sorts of Legumina, and sallets, and will scarce abstain from it in hot diseases."[17] This observation, though specific to Jamaica, is important for several reasons.[18] First, it shows the familiar hot sauce formula of chilli, vinegar, and salt. These early sauces were often called "cayenne vinegar," "chili vinegar," or "pepper vinegar." Both *The Virginia Housewife*, by Mary Randolph, and *The Carolina Housewife*, by Sarah Rutledge, have a recipe for "pepper vinegar" that is essentially the same as that used by Native Americans and enslaved blacks in the Jamaica colony.[19] Curiously, cookbooks by African Americans Malinda Russell and Abby Fisher do not have a hot sauce recipe. There are pepper relish recipes in the cookbooks published by the Montana Federation of Negro Women's Clubs and the New Jersey State Federation of Colored Women's Clubs, but they are not hot sauces.[20]

Second, the traveler's account of the colony also demonstrates the extensive use of cayenne chillis, which still remain the chosen one for soul food seasoning. Unfortunately, we don't know if enslaved Africans actually preferred cayenne chillis or if they were merely what the plantation master provided. For the cost-conscious planter, cayenne chillis were a popular supplement because they were easy to grow and cheaper than black pepper, and they could meet the enslaved Africans' desire for pungent spices.[21] The enslaved could also forage for chillis in some areas, for cayenne was reportedly growing wild in Louisiana as early as 1804.[22] Last, the traveler's passage shows that enslaved Africans in Jamaica used hot sauce both as a condiment and as a medicine for "hot diseases." It's the medicine angle that gets us back to the American South and to Col. Maunsel White, who touted hot sauce for medicinal use.

In the early decades of the nineteenth century, pharmacists in the United States touted cayenne chillis as a new remedy for a variety of mouth, throat, and digestive ailments.[23] A medical publication in 1822 advised, "Take two table spoonfuls of small red pepper, or three of common Cayenne pepper, and two of fine salt, and beat them into a paste; add a half pint of boiling water, strain off the liquor when cold, and add to it half a pint of very sharp vinegar. Give a table spoonful every half hour as a dose for an adult, and so in proportion for younger patients. Perhaps this medicine might merit a trial in the yellow fever."[24] Does the combination of dried cayenne chillis, water, vinegar, and salt seem familiar? It should, because this medicine is the same formula for hot sauce!

Europeans introduced chillis as food into eastern North America as early as the seventeenth century. Swedish settlers in the Delaware River Valley were farming the fiery habanero chilli (*Capsicum chinense*) by 1642.[25] Southern planters were growing chillis and spicing slave food with chillis by the eighteenth century. Thomas Jefferson grew cayenne chilli in his private garden by 1773.[26] Though there is little documentation that African slaves used chillis in the seventeenth and eighteenth centuries, it is well documented that in the nineteenth century enslaved African Americans grew chillis in their private gardens. Red chillis played an important role in plantation life. Given their meager diet, inadequate clothing, extended time spent in the elements, and squalid living conditions, slaves often succumbed to disease. Planters often scrimped on paying a physician to provide health care, so the enslaved relied on folk remedies and plant-based treatments like red pepper medicines to fight and cure diseases.

Several beliefs regarding red chillis also survive slavery. Folklorist Newbell Puckett collected this anecdote while compiling African American beliefs in the early twentieth century: "One old Negro mammy told me that she purposefully made her step-daughter as angry as possible and then put her at once to planting peppers, the idea being that peppers, to grow, must be planted by an angry person. Others say a red-headed or high-tempered person should plant them."[27] The enslaved also believed that rubbing their feet with red pepper while trying to escape would obscure the scent the dogs were trying to track. When escaped slaves were caught, planters would sadistically rub hot sauce's ingredients—pepper, vinegar, and salt—into the fresh whipping wounds to put the slave in excruciating pain.[28] Most importantly, chilli was used to spice bland plantation food. This was a workable arrangement because enslaved Africans already had an appetite for chillis. Also, chillis could be reused by simply adding more vinegar to them to create pepper vinegar.

Since hot sauce was already known as a condiment and medicine, why did Colonel White get so much favorable publicity? The big difference was his "discovery" of the Tabasco chilli, which proved to be a significant upgrade from cayenne chilli. Col. Maunsel White was an orphan, an Irish émigré, a Louisiana transplant, an entrepreneur, a hero of the War of 1812, a politician, a sugar planter, a slave owner, a philanthropist, and an epicure. He was a larger-than-life figure—someone you definitely wanted to know if you lived in antebellum Louisiana. Most importantly for our purposes, he was a chilli cheerleader and a pepper sauce promoter—probably the biggest one of his time. If there ever is a pepper pantheon, Colonel White deserves a place of honor. The *Daily True Delta* article on Maunsel White that opened this chapter created a sensation when it was published in 1850. It was widely reprinted in contemporary newspapers and agricultural journals. Planters in the antebellum South were eager to share success stories and to brag about their best practices on successfully raising crops and managing their slaves.

Planters were particularly proud of their successes with managing their laborers' hygiene. According to newspaper reports of the time, a significant cholera epidemic struck the Lower Mississippi Valley in the late 1840s, killing thousands, white and black.[29] Undoubtedly, White and his slaves were already familiar with the use of cayenne chilli for medicine. After White got word of the new chilli and received the seeds from a returning soldier who fought in the Mexican-American War, he began experimenting on how to grow the Tabasco plant. White successfully raised the Tabasco chilli, and the *Daily True Delta* reported on 7 December 1849, "I must not omit to notice the Colonel's [Maunsel White's] pepper patch, which is two acres extent, all planted with a new species of red pepper, which Colonel White has introduced into our country, called Tabasco red pepper."[30] As the 1850 article indicates, the new chilli concoction was very effective in stemming the cholera epidemic. White shared the Tabasco chilli and the results of his medical trials with fellow Louisianans, possibly including the McIlhenny family of Avery Island in southern Louisiana who started building the Tabasco Brand Pepper Sauce empire in 1868.[31] In the intervening decades between when White introduced the Tabasco chilli to Louisiana soil and the birth of Tabasco Brand Pepper Sauce, Colonel White was busy marketing his own Tabasco chillis.

White first intended to use the Tabasco chilli the same way as dried cayenne, but he found the Tabasco chilli so oily that it was "impossible to preserve it by drying." This distinctive property inspired Colonel White to find another way to stretch Tabasco chillis. They were, and still are, difficult to grow in Louisiana's climate, and the plant's low yields make farming Tabasco chillis an expensive endeavor. Yet the oily characteristic was also a blessing. One author conjectured that "the Tabasco must have drawn White's attention because, unlike other hot peppers, it is juicy: a squeeze yields six to eight fiery drops. There were other peppers available at that time, brought by slaves from Africa and by the Spaniards from Mexico, but they were good for garnishing a dish or for use in cooking. Now here was a pepper that didn't need to be chopped or puréed to extract its pungency, just squeezed like a lemon. It was ideal for making a refined pepper sauce."[32] At some point, the mid-nineteenth-century equivalent of a light bulb went off over Colonel White's head. By 1853, Colonel White was manufacturing and marketing a hot sauce he called Maunsel White's Concentrated Essence of Tabasco Peppers. He made this sauce with the boiling process described in the *Daily True Delta* article. This was an innovation from the steeping or fermentation methods that typified other hot sauces and the pepper vinegars of the time.

Colonel White gets so much attention here because, unlike other hot sauce barons, he at least acknowledged a debt to his enslaved African Americans. Any commercial success Colonel White earned from his pepper sauce depended on enslaved laborers. African Americans farmed and harvested the acres of Tabasco chillis. White's Parisian-trained, Big House kitchen slaves were most likely executing White's early experiments in concocting a pepper sauce.[33] Alternatively, if the task were not left to the Big House slaves, field slaves may also have used their expertise in making chilli vinegars to develop the new Louisiana-style hot sauce.

Thanks to White's boosterism, hot sauce went "big time" in no time. Supposedly, White unveiled his perfected sauce at a dinner he gave for former president Andrew Jackson.[34] By 1858, word of mouth had created a demand for his sauce, and White decided to sell it commercially to apothecaries, grocers, private clubs, and restaurants.[35] White had his slaves deliver bulk orders of his hot sauce in large bottles, and retailers would then transfer the hot sauce into much smaller bottles for resale.[36] Restaurateurs, particularly in places where oysters were sold, offered a half-cup of the Maunsel White hot sauce as a lagniappe (the Louisiana French term for a bonus) to customers.[37] Ever the booster, White reportedly always brought a bottle of his own sauce when he dined in New Orleans oyster saloons like the Gem Restaurant.[38]

The hot sauce collection at Mert's, Charlotte, N.C.

Maunsel White's hot sauce made such a spicy splash that, as indicated by this testimonial from *The Picayune Creole Cook Book*, it became closely associated with New Orleans itself:

A daily sight in our New Orleans streets is to see the negro servants going at lunch or suppertime, to the nearest oyster saloon with a great salver for oysters on half-shell. They return with the dainty bi-valves ranged closely in their open shells on the salver, and with a small glass of Maunsell White, and a plate of "hard tack" (oyster bread) or crackers. Those who do not like the taste of pepper often use Worcestershire Sauce instead of the Maunsell White. But the piquant Maunsell White is essentially Creole, originated in New Orleans, and gives the oyster a toothsome touch that must be tasted in order to be appreciated.[39]

Yet White's hot sauce fame was not everlasting. Colonel White died on 17 December 1863, and his heirs sold the sauce until the 1920s. However, the marketing efforts of the McIlhennys catapulted their Tabasco-based hot sauce to tremendous commercial success. By the mid-twentieth century, Col. Maunsel White and his sauce would be virtually unknown to devoted hot sauce consumers. Regardless, from field to table, African Americans were heavily involved in the production and proliferation of one of Louisiana's earliest and most popular hot sauces.

Southern media were constantly filled with planters giving one another advice on how to keep their slaves healthy. As early as the mid-nineteenth century, magazines like *DeBow's Review* became a megaphone advocating the use of chillis in slave rations. In 1851, *DeBow's Review* printed a letter from a "Small Farmer" who wrote, "My negroes get baits of fresh meat occasionally, but always seasoned high with red pepper."[40] In 1854, *DeBow's Review* advised planters that "a bountiful supply of red pepper should be cultivated, kept on hand and used freely, in damp sections, where sore throats are apt to prevail, and also a fall in [the number of] complaints. It acts by creating a glow over the whole body, without any narcotic effect; it produces general arterial excitement, and prevents, in a considerable degree, that languor and apathy of the system, which render it so susceptible to chills and fevers; it may be given in any way or form which their taste or fancy may dictate."[41]

After Emancipation, hot sauces traveled wherever African Americans went, either as a simple, clear-colored chilli vinegar or as a red-hued, Louisiana-style hot sauce. Emancipation also fueled the need for convenience and economy as African Americans fled the rural South for opportunities in other parts of the country. William A. Brown, a freeborn black man from Massachusetts, arrived in Virginia City, Nevada, in 1862, probably lured there by potential riches from mining. After a short stint as a street shoe-polisher, Brown opened up the Boston Saloon in 1864. One of the few black-owned establishments in Virginia City, it catered to moneyed African Americans in the 1860s and 1870s. The saloon moved to its final location by 1866. In 2002, archaeologists conducting an excavation of the saloon made a remarkable discovery: Amidst the shattered champagne bottles and gold coins stuck in the floorboards were the remains of a 130-year-old bottle of Tabasco Brand Pepper Sauce.[42] It is believed to be the oldest hot sauce bottle in existence.

In a strict historical sense, a Louisiana-style hot sauce must be made of Tabasco chillis. However, Tabasco chillis, because of their intensive farming requirements and lower yield, were consistently more expensive than cayenne chillis. Thus, the less-hot cayenne chillis were a frequent substitute in Louisiana-style hot sauces. Cayenne chillis were most prevalent in American cooking, and more pungent chillis were shunned. As food historian William Woys Weaver notes, "Because of its intense heat, the habanero was generally viewed as vulgar by well-to-do whites who consistently substituted cayenne peppers instead, and in very small quantities I might add. Cayenne peppers are by far the most commonly mentioned peppers in our regional culinary sources, at least until the 1830s."[43]

A soul food experience is not complete without some heat. Even after adding red cayenne chillis (dried whole chillis or dried chilli flakes) during the cooking process, many soul foodies will douse some of their favorite hot sauce on top. Cayenne chillis are still the capsicums of choice for Louisiana-style hot sauce manufacturers and soul foodies, though the latter group is turning up the heat. Some soul food diners have shared with me that they are switching to hotter chillis like habaneros, particularly to season stewed dishes like greens and beans. In addition, a growing number of soul foodies are using Mexican- and Asian-style hot sauces, though a Louisiana-style hot sauce is still the likely choice.

No doubt there's been a "global warming" of culinary palates in the United States, in which foods and condiments are getting hotter and hotter. However, a distinctive aspect of African American foodways has always been the number of specialty dishes infused or drenched with hot sauce. For example, a half-century ago, if you wanted a fiery barbecue sauce, you went to a black-run barbecue place. Fried fish bathed in hot sauce is another example. In 2007, the peripatetic gourmands Jane and Michael Stern located soul food's hot spot in Nashville, Tennessee: "Hot-fish sandwiches are a staple at soul-food restaurants throughout the South, but the tradition is strongest in Nashville, where they are the specialty of shacks, stands, and drive-throughs. Donald 'Bo' Boatright, who started Eastside Fish in 2003, grew up eating them as part of what he calls 'summer nights of fun'—evenings when neighbors gathered to play cards and to eat hot fish."[44] The fish in question is doubly "hot"—warm from being recently fried in hot oil and spicy from a liberal hand with the hot sauce bottle.

There's also a soul food backstory with what is arguably America's favorite spicy snack food—the buffalo chicken wing. When Calvin Trillin wrote "An Attempt to Compile a Short History of the Buffalo Chicken Wing" in 1980, he raised the distinct possibility of an African American provenance for one of America's favorite bar foods. He interviewed a guy named John Young who claimed that in the mid-1960s he invented the signature hot sauce necessary for buffalo wings. He called his sauce "mambo sauce." Young's claim contradicts the Bellissimo family who own and operate the Anchor Bar in Buffalo, New York, and are widely believed to have originated the buffalo chicken wing. Trillin's investigation shows that even within the Bellissimo family there are two separate versions of the story—which is problematic to say the least.[45] Though no one really knows for sure, a chicken wing drowning in hot sauce fit squarely within the soul food tradition, and less so with Italian American foodways. That history should cause us to consider another plausible origin for buffalo wings other than the one commonly accepted.

Aside from these hot fish and chicken offerings, African American–run barbecue joints have a deep tradition of featuring at least one incendiary barbecue sauce on their menu. One of the most famous barbecue purveyors of the Down Home Cooking period was a guy named Eugene "Hot Sauce" Williams. Williams ran successful barbecue restaurants in Cleveland, Ohio, and Pittsburgh, Pennsylvania, in the 1940s and 1950s and earned a reputation for a good barbecue product and a tongue-blazing sauce. In 1942 the *Cleveland Call and Post* reported on how Williams got a "copyrighted label" for his nickname: "It so happened that his press agent, one Mitch Plotkin, known very well in Cleveland, had his first taste of Mr. Williams' ribs. . . . As Mitch, later explained . . . 'That sauce was the hottest thing that ever touched my tongue.'"[46] Then the *Pittsburgh Courier* exposed a Louisiana connection in 1952: "Williams has refused thousands of dollars for his exclusive formula, and it is believed that his annual trips to the Mardi Gras at New Orleans brings him into further contacts with old Southern chefs who, it is believed helped 'Hot Sauce' develop this sauce many years ago."[47] Given hot sauce's history, having Louisiana credentials could only have burnished Williams's reputation.

You would think I would have learned my lesson by now, but I continue to try hot barbecue sauces in black-run barbecue joints. Ordering barbecue with the hottest sauce on the menu usually follows a familiar pattern, one you will likely experience should you choose to go this route:

WAITSTAFF "What can I get for you, baby?"
    (Here, "baby" is a term of endearment, not sexual harassment.)
ME "I would like the rib sandwich."
WAITSTAFF "Hot, medium or mild?"
ME "I'll get the hot."
WAITSTAFF "No, you won't."

In such cases, I always wonder why the "hot" barbecue sauce is even an option. I insisted and was served the hot rib sandwich. After taking a bite, I felt like my lips had burned off and that I was walking around with a permanent smile. I didn't complain one bit, and I took my hot sauce medicine like a man.

13

What's Sweet, Red, & Drunk from a Jelly Jar?

HINT: LIQUID SOUL!

Cuzzin Cora, a soul food restaurateur has the following on-air conversation with local radio DJ Cee-Cee Lovely:

LOVELY "Whew, it all sounds so delicious," Cee-Cee saluted.
"You said a mouthful."

CORA "I usually do, baby. By the way, we also have red Kool-Aid."

LOVELY "What flavor?"

CORA "I said red! Red!"

—Adapted from Victor McGlothin's novel *Every Sistah Wants It.*

★　★　★　★　★

"What? Red Kool-Aid was invented by *a white dude living in Nebraska in the 1920s*? Well, he had a black assistant, right?" asked a couple of my African American friends as I was dropping knowledge on the latest version of my Unifying Theory of Why Black People Love Red Drinks. I felt compelled to inform them that a white man named Edwin Perkins—a traveling salesman from Hastings, Nebraska—invented Kool-Aid in 1927. Obviously unaware of what would become proper soul food nomenclature, Perkins included strawberry (as opposed to "red") as one of the product line's original flavors. Kool-Aid went national in 1929, selling for 10 cents a package, but Perkins soon slashed the price in half to make his product an affordable "luxury" during the Great Depression.[1] Shock could explain my friends' reaction, but I really think it was heartbreak. African Americans have long had a strong affinity for red drinks that stretches back in time beyond Nebraska, believe it or not, all the way back to West Africa. Put in stark terms, red drinks are liquid soul.

By red drink, I mean any nonalcoholic beverage ("soft drink") that is primarily red in color and secondarily has cherry, strawberry, or tropical fruit as its flavor. As Cuzzin Cora emphasizes, the drink's flavor is almost immaterial. It's about the color. Red drinks are omnipresent at African American social gatherings, yet they are one of the most unexamined aspects of African American foodways. Any time black people get together for a special occasion, if there's food there, there's going to be a red drink. Go to any restaurant that has a predominantly black clientele, and there's going to be a red drink available. Sure, other beverages like lemonade and sweet tea will make an appearance, but they're more southern than soulful. Red drinks have the most "juice" within soul food culture because, more than any other beverage, they symbolize a social connection to family, friends, and strangers and, unwittingly, a bond with the African diaspora. With sincere apologies to Alice Walker, Whoopi Goldberg, Oprah, and even Prince, it's all about the color red, not The Color Purple.

Why red drinks? That answer seems to be lost in antiquity. Writing in 1926, Newbell Puckett, a southern folklorist and chronicler of African American folk beliefs, suggested a cultural and historical continuity to West African societies where red had been an important royal and ritual color for at least two centuries:

[William] Bosman (A.D. 1795) says that red was the royal color at Ardra (one home of Vodu-worship) which is the probable reason for its being the favorite vodu color in Hayti. Red flannel is always used by the American Negro in making his "tricks," but we cannot be too sure of its African origin. . . . Thus, while it seems probable that the use of red is of African origin in the case of Negroes, since the Negro practices the voodoo rites associated in Africa with this color, we cannot be absolutely sure that there has been no European infiltration. In both Europe and Africa it may well be that the red color represents what was formerly sacrificial blood offered to the fetish in question.[2]

Puckett suggests the real possibility of a voodoo connection to West Africa but also hints at a European influence. Red could be operating as a metaphor for blood sacrifice as well as for kinship. This is not unlike how some Christians use wine or grape juice to represent the blood of Jesus Christ during their Holy Communion ritual, which denotes a connection with other Christians around the world.

That appreciation for the color red connects African Americans with other parts of the African diaspora was not lost on whites who were somewhat familiar with black culture. A 1902 *Washington Post* article captured an interesting exchange between two southern U.S. senators, Hernando Money of Mississippi and Ben Tillman of Georgia. It began with imitation butter but quickly included a broader accounting of how blacks in the Caribbean loved the color red. Senator Money said that imitation butter made in the United States that was going to the Caribbean was a "brilliant red" color. " 'The darkies down there,' he says, 'won't have any other color. They like red butter just as they adore red shirts and red cravats.' 'Like red lemonade at a circus,' suggested Senator Tillman, as he listened to the story about red butter. 'Yes,' replied Senator Money, 'or the red label on a tomato can. I have been told by grocers that if a black and white label should be placed on canned tomatoes, there would be no sales at all. It's all a matter of taste.' "[3]

Today, market researchers know that red sells. With food purchases, consumers want to buy red steaks and red fruit because we've somehow learned to associate red with fresh meat and ripe fruit.[4] The discussion between the two senators shows that such "matters of taste" apply across several categories beyond food and drink. Several red drinks appear at different points in the soul food story and open a window on African American foodways. In this chapter, we'll take a swig of two traditional West African drinks, kola tea and hibiscus tea; a gulp of two traditional Emancipation celebration drinks, red lemonade and red soda pop; and then guzzle some red Kool-Aid.

Like people in other parts of the Old World, West Africans were faced with drinking water that didn't taste very good. Tadeusz Lewicki notes, "During the Middle Ages, water was not regarded as the most salubrious drink in West Africa. Ibn Battua, for instance, declares that plain water disagreed with the people of the banks of the Middle Niger, and that for this reason they used various other beverages."[5] So they came up with a number of drinks that either made water more palatable or avoided water altogether. I won't comment on the West African traditions of making palm wine and lightly brewed beers. My focus is on nonalcoholic beverages, and the medieval record shows West Africans consumed milk (especially sour milk), water mixed with honey, drinks thickened with millet or sorghum, and kola tea (which the local Arabs of the time called "coffee of the Negroes").[6] Of these beverages, only the kola tea was identifiably red, though some varieties of millet and sorghum are reddish, so they may have given drinks a reddish hue.

By the time of the Atlantic slave trade, there were two prominent red drinks in West Africa: kola tea and hibiscus tea. Both appear to have been enjoyed and modified through the centuries, demonstrating the enduring popularity of red drinks. Kola tea's key ingredient is the kola nut. Kola nuts are the fruit of West African trees, some indigenous and others introduced into the region. Of the forty known varieties, *Cola nitida* and *Cola acuminate* were the most utilized.[7] Of the two, *Cola nitida* has been the most common and commercially important kola nut.[8] Kola nuts tend to be white or red, and one authority notes that the white variety "was much more valuable and rare, occurring in the same pod as white and pink or red nuts. . . . Red kola was the preferred kola of trade because of its long-lasting quality."[9] A brisk trade for kola nuts was under way within the region as early as the sixteenth century. West Africans put kola nuts to a lot of uses: anticoagulant, aphrodisiac, appetite suppressant, condiment, currency, digestive aid, hangover cure, negotiating tool (especially for wars and weddings), stimulant, and water purifier and sweetener.[10] I am most interested in its uses as a water purifier and a stimulant and as a vehicle for social bonding.

Some of the earliest written accounts by Europeans about kola describe its ability to change the taste of nasty water. In 1591, a Portuguese trader named Odoardo Lopez wrote of kola nuts for a book published in Rome, "There are other trees which produce fruits called cola; which are as big as a pine cone and contain other fruits like chestnuts, in which there are four different [separate] pulps of a red, fleshy colour, people keep them in their mouth and chew them to quench their thirst and make the water tasty."[11] We get a more complete description of the palate-altering effects of chewed kola and water from a European in Central Africa in 1871: "There is a peculiar fruit called the *kola*, or *gooroo*, somewhat resembling the chestnut in shape, very bitter, but which has the effect of making water that is drunk afterward taste like *eau sucrée* or, according to one observer, 'like white wine and sugar.' It is most eagerly sought after by all Mohammedan tribes."[12] With their ability to improve the taste of bad water, kola nuts became a valuable commodity.

Besides enhancing taste, kola was known to wake a person up. One authority writing in the late 1800s indicated that kola nuts were "used to form a refreshing and invigorating drink throughout a large portion of tropical Africa."[13] The traditional ways to drink kola varied throughout West Africa. In some places kola nuts could be chewed while the beverage was in one's mouth or immediately afterward, added to hot or cold water, added to alcoholic beverages, consumed "as an aperitif before meals, or 'like coffee' after meals."[14] Though the color of kola nut drinks was not documented in the medieval sources, they were likely to be red. A "Kola drink" recipe from a 1950s Nigerian cookbook testifies to red's longevity as a popular drink color:

> Ingredients: 6 Kola Nut, Water, Sugar. Method: (1) Choose red kola nut's (2) Beat them in a mortar or blender in a vessel free from pepper or grate or chop up (3) Add hot water and sugar leave to cool (4) Strain. Only people who eat kola like this drink, and they prefer it hot.[15]

Whenever someone eats red kola nuts, their saliva turns red. In some West African cultures, this was a sign of wealth and social status because red kola nuts were scarce and thus a luxury. Ex post facto, red slobber was proof that a person was wealthy enough to have their kola nuts and eat them too.[16]

In the United States, kola nut drinks are called "colas." You might be wondering why I consider cola a red drink when most colas are brown. There are two plausible explanations. One is that American cola manufacturers were probably using dried kola nuts, which are brown. The other is that they may have purposefully dyed the drinks brown in order to have a similar look to the popular dark drinks of the time, Moxie and root beers. Regardless, all colas are now dyed brown, even though kola nuts are no longer used in making the drinks. Next time you get a cola, check the label and you'll see "caramel coloring" as an ingredient. So when you walk into a soul food restaurant that offers beverages like Kool-Aid and cola, remember—you're really getting a choice of two red drinks. It's just that one is in disguise.

In the Caribbean and South America, planters got really interested in kola nut because they thought it would help get more productivity out of their enslaved labor force. Judith Carney notes that kola nuts made their way to the New World as slave ship provisions and were later used on plantations. Planters in Cayenne, Guadeloupe, Jamaica, and Martinique dispensed kola nuts to their slaves with the hopes of avoiding having to provide fresh water and health care for small stomach ailments.[17] Some

West Indian slaves planted kola trees in their private gardens, showing the cultural value of the kola nuts.[18] Accordingly, kola drink references pop up during the eighteenth and nineteenth centuries. George Washington reportedly grated some kola nut into a cocktail called the "swizzle" while visiting his brother in Barbados.[19] The earliest reference I found for a standard kola tea is in a revised edition of Caroline Sullivan's *The Jamaican Cookery Book* (1893). No recipe is provided, and the drink is part of a suggested Wednesday menu of "Tea, prepared kola, Salt fish and ackees, Scaveeched kingfish, Cassava cakes, Roasted cocos, Tomatoes and vinegar."[20]

In British North America, no similar documentation of kola nut use for energy or cures, nor for teas, exists during the antebellum period, but some linguistic evidence raises the possibility. Lorenzo Dow Turner's groundbreaking work on African word survivals among the Gullah people of the coastal islands of Georgia and South Carolina includes *bise* and *bisi* as words he commonly heard in Gullah conversation. He links each word to the terms for kola nut used by the Twi people of the Gold Coast and the Ewe people of Togo and Benin, respectively.[21] Turner conducted his research over two decades and published his work in 1949. Proof of kola nut drinks in early British North America is scant. The only hint of their possible existence is the linguistic evidence from Turner's research showing that kola nut names remained part of the Gullah language well into the twentieth century.

During the nineteenth century, American and European pharmacists saw real therapeutic and financial potential in the kola nut, and it became one of the most celebrated wonder drugs of that period. All kinds of clinical trials were conducted to pinpoint what the kola nut could do. Physicians and pharmacists hoped it would alleviate or cure mental illness and nervous disorders. According to one source, "Messrs. F. Stearns & Co. were the introducers of Kola nuts to the medical and pharmaceutical professions of the United States, being the first to offer the drug for sale in the beginning of the year 1881. They are headquarters for Kola nuts in this country, importing them in the fresh state in immense quantities direct from Africa."[22]

The kola nut seemed to have the same ability as the coca plant, "whose leaves when chewed, not only revive the exhausted, but also lessen hunger and thirst, and enable much more work to be done than can be performed otherwise."[23] Given this, Dr. Pemberton's pairing of coca leaves and kola nuts in 1886 to make a new brain tonic called "Coca-Cola" doesn't seem so strange. Several other southern pharmacists followed suit by "inventing" other drinks using colas (e.g., Pepsi-Cola in New Bern, North Carolina, in 1896, and Royal Crown Cola in Columbus, Georgia, in 1902).[24] The essential formula for these drinks is a kola tea with carbonated water.

The other traditional West African drink that draws our attention is a tea made from the hibiscus plant (*Hibiscus sabdariffa*), and it is a botanic relative of okra. The dried red flowers of this plant are used to make a tea called by its French name, *jus de bissap*, or just *bissap*. It is known as the "national drink of Senegal." The red flower tea is also popular in Gambia (called *wanjo* there) and in northern Nigeria.[25] In West Africa, this tea is typically made by boiling water, adding the dried flowers, and sweetening it with sugarcane and additional pungent flavors like ginger and grains of paradise.[26] Unlike for kola nuts, there really isn't a documented reason for why *bissap* crossed the Atlantic. It wasn't known as an energy drink that could bolster slave productivity. Judith Carney has raised the possibility that West Africans ate and used hibiscus leaves for religious ceremonies.[27] The religious purpose may be lost to us now, but the plant and its flowers made it to Jamaica by 1700 and were considered a common drink for enslaved Africans by that early date.[28] Maybe the only reason that matters is that it tastes really good.

In the Americas, *bissap* was called hibiscus, red sorrel, or sorrel tea. As in West Africa, the hibiscus plant blooms around Christmastime in the Caribbean and is a popular holiday drink. Hibiscus tea is prepared the same way as *bissap* is in West Africa, but without the grains of paradise. Over time, hibiscus tea spread throughout the Caribbean and Latin America, where it is also known today as *agua de Jamaica* (Jamaica water). If you ordered that drink at a Latino market or restaurant or bought some Celestial Seasonings Red Zinger tea, you actually consumed a traditional West African drink. As with kola nut tea, there's scant evidence of hibiscus tea being made in the antebellum South. In 1847, at least one agricultural journal argued that hibiscus should be cultivated in the American South. Yet the article's tone suggested that if hibiscus were indeed present, its cultivation and use were limited.[29]

So we have two West African drinks associated with and consumed on special occasions that clearly made their way to the Caribbean, but we're unsure if they were regular drinks on plantations in the American South. Even if kola nut and hibiscus teas were not available on the plantation, the slaves still had to drink something. On one hand, West African slaves replicated their fermented milk drinks and tea traditions in the Americas using substituted ingredients. On the other hand, plantation slaves drank buttermilk (a by-product of churning butter), herbal teas, fermented rice and corn drinks, spring tonics, and sweet potato beer. The big caste distinction was the enslaveds' heavy reliance on water. Well into the nineteenth century, whites often drank mildly alcoholic beverages — "small beers" and ales — instead of water. Thus, to drink a lot of water, from the whites' perspective, reinforced the idea that the enslaved were savages like the Native Americans. Still, slaves were able to transform stigmatized water into a flood of red drinks.

The FWP interviews raise the tantalizing possibility that there were more red drinks for the North American enslaved than previously believed. Larkin Payne of Arkansas speaks of a red molasses supplied to his family by poor whites near his plantation. "When my folks was set free they never got nothing. The mountain folks raised corn and made whiskey. They made red corn cob molasses; It was good."[30] The concoction of molasses and water could have been, on occasion, a red rather than a brown drink, and that blend had a long association as an energy drink for laborers in and outside the South. After Emancipation, African Americans throughout the South reinterpreted molasses and water, changing it from a work drink to one appropriate for play, and South Carolina was the epicenter of this shift. Molasses and water was, for example, served at a New Year's Day celebration held in Port Royal, South Carolina, in 1863.[31] Additional Reconstruction-era newspapers and travel accounts show that in the Carolinas, molasses and water was a popular drink on the Fourth of July and described as "the favorite beverage of the negroes."[32] The concoction was also a communion wine in black churches across South Carolina and the Sea Islands.[33] If the molasses made the water red, its religious use as a sacramental wine makes a lot of sense.

Though I've focused on soft drinks, alcoholic drinks should not be overlooked in the red drink story. There are references to "red whiskey" in the antebellum South's magazines and newspapers and in slave testimony. "Uncle" Henry Barnes of Alabama adds this memory: "Cose us hab our med'cin' sich lak elderbush tea. Hit was red 'mos' lak whiskey an' used hit for feber. Den dere was red sassafrac tea fer spring feber." Barnes's testimony reveals that teas made from the elderbush and red sassafras plants were used as medicine, especially for fever. But he also sheds light on two drinks that I would not have linked — I don't want to put too much stock into one reference, but when he says the tea "was red 'mos' lak whiskey," he reveals indirectly that plantation whiskey was commonly red in color. As a reward for work, planters let whiskey flow on holidays as well as after (and sometimes during) cornshuckings and hog killings. We can deduce, then, that red drinks took on special occasion value yet again, but in an entirely new context. Lew Bryson, managing editor of *Whiskey Advocate* magazine, shared with me why whiskey was red for a time. "It's that the process—barrel-aging—that gives the whiskey the red color also makes it taste smoother, and better. . . . Whiskey—rye or bourbon—that is aged in charred oak does have a reddish color to it. It comes from caramelization of sugars in the oak during the charring process. The whiskey soaks into the oak during aging and picks up flavor and color. The aging 'smoothes' the whiskey as well, as the char filters out some of the rougher tastes in the unaged 'moonshine.'"[34] I don't have accurate numbers of how much barreled whiskey got to slaves. Given the caste considerations of the time, it seems more probable that slaves would have received the cheaply made, clear moonshine rather than aged, and hence more valuable, whiskey.

Henry Barnes also mentions another common red drink for the enslaved—sassafras tea. Sassafras tea could be red or white, depending on which part of the root was used. During the desperate times of the Civil War, sassafras tea was one of the few drinks that southern blacks and whites shared in common. Mary Elizabeth Massey writes in *Ersatz in the Confederacy*, "To a lesser extent than coffee, tea was missed during the war. It was never as popular as coffee, yet there were those who wanted it sufficiently to search for substitutes. Most common of the expedients was sassafras tea, a beverage long familiar to many, especially Negroes."[35]

Red drinks were plentiful in the plantation Big House. Antebellum southern cookbooks are replete with recipes for homemade cherry, raspberry, and strawberry liqueurs, syrups, and vinegars, kept on hand to color a wide range of hard and soft drinks.[36] Big House mistresses also could have added red fruits to lemonade to get the desired effect. By the latter half of the nineteenth century, artificial food colorings were commercially available to African Americans, providing another option for making a red drink. Mrs. Russell's cookbook contains a recipe for a strawberry cordial that's the earliest printed in an African American cookbook:

> Strawberry cordial. Two and a half lbs sugar to one gallon juice; put the berries in a stone pot, setting it in hot water, boil and strain through a bag, mix the sugar with the juice, simmer half an hour; when cold, add a quart of peach brandy, bottle and cork.[37]

Like other cordials of the time, this would have been stored and consumed when needed. The scarcity of red drink recipes in early African American cookbooks suggests that they had limited appeal to class-conscious blacks, or that their consumption was a vernacular practice that needn't be recorded in a cookbook.

It's not until after Emancipation that we see clearer, documented links between African Americans, red drinks, and special occasions. Red lemonade was the preferred drink during the Southern Cooking era. The connection became so strong that red lemonade was wedded in the white press to other traditional African American foods, like fried chicken, fried fish, and watermelon, for the purpose of ridicule and stereotyping. In 1897, the *Atlanta Constitution* reported, "There was the most enthusiastic celebration of the glorious Fourth in the city yesterday. Every negro in Atlanta . . . was there." The paper went on to note that "barbecue with barrels of pink and red lemonade and pug dog sausages" were available.[38] In 1899, the *Dallas Morning News* wrote, "The housekeepers of Dallas need not be surprised if they find that their Afro-American cooks 'turn up missing' this morning for to-day is Emancipation day. . . . Red lemonade and fried chicken will disappear with remarkable rapidity."[39] Even the black press took note of the seemingly endless gulping down of red drinks. The *Augusta Sentinel* wrote, "Summer excursions and picnics have started. Negroes in the South spend every summer on these silly things twice enough money to carry them through each succeeding fall and winter. . . . It would be a thousand times better if we as a race, put one half as much in savings banks as we invest on excursions and red lemonade."[40]

Why red lemonade? African Americans in the North and South have loved going to the circus since its beginnings in the early 1800s, and possibly, red lemonade was born at the circus. According to a funny (and pretty disgusting) creation myth reported by the *Morning Oregonian* in 1897, red lemonade was born forty years earlier at a Texas circus. A former circus clown became a pink lemonade vendor, and he used water, tartaric acid (for the color), and lemon to make the beverage. One day, the vendor ran out of plain water, and in a fit of desperation, he substituted used wash water stained pink from laundering pink tights. He added tartaric acid and a lemon to the solution and sold it as "strawberry lemonade." The inventive vendor quipped, "My sales were doubled that day, and since then no well-regulated circus is without pink lemonade."[41] Whether or not this origin is true, pink lemonade did become so associated with the circus that it was eventually called "circus lemonade."

During the Southern Cooking era, African Americans publicly claimed ownership of circus lemonade. In the late 1880s, Elizabeth Tines ran a restaurant on 71 Peachtree Street in Atlanta, Georgia, "where the hungry are fed and where ice cream and red lemonade are served in the summer to the thirsty colored population."[42] In 1890s New York City, red lemonade was sold on Broadway to whites and was a prominent offering of street vendors in the "negro quarters," along with hot corn and hot sweet potatoes.[43]

A soul food restaurant is immediately suspect if it doesn't offer at least one type of red drink. It's like to going to a craft brewery that doesn't offer an India Pale Ale. Typically, the menu includes some sort of punch or carbonated beverage. Yet many soul food joints still sell the old family favorite — Kool-Aid. What's the magic of Kool-Aid? I think its enduring appeal is that you can make it the way you want it. Most restaurants go way overboard on the sugar, as if tartness is a sign of failure.

Sometimes, you walk into a soul food establishment, and you just know you're going to get really sweet Kool-Aid. I felt that way when I walked into Alcenia's in Memphis, Tennessee. If there ever was such a thing as a "Kool-Aid aesthetic," it's in full effect at this place. The décor is in vivid colors, like a well-coordinated Kool-Aid riot. B. J. Tamayo, owner of the joint named after her mother, gives you a steady diet of "honeys" and "sugars" that one expects from sweet southerners. Then, you get hit with "Ghetto Aid," the apotheosis of Kool-Aid. Three fruit flavors, each glued together with pure sugar. It's magnificent.

Some soul food places commit what I call red drink heresy. The Southern Kitchen in Tacoma, Washington, does so with its resident red drink — a strawberry lemonade. It sounded harmless enough when I ordered it. It's served in a culturally appropriate mason jar, but without warning, a culturally inappropriate mound of whipped cream appeared on top. I asked the waiter if that was the strawberry lemonade, and I think he could tell that I was perplexed. He told me "that's how we roll at the Southern Kitchen." That response made me laugh. It was a pretty presentation to be sure, but it ended rather ugly when the whipped cream melted.

During the Southern Cooking era, molasses and water and red lemonade were inexpensive, refreshing drinks that could be made easily and quickly; their popularity reflected the poor economic condition of African Americans in the rural South. As African Americans prospered, a new range of purchased drinks was added to the menu, particularly carbonated water beverages, commonly known as "soda pop."[44] Take, for example, this 1897 depiction of an African American camp meeting outside Colum-

Alcenia's Ghetto Aid,
Memphis

bus, Georgia: "There were booths everywhere—it was a regular Atlanta midway in this respect—and the people were crying, shouting and singing their wares—all eatables—at the top of their voices. The din which resulted was great. There was on sale red lemonade, soda water, *which also, was red*; fried fish, sausage, bananas, apples, candies, and everything else that tickles the colored palate."[45]

Here we see an important transition taking place. As carbonated beverages became cheaper and more widely available, they were slowly incorporated into special occasions until they became the signature drink. By the 1920s, red lemonade was infrequently mentioned in written accounts of African American celebrations. Red soda pop became the prominent drink at public celebrations, especially the "Juneteenth" celebrations of East Texas.

Juneteenth is an Emancipation anniversary celebration. It commemorates when federal troops, under the command of General Gordon Granger, arrived in Galveston, Texas, to inform enslaved African Americans that they were free. However, the troops arrived on 19 June . . . 1865— a full two and one-half years after the Emancipation Proclamation went into effect. The planters delayed the news for obvious economic reasons. "Many plantation owners knew of the order but didn't act on it because slaves, who made up a third of Texas's population at the time, were integral to the way of life and to the war effort. Cotton was being sold in Britain to pay for munitions, and without the large unpaid labor force, the source of funds would have collapsed," according to Lula Briggs Galloway, president of the National Association of Juneteenth Lineage.[46]

Juneteenth is an unusual holiday because it commemorates getting the news about freedom late, but in the spirit of "better late than never." The good news was celebrated primarily in East Texas, western Louisiana, southwestern Arkansas, and southeastern Oklahoma—the home field of Juneteenth celebrations. Galloway explains Juneteenth's historical continuity through drinks. "Besides barbecue, a staple of the festivities is red soda water. Some sources describe it as strawberry soda pop, like the kind made by Nehi or Fanta, but some historical sources describe a strawberry lemonade. . . . The color red had a significance that has been lost, but red soda water is still served at many celebrations because that's what the former slaves drank."[47]

Texan expatriates who settled in other parts of the United States took Juneteenth celebrations and red drinks with them, often supplanting the local traditions of celebrating Emancipation on different dates. As examples, some used to celebrate Emancipation Day on 1 January (the anniversary of when the Emancipation Proclamation went into effect), while others celebrated on 22 September (the anniversary of when Lincoln issued a "preliminary" Emancipation Proclamation).[48] As a result, Juneteenth is now the closest thing to a national Emancipation celebration. In most places, the original Emancipation celebrations have died out, but Juneteenth endures. Edna Lewis discussed the Emancipation holiday in a 1983 interview: "We don't celebrate it anymore; I was thinking about it in relation to Thanksgiving[.] I think it was discontinued in the 1930s. I remember the last one that I attended was in the '30s. As the older generation died out and life changed[,] the young people moved to the cities [and] it sort of broke up that custom of celebrating Emancipation Day."[49] Fortunately, Juneteenth has bounced back and now thrives in different parts of the country even where there are small numbers of black people. Even Alaska, Hawaii, and Vermont now have Juneteenth celebrations.

The allure of red drinks within the black community isn't limited to just special occasions. Like we saw with chitlins, Kool-Aid became an important feature of military life for black troops serving in the Vietnam War. Kool-Aid served a slightly different, but related, function. Chitlins were about building a community while in a foreign environment. Kool-Aid was about connection to their home back in the United States. James E. Westheider writes in *The African American Experience in Vietnam*,

> For the men and women stationed overseas, these [black] items were particularly important because most of the service personnel in Vietnam often felt vulnerable and alone, and needed that tangible connection with life back in the United States, or what they called "the real world." African Americans stationed in the United States could shop off-base for black magazines, hair-care products, and other necessities that were not available on-base, but for blacks posted outside of the United States, especially in South Vietnam, this option was seldom available. . . . In 1968, Kraft Foods shipped a free supply of Kool-Aid for the entire base at Kontum after Sgt. [Allen] Thomas wrote to the manufacturers and told them that the GIs stationed there missed the soft drink.[50]

Vietnam veterans like J. Carle Abernathy, a staff sergeant E-6 stationed near Denang, underscore the bond with home. He told me that getting a package of Kool-Aid was like getting a letter from home, and it was always red. "The brothers would call home for red Kool-Aid," Abernathy told me, "but they wouldn't even have to ask for it." If the troops came upon a good source of drinking water that was pure enough, they would whip out the package and make some Kool-Aid right on the spot with the sugar in their rations.[51] Black media also reinforced the importance of Kool-Aid for the troops. In 1966, Cleveland's black newspaper *The Call and Post* reported that Private First Class Samuel Malone, a graduate from the local Glenville High School, "wrote his family that he had received the food package that they sent to him last March. Most of all he enjoyed the packages of Kool-Aid."[52] In 1968, the same newspaper reported, "Men in Vietnam have asked for items such as assorted greeting cards, plastic containers for Kool-Aid and Kool-Aid to put in it among other things."[53] When the *Phila-*

delphia Tribune held its First Annual Paddy Poll of servicemen in Vietnam, one of their ten worst experiences was "a fly in your Kool-Aid."[54]

Much of this discourse on red drink has been related to public celebrations, but when drinking alone, a favorite choice has, once again, been red Kool-Aid. In fact, I believe that red Kool-Aid is the official soul food drink. It's nourished untold generations of African American children, including yours truly. It's fun, it's easy to make, and it's sugar water. If cups weren't available—which happened a lot in poor households—a washed-out, used jelly jar was a good substitute. What's not to like? Yet, Kool-Aid's liberating, do-it-yourself quality may ultimately be the undoing of powdered drinks. I've asked several in the Millennial Generation (born between 1980 and 2000) how they feel about red Kool-Aid. They tell me that they like it, but it takes too much time to make. They'd rather just grab a soda pop. Put another way, they think of Kool-Aid as "too slow food." I know, I know, that's sacrilege for some.

There is another generational shift currently under way, and it's alarming. Young people under twenty appear to have a pronounced preference for grape Kool-Aid, or "purple drank," as they say. This is really throwing me—because I believe the children are our future, that we should teach them well and let them lead the way. But when it comes to abandoning red Kool-Aid for purple, well, I just don't know.

Of late, people have seemed more interested in eating Kool-Aid than in drinking it. High school kids and younger have something called "Happy Crack." It's Kool-Aid powder mixed with white sugar and then eaten *sans* anything else. No liquid added. *Nada*. In 2007, John T. Edge ignited a wave of curiosity about another trend when he wrote a *New York Times* article on Kool-Aid pickles (or "Koolickles" in some circles) and grossed out half of America. I have had Kool-Aid pickles in the Mississippi Delta, their native habitat. The one I got at Delta Fast Food in Cleveland, Mississippi, wasn't that bad, basically a sweet-and-sour pickle with the sourness hitting you first, followed by that familiar Kool-Aid sweetness. I thought this was a unique phenomenon completely thought up by kids, but it may just be a new twist on something their parents did when they were kids. Several older African Americans remember dipping pickles in Kool-Aid powder and eating it. They also remember sticking a peppermint stick in a pickle's soft center and letting it dissolve, thus creating the same sweet and sour effect. You think that's strange? Just check out some of the weird things that often get served at state fairs, and 2011 was no exception. That year,

Red Drinks Tasting Notes

If you are eating something spicy, I recommend an *agua de Jamaica*, less than a day old with a great body—it's floral and foxy with hints of cranberry.

Barbecue calls for a red drink with a big personality. I suggest the effervescence of a 2013 Big Red soda born from the *terroir* of Waco, Texas. It has the crisp structure of red berries, with undertones of cotton candy.

For anything else, I recommend a 2012 Tropical Punch Kool-Aid. It pleases the eye with hints of seduction. The attack on the nose is vigorous without being overbearing. The true connoisseur doesn't object to the proper sweetness, especially when there is a great aftertaste. Naturally, it must be consumed from a jelly jar.

Charlie Boghosian invented "fried Kool-Aid," which went viral and did a brisk business.[55]

The continuity of red drinks from West Africa swirls full circle with an interesting story of the last Africans who arrived in the American South. In 1860, the slave ship *Clotilda* landed near Mobile, Alabama, with 110 captive West Africans aboard. Stranded in a strange land, they decided to found their own community near Mobile, a place that was eventually called "Africa Town." They held a picnic on New Year's Day 1900 at a place where, "along with the church, the Africans had built a long shed that accommodated a table for picnics."[56] Eva, who grew up in Africa Town, remembers her experience as a little girl: "Everybody who knew the way out to Plateau came for the free picnic. A half cow was cooked all at once, and everything was free. The deacons spent all night making the barbeque. There were two or three hundred pounds of ice in huge pots cooling down a wonderful red drink which was made with fruit and food coloring."[57] In this instance, the African refugees used a red drink to invite, and unite, people inside and outside their community the same way they probably used red drinks in Africa. It was a social occasion, but the red drinks were served to connect them with their new neighbors.

The mention of red drinks will get a knowing nod from most African

Americans, even the ones under the sway of grape drinks. More than any other soft drink, red drinks evoke memories of shared moments with other African Americans. If you're still not convinced about the special role that red drinks have in soul food culture, I'll just have to use a well-worn phrase from the 1990s: It's a black thing, and you wouldn't understand!

Alcenia's Ghetto Aid

While at Alcenia's in Memphis, Tennessee, I couldn't resist ordering the Ghetto Aid. This red drink arrived in a tall, lime-colored glass, putting my eyes on overload. I like that Alcenia's has tried to bridge the generational divide by mixing red and grape Kool-Aid together.

Makes 4 to 6 quarts

> 1 envelope cherry Kool-Aid
> 1 envelope tropical punch Kool-Aid
> 1 envelope grape Kool-Aid
> 4 cups sugar, or to taste
> 4 to 6 quarts water
> Lemon slices, for serving (optional)

1 Empty the Kool-Aid envelopes into a very large pitcher. Add the sugar. Pour in water until the mixture is as sweet and concentrated as you like. Stir until the sugar dissolves. Refrigerate until chilled.
2 Serve over ice with a slice of lemon if you wish.

Hibiscus Aid

Dried hibiscus flowers should be available in your supermarket produce section or at any market catering to a Latino clientele. Showing the association with Latino culture, my grocery store displays them alongside various fresh and dried chillis. This recipe comes courtesy of the College of the Virgin Islands Cooperative Extension Service's cookbook *Native Recipes* that was published in 1978. I made it to the Virgin Islands in 2010 when my twin sister, April, got married there. What a beautiful place! I like this recipe because of the way the tartness of the hibiscus and lime, the spiciness of the ginger, and the sweetener all play off each other.

Makes 2 quarts

> 2 quarts water
> 1 ounce fresh or dried food-grade hibiscus blossoms (about ½ cup)
> 1 ounce fresh ginger, finely chopped (about 2 tablespoons)
> 1 cup sugar, honey, or agave syrup, or to taste
> Juice of 1 fresh lime (about 3 tablespoons)
> ½ to 1 cup of a sweetener (e.g., sugar, honey, agave syrup)
>   depending upon the level of sweetness desired

1 Bring the water to a boil in a medium saucepan. Remove the pan from the heat and add the ginger, hibiscus, and sugar. Stir until the sugar dissolves.
2 Cover and let cool to room temperature. Strain into a large pitcher.
3 Stir in the lime juice and refrigerate until chilled. Serve cold.

14

Give Me Some Sugar

THE GLORY OF SOUL FOOD DESSERTS

A peach cobbler is an inspiration, not an accident. It is a melody, not a tumult. It is a soft zephyr blowing through the peach tree and turning a woman's hand into a deed of grace. Is there too much poetry about that? Well, go and buy a pie for 15 cents at the grocer—your soul was never built for peach cobbler.—"Peach Cobblers," *State*, 10 July 1908

Sweet potato pies, a good friend of mine asked recently, "Do they taste anything like pumpkin?" Negative. They taste more like memory, if you're not uptown.—LeRoi Jones, *Home*, 1966

★   ★   ★   ★   ★

"Come over here and give me some sugar!" I heard that a lot during my childhood, mainly on our family summer trips to Chattanooga, Tennessee—my mother's hometown. That's how southerners let shy kids like me know that they wanted a kiss, regardless of whether I wanted to give one or not. I don't hear that expression very often now that I'm grown and live outside of the South. Yet I remember that hearing those words and feeling the kisses and hugs that ensued were the appetizer for a long afternoon or evening of adults socializing, kids playing, and everyone eating. There was always the long table covered with myriad soul food specialties, and next to that was a separate table, beckoning me with not one but several desserts.

When I talk soul food with others, it's the desserts that evoke the deepest sighs and the most wistful looks off into the distance, as if those reminiscing were literally *eating* nostalgia. It's an interesting historical twist because "dessert" is the most foreign concept on the soul food plate. Before European colonization, West Africans didn't have dessert—a composed sweet course to end the sequence of an otherwise savory meal. If desired, one could eat a piece of fruit. During the slave trade period, however, African Americans began to develop and include sweet dishes in their meals. For slaves in the antebellum South, "dessert" was typically a piece of cornbread doused with molasses or sorghum or a piece of fruit. Specifically composed desserts were prepared by enslaved cooks in the Big House, and eventually in slave quarters on weekends and holidays. As with other foods, African Americans soon earned a reputation for being adept dessert makers, and many have used their skill to make a living.

Pam Wright belongs to this group, and she knows how effectively dessert pairs with nostalgia. Self-described as "The Cobbler Lady," Wright runs the "Cobblers, Cakes and Cream" dessert-and-coffee shop in Los Angeles. Many a passerby pauses as Wright makes cobblers in the shop's window. Some tell their children, "See, she's over there making the cobblers your grandmother used to make." Others just stare. Take, for instance, the older white guy who would just come by every day like clockwork to watch her practice her craft. One day he came into the store and professed that after watching her for the umpteenth time, "I've been transported to my mother's kitchen." Riffing off LeRoi Jones's quote above, that's memory talking.

Today, no soul food gathering would be right without several dessert offerings, and it's hard to focus on just one. As food writer Shaun Chavis put it, "I know everyone's family did this on holidays: You don't pick one. You get a 'dessert plate' with a little slice of everything."[1] That's exactly how I'm going to handle this desserts chapter. Rather than gorge on the history of one particular dessert, we're going to taste a select few. If the Soul Food Hall of Fame has a dessert category, its first induction class would be banana pudding, peach cobbler, pound cake, and sweet potato pie. Though they took unique paths to the soul food plate, these disparate desserts have more in common than you think. All share a British heritage, a strong association with slavery, and a change in status from luxury item to convenience food.

Peaches, like so many other things in this meal, began as rich people's food. Legendary nineteenth-century French chef Alexis Soyer tells us that peaches, the fruit of the peach tree (Prunus persica), were "still quite a novelty in Rome towards the middle of the 1st century of the Christian era, and the rich alone could eat peaches."[2] Believed to be native to portions of China and Tibet, the peach tree is remarkably adaptive and thrives in any temperate climate that has a cold enough winter.[3] For this reason, peach trees were never extensive in tropical areas like West Africa, and most of the enslaved got their first look at and taste of peaches in the Americas.

The Spanish introduced peach trees in several parts of North America in the 1500s, but it was Native Americans who quickly embraced its fruit and planted peach trees throughout the South.[4] By the time enslaved West Africans arrived, peach trees were a frequent part of the rural South's landscape, and their fruit was used extensively. As food historian Sandy Oliver observes, "Peaches were among the most common stone fruits grown in early America. . . . Along with apple trees, a peach orchard provided evidence of an established homestead for claim purposes. Peaches were eaten fresh, were used in pies and other sweet dishes, and often were preserved as wet sweetmeats."[5] Given their ubiquity, peaches were also a cheap source of food for slaves and plantation hogs.[6] "Uncle" Henry Barnes recalls, "Us had a big orchard wid apples an' peaches an' pears, more 'n us an' de hawgs togedder could eat up."[7] Barnes's experience mirrors that of slaves across the region. Despite its strong association as both slave and animal food, the peach was not condemned to a low social status. Peaches were enjoyed by all classes of people.

Of the various confections made with peaches, peach cobbler has long been beloved. Writing in 1897, Louis Hughes best captures peach cobbler sentiment with this vivid memory of an antebellum Fourth of July barbecue near Charlottesville, Virginia:

Not far from this trench were the iron ovens, where the sweetmeats were cooked. Three or four women were assigned to this work. Peach cobbler and apple dumpling were the two dishes that made old slaves smile for joy and the young fairly dance. The crust or pastry of the cobbler was prepared in large earthen bowls, then rolled out like any pie crust, only it was almost twice as thick. A layer of this crust was laid in the oven, then a half peck of peaches poured in, followed by a layer of sugar; then a covering of pastry was laid over all and smoothed around with a knife. The oven was then put over a bed of coals, the cover put on and coals thrown on it, and the process of baking began. Four of these ovens were usually in use at these feasts, so that enough of the pastry might be baked to supply all. The ovens were filled and refilled until there was no doubt about the quantity.[8]

Convenience Pies

COBBLERS AND THEIR CULINARY KIN

A wide variety of easy-to-make pielike desserts emerged in the eighteenth and nineteenth centuries. They often had fanciful names and strong regional affinities. Karen Barker, pastry chef extraordinaire at the Magnolia Grill in Durham, North Carolina, provides a good summary in her book *Sweet Stuff*.

There are some regional differences in exact definitions, but in general *cobblers* are baked fruit topped with a pastry or biscuit crust. If it's a pastry crust, the dessert is sometimes called a *deep-dish pie*. Occasionally you will see cobblers with a bottom crust as well. *Crisps* fall into the category of fruit baked with a crumb topping (usually made from butter, flour, sugar, and, at times, nuts). If buttered, sweetened breadcrumbs are used, the dessert becomes a *betty*. *Crunches* and *crumbles* are closely related and usually contain oats. If you have a cake base that's topped with fruit and then covered with a layer of crumbs, you wind up with a *buckle*. *Grunts* and *slumps* are topped with steamed biscuits or dumplings and are cooked covered, on top of the range.[1]

Though different from cobblers, fried pies were also a popular and convenient dessert. Typically, a small amount of pastry was filled with preserved fruit, folded in half, pinched to seal off the edges, fried, and then sugared to taste. Though fried pies originated in medieval Europe and not in soul food culture, they are a popular dessert with African Americans.

---

1 Barker, *Sweet Stuff*, 125

Hughes gives us a good sense of why cobblers were so popular, particularly for events with large crowds: The filling could be made with varying types of fruit; it requires little preparation; its ingredients aren't measured precisely, as is necessary for a cake or pie; like a banana pudding, cobbler has a simple layering formula; and, most importantly, a cobbler can be stretched to fill the space of whatever container the cook has available, provided enough fruit and piecrust are on hand. In many instances, cooks only prepared a top crust so they could stretch the dessert and prepare more cobblers with a lot more fruit and with less flour.

How peach cobbler got its name is a mystery. The earliest definitions for the word "cobbler" applied to a type of alcoholic drink. It wasn't until the mid-1800s that "cobbler" was used to describe a particular type of dessert. Soon after its "invention," cobbler became a popular dessert and appeared in the earliest African American cookbooks. Mrs. Russell and Mrs. Hayes have recipes for a peach cobbler, and Mrs. Fisher has one for a peach pie (no top crust). Mrs. Russell's recipe is a very traditional, two-crust approach instructing the cook to stew some sweetened peaches, pour them into a pan lined with piecrust, cover with another piecrust, and bake.[9] Mrs. Hayes, on the other hand, has the cook mix up a batter, which is then poured over sweetened, sliced peaches; then the mixture is baked.[10] Many soul food cooks will recognize the Hayes method as something often called "miracle pie." Thus, a legitimate peach cobbler could appear in three forms: one piecrust under the filling, a filling enveloped by two crusts, or a batter poured over the filling that forms a top crust while baking.

If peach cobbler ever had a reputation of being reserved for society's upper crust, it was gone by the beginning of the twentieth century. Peaches became more widely available because more people took up peach farming in the latter half of the nineteenth century. For those who couldn't get fresh peaches, significant advances in canning technology transformed peaches from a seasonal summer fruit into an inexpensive fruit that was available year-round. Given these developments, home economists were touting peach cobbler in newspapers like the *Kansas City Negro Star* as an affordable way "to make a few peaches go as far as possible."[11] A little more than a decade later, DeKnight's *Date with a Dish* (1948) also emphasized the cobbler's staying power: "Deep dish cobblers are country favorites. When all else in desserts fail, the unforgettable cobbler takes a bow. When sugar was scarce and pennies low, maple syrup and even molasses made delightful eating added to apples which were topped with a crunchy, flaky crust."[12]

Despite its apparent simplicity, some cobbler cooks have created their own strict code for correctly making a cobbler. I return to Pam Wright, "The Cobbler Lady" in Los Angeles. During Wright's childhood, her mother occasionally made peach cobbler. Wright loved cobblers so much that, while still a little girl, she began experimenting with making them and continued to hone the art. As an adult, she decided to dive full in and

Pear cobbler, "The Cobbler Lady," Los Angeles

turn the hobby into a business. She opened up her own place in 1989. According to Wright, a good peach cobbler is not overspiced (i.e., too much nutmeg) or overly sweet (i.e., too much added sugar or peach syrup from the can). Wright uses canned peaches because her business has such high volume that she can't risk the inconsistency that comes with using fresh or frozen peaches. In her words, "It would take too long to get the taste right." Wright belongs to the top-crust-only cohort of cobbler makers. A bottom crust absorbs too much of the cobbler's juice, and without a good amount of juice, cobbler becomes a pie. I've had plenty of top-notch, juicy cobblers that did have a bottom crust. So alas, the worthiness of a bottom crust seems a matter of personal preference. Wright even conceded that some cooks love crust so much that they add a middle layer of it to their cobblers "to get a dumpling effect."

Peach cobbler is celebrated as a source of comfort, but it can also cause consternation. Wright no longer offers a frozen, take-home, bake-it-yourself cobbler. "The customers were scared that they would somehow mess it up," Wright told me. "One young woman asked me, 'Do I take the top off of it?' in order to cook it!" I was so taken aback by this story that, despite the risk of being politically incorrect, I had to ask if the woman in question was African American. She was. Sigh.[13] I know it's just one example, but it may be an indicator of just how much home cooking has declined. Though sad news for me, it's good news for entrepreneurs like Wright who are maintaining a tradition and sharing it with others. However, I do hope more people will get in their own kitchen and make cobbler. It's as easy as pie.

Banana pudding inspires shouts of joy at the mere mention of its name. Since the nineteenth century, it has become easier for the home cook to prepare. Like the cobbler, it journeyed from elite homes to those of working families and went from requiring careful preparation to becoming a quick convenience food. Banana pudding didn't appear on American tables regularly until the decades after the Civil War. Scattered slave testimony describes eating bananas on the plantation, usually around Christmas, but it wasn't a widespread practice. At the time, only wealthy people in the United States enjoyed the privilege of eating banana pudding, because bananas themselves were a luxury item. Bananas are native to South Asia and, by the time of the Atlantic slave trade, were well established in West Africa. European slavers figured out that the fruit was a great food source for their human captives; they used bananas to provision their slave ships and Caribbean plantations whenever and wherever the plants could grow. Since bananas were cheap in that region, British Caribbean cooks experimented with putting bananas in their traditional desserts at a much earlier date than those in British North America. The British trifle was one such dessert that got a makeover.

Banana pudding's acknowledged immediate ancestor is the British trifle—a dessert in which a bread element (cake, shredded bread, or cookies) was covered with a boiled custard and then topped off with a meringue. Trifles were commonplace in American and southern cookbooks, and we find one in Malinda Russell's cookbook called a "Boiled Trifle." It includes a rich custard seasoned with cinnamon or lemon peel poured over brandy-soaked sponge cakes. Caroline Sullivan's *The Jamaican Cook Book* (1893) has three different recipes for banana pudding. Though the dessert has variables—its base could be a cake or shredded bread and the topping could be a meringue or whipped cream—custard and sliced bananas are constants.[14]

By the twentieth century, home economists were positioning banana pudding as an economical dessert using leftover bread or cake as the base. What really made the dessert inexpensive was the stunning success of commercial banana growers, importers, and transportation magnates who flooded the U.S. market with cheap bananas. The earliest known recipe in an African American cookbook for something akin to a banana pudding shows up in the *Montana Federation of Negro Women's Clubs Cook Book* (1927) as a "banana cream pie." The recipe, submitted by Mrs. Chas. L. Evans of Kalispell, Montana, goes,

> Slice two bananas into a baked pie crust and cover with the following cream: 2 cups milk, yolks of 2 eggs, 1 scant cup sugar, 1 tablespoon flour or cornstarch, dissolved in 2 tablespoons of milk[.] Cook until thick, flavor with vanilla. Cool and pour over bananas. Make a meringue of the egg whites and 2 tablespoons powdered sugar, put over pie and brown in the oven.[15]

Since this auspicious beginning, the recipe for banana pudding has undergone few structural changes. But how ingredients were sourced changed quite a bit. First off, within a couple of decades of Mrs. Evans's recipe getting printed, vanilla wafer cookies had become the standard bread element for banana pudding. No more need to make a cake or shred some bread. Also, more home cooks can prepare it and serve it cold now that refrigerators are widely available. The biggest change, however, is that one no longer needs to go through the trouble of making a custard for filling and whipping up cream or a meringue as a topping. The home cook can purchase a package of banana-flavored instant pudding mix and a container of already-whipped cream that will do the trick. The downside is that using commercially prepared pudding, wafers, and whipped cream means that probably more sugar, salt, and artificial ingredients are added to the dessert. This is a trade-off that many home cooks have been willing to make. In order for banana pudding to remain a regular part of the soul foodie's repertoire, it had to become more convenient to make.

By the turn of the twentieth century, pie was the most popular dessert in the United States. If Janet Jackson had been alive and writing songs at the time, she would have declared, "We are a slice of the Pie Nation."[16] As one authority wrote in 1901, "Pie is eaten mainly by the native population. Foreigners eat very little of it. . . . The area of greatest consumption is in New England and the Middle States, though pie is eaten extensively all through the West. Pie is eaten much more commonly in the North than in the South."[17]

Thus, we see that even "Pie Nation" was divided along geographic lines, like most things in the latter nineteenth century. The *Ladies' Home Journal* explained in 1891 that we couldn't even agree on what to call a pie. "At the South, any dessert made of eggs, butter, sugar and milk, cooked in paste, with one crust, is known as a 'pudding.' At the North a similar compound with like ingredients, baked in the same way, is by the rank and file, commonly called 'pie.'"[18] We should cut southerners some slack here because they were merely following the example set forth by their British ancestors, who have been eating pie but calling it "pudding" since the time of Queen Elizabeth I.[19]

According to culinary historian William Woys Weaver, "The word *pie* derives from the medieval Latin words *petia* or *pecia* and referred to 'a morsel which could be eaten with the fingers and which also contained some type of filling'—in short, a pastry envelope."[20] Before the Brits got to pies, though, there was pudding—a savory combination of meat, grains, and spices placed inside animal parts that served as containers (e.g., a stomach or intestines) and boiled in water. Sometime during the sixteenth century, someone invented pudding cloth, which made the dish much easier to cook, since animal parts, which were only available seasonally during slaughtering times, were no longer necessary. Pudding eating proliferated as a result, and cooks sought new ways to make the dish besides the usual boiling. That led to the culinary innovation in which "the baking dish was lined with a thin sheet of pastry before the pudding mixture went into it." In other words, they came up with pie, though it was often called "baked pudding."[21] Like pudding, the earliest pies were savory, but sweet pies came into vogue soon afterward.

The transition from pudding to pie happened during the sixteenth century, around the same time that sweet potatoes were being introduced into Britain as an exotic import from the Americas via Spain. That's why sweet potatoes were often called Spanish potatoes in the cookbooks of that era. Whatever name given them, sweet potatoes were a luxury item in Britain well into the seventeenth century. Any savory or sweet dish containing sweet potatoes was considered rich people's food.

Sweet potato pie arrived in America as an upper-class English dessert, and it immediately took its place in upper-class colonial kitchens. In 1756, South Carolina's renowned matriarch Eliza Lucas Pinckney, for example, had a "Yam Puding" recipe in her manuscript cookbook.[22] There's much more evidence that it was regularly eaten in the Big House—*The Virginia Housewife*, *The Kentucky Housewife*, and *The Carolina Housewife* all have recipes for sweet potato pudding, sweet potato pie, or both—all tracing a direct heritage from the Elizabethan Age kitchens of Hannah Glasse and her contemporaries.[23] In these wealthy kitchens, enslaved and free African American cooks learned the art of making sweet potato pie. For all of its popularity in the Big House, it's difficult to gauge where sweet potato pie ranked in the slave quarters. Emma Vergil of Athens, Georgia, gave the only explicit sweet potato pie reference in the FWP interviews, and she described it as the finale of a post-cornshucking meal.[24]

After Emancipation, African American cooks embraced two versions of sweet potato pie. Malinda Russell's pie is made of sweet potatoes sliced lengthwise and moistened with water, brandy, vinegar, and lemon juice. It mimicked her apple pie's spicing and use of two crusts. George Washington Carver, the famous scientist, was a big proponent of this pie, and he revived its popularity by including its recipe in his widely read agricultural bulletins of the 1930s. Over the next several decades, sliced sweet potato pies became a rarer sight in cookbooks and restaurants. If you're like I was before I started writing this book, you've probably never eaten or heard of one. Of the two, the custard-style pie enriched with eggs and milk or cream has endured as the most popular option. Abby Fisher's 1881 cookbook has a recipe that would be at home in any of today's soul food kitchens. In 1948, Freda DeKnight's cookbook *A Date with a Dish* offered up three versions of custard-style sweet potato pie.[25]

Innumerable cooks can say that their sweet potato pie artistry earned them a great reputation, and possibly a good living, but how many can say that their sweet potato pie helped others earn an education? Dr. Mary McLeod Bethune (1857–1955) is the only one who comes to my mind. Bethune was an extraordinary woman who founded the Daytona Educational and Industrial Training School for Negro Girls in Daytona Beach, Florida, in 1904. Dr. Dorothy Height, longtime head of the National Council of Negro Women, once said, "I loved to hear Mary McLeod Bethune tell the story of the school she founded in 1904 with five little girls, $150 and faith in God. Times were hard. When she needed money to keep the school doors open, Mrs. Bethune would bake and sell sweet potato pies." Bethune could often be seen bicycling in the mornings to nearby resort towns in order to sell her pies to an extensive white clientele. Since Bethune left us long ago, we can no longer taste those sweet potato pies, but we can bear witness to their legacy. Bethune was the first "African-American, or woman of any race, to be honored in a monument in a public park in the Nation's Capitol [sic]—The Bethune Memorial in Lincoln Park."[26] Yet the most enduring monument to Dr. Bethune and her sweet potato pies is the fact that that little school she founded has become Bethune Cookman University, which continues to educate scores of young people.

Pound cake gives us a good, sugary finish to this chapter. Though it doesn't follow the slave-food-cum-special-occasion-food narrative, per-haps no dish better captures the soul food ethos. Cake connoisseur Warren Brown, known for his Cakelove bakeries in the Washington, D.C., area, his cake cookbooks, and his Food Network TV show *Sugar Rush*, puts it best: "Pound cake is one of my favorite cakes to bake and eat. It's versatile and easy to mix, lasts a long time, and goes with just about anything."[27] To use a well-worn analogy, pound cake is the soul food dessert equivalent of a black dress.

The earliest pound cakes in America were essentially fruitless versions of the venerable "plum cakes" popular in seventeenth- and eighteenth-century British kitchens.[28] British food historian Anne Wilson writes, "A typical recipe gives as ingredients fourteen pounds of flour, three of but-ter, one and a half of sugar and some spices."[29] Along with some yeast, several pounds of fruit (or seeds to "seed cake") were added before final baking. By the eighteenth century, cooks had traded in the yeast to make a richer cake with eggs as the leavening agent. These "rich cakes" are pro-genitors of the pound cakes we know and love today.

During slavery, pound cakes were high up on the cake pedestal. Nellie Smith, formerly enslaved in Georgia, recalled, "Why, Child, two of the best cake-makers I ever knew used them old ovens for bakin' the finest kinds of pound cakes and fruit cakes, and everybody knows them cakes was the hardest kinds to bake we had in them days."[30] Gus Smith, formerly enslaved in Missouri, exclaimed, "My! women in those days could cook. Great big 'pound cakes' a foot and a half high. You don't see such things now-a-days."[31] During the Slave Food era, pound cakes were devoured at lavish plantation weddings by the planter's family and slaves alike. Smity Hodges of Mississippi remembered, "When Miss July got mar'ied dey had two cooks de kitchen makin' pound cake for more'n a week."[32] Not every-one was thrilled about wedding pound cake. Sylvia Durant of South Caro-lina said of her own postslavery experience, "I was married over dere in Bethel M.E. Church en served a little cake and wine dere home afterwards en dat ain' no weddin. Didn't have nothing but pound cake en wine."[33]

By the twentieth century, pound cakes had lost some luster and were considered a simpler, less expensive cake to prepare than they were in years past. Yet, that didn't mean that pound cakes weren't prized. "There is *always* a pound cake on church and birthday buffets," asserted Ruth Gaskins in her 1969 book, *A Good Heart and a Light Hand*. Edna Lewis ex-plained its ubiquity in *The Taste of Country Cooking*: "The keeping quality of pound cake made it a popular favorite, plus the fact that the main ingredients were always available: butter, eggs, and flour. I learned that the formula for a good pound cake is a slow oven, cold butter, carefully measured flour (too much flour will cause the cake to crack on top), and proper mixing of butter, sugar and eggs."[34] Because of their "keeping quality," pound cakes could be prepared on Sunday and kept through the week in case unexpected company dropped in. For the same reason, and because they didn't need a frosting, pound cakes were also great for long trips or for sending overseas to homesick soldiers. Within a half-century, pound cakes went from special occasion food to an immensely practical treat.

Thanks to the technological advances of mixers, soul food cooks often stress the pound cake's simplicity. Again, I think Warren Brown channels the general consensus on why we have such warm feelings about this particular dessert. "Pound cake was my starter cake. I found the county fair–winning recipe published in the local newspaper and went for it. . . . Whenever I teach a class, I always fall back on the pound cake because it's almost foolproof, the ingredients are readily available, and it bakes evenly (especially in a Bundt pan). I also like it because once it's out of the oven, it can be served plain or with minimal finishing touches."[35] Speaking of channeling, when I hear Warren Brown's story, I feel I'm connecting with a kindred spirit. Brown was a lawyer for the inspector general's office of the U.S. Department of Health and Human Services who left litigation in 2000 to embark on an eventually successful career making layer cakes and other delicious items. Back when I was a litigator, I too felt the siren call of a food career, which at the time I interpreted as opening up a soul food restaurant. Unlike Brown, I didn't immediately take that path. As such, I endured by singing spirituals in my law firm office until I finally got a change of venue.

Back to pound cake because something kept bugging me. I couldn't understand why so many people stake their cooking prowess on their pound cake if it's so simple. I "tweeted" this burning question out on social media, and "Sir_Geechie" Jamara Newell put things together. Newell answered, "Being that it [has] such a neutral flavor even minor distinctions in technique and ingredient can make a noticeable difference."[36] A Holly Hobbie baking oven lightbulb lit up over my head. Instead of having to meet a high standard, pound cake should be properly viewed as the cake standard, comparable to a jazz standard. With many great jazz singers, it was less about creating new songs than about what they brought to a known lyric or melody and how they put their spin on it. Pound cake gives bakers more room to highlight their skill in a way that other cooks can't match. As cake expert Maida Heatter wrote in of one of her pound cake recipes, "Although I think this is easy, you can spoil it, easily, by under-beating the eggs at the beginning and/or overbeating after adding the butter and flour. So be careful. Good luck."[37] So the cook is forewarned. Just as it is possible for a jazz singer to make a mess of even a reliable standard—say by improvising a song to the point of cacophony—a baker must tread carefully and avoid putting too much spin on a pound cake.

Speaking of spin, these classic soul food desserts reverse the old adage that reflects the prevailing attitude on soul food: "One man's garbage is another man's treasure." They began as high-end dishes in Elizabethan England's royal kitchens (sweet potato pie), in antebellum Big Houses (peach cobbler and pound cake), and in urban American hotels and restaurants during the Southern Cooking era (banana pudding). African American cooks took what they learned in wealthy white kitchens and incorporated these desserts into the soul food tradition. As African Americans prospered, cooks embraced all of the innovations that made dessert-making easier (electric appliances, commercial mixes, premade pastry shells, etc.), particularly for the preparation of Sunday dinner. With the decline of home cooking, it's much easier today to purchase an already-made confection than to prepare one from scratch. Eating peach cobbler, banana pudding, sweet potato pie, and pound cake won't soon become a memory, but the joy of making these desserts from scratch probably will become rarer.

Banana Pudding

My mom's banana pudding recipe embraces the old and the new. It's got an old-fashioned custard to bring the main ingredients together and a homemade meringue to top it all off. Instead of making the bread component from scratch, I use vanilla wafer cookies. This is a very sweet dessert and a definite crowd-pleaser.

Makes 12 servings

PUDDING
   1 cup sugar
   ½ cup all-purpose flour
   ½ teaspoon salt

4 cups whole milk

4 large egg yolks

2 teaspoons pure vanilla extract

6 small, ripe, firm bananas, cut into thin rounds (about 6 cups)

8 ounces vanilla wafers (about 60 cookies)

MERINGUE

4 large egg whites

½ teaspoon cream of tartar

½ cup sugar

1 For the pudding: In a large, heavy saucepan or in the top of a double boiler, whisk together the sugar, flour, and salt. (If using a double boiler, fill the bottom about one-third full of water and bring to a simmer.)

2 Whisking continuously, add the milk in a slow, steady stream, whisking until smooth. Whisk in the egg yolks. Cook over medium heat, stirring continuously with a heatproof spatula, until the mixture thickens to the consistency of thick pudding, about 15 minutes. Remove the pan from the heat and stir in the vanilla.

3 Line the bottom of a large glass baking dish with vanilla wafers. Top with a layer of banana slices. Pour a thin layer of custard over the bananas, spreading it with the spatula. Repeat the layers until you have used all of the remaining ingredients, ending with a top layer of custard.

4 For the meringue: Preheat the oven to 350°F. Place the egg whites and cream of tartar in a clean, dry, spotless metal or glass bowl. Beat with an electric mixer set to high speed until the whites begin to hold soft peaks. With the mixer running, add the sugar in a slow, steady stream. Continue beating until the whites are glossy and hold stiff peaks. Spoon the meringue over the warm pudding, making sure it touches the edges of the baking dish. Use the back of the spoon to make a pretty design in the meringue.

5 Bake until the tips of the meringue are golden brown, about 15 minutes.

6 Let cool for 15 minutes and then refrigerate until the pudding is chilled. Serve cold.

Summer Peach Crisp

This is a riff on a peach cobbler that I found while flipping through the National Cancer Institute's 1995 publication *Down Home Healthy Cookin': Recipes and Healthy Cooking Tips*. The tartness of the berries complements the vivid sweetness of the peaches. For more reinterpretations of soul food classics, visit the NCI website at www.cancer.gov.

Makes 6 servings

FILLING

    ½ cup granulated sugar
    3 tablespoons all-purpose flour
    1 teaspoon grated lemon peel
    4 cups peaches (fresh or unsweetened frozen)
    1 cup blueberries or blackberries (fresh or unsweetened frozen)

TOPPING

    ⅔ cup rolled oats
    ⅓ cup packed brown sugar
    ¼ cup whole wheat flour
    2 teaspoons ground cinnamon
    3 tablespoons soft margarine, melted

    If using frozen fruit, make sure that it is completely thawed, but don't drain the juice.

1   In a medium bowl, combine sugar, flour, and lemon peel; mix well.
2   Add peaches and berries; stir to mix.
3   Spoon into a 6-cup baking dish.
4   In a small bowl, combine oats, brown sugar, flour, and cinnamon.
5   Add melted margarine; stir to mix.
6   Sprinkle topping over filling.
7   Bake in a 375°F oven for 40 to 50 minutes or until filling is bubbly and top is brown.
8   Serve warm or at room temperature.

Whither Soul Food?

"Southern cooking is about to become extinct. . . . It's mostly black, because blacks—black women and black men—did most of the cooking in private homes, hotels and on the railroads. So the tradition carried on until the Depression." Fast food, industrialization and the migration to Northern cities helped speed its demise. —Edna Lewis

★　★　★　★　★

It's time to revive soul food, before it's too late. When Edna Lewis worried aloud about southern cooking becoming extinct, one of the things foremost on her mind was the fading significance of black cooks who practiced that cuisine. The same dynamic now challenges soul food. Without more home cooks and professional chefs among the cuisine's devotees, more restaurants showcasing this particular culinary art, and a shift in perception, soul food's days as a culturally relevant cuisine are numbered.

Chef Joe Randall, who runs the Savannah Cooking School, gives some historical perspective on the challenges in recruiting professional chefs: "With the passage of the 1964 Civil Rights Act, civil rights leaders said, 'We no longer have to cook in your kitchens because it opened up other opportunities. [Today,] black chefs are afraid that they will be considered less than professional if they are associated with soul food. They want to be a chef who "happens to be black."' If they were Austrian, they wouldn't deny being Austrian to be a chef."[1]

Chef Randall hopes to attract more African Americans back to the kitchen with the Edna Lewis Foundation he founded and based in Atlanta, Georgia. "The Foundation is dedicated to honoring, preserving and nurturing African Americans' culinary heritage and culture," said Randall, "and to elevating the appreciation of our culinary excellence." With a variety of programming and events, Randall hopes that the foundation will give African American chefs the well-deserved recognition they've sorely lacked. A wide variety of African American heritage cooking will be celebrated by the foundation, with soul food being just one of those traditions.

As more African Americans enter the culinary field, they'll need places to cook. That won't happen without a rejuvenated soul food restaurant culture that gives birth to thriving places more likely to have an afterlife beyond their original owners. However, opening up a restaurant is not as easy as it once was, particularly due to high start-up costs. Chef Randall estimates that it takes $2 million to $3 million to open up and operate a nice restaurant these days. African Americans have long had difficulty getting enough capital to open any kind of business, and restaurant financing is even more elusive, given the high-risk nature of the industry. In the past, soul food restaurants sprouted up and stayed where their operating costs were low, and that usually meant the poorest parts of town. The lack of financing also explains in part why soul food has rarely left urban black neighborhoods. Yet, there are some bright signs.

After eating my way across the country, it's clear to me that soul food's creative energy burns brightest in the restaurants that are targeting an upscale, vegetarian or vegan clientele. This new breed of restaurateurs is playing off the soul food moniker or they're abandoning it altogether, calling themselves Down Home Healthy, Neo-Soul, Vegan Soul, or southern cooking. This trend makes sense to Chef Nyesha Arrington of the Wilshire Restaurant in Santa Monica, California, who tells me, "I see the lines between cuisines are being blurred. Chefs are adapting and changing styles in terms of eating habits. People are not going for butter, fat, deep frying for flavor, so I'm not surprised that soul food is going to be healthier." Even with the adaptation to current trends, Chef Arrington adds that she hasn't abandoned the home cooking vibe. "When someone comes into my restaurant, I will make a well-executed, delicious dish. I cook to give a family-style experience which is really soulful. I want the atmosphere to be comfortable, unpretentious, like being at home. I want them to feel excitement."[2] In an interesting twist, southern cooking is no longer code for poor, rural cooking as it was a century ago. Now, southern cooking is an invitation for chefs of any background to borrow, experiment, fuse, rediscover, and reinterpret the region's varied ingredients, techniques, and traditions . . . all the while charging a premium for the excitement they create.

Speaking of excitement, Chef Marcus Samuelsson generated a lot of it in December 2010 when he opened Red Rooster Restaurant in Harlem. Born in Ethiopia and adopted and raised by Swedish parents, Samuelsson has an interesting mission. When I asked him to define soul food,

Chef Samuelsson said, "Comfort food has been around longer than soul food, and it's not defined as much by geography the way that southern food and soul food are aligned. We offer comfort food through the lens of Harlem, and pay homage to the comfort food of all the ethnicities that make up Harlem today, from our Latin immigrants to our West African community."

Chef Samuelsson lays out a possible road map when he says of soul food's future, "Like many cuisines, I think its number of platforms will increase with time. As American African heritage gets more diverse, I think there will be more and more takes on 'soul food,' such as health-focused soul food, high end soul food, fast-casual soul food concepts, and more." At his Red Rooster restaurant in Harlem, Chef Samuelsson's vision is reflected in a menu that caters to several tastes while remaining in a particular culinary framework. He tells me that the Red Rooster's most popular items are "Helga's Meatballs, a Swedish comfort food that I named in homage to my Grandmother." Other popular menu items are "traditional Southern comfort food, like our Fried Yard Bird and Corn Bread. Also, dishes like the Snapper, which reflect Harlem's West African immigrants; and the Fish Taquitos, which are a nod to our Latin American community."[3] Samuelsson's perspective shows us that soul food need not be abandoned. Soul food can be featured on menus as part of a culinary continuum presented to diners, while its uniqueness remains preserved.

There are some who feel that soul food is diminished in profile only because no one has really gone "big" with a national soul food franchise. Jamawn Woods tried to do so with the "Soul Daddy" healthy soul food concept on *America's Next Great Restaurant*, but it didn't fly. Still, Michael Moore of Glory Foods says, "I've wondered why there isn't a national soul food chain, fast food or medium like the Olive Garden. It celebrates Italian cuisine, and a soul food place could have a similar footprint. Cracker Barrel is totally southern and southern food is seasoned a little different [than soul food is]. There is some overlap, but southern food is usually a bland experience. When you go to Paschal's [in Atlanta] you know you're going to get well-seasoned food." Someone just might pull off a national soul food chain, but Moore thinks the effort will need savvy marketing, and possibly a name change. "Soul food still scares people for whatever reason. White Americans are not comfortable with that term. We can maintain the integrity of soul food, but it needs to be packaged a certain way. Soul food can exist anywhere in the same sense that Chinese food does."[4]

Across the Atlantic Ocean, Charita "Momma Cherri" Jones has been thinking along the same lines. Momma Cherri, who once operated a popular soul food restaurant in England (and hopes to again sometime in the future) thinks franchising should be the goal. She tells me passionately, "Soul Food needs to hit the world on a large scale, with financial backing. The beauty of it is that the ingredients aren't expensive and because of the history attached to it could be a 'win-win' situation for all. After all everyone loves fried chicken, ribs, sweet potatoes and with the imagination of the talented chefs of today, a soul food menu could be endless, just as long as you put your heart and soul into each and every dish."[5]

The international prospects for soul food got me thinking whimsically about its intergalactic prospects. Why should I limit soul food's future to our planet? After all, the National Aeronautics and Space Administration (NASA) isn't. In 2012, NASA announced a project to run a controlled simulation of life on Mars in which six selected volunteers would help determine the best food to feed astronauts on an extended Mars mission.[6] I do hope that a soul foodie made the short list; otherwise the cuisine will be woefully underrepresented on Martian menus. That would be a shame because astronauts should be primed for a soul food experience in space. They've been dousing Louisiana-style hot sauce on space food for decades (evidently it was the only way to give the food some taste). NASA scientists are also wise to the fact that the sweet potato has long proved its mettle in World War II as a provision that can be dehydrated and reconstituted to great effect, making it a perfect food for the nine-month trip from Earth to Mars. Lastly, what else could be more appropriate for the Red Planet than a steady flow of one of soul food's traditional red drinks?

Thinking big about soul food's prospects seems futile at a time when so many folks think so little of this cuisine. More of us need to shed soul food's negative associations and learn its history, in order to appreciate it. Chef Szathmary's Theory of Special Edibility from Chapter 1 helps us do so. He argued that when ethnic groups migrate to the United States, the festive foods of their former homeland become more commonplace in their adopted country. For the most part, the development of African American cuisine fits the theory. The festive foods established during the Slave Food period—much of it in high-end cooking—persisted through the Southern Cooking and Down Home Cooking eras to become the most identifiable aspects of what we now call soul food. When proponents and critics of soul food emphasize its slavery and poverty background, they obscure the cuisine's high-class pedigree.

Enslaved West Africans certainly tried to reconstruct their foodways under the strictures of America's slave society. They grew familiar foods in their private gardens with varying success (true yams and black-eyed peas), raised animals like the ones back home (chickens and goats), and substituted New World foods that tasted enough like the foods they remembered (mud-dwelling fish, bitter greens, sweet potatoes, cornbread, and chillis). As a common culture was forged during slavery, a common cuisine emerged as well. Earlier, I called this emergent cuisine Slave Food—a misnomer, given that whites ate many of the same foods in the Big House and rural cabins.

As the cuisine of enslaved people changed, their festive foods changed as well. West African religious meaning given to certain foods (chickens and red drinks) diminished to the point where the food retained a vague association with special days. Because whites so outnumbered blacks in British North America, European American cultural norms gave little space for West African culture to thrive except in limited situations. While holding onto their own beliefs, the enslaved borrowed ideas and traditions from the whites and Native Americans they encountered. In some instances, the enslaved adopted European notions of good food (candied yams, pound cake, and sweet potato pie); revived West African food beliefs using new ingredients (chitlins retaining the life force of the animal); or created new traditions using old, familiar ingredients (catfish at the fish fry and black-eyed peas on New Year's Day).

After Emancipation, agriculture and the black church's events set the social calendar in the rural South. Not by coincidence, most special occasions happened in the fall and early winter when the agricultural work associated with the harvest was over. Almost every single food in our representative meal was available around that time of year. The festive nature of these foods was further enhanced because they were so labor-intensive to prepare: Corn had to be shucked, catfish had to be skinned, greens had to be stripped from the stalk, hogs had to be killed, chitlins had to be cleaned, and everything had to be expertly cooked. That was life in the rural South, a life tied to the seasons.

Once black migrants in urban areas prospered, an increasingly industrial food system changed their foods and food choices in significant ways. Whether from a street vendor or at a grocery store or a restaurant, their favorite southern foods were now available outside the South. Black-eyed peas were easier to farm, dry, and ship nationwide than other southern beans. Cabbages, collard, kale, mustard, and turnip greens were easier to grow up north than other greens. Catfish, chickens, and pigs were easy to farm on a large scale, which made them easy to supply at markets across the country. Thus it was easier to re-create home through food. Technological improvements in food preservation and the development of convenience foods made a difference as well. Dishes like peach cobbler could now be made from canned or frozen ingredients at any time. For the transplants from the rural South, city life meant that certain special occasion foods could now be consumed more regularly, year-round.

Holding on strong to tradition, many African Americans ate particular foods in what they believed to be the appropriate season. They fried chicken in the spring and stewed chitlins in the fall. They waited to eat certain greens and sweet potatoes after the first frost hit them and made them sweeter. Urban blacks revived the Sunday dinner tradition, and they brought back the fish fry on Friday or Saturday. When it came time for the fall holidays, they replicated the festive foods one would expect to see in the rural South. Though the preacher was no longer the regularly expected guest of honor on these occasions, urban households certainly welcomed family, friends, and anyone else who might drop by. The more people cooked at home, the less they ate out. As a result, public eating options that had long held a dominant role in providing festive foods were patronized less often by black people. Street vendors disappeared because the ingredients one needed could be purchased at a nearby grocery store. As the home became more of a focal point for great food and connecting with loved ones, down home cooking became less about connections to the South and more about the black migrants' stronger connections to their new, adopted communities where they settled outside the South.

In the Soul Food era, Stokely Carmichael and other black public figures tried to consciously build a national black community that seemed culturally and socially fractured by the Great Migrations. They did so by taking down home cooking and marinating it in a rich gravy of racial identity politics and then transforming "soul food"—a phrase with layers of biblical, commercial, and historical meaning—into a race-based rallying cry. The effort worked at first, with many blacks adding the cooking and eating of soul food to the short list of acceptable cultural signifiers, like wearing an Afro or sporting a dashiki. During its surge in popularity among blacks and whites, articles were written, cookbooks published, school menus changed, and restaurants opened (or renamed) to showcase this new cuisine.

This might have worked out for everyone if the term hadn't been so vague and politically and racially charged. Soul food unraveled for African Americans because it focused too heavily on what was perceived as a poverty cuisine rooted in the rural South. As African Americans prospered, that reference point seemed more foreign. One of the ways that Americans accept immigrants is by accepting their food on the majority's terms by eventually make the new cuisine nonethnic. Immigrant groups, eager for social acceptance, have been more than willing to strike that bargain. Soul food endeavored to do the exact opposite. African Americans wanted acceptance on their own terms, by keeping racial identity, not terms dictated by the majority. Whites were confused because blacks seemed to want acceptance and rejection at the same time.

Yet many African Americans still responded to soul food. Understandably, blacks across the country gravitated toward the celebration foods rather than the everyday fare. It's what they were already eating on their special occasions, and now they had license to eat more of it as a show of racial solidarity and of improved economic status. In this way, embracing soul food was an extremely conservative move. Rather than advocating for a clean break from established food traditions shaped by whites, Black Power advocates picked the most common culinary denominator among blacks to bring them together. A really bold move for blackness would have been to advocate for the wholesale adoption of African foods and cooking techniques in order to help foment a truly pan-African cuisine. Yet that would have been impractical, given the difficulty and expense of importing West African ingredients and spreading that culinary expertise to millions of African Americans. In short, African Americans would have had to reverse centuries of acculturation and attempted assimilation and relearn being African. So instead, cultural advocates pushed for pork, greens, and cornbread to create the ties that bind.

But soul food had too many internal inconsistencies to overcome before it could endure as a national cuisine. The notion of "soul food" glosses over the strong subregional food traditions among blacks in the South and the ways that urban blacks outside the South had translated southern food in their new homes. People know the difference. As Michael Moore, chairman of Glory Foods, states succinctly, "There are a lot of different takes on soul food depending on where you grew up. It's different in Texas than it is in Alabama." He could have added San Francisco, Philadelphia, and Denver to that list. Though "soul food" had a great run initially as a marketable term, it didn't take hold in the South the way it did in the North. Black southerners are just as likely to call our representative meal "southern food" or "home cooking" (just as southern whites do) as "soul food."

Chef Sonya Jones of the Sweet Auburn Bread Company in Atlanta, Georgia, drives the point home: "Soul food is what black people call home cooking. Soul food is more limiting than southern, and it's our personal niche pulled from southern food." Outside the South, soul food contrasts sharply with other cuisines, but within the South, the culinary lines are blurred.[7]

Soul food has a stronger cultural meaning outside the South, but that by no means implies that there's a consensus as to its meaning. As an experiment, I posed the question "What is Soul Food?" on my social media outlets and got some very interesting responses that fell into three broad categories, a progression from the general to the particular. The first was that soul food is universal. Chef Scott Barton in New York City states eloquently, "Soul food is everyone's food. Every culture has its 'soul food' that reflects the provincial cuisine, the cuisine of labor, of struggle, of heritage and making do with little. But, enjoying the respite at the table where together the gathered collective that may be a family, a community, a church, a rehab center or whatever can appreciate each other, their gifts and the sustenance that nourishes them in that brief moment."[8]

For others, soul food is peculiar to the African American experience. Chef Hardette Harris from Minden, Louisiana, expresses it this way: "'Soul food' as we know it in this country originated from the rural South, and it was prepared by slaves, and sharecroppers. It was primarily made up of dishes that consisted of items that were grown, left over or given to them. So since there wasn't much else, the meal represented a whole lot more than just nourishment."

Chef Harris then pivots to a third commonly held definition of soul food—that it's love. "A lot of the 'love' poured into preparing the meal may have made up for the humiliation of being thought of as less than [a human being] and having less to share. So, as it is now in true Southern homes, offering a meal to almost anyone that steps foot in the home comes from a history of offering the best of what one has: 'good' food prepared and offered with 'love' . . . because there may not be much else to offer. But we always have 'love.'"[9] For Chef Wayne Johnson of Seattle, Washington, cooking soul food is a very personal expression. "Soul food is not a cuisine. It's a product of who's cooking it and where it's coming from. You should put love in your food." For emphasis, Chef Johnson adds, "Machines don't have soul. You can't get it from something that's manufactured."[10]

If soul food is about love, then, I must ask, Why are so many people "hating on" the cuisine? Shaun Chavis, a food writer, hits the nail on the head with three solid points. First, she notes the cuisine's unhealthy image, but she also explains, "What most people think of soul and Southern today is a commercialized version of the real thing, and we all know that, when food is commercialized, it picks up fat, sugar, salt, and size, and loses flavor." Chavis also notes that many have internalized that soul food is slave food, though as we've seen, whites of all classes were eating the same foods. Since soul food is comprised of a lot of celebration foods, it is not a cuisine composed entirely of rationed foods that were forced upon slave populations. In many instances, African Americans chose these foods. Lastly, Chavis elucidates another stigma: "The fear that eating and enjoying soul food suggests you haven't been assimilated into mainstream society."[11] The outsider status that soul food brazenly conferred on itself in the race-conscious 1960s is now a liability in what is perceived as an increasingly postracial America.

Soul food is also caught within the cross-currents of changing identity within the black community, most notably with questions of post-blackness. Zandria Robinson, professor of sociology at the University of Mississippi, shares that we're

> in the middle of the post-blackness discussion where African Americans are saying "I have no idea what soul food is. I have no connection to it, and you can't make assumptions about what I eat." We're in a moment in Blackness where we're trying to excise our bad habits, not just food. . . . What we're really saying about the food is that it's country. We're trying to get away from the things that black people eat. At the same time, fine dining establishments (read white chefs) are doing an interpretation of soul food that riffs on traditional items. This makes it OK to eat chicken and watermelon in public.

Such conversations are challenging because African Americans have yet to be fully assimilated into mainstream American society as other ethnic groups have. Too many black people remain at the margins. We discussed how, within hip hop culture, southern rappers celebrate soul food, but outside of the South they don't do so as much. She also notes the strong antipork sentiment, whereas steak is a metaphor for achievement and status. Then Professor Robinson said something that will endear her to me forever: "Pork needs a rebirth."[12]

Therese Nelson, who manages the Black Culinary History Group on Facebook, brings things into focus for me when she acknowledges soul food's universal aspects but also says, "I think that the danger in oversimplifying American soul food is that we now marginalize the culture itself. I think that now is definitely the time to have real and complex conversations about our food as it relates to heritage in a much more pivotal context because when we diminish the value of our food we forfeit our legacies in a way that is unacceptable in these delicate cultural times."[13] In other words, it's time to get busy!

Before she died in 2007, Edna Lewis rolled up her sleeves and did things to ensure that the "historical significance of black cooks in the Southern culinary tradition" would not go unsung. She lectured at the Smithsonian Institution. She founded a group, albeit short lived, called the Society for the Revival and Preservation of Southern Food. She was one of the founding members of the Southern Foodways Alliance, a now-thriving organization dedicated to preserving the diverse food cultures of the American South (I served on the organization's board from 2003 to 2009).

Most importantly, she kept cooking. Describing her own approach to cooking in a 1983 Fearrington House interview, Lewis said,

> I think you have to [have] a determination about cooking because otherwise you can drop it or get bored with it. But, I think cooking is scientific, and if you're curious about following the science, then you'll learn about cooking. . . . If you start right in the beginning, and continue that way, you might be successful. But, if you try to do other things while you're cooking—and I think cooking is creative— you find out a lot about it. While you're doing it and other thoughts come to you next time to test it out. . . . And you can't get away from it. Even though sometimes you'd like to do something else but with me it always comes back to cooking. So, it's even, what do you call it?

Lewis ended by laughing and saying, "kind of seductive."[14] Because Lewis was a tireless champion for southern food, it now flourishes as a strongly identifiable mother cuisine with several subregional components.

More people need to cook more soul food at home. I know the pressures of modern life can make this a challenge, but I think you'll find that when you commit to home cooking, particularly healthy home cooking, you'll spend less money overall, eat a lot better food, and have better health outcomes. Soul food has enough building blocks—chicken, fish, greens, legumes, sweet potatoes, etc.—for a healthy cuisine; it's just a matter of how these foods get cooked and how much people eat. This would be a perfect moment for me to give you the definitive, healthy soul food diet, but I'm not going to do so. The messages we get about what is "healthy" tend to shift, and who knows what will be in vogue when you're reading this. In the 1990s, we were told that life would be good if we just cut down on our fat and sodium intake. Now we're paying more attention to processed ingredients like white flour and white sugar.[15]

Home cooks are getting a lot of help keeping up with the latest developments. Numerous black organizations and institutions, including the black church, are educating people on healthy lifestyles and suggesting healthy riffs on traditional soul food favorites. Restaurants have already responded to the consumer demand for healthier options. Give them some of your business when you go out to eat, as millions of Americans do several times a week.

Initially, I defined soul food as the traditional foods of African Americans, but that's imprecise. Soul food is really more about the African Americans who left the Black Belt region of the South, settled across a nation, and reestablished and reinterpreted the Black Belt South's celebration food in their new homes. The foods typically reserved for Sunday dinner and holidays became more commonplace and are now consumed several times during the week. But the migrants also brought with them the poverty foods of the Black Belt, and they embraced other cheap foods because many remained chronically poor. Black cooks had no choice but to continue to stretch most meals by using cheap cuts of meat and lots of inexpensive vegetables and starches—foods that class-conscious whites rejected or ate when no one was watching.

Our representative meal also shows that the celebration food aspect (the source of its unhealthy image) and the slave food aspect (another source for scorn) are not soul food's sum total. Like other cuisines, it's a mixture of many things—some good, some bad. It's up to you to exhibit some moderation in how you prepare and how much you eat of the richer elements of this cuisine while balancing them out with its healthier ingredients. Soul foodies must also recognize that they can eat the glorious stuff, but just not a lot of it, every day, for every meal.

Soul food has a heritage of experimentation. It's a fusion of West African, Western European, and Native American culinary elements. Black cooks have borrowed from other cuisines, collaborated with other ethnic cooks, and played around with the familiar to give soul food life. There's plenty of room on the plate for more innovation. However, soul food needs to lose some of its edge and be more accessible to those who aren't black. Other ethnic cuisines have popularity and longevity because people outside the group, particularly whites, felt empowered enough to make that particular food. If African Americans can excel at making French and Italian food, whites should be free to cook soul food as long as the cook gets the taste right.

"Getting the taste right" means bringing more intense flavors to the table. Soul food has traditionally been saltier, spicier, and sweeter, and, yes, it had more fat than most other foods. That's the place from where soul food has come, but there are so many more places for cooks to take this cuisine. As our food-obsessed society continues its search for new ingredients, it often rediscovers foods from the not-to-distant past. The current heirloom vegetable gardening and the nose-to-tail cooking crazes are just a couple of examples. Soul food has a host of vegetables, particularly greens, just waiting to be introduced to a broader audience.

We must be wary that at some point, though, soul food may become so transformed that it is no longer recognizable. My hope is that when innovative cooks reach that point, they will name and embrace the new culinary form without jettisoning the old. Soul food can keep its flavor without losing its soul.

Notes

PREFACE

1 Egerton, Southern Food, 4.

CHAPTER 1

1 Are We There Yet?
2 "World's Worst Cuisine."
3 Camp, American Foodways, 24.
4 Fisher, "Spoon Bread and Moonlight."
5 Gee, "Gospel of Great Southern Food," 128.
6 Rice, "Louis Szathmary."
7 Algren, America Eats, xvi.
8 Szathmary, "How Festive Foods," 137–38.
9 Ibid., 138.
10 Savela, "Neck Bone's," J35.

CHAPTER 2

1 Lewicki, West African Food, 33.
2 Johnston, Staple Food Economies, 24.
3 "Summary of Evidence."
4 Rediker, Slave Ship, 57.
5 Eltis and Richardson, Atlas of the Transatlantic Slave Trade, 167.
6 Ibid.
7 Gandy, "Evidence with Respect," 168.
8 Wagner, "Introduction and Early Use of African Plants," 113.
9 Falconbridge, "Account of the Slave Trade," 124.
10 Rediker, Slave Ship, 269.
11 Rawick, From Sundown to Sunup, 7.
12 Rediker, Slave Ship, 5.
13 Berlin, "Time, Space," 45.
14 Ibid., 46.
15 Koslow, African American Desk Reference, 8.
16 Rediker, Slave Ship, 5.

17 Fox-Genovese, *Within the Plantation Household*, 71.

18 Wade, *Slavery in the Cities*, 23.

19 Ibid., 57.

20 Ibid., 28.

21 Ibid., 133.

22 Ibid., 61–62.

23 Yeoman, "The South, Number Five."

24 Fox-Genovese, *Within the Plantation Household*, 150.

25 Genovese, *Roll, Jordan, Roll*, 8–9.

26 Sydnor, *Slavery in Mississippi*, 36.

27 "Privations of the Slaves," 27, 31.

28 "Visit to a Rice Plantation," 2.

29 Wade, *Slavery in the Cities*, 277.

30 Abrahams, *Singing the Master*, 41.

31 "Privations of the Slaves," 27–28 (emphasis added).

32 Ibid., 31.

33 Yeoman, "The South, Number Five."

34 Collins, "Essay on the Management of Slaves," 154.

35 Davis, *Black Experience in Natchez*, 134–35.

36 Turner, *Africanisms*, 62, 149.

37 Rawick, *From Sundown to Sunup*, 77–78.

38 Cade, "Out of the Mouths of Ex-Slaves," 301.

39 Fox-Genovese, *Within the Plantation Household*, 150–51.

40 Yeoman, "The South, Number Five."

41 Cade, "Out of the Mouths of Ex-Slaves," 296.

42 Breeden, *Advice among Masters*, 94.

43 Roles, "Twenty-five Years among the Cotton Plantations."

44 Abrahams, *Singing the Master*, 30.

45 Smith, *Starving the South*.

46 Stier, *Mississippi Narratives*, 146–47.

CHAPTER 3

1 Cofer, *Georgia Narratives*, 209.

2 Foner, *Reconstruction*, 68–69.

3 Ibid.

4 Webster, "Freedmen's Bureau in South Carolina," 123.

5 Franklin, *From Slavery to Freedom*, 307.

6 "The Freedmen's Bureau."

7 DuBois, *Negro American Family*, 130.

8 Lewis, Fearrington House interview.

9 Berlin, *Slaves without Masters*, 241–42.

10 Gordon, *Georgia Negro*, 249–51.

11 Murchie, "Life on a Share-Crop Plantation."

12 Simonsen, *You May Plow Here*, 36–37.

13 Joffe and Walker, *Some Food Patterns of Negroes*, 4, 21.

14 Simonsen, *You May Plow Here*, 29–30.

15 Ibid., 134.

16 Sterner, *Negro's Share*, 188.

17 Vance, *Human Geography of the South*, 423–24.

18 Raper, *Preface to Peasantry*, 256–57.

19 Ibid., 258–59.

20 Blackmon, *Slavery by Another Name*, 358.

21 Dodson, Diouf, and Schomburg Center, *In Motion*, 136.

22 Dirks and Duran, "African American Dietary Patterns," 1889.

23 Ibid.

24 Mayer, *Human Nutrition*, 617.

25 See "Eating Outdoors in Boston" and "Chicago's Night Cooks."

26 "Harlem Market Men Sing."

27 "Wealthiest Negro Colony."

28 Joffe and Walker, *Some Food Patterns of Negroes*, 12.

29 Keegan, *Blacktown, U.S.A.*, 141.

30 Joffe and Walker, *Some Food Patterns of Negroes*, 2.

31 Ibid., 9.

32 Ibid.

33 Drake and Cayton, *Black Metropolis*, 573n.

34 Ibid., 13.

35 Jerome, *Northern Urbanization*, 1669.

36 "Saving the Gas Bill," 7.

37 Joffe and Walker, *Some Food Patterns of Negroes*, 34.

38 Peters, "Off the Main Stem."

39 Wells and Taylor, *William Shakespeare*, 12.

40 See Cox, "General Meeting."

41 Jones, "Can the Pew Help Rescue the Pulpit?" (emphasis added).

42 Bennet, "Soul of Soul," 114.

43 Ibid.

44 Joffe and Walker, *Some Food Patterns of Negroes*, 18.

45 Savela, "Neck Bone's," J36.

46 Sugrue, *Sweet Land of Liberty*.

47 Carson, *In Struggle*, 79–80.

48 Ibid., 80.

49 Ibid., 103.

50 Ibid., 101.

51 Ibid., 209–10.

52 [Carmichael and SNCC], "Excerpts from Paper."

53 See "Black Nutritionist Finds Soul Food Unhealthy."

54 Mendes, *African Heritage Cookbook*, 85.

55 Rawlins, "Keeping Fit."

56 White, "Soul Food Battle."

57 "Eating Like Soul Brothers."

58 Cleaver, *Soul on Ice*, 40.

59 "Reuss Survey Shows."

60 Mickler, *White Trash Cooking*, 3.

CHAPTER 4

1   Major, *Juba to Jive*, 209.

2   Erickson, "Hoover and Henri IV."

3   Sokolov, *Jewish-American Kitchen*, 60.

4   "Vied with Voices in Rival Song."

5   McGee, *On Food and Cooking*, 139.

6   Visser, *Much Depends on Dinner*, 120.

7   Simoons, *Eat Not This Flesh*, 67.

8   MacDonald, "Why Chickens?" 52.

9   Ibid., 52–53.

10 Ibid., 55.

11 Lewicki, *West African Food*, 90.

12 Alpern, "European Introduction of Crops," 41 n. 192.

13 Ayensu, *Art of West African Cooking*, 97.

14 Alpern, "European Introduction of Crops," 13–43.

15 Glasse, *Art of Cookery*, 40.

16 Lewis, *Taste of Country Cooking*, 105.

17 "Cuisine of Maryland," 7.

18 Bittman, "Chicken without Guilt."

19 Crawford, "Sketches of Private Life."

20 Morgan, *Slave Counterpoint*, 359.

21 Wood, *Black Majority*, 139.

22 Dodson and Gilkes, "'There's Nothing Like Church Food,'" 524.

23 Watson, "Black Chicken King Still Frying."

24 Gaskins, *Good Heart*, 20.

25 "Chicken Question."

26 Dirks and Duran, "African American Dietary Patterns," 1887.

27 Joffe and Walker, *Some Food Patterns of Negroes*, 14.

28 "Eating Outdoors in Boston."

29 "Licenses for Alley Cook Shops."

30 Innis, "Church Dinner."

31 "Father Divine's More Abundant Life."

32 Braden, *These Also Believe*, 28.

33 Richman, "Praise the Lord."

34 Author interview with Durham.

35 "Mahalia Jackson in Big Business."

36 "Second Mahalia Jackson Chicken Shack Opens."

37 Ibid.

38 Lewis, "N.A.A.C.P Facing a Battle."

CHAPTER 5

1 Hurston, *Mules and Men*, 95.
2 Lewicki, *West African Food*, 99.
3 Dawson, "Enslaved Watermen," 96–101.
4 Given that Kingsley lived toward the end of the nineteenth century, her observations have limited value for defining the role fish played in West African societies during the Atlantic slave trade. Yet, Kingsley's writings should not be overlooked, because they do evidence an interesting connection and continuity with what occurs in the United States.
5 Kingsley, "Fishing in West Africa," 776, 778.
6 Ibid., 779.
7 Dawson, "Enslaved Watermen," 114.
8 *Improved Village Technology*, 173–74.
9 Murphy, "Foods and Cooking of Rural Gambia," 295.
10 Morgan, *Slave Counterpoint*, 63.
11 Oliver, *Saltwater Foodways*, 332.
12 Swanton, *Indians of the Southeastern United States*, 265–66.
13 Ibid., 334.
14 Ibid., 340–41.
15 Ibid., 342.
16 Author interview with Miller.
17 Wood, *Black Majority*, 202.
18 Savitt, *Medicine and Slavery*, 95.
19 Ibid., 94–95.
20 Joffe and Walker, *Some Food Patterns of Negroes*, 31.
21 Singleton, *Archaeology of Slavery*, 170–71.
22 Researchers interviewed 198 informants. Tabulation based on Covey and Eisnach, *What the Slaves Ate*, Appendix D, 247–48.
23 Davis, *Alabama Narratives*, 124–5.
24 Morgan, *Slave Counterpoint*, 361.
25 Parkes, *Georgia Narratives*, 156.
26 Morgan, *Slave Counterpoint*, 359.
27 M, "Alligator Story," 608, 609.
28 Kegley, "Catfish Connoisseur."
29 "Negro as Fisherman."
30 Beard, "Paddle Fish of the Mississippi."
31 "Catfish," *Forest and Stream*.
32 "Mud."
33 Taylor, "Food of the New South," 17.
34 "The Cat."
35 DeKnight, *Date with a Dish*, 193.
36 Glenn, "Eating Habits of Harlem," 83.
37 Ibid.
38 Barnett, "Nation's Largest Consumer of Fish?"

39 Ibid.

40 Forman, "Catfish Achieve Upward Mobility"; Reed, "Cat Fight."

41 Forman, "Catfish Achieve Upward Mobility."

42 Ellis, "Bullheads of Yore Are No Match for Today's Catfish."

43 Forman, "Catfish Achieve Upward Mobility."

44 Woods and Styler, *Sylvia's Soul Food*, 70.

45 Reed, "Cat Fight," SM94.

46 Streitfeld, "Soaring Grain Prices."

47 Ibid.

48 "The Virginians."

49 "Country Fish Fry."

50 Puckett, *Magic and Folk Beliefs*, 72.

51 "Country Fish Fry."

52 "Wind from the North," 3–4.

53 "Bill Will End Fish Fries."

54 Clark, "Wylie Ave."

55 Gaskins, *Good Heart*, 26.

56 "The Haunts," O_4.

57 White, "Fried Fish Joints."

58 Poston, "Harlem Shadows."

59 "Blues Songs Ring."

60 Eskew, "Black South in Chicago."

61 McDonald's advertisement.

62 Liasson, "Democrats Flock to Rep. Jim Clyburn's Fish Fry."

63 Hunter, "Muslims Open a Fish House."

64 Author interview with Powell.

CHAPTER 6

1 Reynolds, "Sexy Beast."

2 Alcock, "Umbles," 20.

3 Sokolov, "Humble Pie," 81.

4 Glasse, *Art of Cookery*, 30.

5 Gray, *History of Agriculture*, 30, 38.

6 McIntyre, "Winter Scene," 41; Holmes, "Dey Kep'," 193.

7 Rountree, *North Carolina Narratives*, 233.

8 Fox-Genovese, *Within the Plantation Household*, 158–59.

9 McIntyre, "Winter Scene," 43.

10 Woodson, *Texas Narratives*, 214.

11 Moss, *Arkansas Narratives*, 159–60.

12 Covey and Eisnach, *What the Slaves Ate*, 106.

13 "We Refreshes Our Hog Meat with Corn Pone."

14 Hall, "Strut."

15 DeKnight, *Date with a Dish*, 86.

16 Roberts, "Salley, S.C."; "Chitlins for Ford."

17 Turner, *Through the Back Door*, 6.
18 Ibid.
19 Ibid., 9.
20 Ibid., 10.
21 Ibid., 9.
22 Edwards and Mason, *Onje Fun Orisa*, 11.
23 Ibid., 28–29.
24 Byrd, "Harlem Rent Parties," 4–5.
25 Snelson, "Harlem, 'Negro Capital of the Nation.'"
26 Byrd, "Harlem Rent Parties," 4.
27 "Rent Parties in Harlem Attract White Patrons."
28 "Is Jim Crowism Growing in Chicago?"
29 Harrington, "Food That Tempts Harlem's Palate."
30 "Chitlin Supper."
31 "Dark Epicures Gobble It Up."
32 Ikeura et al., "Identification of (E, E)-2, 4-Undecadienal."
33 Powers, *Boilin' 'n' Bakin' in Boogar Hollow*, 12; *Cookin' in Rebel Country*, 29.
34 Author interview with Auchmutey.
35 Neal, *What the Music Said*, 31.
36 Lauterbach, *Chitlin' Circuit*, 10.
37 Marx de Salcedo, "Quito's Street-Food Star," 21; Spivey, "Latin American and Caribbean Food."
38 Parry, "Chitterlings in Paris?"
39 Ibid.
40 Hardy, "How Paris Warms Up To."
41 Segura, "Haynes."
42 Author interview with Adams.
43 Drake, "Japanese Soul Club."
44 Lutz, "Cadaver Connection."
45 Casey, "Soul Food in Vietnam."
46 Lewis, "Negro GIs."
47 Ibid.
48 Parks, *GI Diary*; Payne, "Crowded Saigon Is Lonely."
49 Johnson, "U.S. Negro in Vietnam."
50 Ibid.

CHAPTER 7

1 Lundy, *Butter Beans*, 23.
2 Carney and Rosomoff, *In the Shadow of Slavery*, 17; Dunmire, *Gardens of New Spain*, 317.
3 Lewicki, *West African Food*, 54.
4 Albala, *Beans*, 118.
5 Carney and Rosomoff, *In the Shadow of Slavery*, 67.
6 Wagner, "Introduction and Early Use of African Plants," 114–15.

7 Simmons, *American Cookery*, 26.

8 Advertisement, *New York Diary*.

9 Hubbell, "'Hopping John,'" 84.

10 Green, *Beans*, 30.

11 Simmons, *Texas Narratives*, 24.

12 Moore, "Established and Well Cultivated," 81.

13 A planter, in *Debow's*, 325.

14 "Some Dainty Southern Recipes."

15 Dovlo, Williams, and Zoaka, *Cowpeas*, 17.

16 Ibid., 18 n. 4.

17 Randolph, *Virginia Housewife*, 111.

18 Tyree, *Housekeeping in Old Virginia*, 253–54.

19 Richardson, "Foods along U.S. 1 in Virginia," 2–3.

20 Bradley, "Word-List from South Carolina," 38–39.

21 Grime, *Ethno-Botany of the Black Americans*, 20–21.

22 Harris, *Beyond Gumbo*, 8–9.

23 *Picayune Creole Cook Book*, 182.

24 Hubbell, "'Hopping John,'" 87–88.

25 Dovlo, Williams, and Zoaka, *Cowpeas*, 18.

26 Rutledge, *Carolina Housewife*, 83.

27 Eddington, "Cowpeas"; Eddington, "Hoppin' John."

28 Hess, *Carolina Rice Kitchen*, 98.

29 "Black-Eyed Peas."

30 "Chips."

31 Glenn, "Eating Habits of Harlem," 84.

32 Martin interview.

33 "Soul Food Date."

34 Fountain, *Oklahoma Narratives*, 106.

35 Collins, *Texas Narratives*, 244.

36 Dalziel, *Useful Plants*, 225.

37 Dovlo, Williams, and Zoaka, *Cowpeas*, 43.

38 Ibid., 47.

39 Ibid., 59.

40 Ravernell, "12 months of luck."

41 Albala, *Beans*, 119.

42 Mangam, "Magic of the Black-Eyed Pea," 236.

43 Thompson, *Holiday Symbols*, 488; "1752 Calendar Change."

44 Whitlock, "Throughout New Year's," 138–39.

45 Hubbell, "'Hopping John,'" 85.

46 Rowland, *Improvement of the Cowpea*, 144.

47 Poe, "Hopping John Is Magical."

48 "City Greets New Year in Din, Frolic."

49 "Pot of Black-Eyed Peas."

50 "Actors' Watch Night Party."

CHAPTER 8

1 Rice interview.
2 Lewicki, *West African Food*, 112.
3 The word "macaroni" is the Anglicized version of the Italian word *mac-cherone*, which is believed to be based on a Greek word *makaria* (translated as "food made from barley"). See "Macaroni," *Oxford English Dictionary Online*; see also Stephenson, "Etymology of 'Macaroni, Macaroon.'"
4 Del Giudice, "Pasta," 48.
5 Thorne, *Simple Cooking*, 27.
6 "Macaroni," Monticello website.
7 Nathan, "Gourmet President," 33.
8 Author communication with Laudan; Pearl, Cuttle, and Deskins, *Completely Cheese*, 12–14.
9 Author communication with Mendelson.
10 *National Cookery Book*, 162.
11 Randolph, *Virginia Housewife*, 127–28.
12 Rutledge, *Carolina Housewife*, 110–11.
13 Diner, *Hungering for America*, 24.
14 Ibid., 40–41, 44.
15 Ibid., 54–55.
16 Nizzardini and Joffe, *Italian Food Patterns*, 4, 7.
17 Painter, *History of White People*, 206.
18 Folse, *Encyclopedia of Cajun*, 108.
19 Ibid.
20 Ibid.
21 Ibid., 109.
22 *Picayune Creole Cook Book*, 194–95.
23 Richard, *New Orleans Cook Book*, 86.
24 Rorer, *Mrs. Rorer's New Cook Book*, 300.
25 Hayes, *Kentucky Cook Book*, 12.
26 Harris, *Montana Cook Book*, 7, 10.
27 http://www.slate.com/articles/life/permanent_record/features/2011/permanent_record/permanent_record_the_story_of_a_depression_era_macaroni_laborer_.html.
28 "Tavern Topics," 15 March 1941.
29 Joffe and Walker, *Some Food Patterns of Negroes*, 25.
30 King, "Hungry World of Kraftco."
31 Holt, "Short Cuts to Good Meals."
32 DeKnight, *Date with a Dish*, 273.
33 Grant and Groom, "Dietary Study."
34 Opie, *Hog and Hominy*, 62.
35 Dickins, "Food Patterns of White and Negro Families."
36 Starr, *Soul of Southern Cooking*, 101.

37 Swann, "What's Cooking?"
38 "Relief Committee to Feed the Destitute."
39 "No Eggs, Oatmeal or Butter in 'Colored' Relief Orders."
40 Carlson, "Advertising."

CHAPTER 9

1 Pound, "Motherless Greens."
2 Byars, "Traditional African American Foods," 76.
3 Field, "Cruciferous and Green Leafy Vegetables," 290.
4 Ibid.
5 Boswell, "Our Vegetable Travelers," 172.
6 Field, "Cruciferous and Green Leafy Vegetables," 293.
7 Ibid., 291.
8 Moxon, English Housewifery.
9 Wilson, "Pottage and Soup as Nourishing Liquids," 3.
10 Ibid.
11 Spencer, "Food in Seventeenth-Century Tidewater Virginia," 86.
12 Wilson, "Pottage and Soup as Nourishing Liquids," 13.
13 Carney and Rosomoff, In the Shadow of Slavery, 177.
14 Wilson, West African Cookbook, 30.
15 Dalziel, Useful Plants, 419.
16 Boahene, West African Foods, 28–29.
17 Carney and Rosomoff, In the Shadow of Slavery, 178.
18 Osseo-Asare, Food Culture in Sub-Saharan Africa, 11.
19 Liboke de Viande, Congo Cookbook website.
20 Alpern, "European Introduction of Crops," 19; see also Lewicki, West African Food, 57–58.
21 For example, Gibbon, "Central Africa."
22 Haughton, Green Immigrants, 197.
23 Raymond, Reconnaissance Report on Concentrated Rations of Primitive Peoples, 109.
24 Editor, "On Plantation Gardens"; Affleck, "Plantation Garden for the South."
25 Harrison, Arkansas Narratives, 187.
26 Briggs, South Carolina Narratives, 96.
27 Pope, Georgia Narratives, 173.
28 Adams, South Carolina Narratives, 8.
29 Nunn, Alabama Narratives, 279.
30 Sells, Texas Narratives, 10.
31 "Fall and Winter Gardens."
32 Telfair, Georgia Narratives, 3.
33 Tobin, "'And There Raise Yams,'" 172.
34 Editor, "On Plantation Gardens."
35 Breeden, Advice among Masters, 271.
36 Ibid., 273.

37 Atwater and Woods, *Dietary Studies*, 21.
38 Bennett, Smith, and Passin, "Food and Culture," 657.
39 Ibid., 658.
40 Gladney, *Food Practices*, 7.
41 Bennett, Smith, and Passin, "Food and Culture," 657.
42 Glenn, "Eating Habits of Harlem," 83.
43 "Mustard Greens."
44 Joffe and Walker, *Some Food Patterns of Negroes*, 14.
45 Glasse, *Art of Cookery*, 10.
46 Randolph, *Virginia Housewife*, 103.
47 Philip, *Reason Why*, 48.
48 Leslie, *Directions for Cookery*, 183.
49 Hale, *Mrs. Hale's New Cook Book*, 265–66.
50 Corson, *Cooking Manual*, 91.
51 DeKnight, *Date with a Dish*, 246.
52 "Cook Greens in Their Own Juice."
53 Joffe and Walker, *Some Food Patterns of Negroes*, 14.
54 "There's Variety in Greens for Salad."
55 Pound, "Motherless Greens."
56 Hunt, *Bread from Heaven*, 227.
57 Glory Foods website.
58 Author interview with Moore.
59 Owens, *Cracker Kitchen*, 186.
60 Author interview with Betz.
61 Lewis, Fearrington House interview.
62 Sullivan, oral history interview, 16.
63 Author interview with Conwell.
64 Carver, *Nature's Garden for Victory*, 17.

CHAPTER 10

1 Author interview with Conwell.
2 O'Brien, "Sweet Potatoes and Yams," 208.
3 Turner, *Africanisms*, 199, 204.
4 From now on, I will use the terms "sweet potatoes" and "yams" precisely, and I will only use the two interchangeably when discussing candied yams, the dish.
5 O'Brien, "Sweet Potatoes and Yams," 216.
6 Wilson, *West African Cookbook*, 37.
7 Ibid., 71.
8 Johnston, *Staple Food Economies*, 24.
9 Okigbo, *Plants and Food in Igbo Culture*, 20.
10 Thompson, *Holiday Symbols*, 486–87.
11 Johnston, *Staple Food Economies*, 175.
12 La Fleur, "Culture of Crops," 155–56, 159–60.

13 Thompson, *Holiday Symbols*, 486.

14 La Fleur, "Culture of Crops," 155–56, 159–60.

15 O'Hara, "Weird, Wild Dance."

16 Wagner, "Introduction and Early Use of African Plants," 113.

17 Harris, *Plants, Animals, and Man*, 115.

18 Wagner, "Introduction and Early Use of African Plants," 113.

19 Alpern, "European Introduction of Crops," 26.

20 Ibid.

21 Wilson, *West African Cookbook*, 36.

22 Verrill, *Foods America Gave the World*, 43.

23 Ibid., 44.

24 Sokolov, "Columbus's Biggest Discovery," 66.

25 Denker, "The Carrot Purple," 63.

26 Ibid., 65.

27 Sokolov, "Peripatetic Potato."

28 Briggs, *English Art of Cookery*, 389.

29 Morgan, *Slave Counterpoint*, 141.

30 Carney and Rosomoff, *In the Shadow of Slavery*, 113.

31 Ibid.

32 Glover, *Account of Virginia*, 1895.

33 Choice, *Texas Narratives*, 218.

34 Summer, "Culture of the Sweet Potatoe."

35 Old Southhampton, "To Keep Sweet Potatoes."

36 Simonsen, *You May Plow Here*, 107–8.

37 Magoffin, in *American Farmer*, 356.

38 Joffe and Walker, *Some Food Patterns of Negroes*, 10.

39 Summer, "Culture of the Sweet Potatoe."

40 Randolph, *Virginia Housewife*, 109.

41 Bryan, *Kentucky Housewife*, 197.

42 Rutledge, *Carolina Housewife*, 96.

43 Grime, *Ethno-Botany of the Black Americans*, 134–35.

44 Schwaab, *Travels in the Old South*, 512.

45 "Untitled."

46 Ude, *French Cook*, 345.

47 Perry, "Plantation Sweet-Potato Recipes."

48 "Southern Dishes."

49 F——s, "Sweet Potatoes."

50 "The Sweet Potato."

51 *Sweet Potatoes and Yams*, 11.

52 "Southern Soldiers Cry for the Yam."

53 Corrigan, "Wilson Put Sweet Potatoes."

54 "Southern Soldiers Cry for the Yam."

55 "Georgia Yam."

56 Dirks and Duran, "African American Dietary Patterns," 1887.

57 Dickins, "Food Patterns of White and Negro Families," 430.

58 Byrd, "Life in the Harlem Markets," 8–9.
59 Joffe and Walker, *Some Food Patterns of Negroes*, 18.
60 Byrd, "Life in the Harlem Markets," 8–9.
61 Harris, *Montana Cook Book*, 10.
62 Rhett and Woodard, "Better Than Candied."
63 Nutter and Wallace, "Dr. Miller and His Fabulous Yams," 122.
64 Paddleford, "Gold-Mine Potato."
65 Hunt, *Bread from Heaven*, 249.
66 *Sweet Potato Statistical Yearbook*, 3; Lamb, "In Dishes from Soup to Hash."
67 Author communication with Walker.

CHAPTER 11

 1 Bruce, "Rethinking Cornbread," 11.
 2 Ortiz, "Maize as a Staple Food," 134.
 3 Fussell, *Story of Corn*, 19.
 4 Sokolov, "Broken Kernels," 90.
 5 Dalziel, *Useful Plants*, 552.
 6 Osseo-Asare, " 'We Eat First,' " 55; Ortiz, "Maize as a Staple Food," 135.
 7 La Fleur, "Culture of Crops," 167–68.
 8 Usner, *Food Marketing*, 288.
 9 Carr, *Food of Certain American Indians*, 8,
10 Swanton, *Indians of the Southeastern United States*, 274.
11 Ibid., 296.
12 Carr, *Food of Certain American Indians*, 28–29.
13 Hess, "American Loaf," 7.
14 Miller, *Texas Narratives*, 83.
15 "Word Shadows."
16 Gibbs, "Re-creating Hominy," 46.
17 Abrahams, *Singing the Master*, 4–17.
18 Ibid., 60.
19 Van Hook, *Georgia Narratives*, 81.
20 Hurt, *Texas Narratives*, 175.
21 Klein, *Alabama Narratives*, 295.
22 Van Hook, *Georgia Narratives*, 81.
23 Cofer, *Georgia Narratives*, 209.
24 Abrahams, *Singing the Master*, 20.
25 Gibbs, "Re-creating Hominy," 50.
26 Ibid., 47.
27 "Recipes," *Dwight's*, 5 December 1846.
28 "Privations of the Slaves," 27, 31.
29 "White and Yellow Cornmeal."
30 Simonsen, *You May Plow Here*, 56.
31 White, oral history interview.
32 "Recipes," *Dwight's*, 5 December 1846.

33 Ibid.

34 Van Hook, *Georgia Narratives*, 75.

35 "Recipes," *Dwight's*, 5 December 1846.

36 Cofield, "How the Hoe Cake (Most Likely) Got Its Name."

37 Richardson, *Missouri Narratives*, 291.

38 Brown, "Mrs. Pepper's Florida Recipes."

39 Purdue, "Capitol Collard Greening"; *U.S. One*, xxvi; "Sugar and Spice."

40 Russell, *Domestic Cook Book*, 26.

41 L. C. R., "Maize or Wheat?"

42 Neal, *Southern Cooking*, 25.

43 Johnson, "Sugar in Corn Bread!," 5.

44 "Late Confessions."

45 Argyle, "Cry for Bread."

46 Fisher, *What Mrs. Fisher Knows*, 11.

47 Hayes, *Kentucky Cook Book*, 6.

48 Cosmopolitan, "Another Corn Cake Connoisseur."

49 Kretschmar, "Corn Meal Grievance."

50 Friedman, "Africans and African-Americans," 82.

51 Ibid., 80–81.

52 Haskin, "Corn Bread Hot and Fresh Is Popular," 4.

53 "Corn Meal Provides Good Food."

54 Turner, "Corn."

55 "Why the Hoecake Is Going."

56 "Some Mighty Fine Ways."

57 Dirks and Duran, "African American Dietary Patterns," 1882.

58 Joffe and Walker, *Some Food Patterns of Negroes*, 13.

59 Friedman, "Africans and African-Americans," 82.

60 DeKnight, *Date with a Dish*, 315–19.

CHAPTER 12

1 "Chilli" is the spelling of the native Nahuatl word for pungent capsicum fruits. Even though the terms "chile," "chili," "pepper," or "hot peppers" are also used, I join Alan Davidson and Harold McGee in using the name the indigenous people had for this food item. See McGee, *On Food and Cooking*, 420.

2 See Smith, "Condiments."

3 DeWitt and Gerlach, "Seas of Hot Sauces."

4 "Hot."

5 "Pepper Sauce."

6 Ross, "African Cuisine Favors Stew," F3.

7 Wright, "Medieval Spice Trade," 40.

8 "Grains of paradise" are the seeds of a native West African plant called *Aframomum melegueta*. The plant is related to the ginger plant, and the seeds have a peppery taste. The seeds are golden-brown or red-brown, angular and granular, strongly aromatic and pungent, and they have a flavor similar to

that of cardamom. They were at one time important in trade with Europe. Part of the West African coast was known as the Grain Coast (now Liberia). The seeds are also known as "Guinea pepper." See Dalziel, *Useful Plants*, 471.

9 *Abstract of the Evidence*, 97.

10 Alpern, "European Introduction of Crops," 13–43, 27–28; Wright, "Medieval Spice Trade," 35–43.

11 Raghavan, *Handbook of Spices*, 91.

12 Since "Guinea pepper" was applied to a native West African spice and chillis, I cannot say for certain which spice was used. See Grime, *Ethno-Botany of the Black Americans*, 87; Purchas, *Pvrchas his Pilgrimes*, 1274.

13 "Cure for Rheumatism."

14 Wagner, "Introduction and Early Use of African Plants," 115.

15 Ibid.

16 Hudgins, "Hot Sauces," 122.

17 Grime, *Ethno-Botany of the Black Americans*, 88 (quoting H. Sloane, *The Natural History of Jamaica* [London, 1707–25], 1:241).

18 A closer examination of culinary practices shows that chilli consumption in the Caribbean varies from country to country. For that reason, I'm careful not to draw too broad a conclusion.

19 Randolph, *Virginia Housewife*, 163; Rutledge, *Carolina Housewife*, 182.

20 Harris, *Montana Cook Book*, 21; *To Work and Serve the Home*, 31.

21 Karen Hess speculated as much in her annotations in Randolph, *Virginia Housewife*, 283.

22 "Medical," 38.

23 "Management of Slaves."

24 Farquhar, *Angina Maligns*, 266; "Phillip's History"; Barton, *Outlines of lectures*, 2:43, 84.

25 Weaver, "From Turtle to Tripe," 287.

26 Baron, *Farm Books of Thomas Jefferson*, 64.

27 Puckett, *Magic and Folk Beliefs*, 323.

28 Tate, *North Carolina Narratives*, 334.

29 Cholera is a waterborne illness that affects a person's digestive system and can often be fatal, even in a matter of hours.

30 DeWitt and Gerlach, *Spicy Food Lover's Bible*, 42.

31 This assertion is controversial, for there has been a long-running argument about who first brought the Tabasco chilli to Louisiana and who first bottled Tabasco pepper sauce. There is a lot of circumstantial evidence to favor White over McIlhenny, but nothing conclusive. I do not endeavor to add any heat or light to the discussion.

32 Naj, *Peppers*, 159–60.

33 Ibid., 159.

34 Ibid., 160.

35 Ibid.

36 Ibid., 161.

37 *Picayune Creole Cook Book*, 58.

38 Mariani, *American Food and Drink*, 200.

39 *Picayune Creole Cook Book*, 58.

40 Small Farmer, "Art. III—Management of Negroes."

41 "Management of Slaves."

42 Dixon, *Archaeology of the Boston Saloon*. See also "Oldest Known Tabasco Bottle Type."

43 Weaver, "From Turtle to Tripe," 288.

44 Stern and Stern, "Skillet Set."

45 Trillin, "Attempt to Compile."

46 "'Hot Sauce' Williams."

47 "Hats Off."

CHAPTER 13

1 Kool-Aid Museum website.

2 Puckett, *Magic and Folk Beliefs*, 220–21.

3 "Capitol Chat."

4 Parsons, *How to Pick*.

5 Lewicki, *West African Food*, 123.

6 Ibid., 123–29.

7 Agiri, "The Yoruba," 55.

8 Abaka, *Kola Is God's Gift*, 20.

9 Ibid.

10 Ibid., 5–6.

11 Ibid., 1.

12 Reade, "Food in Central Africa."

13 Christy, "Kola-Nut Tree."

14 Sundstrom, "Cola Nut," 138.

15 Williams, *Miss Williams' Cookery Book*, 229; Imam, *Method of Preparing Local & Modern Snacks*, 12–13.

16 Dalziel, *Useful Plants*, 101.

17 "Kola."

18 Carney and Rosomoff, *In the Shadow of Slavery*, 71.

19 "George Washington, Inventor."

20 Sullivan, *Classic Jamaican Cooking*, 177.

21 Turner, *Africanisms*, 65.

22 "Marvelous Kola Nut."

23 "Might Turn a Battle."

24 Egerton, *Southern Food*, 203.

25 "Bissap."

26 Dalziel, *Useful Plants*, 129–30.

27 Carney and Rosomoff, *In the Shadow of Slavery*, 236.

28 Cassidy, *Jamaica Talk*, 203; Browne, *Civil and natural history of Jamaica*, 285.

29 J. W. K., "New or Little Known Vegetables."

30 Payne, *Arkansas Narratives*, 307.

31　"New Year's Day in Port Royal."

32　Ibid.

33　Lebby, *South Carolina Narratives*.

34　Barnes, "He Misses Dem 'Set Down Hawgs,'" 21; author communication with Bryson.

35　Massey, *Ersatz in the Confederacy*, 74.

36　Bryan, *Kentucky Housewife*, 401–2.

37　Russell, *Domestic Cook Book*, 18.

38　"Honor the Day in Warm Style."

39　"This is 'Mancipation Day.'"

40　Haley and Washington, *Afro-American Encyclopedia*, 532.

41　"Origin of Pink Lemonade."

42　"Tines's Troubles."

43　"What We Are All Talking About."

44　I use the term "soda pop" as a compromise, though many say just "soda" or "pop," as I do.

45　"The Camp Meeting in Chunnenuggee" (emphasis added).

46　Hunt, "Traditional Foods."

47　Wiggins, "Juneteenth," 237–352; Hunt, "Traditional Foods."

48　See Wiggins, *O Freedom!*

49　Lewis, Fearrington House interview.

50　Westheider, *African American Experience in Vietnam*, 53–54.

51　Author interview with Abernathy.

52　Polk, "Soldier Completes Viet Nam Missions."

53　"Mail Overseas Gifts Early."

54　"Conrad Clark Send News from Vietnam."

55　Edge, "Sweet So Sour"; Rufca, "Fried Kool-Aid."

56　Diouf, *Dreams of Africa in Alabama*, 214–15.

57　Ibid.

CHAPTER 14

1　Author communication with Chavis, 16 July 2012.

2　Soyer, *Pantropheon*, 104.

3　Dunmire, *Gardens of New Spain*, 190–91.

4　Swanton, *Indians of Southeastern United States*, 294.

5　Oliver, *Food in Colonial and Federal America*, 64.

6　Gray, *History of Agriculture*, 190.

7　Barnes, "He Misses Dem 'Set Down Hawgs,'" 22.

8　Hughes, *Thirty Years*, 49.

9　Russell, *Domestic Cook Book*, 30.

10　Hayes, *Kentucky Cook Book*, 17.

11　"Peaches."

12　DeKnight, *Date with a Dish*, 380.

13　Author interview with Wright.

14 Russell, *Domestic Cook Book*, 24; Sullivan, *Classic Jamaican Cooking*, 90–91.

15 Harris, *Montana Cook Book*, 21.

16 For those of you who weren't listening to Top 40 in the 1980s, I'm referring to Jackson's chart-topping single "Rhythm Nation."

17 "Table Talk."

18 Stearns, "Five Delicious Southern Puddings."

19 Wilson, *Food and Drink in Britain*, 318.

20 Weaver, "Pie," 68–99.

21 Wilson, *Food and Drink in Britain*, 318.

22 Pinckney, *Recipe Book*.

23 Briggs, *English Art of Cookery*, 389.

24 Vergil, *Georgia Narratives*.

25 Russell, *Domestic Cook Book*, 23; Fisher, *What Mrs. Fisher Knows*, 26; DeKnight, *Date with a Dish*, 343.

26 Clark, "Mary McLeod Bethune."

27 Brown, *United Cakes of America*, 160.

28 Wilson, *Food and Drink in Britain*, 269.

29 Ibid.

30 Smith, *Georgia Narratives*, 307.

31 Smith, *Missouri Narratives*, 322.

32 Hodges, *Mississippi Narratives*, 70.

33 Durant, *South Carolina Narratives*, 348.

34 Gaskins, *Good Heart*, 75; Lewis, *Taste of Country Cooking*, 63.

35 Brown, *Cakelove*, 24.

36 Author communication with Newell.

37 Heatter, *Maida Heatter's Best Dessert Book Ever*, 111.

CHAPTER 15

1 Author interview with Randall.

2 Author interview with Arrington.

3 Author communication with Samuelsson.

4 Author interview with Moore.

5 Author communication with Charita Jones.

6 Danneman, "Mars mission."

7 Author interview with Moore; author interview with Sonya Jones.

8 Author communication with Barton.

9 Author communication with Harris.

10 Author interview with Johnson.

11 Author communication with Chavis.

12 Author interview with Robinson.

13 Author communication with Nelson.

14 Lewis, Fearrington House interview.

15 I'm grateful to Sheri Castle for her insight on changes in the conventional wisdom of what is "healthy."

Bibliography

ARCHIVAL SOURCES

Federal Writers' Project, Manuscripts Division, Library of Congress, Washington, D.C.
    America Eats Essays
    "Chitlin Supper." N.d.
    "Cuisine of Maryland." N.d.
    Richardson, Eudora Ramsay. "Foods along U.S. 1 in Virginia." N.d.
    Thomas, John W. "Chicken." N.d.
    "We Refreshes Our Hog Meat with Corn Pone." N.d.
    "Wind from the North, Fish Bite Like a Horse." N.d.
Byrd, Frank. "Harlem Rent Parties." 23 August 1938.
———. "Life in the Harlem Markets." 28 December 1938.
Eskew, Garnett L. "The Black South in Chicago." 3 May 1939.

AUTHOR INTERVIEWS AND PERSONAL COMMUNICATIONS

Abernathy, J. Carle. Interview, 7 April 2012, Denver, Colorado.
Adams, Bob. Interview, 19 March 2012, Denver, Colorado.
Arrington, Chef Nyesha. Phone interview, 28 February 2012.
Auchmutey, Jim. Interview, 21 February 2012, Atlanta, Georgia.
Barton, Chef Scott. Facebook communication with author, 4 February 2012.
Bennet, Rob. Interview, 3 November 2011, Knoxville, Tennessee.
Betz, Ryan. Phone interview, 19 January 2012.
Bryson, Lew. Email communication with author, 16 August 2012.
Chavis, Shaun. Facebook communication with author, 6 February, 16 July 2012.
Conwell, Benita. Phone interview, 1 February 2012.
Durham, Iretha. Interview, 23 April 2011, Savannah, Georgia.
Harris, Chef Hardette. Facebook communication with author, 4 February 2012.
Johnson, Chef Wayne. Phone interview, 17 February 2012.
Jones, Charita. Email communication with author, 15 January 2012.
Jones, Sonya. Phone interview, 18 January 2012.
Laudan, Rachel. Email communication with author, 30 March 2011.
Mendelson, Anne. Email communication with author, 29 March 2011.
Miller, Hyman, Sr. Phone interview, 20 February 2012.

Moore, Michael. Phone interview, 4 January 2012.
Nelson, Therese. Facebook communication with author, 6 February 2012.
Newell, "Sir_Geechie" Jamara. Twitter exchange with author, 2 August 2012.
Powell, Georgette. Phone interview, 24 January 2012.
Randall, Chef Joe. Phone interview, 15 March 2012.
Robinson, Prof. Zandria. Phone interview, 23 January 2012.
Samuelsson, Chef Marcus. Email communication with author, 7 March 2012.
Walker, Charles. Email communication with author, 6 December 2011.
Weaver, William Woys. Email communication with author,7 April 2011.
Wright, Pam. Phone interview, 10 March 2012.

OTHER INTERVIEWS

Lewis, Edna. Fearrington House interview. Conducted by Davia Nelson, 1983.
    Author's collection.
Martin, Dulcina Baker. Ex-slave interview. *African American Experience in Ohio*,
    http://dbs.ohiohistory.org/africanam/page.cfm?ID=13926&Current=003.
    10 January 2012.
Rice, Condoleezza. *700 Club* interview. Christian Broadcasting Network, 23
    November 2011 broadcast, http://www.cbn.com/media/player/index.aspx?s
    =/archive/club/700Club112311_WS. 21 March 2012.
Sullivan, Herman. Oral history interview. Conducted by Amy Evans Streeter at
    the Shiloh Seventh-day Adventist Church, Greenwood, Miss., 23 September
    2011, http://www.southernfoodways.org/documentary/oh/shiloh/herman
    -sullivan.shtml. 4 April 2012.
White, Izola. Oral history interview. Conducted by Amy Evans at Izola's Family
    Dining, Chicago, Ill., 24 March 2008, http://southernfoodways.org/docu
    mentary/oh/chicago_eats/izolas_family_dining/izola_white.shtml. 4 April
    2012.

BOOKS, ESSAYS, ARTICLES, DISSERTATIONS, AND WEBSITES

Abaka, Edmund. *Kola Is God's Gift: Agricultural Production, Export Initiatives & the Kola
    Industry of Asante & the Gold Coast c. 1820–1950*. Athens: Ohio University Press,
    2005.
Abrahams, Roger D. *Singing the Master: The Emergence of African-American Culture in the
    Plantation South*. New York: Penguin, 1992.
*An Abstract of the Evidence Delivered Before a Select Committee of the House of Commons in
    the Years 1790 and 1791 on the Part of the Petitioners for the Abolition of the Slave Trade*.
    Newcastle, England, 1791. http://books.google.com/books?id=nfzXsPPXVyU
    C&pg=PR5&lpg=PR5&dq=An+Abstract+of+the+Evidence+Delivered+Before
    +a+Select+Committee+of+the+House+of+Commons+in+the+Years+1790&
    source=bl&ots=i7eU7qfrr&sig=YhIIIlcKLtNpHhARPo8A9D400E&hl=en&sa=
    X&ei=pFTuUPPjLOec2QW574HIDA&ved=0CEAQ6AEwAw. 7 February 2012.
"Actors' Watch Night Party." *Boston Herald*, 1 January 1905, 12.

Adams, Ezra. *South Carolina Narratives*, vol. 2, pt. 1, 5–8. In Rawick, *American Slave*.

Advertisement. *New York Diary*, 14 August 1792, 3.

Affleck, T. "Plantation Garden for the South." *Southern Cultivator*, February 1846, 23.

"The Africans at Charleston." *Harper's Weekly* 11 (September 1858): 582.

Agiri, B. A. "The Yoruba and the Pre-Colonial Kola Trade." *Odu: A Journal of West African Studies*, July 1975, 55.

Albala, Ken. *Beans: A History*. New York: Berg, 2007.

Alcock, Joan. "Umbles and the Eating of Humble Pie." In *Wild Food: Proceedings of the Oxford Symposium on Food and Cookery 2004*, edited by Richard Hosking, 19–28. London: Prospect Books, 2006.

Algren, Nelson. *America Eats*. Iowa City: University of Iowa Press, 1992.

"Alleged Secret Meeting of Negroes." *New-York Tribune*, 19 August 1895, 3.

Alpern, Stanley B. "The European Introduction of Crops into West Africa in Pre-colonial Times." *History in Africa* (1992), 13–43.

"American Cookery." *Kansas City Star*, 24 November 1913, 7.

Are We There Yet? Television trailer, http://www.youtube.com/watch?v=SxuQxN24RZs&feature=BFa&list=PLD3B37C71122C6D91&lf=results_main. 8 March 2012.

Argyle, Ruth. "A Cry for Bread." *Good Housekeeping*, May 1892, 215.

Atwater, W. O., and Chas. D. Woods. *Dietary Studies With Reference to the Food of the Negro in Alabama in 1895 and 1896*. Washington: Government Printing Office, 1897.

Ayensu, Dinah Ameley. *The Art of West African Cooking*. New York: Doubleday, 1972.

Barbour, Charlie. *North Carolina Narratives*, vol. 14, pt. 1, 74–77. In Rawick, *American Slave*.

Barker, Karen. *Sweet Stuff: Karen Barker's American Desserts*. Chapel Hill: University of North Carolina Press, 2004.

Barnes, "Uncle" Henry. "He Misses Dem 'Set Down Hawgs.'" *Alabama Narratives*, 6:20–24. In Rawick, *American Slave*.

Barnett, Albert. "Do You Know What Racial Group Is the Nation's Largest Consumer of Fish?" *Chicago Defender*, 1 August 1953, 11.

Baron, Robert C. *The Garden and Farm Books of Thomas Jefferson*. Golden, Colo.: Fulcrum, 1987.

Barton, William C. (William Paul Crillon). *Outlines of lectures on materia medica and botany, delivered in Jefferson medical college, Philadelphia*. 2 vols. Philadelphia, 1827–28.

Beard, Daniel C. "The Paddle Fish of the Mississippi." *Scientific American*, 21 December 1878, 391.

Bennet, Lerone, Jr. "The Soul of Soul." *Ebony*, December 1961, 111–14.

Bennett, John W., Harvey L. Smith, and Herbert Passin. "Food and Culture in Southern Illinois: A Preliminary Report." *American Sociological Review* 7 (October 1942): 645–60.

Berlin, Ira. *Slaves without Masters: The Free Negro in the Antebellum South*. New York: New Press, 1974.

———. "Time, Space, and the Evolution of Afro-American Society in British Mainland North America." *American Historical Review* 85, no. 1 (February 1980): 44–78.

Berman, Judy. "Mark Twain's Rapturous List of His Favorite American Foods," http://flavorwire.com/265604/mark-twains-rapturious-list-of-his-favorite-american-foods?all=1. 13 March 2012.

Bianco, Marie. "South's Fare Still Big Hit." *Los Angeles Times*, 11 October 1984, O55.

Bilger, Burkhard. *Noodling for Flatheads: Moonshine, Monster Catfish, and Other Southern Comforts.* New York: Scribner, 2000.

"Bill Will End Fish Fries." *Boston Daily Globe*, 21 June 1914, 51.

"Bissap." The Congo Cookbook, http://www.congocookbook.com/beverages/jus_de_bissap.html. 17 September 2011.

Bittman, Mark. "A Chicken without Guilt." *New York Times*, 9 March 2012, http://www.NewYorkTimes.com/2012/03/11/opinion/sunday/finally-fake-chicken-worth-eating.html?_r=1&scp=1&sq=%22fake%20chicken%22&st=cse. 16 March 2012.

"Black-Eyed Peas: A Delicate and Delicious Dish." *Christian Science Monitor*, 31 January 1928, 9.

Blackledge, William. "On the Pea—As Cultivated in North Carolina." *American Farmer*, 28 February 1823, 388–89.

Blackmon, Douglas A. *Slavery by Another Name: The Re-enslavement of African Americans from the Civil War to World War II.* New York: Anchor Books, 2009.

"Black Nutritionist Finds Soul Food Unhealthy." *Jet*, 8 April 1971, 23.

"Blues Songs Ring along Lenox Avenue, Because It's Pork Chop Time in Harlem." *Washington Post*, 14 October 1933, 2.

Boahene, Christine Joyce. *Recipes for West African Foods.* Accra, Ghana: Black Mask LTD, 1994.

Bolden, Frank E. "Courier Survey in Pittsburgh Reveals: Majority of Chinese Restaurants Follow a Policy of Segregation." *Pittsburgh Courier*, 5 February 1944, 10.

Boswell, Victor R. "Our Vegetable Travelers." *National Geographic*, August 1949, 145–217.

Braden, Charles Samuel. *These Also Believe: A Study of Modern American Cults & Minority Religious Movements.* New York: Macmillan, 1949.

Bradley, F. W. "A Word-List from South Carolina." *Publications of the American Dialect Society*, no. 14 (November 1950): 38–39.

Bragg, Rick. "A Delicacy of the Past Is a Winner at Drive-In." *New York Times*, 10 November 1996, 20.

Breeden, James O. *Advice among Masters: The Ideal in Slave Management in the Old South.* Westport, Conn.: Greenwood Press, 1980.

Briggs, George. *South Carolina Narratives*, vol. 2, pt. 2, 93–97. In Rawick, *American Slave.*

Briggs, Richard. *The English Art of Cookery, According to the Present Practice.* London: G. G. J. and J. Robinson, 1788.

Brown, Lucia. "Mrs. Pepper's Florida Recipes: Good Eating from the Sunshine State." *Washington Post*, 13 August 1948, C3.

Brown, Marion. *Marion Brown's Southern Cook Book*. New ed. Chapel Hill: University of North Carolina Press, 1968.

Brown, Warren. *Cakelove: How to Bake Cakes from Scratch*. New York: Stewart, Tabori & Chang, 2008.

———. *United Cakes of America: Recipes Celebrating Every State*. New York: Stewart, Tabori & Chang, 2010.

Browne, Patrick. *The civil and natural history of Jamaica: in three parts*. London: T. Osborne and J. Shipton, 1756.

Bruce, Erika. "Rethinking Cornbread." *Cook's Illustrated*, no. 72 (January/February 2005): 10–11.

Bryan, Mrs. Lettice. *The Kentucky Housewife*. 1839. Facsimile ed., Bedford, Mass.: Applewood Books, 2001.

Byars, Drucilla. "Traditional African American Foods and African Americans." *Agriculture and Human Values* 13, no. 3 (1996): 74–78.

Cade, John B. "Out of the Mouths of Ex-Slaves." *Journal of Negro History* 20, no. 3 (July 1935): 273–337.

Camp, Charles. *American Foodways: What, When, Why, and How We Eat in America*. Little Rock, Ark.: August House, 1989.

"The Camp Meeting in Chunnenuggee." *Columbus Daily Enquirer*, 2 October 1898, 1.

"Capitol Chat." *Washington Post*, 28 March 1902, 6.

Carlson, Walter. "Advertising: Product Use among Negroes." *New York Times*, 7 February 1966, 41.

[Carmichael, Stokely, and SNCC]. "Excerpts from Paper on Which the 'Black Power' Philosophy Is Based." *New York Times*, 5 August 1966, 10.

Carney, Judith, and Richard Nicolas Rosomoff. *In the Shadow of Slavery: Africa's Botanical Legacy in the Atlantic World*. Berkeley: University of California Press, 2009.

Carr, Lucien. *The Food of Certain American Indians and Their Methods of Preparing It, From Proceedings of the American Antiquarian Society, at the Semi-annual Meeting, April 24, 1895*. Worcester, Mass.: C. Hamilton, printer, 1895.

Carson, Clayborne. *In Struggle: SNCC and the Black Awakening of the 1960s*. Cambridge, Mass.: Harvard University Press, 1995.

Carver, George W. *How the Farmer Can Save His Sweet Potatoes: And Ways of Preparing Them for the Table*. Tuskegee, Ala.: Tuskegee Institute Press, 1937.

———. *Nature's Garden for Victory and Peace*. Bulletin 43. Tuskegee, Ala.: Tuskegee Institute, March 1942.

Casey, Sgt. Leon A. "Soul Food in Vietnam." *Virgin Islands Daily News*, 7 September 1971, 4–5.

Cassidy, Frederic G. *Jamaica Talk: Three Hundred Years of the English Language in Jamaica*. London: Macmillan, 1961.

———, ed. *Dictionary of American Regional English*. Vol. 1, *Introduction and A–C*. Cambridge, Mass.: Belknap Press of Harvard University Press, 1985.

Cassidy, Frederic G., and Joan Houston Hall, eds. *Dictionary of Regional American English*. Vol. 2, D–H. Cambridge, Mass.: Belknap Press of Harvard University Press, England, 1991.

"The Cat." *Hartford Courant*, 11 February 1901, 14.

"Catfish." *Forest and Stream*, 14 September 1882, 131.

"Catfish Eaters Sadly Admit Decline in Supply of Their Favorite Dish." *Atlanta Constitution*, 19 October 1937, 3.

"Catherine Market." *New York Herald*, 31 March 1853, 2.

"Chesapeake Bay Fishing." *Baltimore Sun*, 28 July 1898, 8.

Chester-Tamayo, B. J. *Alcenia's: Healing the Soul*. Published by the author, 2011.

"Chicago's Night Cooks." *Knoxville Journal*, 29 January 1890, 7.

"The Chicken Question." *New York Times*, 15 April 1882, 4.

"Chinese Eat Here." *Rockford Gazette*, 19 May 1892, 3.

"Chips." *Broad Ax*, 9 January 1904, 1.

"Chitlins for Ford." *Chicago Defender*, 1 December 1975, 4.

Choice, Jeptha. *Texas Narratives*, vol. 4, pt. 1, 217–19. In Rawick, *American Slave*.

"Chop Suey Resorts." *New York Times*, 15 November 1903, 20.

Christy, Thomas. "The Kola-Nut Tree." *American Journal of Pharmacy* 55 (January 1883): 27.

"City Greets New Year in Din, Frolic." *Baton Rouge Advocate*, 1 January 1936, 2.

Clark, John H. "Wylie Ave." *Pittsburgh Courier*, 26 October 1957, A1.

Clark, Libby. "Mary McLeod Bethune (1857–1955) Founded Bethune-Cookman College with Sweet Potato Pies." *Los Angeles Sentinel*, 28 February 1991, C7.

Cleaver, Eldridge. *Soul on Ice*. 12th printing. New York: Dell, 1974.

Clemmens, Jane E. "The Cooking of Fish." *Good Housekeeping*, January 1900, 132–35.

Clinton, Catherine. *Plantation Mistress: Woman's World in the Old South*. New York: Pantheon, 1982.

"Cobbler." *Oxford English Dictionary Online*, http://www.oed.com.ezproxy.denver library.org:2048/view/Entry/35218?redirectedFrom=cobbler#eid. 23 March 2012.

Cofer, Willis. *Georgia Narratives*, vol. 12, pt. 1, 201–11. In Rawick, *American Slave*.

Cofield, Rod. "How the Hoe Cake (Most Likely) Got Its Name." *Food History News*, vol. XVIV [sic], no. IV, n.d., 6.

Collins, Harriet. *Texas Narratives*, vol. 16, pt. 1, 242–45. In Rawick, *American Slave*.

Collins, Dr. Robert. "Essay on the Management of Slaves." *DeBow's Review*, January/February 1862, 154.

"Conrad Clark Send News from Vietnam." *Philadelphia Tribune*, 3 August 1968, 8.

"Cook Greens in Their Own Juice." *New York Amsterdam News*, 19 August 1950, 19.

Cookin' in Rebel Country. Amarillo, Tex.: Baxter Lane Company, 1972.

"Corn Meal Provides Good Food at Minimum Expense." *Columbus Ledger*, 24 January 1921, 8.

"Cornpone Factions Vie in Radio Debate." *New York Times*, 5 March 1931, 2.

Corrigan, John, Jr. "Wilson Put Sweet Potatoes on Bill of Fare of Army." *Atlanta Constitution*, 20 August 1917, 2.

Corson, Juliet. *The Cooking Manual of Practical Directions for Economical Every-day Cooking*. New York: Dodd, Mead, 1879.

Cosmopolitan. "Another Corn Cake Connoisseur." *New York Times*, 3 September 1892, 10.

"The Counterpart Cousins." In *Three Courses and a Dessert Comprising Three Sets of Tales, West Country, Irish and Legal; and a Melange*, 26. 4th ed. London: Henry G. Bohn, 1830.

"A Country Fish Fry." *Canton's Weekly* (Seattle), 18 May 1918, 1.

Covey, Herbert C., and Dwight Eisnach. *What the Slaves Ate: Recollections of African American Foods and Foodways from the Slave Narratives*. Santa Barbara, Calif.: Greenwood Press/ABC-CLIO, 2009.

Cox, Isham. "General Meeting Near Goldsboro, N.C." *Friend's Review*, 28 October 1871, 154.

Crawford, William H. "Sketches of Private Life and Character of William H. Crawford." *Southern Literary Messenger*, May 1837, 273.

"Cure for Rheumatism." *New Star*, 23 May 1797, 54.

Dalziel, J. M. *The Useful Plants of West Tropical Africa*. London: Crown Agents for Oversea Governments and Administrations, 1937.

Danneman, Matthew. "Mars Mission to Be Simulated to Find Best Food for the Trip." *USA Today*, 20 February 2012, http://www.usatoday.com/tech/science/space/story/2012-02-17/research-mars-food-hawaii/53160760/1. 21 February 2012.

"Dark Epicures Gobble It Up." *Chicago Daily Tribune*, 25 October 1908, 7.

Davis, Clara. *Alabama Narratives*, sup. ser. 1, 1:121–25. In Rawick, *American Slave*.

Davis, Ronald L. F. *The Black Experience in Natchez, 1720–1880*. N.p.: Eastern National, 1994.

Dawson, Kevin. "Enslaved Waterman in the Atlantic World, 1444–1888." Ph.D. diss., University of South Carolina, 2005.

DeKnight, Freda. *A Date with a Dish: A Cook Book of American Negro Recipes*. New York: Heritage Press, 1948.

Del Giudice, Luisa. "Pasta." In *Encyclopedia of Food and Culture*. Vol. 3, *Obesity to Zoroastrianism, Index*, edited by Solomon H. Katz and William Woys Weaver, 46–52. New York: Scribner, 2003.

Denker, Joel. "The Carrot Purple." In *Vegetables: Proceedings of the Oxford Symposium on Food and Cookery 2008*, edited by Susan R. Friedland, 63–70. London: Prospect Books, 2009.

DeWitt, Dave, and Nancy Gerlach. "Seas of Hot Sauces," *Chile Pepper*, May/June 1990, 37.

———. *The Spicy Food Lover's Bible: The Ultimate Guide to Buying, Growing, Storing, and Using the Key Ingredients That Give Food Spice, with More Than 250 Recipes from Around the World*. New York: Stewart, Tabori & Chang, 2005.

Dickins, Dorothy. "Food Patterns of White and Negro Families, 1936–1948." *Social Forces* 27, no. 4 (May 1949): 425–30.

Diner, Hasia R. *Hungering for America: Italian, Irish, and Jewish Foodways in the Age of Migration*. Cambridge, Mass.: Harvard University Press, 2001.

Diouf, Sylviane A. *Dreams of Africa in Alabama: The Slave Ship Clotilda and the Story of the Last Africans Brought to America*. Oxford: Oxford University Press, 2007.

Dirks, Robert T., and Nancy Duran. "African American Dietary Patterns at the Beginning of the 20th Century." *Journal of Nutrition* 131 (2001): 1881–89.

Dixon, Kelly. *Archaeology of the Boston Saloon*. The African Diaspora Archaeology Network, June 2006 newsletter, ISSN: 1933-8651, http://www.diaspora.uiuc.edu/news0606/news0606.html#2. 5 June 2011.

Dodson, Howard, Sylviane A. Diouf, and Schomburg Center for Research in Black Culture. *In Motion: The African American Migration Experience*. Washington, D.C.: National Geographic, 2004.

Dodson, Jualynne E., and Cheryl Townsend Gilkes. "'There's Nothing Like Church Food.' Food and the Afro-Christian Tradition: Re-membering Community and Feeding the Embodied S/spirit(s)." *Journal of the American Academy of Religion* 63, no. 3 (Fall 1995): 519–38.

Dovlo, Florence E., Caroline E. Williams, and Laraba Zoaka. *Cowpeas: Home Preparation and Use in West Africa*. Ottawa, Canada: International Development Research Centre, 1976.

Down Home Healthy Cooking. Washington, D.C.: National Cancer Institute at the National Institutes of Health. NIH Publication No. 95-3408SV, March 1995.

Drake, Hal. "Japanese Soul Club." *Sepia*, September 1974, 26–32.

Drake, St. Clair, and Horace R. Cayton. *Black Metropolis: A Study of Negro Life in a Northern City*. 2 vols. New York: Harper & Row, 1962.

DuBois, William E. B. *The Negro American Family*. Atlanta: Atlanta University Press, 1908.

Dull, Mrs. S. R. *Southern Cooking*. New York: Grosset & Dunlap, 1941.

Dunmire, William W. *Gardens of New Spain: How Mediterranean Plants and Foods Changed America*. Austin: University of Texas Press, 2004.

Durant, Sylvia. *South Carolina Narratives*, vol. 14, pt. 1, 342–48. In Rawick, *American Slave*.

"Eating Like Soul Brothers." *Time*, 24 January 1969, 57.

"Eating Outdoors in Boston." *Boston Daily Globe*, 9 February 1908, 35.

Eddington, Jane. "Cowpeas." *Washington Post*, 14 May 1924, 10.

———. "Hoppin' John." *Washington Post*, 13 May 1924, 12.

Edge, John T. "A Sweet So Sour: Kool-Aid Dills." *New York Times*, 9 May 2007, D1.

———, ed. "Seventh Ward Ramen." *Lucky Peach*, 12 July 2011, 45–47.

Editor. "On Plantation Gardens, and the Culture of Vegetables." *Southern Agriculturalist and Register of Rural Affairs*, August 1830, 417.

Edna Lewis Foundation website, http://ednalewisfoundation.org/index2.html. 7 April 2012.

Edwards, Gary, and John Mason. *Onje Fun Orisa (Food for the Gods)*. New York: Yoruba Theological Archministry, 1981.

Egerton, John. *Southern Food: At Home, on the Road, in History*. Chapel Hill: University of North Carolina Press, 1993.

Ellis, Merle. "Bullheads of Yore Are No Match for Today's Catfish." *Chicago Tribune*, 20 May 1982, A8.

Eltis, David, and David Richardson. *Atlas of the Transatlantic Slave Trade*. New Haven: Yale University Press, 2010.

Erickson, E. E. "Hoover and Henri IV." *American Speech*, February 1937, 9.

F——s. "Sweet Potatoes." *New England Farmer*, July 1856, 308.

Falconbridge, Alexander. "An Account of the Slave Trade on the Coast of Africa (London, 1788)." In *Slavery, Abolition, and Emancipation: Writings in the British Romantic Period*. Vol. 2, *The Abolition Debate*, edited by Peter J. Kitson, 121–34. London: Pickering & Chatto, 1999.

"Fall and Winter Gardens." *Charleston Mercury*, 22 August 1855, 2.

Fambro, Theresa. "A Mess o' Greens." *Chicago Daily Defender*, 27 June 1963, 15.

———. "Down Home Cooking." *Chicago Defender*, 9 May 1963, 13.

Farquhar, George, M.D. *The Angina Maligns Successfully Treated by Mercury and Capsicum Gargle*. Conducted by John Redman Coxe, M.D., at The Philadelphia Medical Museum, 3 January 1805, 266.

"Father Divine's More Abundant Life." *Chicago Daily Tribune*, 10 August 1938, 10.

Ferguson, Sheila. *Soul Food: Classic Cuisine from the Deep South*. New York: Grove Press, 1989.

Field, Robert C. "Cruciferous and Green Leafy Vegetables." In *The Cambridge World History of Food*, edited by Kenneth F. Kiple and Kriemhild Conee Ornelas, 1:288–98. Cambridge: Cambridge University Press, 2000.

Fisher, Mrs. Abby. *What Mrs. Fisher Knows About Old Southern Cooking, Soups, Pickles, Preserves, Etc.* San Francisco: Women's Cooperative Printing Office, 1881. Facsimile ed. with historical notes by Karen Hess, Bedford, Mass.: Applewood Books, 1995.

Fisher, M. F. K. "Spoon Bread and Moonlight." *Atlantic Monthly*, April 1947, 128–29.

"Fishing in the South." *New-York Tribune*, 28 April 1895, 10.

Fitz, James. "American Apples and Apple Culture." *Southern Cultivator and Dixie Farmer*, May 1886, 183.

Folse, Chef John D. *The Encyclopedia of Cajun & Creole Cuisine*. 2nd printing. Gonzales, La.: Chef John Folse and Company, January 2005.

Foner, Eric. *Reconstruction: America's Unfinished Revolution, 1863–1877*. New York: Harper & Row, 1988.

Forman, Gail. "Catfish Achieve Upward Mobility: Muddy, Oily Taste Is Gone." *New York Times*, 1 February 1989, C1.

Fountain, Della. *Oklahoma Narratives*, 7:102–7. In Rawick, *American Slave*.

Fox-Genovese, Elizabeth. *Within the Plantation Household: Black and White Women of the Old South*. Chapel Hill: University of North Carolina Press, 1988.

Franklin, John Hope. *From Slavery to Freedom: A History of Negro Americans*. 3rd ed. New York: Knopf, 1967.

"The Freedmen's Bureau: The Issue O Rations Stopped—Letter from Gen. Howard." *New York Times*, 29 August 1866, 1.

Friedman, Carolyn G. "Africans and African-Americans: An Ethnohistorical View and Symbolic Analysis of Food Habits." In *Encounters with American Ethnic Cultures*, edited by Philip L. Kilbride, Jane C. Goodale, and Elizabeth R. Ameisen, in collaboration with Carolyn G. Friedman, 77–98. Tuscaloosa: University of Alabama Press, 1990.

Fulton, J. Alexander. *Peach Culture*. New York: Orange Judd Co., 1889.

Fussell, Betty. *The Story of Corn: The Myths and History, the Culture and Agriculture, the Art and Science of America's Quintessential Crop*. New York: North Point Press, 1992.

Gaige, Crosby. *The New York World's Fair Cook Book*. New York: Doubleday, Doran, 1939.

Gandy, Harry. "Evidence with Respect to Carrying Slaves to the West Indies, &c. &c. &c." In *Slavery, Abolition, and Emancipation: Writings in the British Romantic Period*. Vol. 7, *Medicine and the West Indian Slave Trade*, edited by Alan Bewell, 167–68. London: Pickering & Chatto, 1999.

Gaskins, Ruth L. *A Good Heart and a Light Hand*. New York: Simon and Schuster, 1968.

Gee, Denise. "The Gospel of Great Southern Food." *Southern Living*, June 1996, 126–28.

Genovese, Eugene D. *Roll, Jordan, Roll: The World the Slaves Made*. New York: Pantheon, 1974.

"George Washington, Inventor." *New York Times*, 2 September 1906, SM4.

"The Georgia Yam." *Atlanta Constitution*, 26 December 1921, 6.

Gibbon, Ed. "Central Africa." In *Encyclopedia of Food and Culture*. Vol. 1, *Acceptance to Food Politics*, edited by Solomon H. Katz and William Woys Weaver, 21–27. New York: Scribner, 2003.

Gibbs, Patricia A. "Re-creating Hominy: The One-Pot Breakfast Food of the Gentry and Staple of Blacks and Poor Whites in the Early Chesapeake." In *Oxford Symposium on Food and Cookery 1988*, 46–54. London: Prospect Books, 1989.

Gillison, J. "They Call it Soul Music: 'Down Home' Jazz Feeling Scoring a 'Swinging' Hit with the Public." *Philadelphia Tribune*, 16 May 1961, 5.

Gladney, Virginia M., M.P.H., R.D., Senior Public Health Nutritionist. *Food Practices of Some Black Americans in Los Angeles County, Including a Method for Evaluating the Diet*. County of Los Angeles Department of Health Services, Community Health Services, 1972.

Glasse, Hannah [By a Lady]. *The Art of Cookery Made Plain and Easy*. 1747. Facsimile ed., London: Prospect Books, 1983.

Glenn, Viola. "The Eating Habits of Harlem." *Opportunity*, March 1935, 82–85.

Glory Foods website, http://www.gloryfoods.com/our_roots. 24 February 2012.

Glover. Thomas. *An Account of Virginia, its situations, temperature, productions, inhabitants, and their method of planting and ordering Tobacco &c*. Royal Society, London, Philosophical Transactions, XI, 20 June 1676. Reprint, Oxford: Blackwell, 1904.

Good, Paul. "The Thorntons of Mississippi: Peonage on the Plantation." *Atlantic Monthly*, September 1966, 95–100.

"Good Living." *Gourmet*, July 2007, 39.

Gordon, Asa H. *The Georgia Negro: A History*. Ann Arbor, Mich.: Edwards Brothers, 1937.

Grant, Faye W., and Dale Groom. "A Dietary Study among a Group of Southern Negroes." *Journal of the American Dietetic Association* 35 (September 1959):
914–15.

Gray, L. C. *History of Agriculture in the Southern United States until 1860.* Washington,
D.C.: Carnegie Institution of Washington, 1933.

Greaves, B. Frank. "Negroes Ask Civil Rights." *Los Angeles Times,* 26 February
1907, I2.

Green, Aliza. *Beans: More Than 200 Delicious, Wholesome Recipes from Around the World.*
Philadelphia: Running Press, 2004.

Green, Blake. "There's Hard Work before These Virginians Can Eat That Ham."
New York Times, 10 January 1972, 24.

"'Green' Greens." *New York Amsterdam News,* 20 March 1971, 17.

"Greens in Our History." *Chicago Daily Defender,* 6 February 1969, 24.

Grime, William Ed. *Ethno-Botany of the Black Americans.* Algonac, Mich.: Reference
Publications, March 1979.

Hale, Sarah J. *Mrs. Hale's New Cook Book: A Practical System for Private Families in Town
and Country.* Philadelphia: T. B. Peterson and Brothers, 1857.

Haley, James T., and Booker T. Washington. *Afro-American Encyclopedia, or the
Thoughts, Doings and Sayings of the Race.* Nashville, Tenn.: Haley & Florida, 1895,
http://books.google.com/books?id=6cptAAAAMAAJ&pg=PA532&lpg=PA5
32&dq=poem+%22red+lemonade%22&source=bl&ots=7vGRreguc8&sig
=W_HlgbsbcsXOx_AsWJmuLVczPo&hl=en&sa=X&ei=D4xgUPjxLcKFywHau
oHICg&sqi=2&ved=0CFMQ6AEwBw#v=onepage&q=poem%20%22red%20
lemonade%22&f=false. 25 September 2012.

Hall, Joan Huston, ed. "Strut." In *Dictionary of American Regional English.* Vol. 5,
Sl–Z, 348. Cambridge, Mass.: Belknap Press of Harvard University Press,
2012.

Hardy, Clifton S. "How Paris Warms Up To, Eats Down To, Bones on American
Type Spareribs." *Chicago Defender,* 18 June 1955, 19.

"Harlem Market Men Sing while They Sell." *New York Times Magazine,* 16 June 1935,
sec. 7, p. 17.

Harrington, John Walker. "Food That Tempts Harlem's Palate." *New York Times,*
15 July 1928, XX2.

Harris, David R. *Plants, Animals, and Man in the Outer Leeward Islands, West Indies: An
Ecological Study of Antigua, Barbuda, and Anguilla.* Berkeley: University of California Press, 1965.

Harris, Emma G., comp. *Montana Federation of Negro Women's Clubs Cook Book.* Billings: N.p., 1927.

Harris, Jessica. *Beyond Gumbo: Creole Fusion Food from the Atlantic Rim.* New York:
Simon and Schuster, 2003.

Harrison, William H. *Arkansas Narratives,* ser. 2, vol. 10, pt. 5, 306–7. In Rawick,
American Slave.

Haskin, Frederic J. "Corn Bread Hot and Fresh Is Popular." *Salt Lake City Telegram,*
26 August 1913, 4.

"Hats Off to 'Hot Sauce' of Cleveland!" *Pittsburgh Courier,* 22 March 1952, 24.

Haughton, Claire Shaver. *Green Immigrants: The Plants That Transformed America.* New York: Harcourt Brace Jovanovich, 1978.

"The Haunts." *Daily (Atlanta) Constitution,* 20 July 1881, O_4.

Hayes, Mrs. W. T. *Kentucky Cook Book: Easy and Simple for Any Cook, By A Colored Woman.* St. Louis: J. H. Tomkins, 1912.

Hearn, Lafcadio. *Gombo Zhèbes: Little Dictionary of Creole Proverbs Selected from Six Creole Dialects.* New York: Will H. Coleman, 1885.

Heart Healthy Cooking African American Style. U.S. Department of Health and Human Services, National Institutes of Health and National Heart, Lung, and Blood Institute. NIH Publication No. 08-3792, rev. 2008.

Heatter, Maida. *Maida Heatter's Best Dessert Book Ever.* New York: Random House, 1990.

Hess, Karen. "The American Loaf: A Historical View." *Journal of Gastronomy* 3, no. 4 (Winter 1987): 3–23.

———. *The Carolina Rice Kitchen: The African Connection.* Columbia: University of South Carolina Press, 1992.

Hodges, Fannie Smith. *Mississippi Narratives,* 9:68–71. In Rawick, *American Slave.*

Holmes, Joseph. "Dey Kep' Niggers in Good Condition to Sell." *Alabama Narratives,* 6:190–94. In Rawick, *American Slave.*

Holt, Jane. "Short Cuts to Good Meals." *New York Times,* 22 August 1943, SM18.

"Honor the Day in Warm Style." *Atlanta Constitution,* 6 July 1897, 2.

"Hot." *Oxford English Dictionary Online,* http://dictionary.oed.com.ezproxy.denver library.org:2048/cgi/entry/50108420?query_type=word&queryword=hot& first=1&max_to_show=10&sort_type=alpha&result_place=2&search_id= RLn9-87MOWL-22037&hilite=50108420. 30 March 2012.

"'Hot Sauce' Williams Tickles Your Ribs." *Cleveland Call and Post,* 21 March 1942, 5.

Hubbell, Sue. "'Hopping John' Gets the Year off to a Flying Start." *Smithsonian,* December 1993, 83–88.

Hudgins, Tom. "Hot Sauces: Fiery Flavorings from the USA." In *Spicing Up the Palate: Studies of Flavourings—Ancient and Modern. Proceedings of the Oxford Symposium on Food and Cookery 1992.* London: Prospect Books, 1993.

Hudson, Carrie. *Georgia Narratives,* vol. 12, pt. 2, 211–19. In Rawick, *American Slave.*

Hughes, Langston. "Mail Me Some More Kinds of Greens If I Missed Any, Says Simple." *Chicago Defender,* 16 September 1950, 6.

Hughes, Louis. *Thirty Years a Slave: The Institution of Slavery as Seen on the Plantation and in the Home of a Planter. Autobiography of Louis Hughes.* Milwaukee: South Side Printing Co., 1897, http://docsouth.unc.edu/fpn/hughes/hughes.html. 14 August 2012.

Hunt, Maria C. "Traditional Foods Help Mark End of Slavery." *San Diego Union-Tribune,* 17 June 1998, FOOD-1.

Hunt, Sharon Kaye. *Bread from Heaven; or, A Collection of African Americans' Home Cookin' and "Somepin't'Eat" Recipes from Down in Georgia.* Warner Robins, Ga.: Queen Hunt Productions, 1992.

Hunter, Charlayne. "Muslims Open a Fish House in Harlem." *New York Times*, 22 October 1974, 45.

Hurston, Zora Neale. *Mules and Men*. 1935. Reprint, New York: Harper Perennial, 1990.

Hurt, Charley. *Texas Narratives*, 4, pt. 2, 172–75. In Rawick, *American Slave*.

Ikeura, Hiromi, Kaori Kohara, Xin-Xian Li, Fumiyuki Kobayahsi, and Yasuyoshi Hayata. "Identification of (E, E)-2, 4-Undecadienal from Coriander (Coriandrum sativum L.) as a Highly Effective Deodorant Compound against the Offensive Odor of Porcine Large Intestine." *Journal of Agricultural and Food Chemistry* 58, no. 20 (2010): 11014–17.

Imam, Binta. *Method of Preparing Local & Modern Snacks*. Nigeria: Hajiya Binta Iman, 2004.

Improved Village Technology for Women's Activities: A Manual for West Africa. Geneva: International Labour Office, 1984.

Innis, Doris Funnye. "The Church Dinner: A Harlem Tradition." *New York Times*, 26 August 1981, C1.

"Introducing the Cowpea." *Hartford Courant*, 1 June 1917, 8.

"Is Jim Crowism Growing in Chicago?" *Broad Ax*, 31 December 1910, 4.

"The Italian's Cookery." *Current Literature*, July 1901, 68.

J. W. K. "New or Little Known Vegetables." *Horticulturalist and Journal of Rural Art and Rural Taste*, January 1847, 342.

Jerome, Norge W. "Northern Urbanization and Food Consumption Patterns of Southern-Born Negroes." *American Journal of Clinical Nutrition* 22, no. 12 (December 1969): 1667–69.

"Jim Crow Eat Shops Pay Dearly." *Chicago Defender*, 25 January 1941, 7.

Joffe, Natalie F., and Tomannie Thompson Walker. *Some Food Patterns of Negroes in the United States of America and Their Relationship to Wartime Problems of Food and Nutrition*. Washington, D.C.: Prepared for the Committee on Food Habits, National Food Council, n.d.

Johnson, Nunnally. "Sugar in Corn Bread!" *Saturday Evening Post*, 1 March 1930, 5, 66.

Johnson, Thomas A. "The U.S. Negro in Vietnam." *New York Times*, 29 April 1968, 1.

Johnston, Bruce. *The Staple Food Economies of Western Tropical Africa*. Stanford: Stanford University Press, 1958.

Jones, Williams. "Can the Pew Help Rescue the Pulpit?" *Baltimore Afro American*, 27 August 1927, 7.

Keegan, Frank L. *Blacktown, U.S.A*. Boston: Little, Brown, 1971.

Kegley, Howard. "Catfish Connoisseur Recites His Difficulties." *Los Angeles Times*, 12 October 1949, A5.

Kerr, Nora. "Salute to a Southern Master Chef." *New York Times Sunday Magazine*, 1 November 1992, SMA12.

King, Seth S. "The Hungry World of Kraftco: The Challenge Is to Keep Up with Changing Attitudes about Food." *New York Times*, 4 July 1976, F1.

Kingsley, Mary H. "Fishing in West Africa." *Eclectic Magazine of Foreign Literature*, June 1897, 773–83.

Kinnaird, Clark. "The Diary of a New Yorker." *Aberdeen Evening News*, 27 July 1928, 7.

Kiple, Kenneth F. *The Caribbean Slave: A Biological History*. Cambridge: Cambridge University Press, 1984.

Klein, Preston. *Alabama Narratives*, sup. ser. 1, 1:294–96. In Rawick, *American Slave*.

"Kola." *Scientific American*, 24 January 1891, 56.

"The Kola Nut: Its Uses and Cultivation." *Current Literature*, February 1894, 126–28.

Kool-Aid Museum website, http://www.hastingsmuseum.org/koolaid/kahistory .htm. 23 January 2011.

Koslow, Phillip, ed. *African American Desk Reference*. Schomburg Center for Research in Black Culture–New York Public Library. New York: Stonesong Press, 1999.

Kretschmar, Ella Morris. "The Corn Meal Grievance, and Some Recipes." *Good Housekeeping*, April 1901, 308–10.

L. C. R. "Maize or Wheat?" *Augusta Chronicle*, 26 November 1888, 2.

La Fleur, James Daniel. "The Culture of Crops on the Gold Coast (West Africa) from the Earliest Times to Circa 1850." Ph.D. diss., University of Virginia, 2003.

Lamb, Yanick Rice. "In Dishes from Soup to Hash, the Sweet Potato Shows Off: A Beloved Old Staple Has Not Lost Its Appeal." *New York Times*, 21 December 1994, C3.

"Late Confessions." *Crisis*, 22 August 1861, 1.

Lauterbach, Preston. *The Chitlin' Circuit and the Road to Rock 'n' Roll*. New York: Norton, 2011.

Lebby, R. Bee. *South Carolina Narratives*, sup. ser. 1, 11:238. In Rawick, *American Slave*.

Lee, Jennifer 8. *The Fortune Cookie Chronicles: Adventures in the World of Chinese Food*. New York: Twelve, 2008.

Leggett, Vincent O. *The Chesapeake Bay through Ebony Eyes*. Annapolis, Md.: Blacks of the Chesapeake Foundation, Inc., 1999.

Leslie, Eliza. *Directions for Cookery in Its Various Branches*. 12th ed. Philadelphia: Carey & Hart, 1844.

"A Letter from Capt. Horace James to Lt. Col. J. S. Fullerton," 10 July 1865. In *Freedom: A Documentary History of Emancipation, 1861–1867*. Ser. 1, vol. 2, *The Wartime Genesis of Free Labor: The Upper South*, edited by Ira Berlin, Steven F. Miller, Joseph P. Reidy, and Leslie S. Rowland, 235. Cambridge: Cambridge University Press, 1993.

Lewicki, Tadeusz. *West African Food in the Middle Ages*. London: Cambridge University Press, 1974.

Lewis, Edna. *The Taste of Country Cooking*. 1976. Reprint, New York: Knopf, 2000.

Lewis, Jesse W., Jr. "Negro GIs Find 'Real Soul Food' in Saigon." *Washington Post*, 6 April 1967, G5.

Lewis, Neil A. "The N.A.A.C.P. Facing a Battle over Its Future." *New York Times*, 31 March 1993, A14.

Liasson, Mara. "Democrats Flock to Rep. Jim Clyburn's Fish Fry." 28 April 2007, http://www.npr.org/templates/story/story.php?storyId=9896347. 14 April 2012.

Liboke de Viande recipe notes. Congo Cookbook website, http://www.congo cookbook.com/meat_recipes/liboke_de_viande.html.

"Licenses for Alley Cook Shops." *Washington Post*, 1 January 1897, 2.

"Life in Mississippi." *Daily Missouri Republican*, 3 September 1851, 2.

Louisiana, a Guide to the State. Compiled by workers of the Writers' Program of the Work Projects Administration in the State of Louisiana. 1941.

Lundy, Ronni. *Butter Beans to Blackberries.* New York: North Point Press, 1999.

Lutz, Charles H. "The Cadaver Connection." *Vietnam Magazine*, April 2011. Published online on 16 March 2012, http://www.historynet.com/the-cadaver -connection.htm. 19 March 2012.

M. "Alligator Story." *American Turf*, August 1830, 608–9.

"Macaroni." Monticello website, http://www.monticello.org/site/research-and -collections/macaroni. 22 March 2012.

"Macaroni." *Oxford English Dictionary Online*, http://www.oed.com.ezproxy.denver library.org:2048/view/Entry/111762?redirectedFrom=macaroni#eid. 24 March 2012.

"Macaroni and Cheese Stand-bys." *Chicago Defender*, 27 October 1956, 15.

MacDonald, Kevin C. "Why Chickens? The Centrality of the Domestic Fowl in West African Ritual and Magic." In *The Symbolic Role of Animals in Archaeology*, edited by Kathleen Ryan and Pam J. Crabtree, 52–55. Philadelphia: University of Pennsylvania Press, 1995.

Magoffin, James. In *The American Farmer and Spirit of the Agricultural Journals of the Day*, 1839, 27 March 1844, 356.

"Mahalia Jackson in Big Business." *New York Amsterdam News*, 18 January 1969, 48.

"Mail Overseas Gifts Early." *Call and Post*, 28 September 1968, 2C.

Major, Clarence. *Juba to Jive: A Dictionary of African-American Slang.* New York: Penguin, 1994.

"Management of Slaves." *DeBow's Review and Industrial Resources, Statistics, etc. Devoted to Commerce.* October 1854, 421.

Mangam, Charles R. "The Magic of the Black-Eyed Pea." *New York Folklore Quarterly* 27, no. 2 (June 1971): 236–39.

Mariani, John F. *The Dictionary of American Food and Drink.* New Haven: Ticknor and Fields, 1983.

"The Marvelous Kola Nut." *Times and Register*, 1 December 1894, 351.

Marx de Salcedo, Anastacia. "Quito's Street-Food Star." *Saveur*, no. 103, July 2007, 21.

Massey, Mary Elizabeth. *Ersatz in the Confederacy: Shortages and Substitutes on the*

Southern Homefront. 1st paperback ed. Columbia: University of South Carolina, 1993.

Mathews, Mitford M. A Dictionary of Americanisms on Historical Principles. Chicago: University of Chicago Press, 1951.

Mayer, Jean. Human Nutrition: Its Physiological, Medical and Social Aspects. A Series of Eighty-Two Essays. Springfield, Ill.: Charles. C. Thomas, 1972.

McDonald's Filet-O-Fish Sandwich Advertisement. Jet Magazine, 9 March 1978, 27.

McGee, Harold. On Food and Cooking: The Science and Lore of the Kitchen. Completely revised and updated. New York: Scribner, 2004.

McGlothin, Victor. Every Sistah Wants It. New York: St. Martin's Press, 2004.

McIntyre, Constance Fuller. "A Winter Scene on the Southern Plantation." Current Literature, February 1902, 41–43.

"Medical." Philadelphia Repository and Weekly Register, 4 February 1804, 38.

Mendes, Helen. The African Heritage Cookbook. New York: Macmillan, 1971.

Mickler, Ernest. White Trash Cooking. Berkeley, Calif.: Ten Speed Press, 1986.

"Might Turn a Battle." Washington Post, 31 January 1897, 23.

Miller, Anna. Texas Narratives, vol. 5, pt. 3, 82–84. In Rawick, American Slave.

"Miscellaneous." Southern Utonian, 24 October 1884, 4.

Moore, Stacy Gibbons. "Established and Well Cultivated: Afro-American Foodways in Early Virginia." Virginia Cavalcade 39 (Autumn 1989): 70–83.

Morgan, Phillip D. Slave Counterpoint: Black Culture in the Eighteenth-Century Chesapeake and Lowcountry. Chapel Hill: University of North Carolina Press, 1998.

Moss, Claiborne. Arkansas Narratives, vol. 10, pt. 5, 155–66. In Rawick, American Slave.

Moxon, Elizabeth. English Housewifery: Exemplified in above four hundred recipes, giving directions in most parts of cookery . . . . Ca. 1752. Ann Arbor: University of Michigan Library, 2005, http://quod.lib.umich.edu/e/eccodemo/K106011.0001.001/1:4.12?rgn=div2;view=fulltext. 23 February 2012.

"Mud." Oxford English Dictionary Online, http://www.oed.com.ezproxy.denverlibrary.org:2048/view/Entry/123228?rskey=ynifnd&result=4&isAdvanced=false#eid. 17 March 2012.

Murchie, Guy, Jr. "Life on a Share-Crop Plantation." Chicago Daily Tribune, 5 December 1937, G4.

Murphy, P. K. "The Foods and Cooking of Rural Gambia." In Oxford Symposium 1981: National and Regional Styles of Cookery, Proceedings, 290–99. London: Prospect Books, 1982.

"Mustard Greens Now a Delicacy in Chicago." Chicago Defender, 28 July 1928, 3.

Naj, Amal. Peppers: A Story of Hot Pursuits. New York: Knopf, 1992.

Nathan, Joan. "The Gourmet President: Jefferson, Not Reagan, Introduced Macaroni and Cheese to the White House." Washington Post Magazine, 18 April 1982, 33–35.

National Cookery Book Compiled from Original Receipts for the Women's Centennial Committees of the International Exhibition of 1876. Facsimile, Bedford, Mass.: Applewood Books, n.d.

Native Recipes. Virgin Islands Cooperative Extension Service. Extension Bulletin No. 1, February 1978, 16.

Neal, Bill. *Bill Neal's Southern Cooking*. Rev. ed. Chapel Hill: University of North Carolina Press, 1989.

Neal, Mark Anthony. *What the Music Said: Black Popular Music and Black Public Culture*. New York: Routledge, 1999.

"Negro as Fisherman." *Kansas City Times*, 16 May 1886, 2.

Nelson, Susan. "'Forest' a faithful servant." *South Carolina Narratives*, vol. 3, pt. 3, 214–16. In Rawick, *American Slave*.

"New Year's Day in Port Royal, South Carolina." *Christian Recorder*, 17 January 1863, 198.

Nizzardini, Genoeffa, and Natalie F. Joffe. *Italian Food Patterns and Their Relationship to Wartime Problems of Food and Nutrition*. Washington, D.C.: The Committee of Food Habits, National Research Council, 1942.

"No Eggs, Oatmeal or Butter in 'Colored' Relief Orders." *Afro-American*, 27 May 1933, 4.

"Note of Agricultural Practices on the Great Peedee, S.C." *Farmer's Register*, 31 October 1840, 636.

Nunn, General Jefferson Davis. *Alabama Narratives*, sup. ser. 1, 1:278–285. In Rawick, *American Slave*.

Nutter, Charles, and Ralph Wallace. "Dr. Miller and His Fabulous Yams." *Reader's Digest*, November 1949, 121–23.

O'Brien, Patricia J. "Sweet Potatoes and Yams." In *The Cambridge World History of Food*, edited by Kenneth F. Kiple and Kriemhild Conee Ornelas, 1:207–18. Cambridge: Cambridge University Press, 2000.

O'Hara, Delia. "A Weird, Wild Dance with a Long History." *Christian Science Monitor*, 18 October 1977, 16.

Okigbo, Dr. Bede Nwoye. *Plants and Food in Igbo Culture*. Ahiajoku Lecture. Owerri, Nigeria: Ministry of Information and Social Development, 1980.

"Old English Farm Fare." *Massachusetts Ploughman and New England Journal of Agriculture*, 22 July 1905, 4.

"Oldest Known Tabasco Bottle Type Discovered at Nevada Archeological Site." Tabasco Company website, http://www.tabasco.com/info_booth/news/old_tabasco_bottle_exc.cfm. 7 April 2012.

Old Southhampton. "To Keep Sweet Potatoes." *Southern Planter*, October 1846, 238.

Oliver, Sandra L. *Food in Colonial and Federal America*. Westport, Conn.: Greenwood Press, 2005.

———. *Saltwater Foodways: New Englanders and Their Food, at Sea and Ashore, in the Nineteenth Century*, Mystic, Conn.: Mystic Seaport Museum, 1995.

Opie, Frederick Douglass. *Hog and Hominy: Soul Food from Africa to America*. New York: Columbia University Press, 2008.

"Origin of Pink Lemonade: How a Circus Clown Met a Texas Emergency." *Morning Oregonian*, 26 December 1897, 18.

Ortiz, Elisabeth Lambert. "Maize as a Staple Food." In *Staple Foods: Proceedings* of the Oxford Symposium on Food and Cookery, 1989, edited by Harlan Walker, 134–41. London: Prospect Books, 1990.

Osseo-Asare, Fran. Food Culture in Sub-Saharan Africa. Westport, Conn.: Greenwood Press, 2005.

———. "'We Eat First with Our Eyes': On Ghanaian Cuisine." Gastronomica: A Journal of Food and Culture 2, no. 1 (Fall 2002): 49–57.

Owens, Janis. The Cracker Kitchen: A Cookbook of Cornbread-Fed, Down-Home Family Stories and Cuisine. New York: Scribner, 2009.

Padda, Darshan S. Native Recipes. St. Croix: College of the Virgin Islands Cooperative Extension Service, February 1978.

Paddleford, Clementine. "Gold-Mine Potato," Sun, 20 October 1946, TW29.

Painter, Nell Irvin. The History of White People. New York: Norton, 2010.

Parkes, Anna. Georgia Narratives, vol. 13, pt. 3, 153–64. In Rawick, American Slave.

Parks, David. GI Diary. New York: Harper & Row, 1968.

Parry, John D. "Chitterlings in Paris? Mais Oui, at Leroy's." Chicago Defender, 23 April 1966, 14.

Parsons, Russ. How to Pick a Peach: The Search for Flavor from Farm to Table. Boston: Houghton Mifflin, 2007.

Payne, Ethel L. "Crowded Saigon Is Lonely, Black GIs Find." Chicago Defender, 7 February 1967, 6.

Payne, Larkin. Arkansas Narratives, vol. 2, pt. 5, 306–7. In Rawick, American Slave.

"Peach Cobblers." State, 10 July 1908, 4.

"Peaches." Kansas City Negro Star, 12 July 1935, 1.

"The Peach Trade." New York Times. 22 August 1870, 2.

Pearl, Anita May, Constance Cuttle, and Barbara B. Deskins. Completely Cheese: The Cheeselover's Companion. Edited by David Kolatch. Middle Village, N.Y.: Jonathan David, 1978.

Pei, Mario. "Language of Black Relations." New York Amsterdam News, 18 April 1970, 4.

"Pepper." Southern Planter, August 1850, 8. Courtesy of ProQuest LLC.

"Pepper Sauce." Oxford English Dictionary Online, http://www.oed.com.ezproxy .denverlibrary.org:2048/view/Entry/140433?redirectedFrom=pepper%20 sauce#eid31150498. 23 March 2012.

Perry, Armstrong. "Plantation Sweet-Potato Recipes." Better Homes and Gardens, October 1937, 8.

Peters, Art. "Off the Main Stem." Philadelphia Tribune, 6 December 1960, 5.

"Phases of City Life." New York Times, 8 November 1891, 12.

Philip, Robert Kemp. The Reason Why—Domestic Science. London: Houlston & Wright, 1864.

Phillips, Kenneth E. "Sharecropping and Tenant Farming in Alabama," http:// www.encyclopediaofalabama.org/face/Article.jsp?id=h-1613. 31 January 2012.

"Phillip's History." The Atheneum; or, Spirit of the English Magazine 1 (May 1822): 118.

The Picayune Creole Cook Book. Facsimile of 2nd ed. New York: Dover Publications, 1970.

Pierce, William C. "Kola." *Medical and Surgical Reporter* 74, no. 17 (25 April 1896): 513.

Pinckney, Eliza Lucas. *Recipe Book*. N.p., 1756.

A planter. In *DeBow's Review of the Southern and Western States*, March 1851, 325.

Poe, Elisabeth E. "Hopping John Is Magical, Dainty and Easy to Make." *Washington Post*, 11 November 1936, X17.

Polk, Anita Lewis. "Soldier Completes Viet Nam Missions." *Call and Post*, 16 July 1966, 3A.

Pope, Alec. *Georgia Narratives*, vol. 13, pt. 3, 172–77. In Rawick, *American Slave*.

Poston, T. R. "Harlem Shadows." *Pittsburgh Courier*, 31 January 1931, A1.

"Pot of Black-Eyed Peas, Pork Bring Heap O' Luck." *Atlanta Constitution*, 31 December 1939, 1A.

Pound, Louise. "Motherless Greens." *American Speech* 11, no. 3 (October 1936): 272.

Powers, Nick. *Boilin' 'n' Bakin' in Boogar Hollow: A Country Cookbook*. Boogar Hollow, Lindale, Ga.: Country Originals, 1971.

"Privations of the Slaves." In *American Slavery As It Is: Testimony of A Thousand Witnesses*. New York: American Anti-Slavery Society, 1839.

Puckett, Newbell Niles. *The Magic and Folk Beliefs of the Southern Negro*. Facsimile of 1926 ed. New York: Dover Publications, 1969.

Purchas, Samuel. *Pvrchas his Pilgrimes: in five bookes: the first, contayning the voyages and peregrinations made by ancient kings . . . and others, to and thorow . . . . 4* vols. London, 1625.

Purdue, Lewis. "A Capitol Collard Greening." *Washington Post*, 5 January 1977, F1.

Raghavan, Susheela. *Handbook of Spices, Seasonings, and Flavorings*. 2nd ed. Boca Raton, Fla.: Taylor & Francis, 2006.

Randolph, Mrs. Mary. *The Virginia Housewife; or, Methodical Cook*. 1828. Special reprint ed., Birmingham, Ala.: Oxmoor House, 1984.

Raper, Arthur F. *A Preface to Peasantry: A Tale of Two Black Belt Counties*. Reprint of 1936 ed., New York: Arno Press & The New York Times, 1971.

Ravernell, Wanda J. "12 Months of Luck in a Humble Legume." *San Francisco Chronicle*, 24 December 2008, http://www.sfgate.com/cgi-bin/article.cgi?f=/c/a/2008/12/23/FDK614Q4OD.DTL. 12 January 2012.

Rawick, George P., ed. *The American Slave: A Composite Autobiography*. 41 vols. Contributions in Afro-American and African Studies. Westport, Conn.: Greenwood Press, 1972–79.

———. *From Sundown to Sunup: The Making of the Black Community*. Westport, Conn.: Greenwood Press, 1972.

Rawlins, E. Elliott. "Keeping Fit—Do You Eat Good Food?" *New York Amsterdam News*, 1 August 1928, 16.

Raymond, Natalie. *Reconnaissance Report on Concentrated Rations of Primitive Peoples*. Washington, D.C.: War Department, Office of the Quartermaster General, 1942.

Reade, Winwoor. "Food in Central Africa." *Appletons' Journal of Literature, Science and Art*, 8 April 1871, 413.

"Recipes." *Dwight's American Magazine*, 5 December 1846, 702.

"Recipes." *Dwight's American Magazine*, 12 December 1846, 718–19.

Rediker, Marcus. *The Slave Ship: A Human History*. New York: Penguin, 2007.

Reed, Julia. "Cat Fight." *New York Times*, 18 May 2003, SM93–94.

"Relief Committee to Feed the Destitute." *New Amsterdam News*, 26 November 1930, 2.

"Rent Parties in Harlem Attract White Patrons." *Atlanta Daily World*, 25 October 1932, 1A.

"Reuss Survey Shows Chittlins Make Merchants Rich." *Milwaukee Star*, 2 November 1968, 16.

Reynolds, Jonathan. "Sexy Beast: For Those Who Like to Do on the Wild Side." *New York Times*, 20 June 2004, SM67.

Rhett, Blanche S., and Helen Woodard. "Better Than Candied." *Atlanta Constitution*, 17 November 1929, J21.

Rice, William. "Louis Szathmary, Noted Chef, Ex-restaurant Owner." *Chicago Tribune*, 5 October 1995, http://articles.chicagotribune.com/1996-10-05/news/9610050031_1_louis-szathmary-illinois-restaurant-association-biblio. 15 April 2012.

Richard, Lena. *New Orleans Cook Book*. 1939. With an introduction by Gwen Bristow. Gretna, La.: Fireside Press, n.d.

Richardson, Charlie. *Missouri Narratives*, 10:290–97. In Rawick, *American Slave*.

Richman, Phyllis C. "Praise the Lord and Pass the Sweet Potatoes." *Washington Post*, 16 November 1986, 53–55.

Roberts, Rebecca. "Salley, S.C., a Town Thankful for Chitlins." *New York Times*, 3 December 1980, C3.

Roles, John. "Twenty-five Years among the Cotton Plantations of Louisiana and Mississippi." *Chicago Tribune*, 30 November 1860, O3.

Rorer, Sarah Tyson Heston. *Mrs. Rorer's New Cook Book: A Manual of Housekeeping*. Philadelphia: Arnold and Co., 1902.

Ross, Nancy L. "African Cuisine Favors Stew." *Washington Post, Times Herald*, 21 August 1966, F3.

Rountree, Henry. *North Carolina Narratives*, vol. 15, pt. 2, 233–35. In Rawick, *American Slave*.

Rowland, W. M. *Improvement of the Cowpea*. Bulletin, Georgia State College of Agriculture, Proceedings of the Georgia State Horticultural Society and Georgia Dairy and Live Stock Association, Athens. Vol. 1, no. 11 (15 January 1913).

Rufca, Sarah. "Fried Kool-Aid: Genius Invention or Sign of the Apocalypse?" *Culturemap Houston*, 21 June 2011, http://houston.culturemap.com/newsdetail/06-21-11-fried-kool-aid-genius-invention-sign-apocalypse/. 16 February 2012.

Russell, Mrs. Malinda. *Domestic Cook Book: Containing A Careful Selection of Useful Receipts For The Kitchen*. Paw Paw, Mich.: T. G. Ward, 1866. Facsimile ed. by William L. Clements Library, Detroit: Inland Press, 2007.

Rutledge, Sarah. *The Carolina Housewife*. With an introduction by Anna Wells

Rutledge. Facsimile of the 1847 ed., 5th printing, Columbia: University of South Carolina, 1999.

Rutledge, "Uncle" Sabe. *South Carolina Narratives*, vol. 3, pt. 4, 65–70. In Rawick, *American Slave*.

Sanders, Dori. *Dori Sanders' Country Cooking: Recipes & Stories from the Family Farm Stand*. John Willoughby, consulting ed. Chapel Hill, N.C.: Algonquin Books, 1995.

Savela, Martin. "The Neck Bone's Connected to the Backbone." *Chicago Tribune*, 22 November 1970, J35–36.

"Saving the Gas Bill." *Afro-American*, 27 October 1917, 7.

Savitt, Todd. *Medicine and Slavery: The Disease and Health Care of Blacks in Antebellum Virginia*. Urbana: University of Illinois Press, 1978.

Schwaab, Eugene L., ed., in collaboration with Jacqueline Bull. *Travels in the Old South*. Lexington: University of Kentucky Press, 1973.

"Second Mahalia Jackson Chicken Shack Opens." *Chicago Daily Defender*, 31 October 1970, 40.

Segura, Jean. "Haynes: 60 Years of an American in Paris." Translated by Christine Madsen, http://www.ruedescollectionneurs.com/magazine/mag/haynes-us.php. 19 March 2012.

Sells, Abram. *Texas Narratives*, vol. 5, pt. 4, 9–14. In Rawick, *American Slave*.

Servanti, Silvano, and Françoise Sabban. *Pasta: The Story of a Universal Food*. Translated by Anthony Shugaar. New York: Columbia University Press, 2002.

"The 1752 Calendar Change." Connecticut State Library website, http://www.cslib.org/CalendarChange.htm. 21 March 2012.

Sheridan, Margaret. "The Top Ten Bestsellers in Chicago." *Chicago Tribune*. 20 September 1984, F1.

Simmons, Amelia. *American Cookery*. Reprint of 1796 ed., Grand Rapids, Mich.: William B. Eerdmans, 1965.

Simmons, George. *Texas Narratives*, vol. 5, pt. 4, 24–26. In Rawick, *American Slave*.

Simonsen, Thordis, ed. *You May Plow Here: The Narrative of Sara Brooks*. New York: Norton, 1986.

Simoons, Frederick J. *Eat Not This Flesh: Food Avoidances in the Old World*. Madison: University of Wisconsin Press, 1967.

Singleton, Theresa A. *The Archaeology of Slavery and Plantation Life*. Orlando, Fla.: Academic Press, 1985.

A Small Farmer. "Art. III—Management of Negroes." *DeBow's Review of the Southern and Western States*, October 1851, 369.

Smith, Andrew F. "Condiments." In *Oxford Companion to American Food and Drink*, edited by Andrew F. Smith, 144. Oxford: Oxford University Press, 2009.

———. *Starving the South: How the North Won the Civil War*. New York: St. Martin's Press, 2011.

Smith, Gus. *Missouri Narratives*, 10:321–332. In Rawick, *American Slave*.

Smith, Nellie. *Georgia Narratives*, vol. 4, pt. 3, 304–19. In Rawick, *American Slave*.

Snelson, Floyd G. "Harlem, 'Negro Capital of the Nation.'" *Cleveland Plaindealer*, 3 March 1939, 3.

Sokolov, Raymond. "Broken Kernels: An International Saga." *Natural History*, September 1991, 88–91.

———. "Columbus's Biggest Discovery." *Natural History*, August 1987, 66–67.

———. "Humble Pie." *Natural History*, April 1977, 80–83.

———. *The Jewish-American Kitchen*. New York: Stewart, Tabori & Chang, 1989.

———. "The Peripatetic Potato." *Natural History*, March 1990, 86–88.

"Some Dainty Southern Recipes." *American Cookery*, June/July 1914, 59.

"Some Mighty Fine Ways of Using Lowly Cornmeal." *Wilkes-Barre Times*, 5 November 1915, 11.

"Soul Food Date." *New York Amsterdam News*, 6 January 1968, 10.

"Southern Dishes." *New-York Tribune*, 12 April 1896, 29.

"Southern Soldiers Cry for the Yam." *Los Angeles Times*, 20 September 1918, 113.

Soyer, Alexis. *The Pantropheon; or, A History of Food and Its Preparation in Ancient Times, Embellished with Forty-Two Engravings Illustrating the Greatest Gastronomic Marvels of Antiquity*. New York: Paddington Press, 1977.

Spencer, Maryellen. "Food in Seventeenth-Century Tidewater Virginia: A Method for Studying Historical Cuisines." Ph.D. diss., Virginia Polytechnic and State University, 1982.

Spivey, Diane. "Latin American and Caribbean Food and Cuisine." *Encyclopedia of African American Culture and History*, 841. Detroit: Thomson Gale 2006.

Starr, Kathy. *The Soul of Southern Cooking*. Montgomery, Ala.: New South Books, 2001.

Stearns, Annie S. "Five Delicious Southern Puddings." *Ladies' Home Journal*, April 1891, 5.

Stephenson, Edward A. "The Etymology of 'Macaroni, Macaroon.'" *American Speech* 39, no. 1 (February 1964): 75–77.

Stern, Jane, and Michael Stern. "Skillet Set." *Gourmet*, October 2007, 58.

Sterner, Richard, in collaboration with Lenore A. Epstein, Ellen Winston, and others. *The Negro's Share: A Study of Income, Consumption, Housing and Public Assistance*. New York: Harper & Brothers, 1943.

Stevens, Charles McClellan. *Encyclopedia of Superstitions, Folklore and the Occult Sciences of the World*. Vol. 3. Chicago: J. H. Yewdale & Sons, 1903.

Stier, Isaac. *Mississippi Narratives*, 7:143–50. In Rawick, *American Slave*.

Streitfeld, David. "Soaring Grain Prices Put Catfish Farms on the Endangered List." *New York Times*, 18 July 2008, A1.

"Sugar and Spice." *Gourmet*, March 1947, 70.

Sugrue, Thomas J. *Sweet Land of Liberty: The Forgotten Struggle for Civil Rights in the North*. New York: Random House, 2008.

Sullivan, Caroline. *Classic Jamaican Cooking*. London: Serif, 2003.

"A Summary of the Evidence Produced before a Committee of the House of Commons, Relating to the Slave Trade." *Connecticut Courant*, 4 August 1794, 1.

Summer, W. M. "The Culture of the Sweet Potatoe." *Cultivator*, February 1845, 65.

Sundstrom, Lars. "The Cola Nut. Functions in West African Social Life." *Studia ethnographica Upsaliensia* 26, no. 2 (1966): 135–42.

Swann, Evelyn, M. "What's Cooking? Newsy Kitchen Notes on Broiling-Baking-Boiling." *New Journal and Guide*, 24 June 1950, D4.

Swanton, John R. *The Indians of the Southeastern United States*. Washington, D.C.: Government Printing Office, 1946.

"The Sweet Potato." *Good Housekeeping*, June 1892, 277.

Sweet Potatoes and Yams. No. 91. New York: Barrett Company Agricultural Department, 1918.

Sweet Potato Statistical Yearbook 2011. Columbia, S.C.: United States Sweet Potato Council, June 2011.

Sydnor, Charles. *Slavery in Mississippi*. Baton Rouge: Louisiana State University Press, 1966.

Szathmary, Louis. "How Festive Foods of the Old World Became Commonplace in the New, Or the American Perception of Hungarian Goulash." In *Food in Motion: The Migration of Foodstuffs and Cooking Techniques. Proceedings, Oxford Symposium on Food and Cookery 1983*, edited by Alan Davidson, 137–42. Leeds: Prospect Books, 1983.

"Table Talk: Concerning Eating and Drinking." *Current Literature*, December 1901, 744.

Tate, Annie. *North Carolina Narratives*, vol. 11, pt. 2, 332–34. In Rawick, *American Slave*.

"Tavern Topics." *New York Amsterdam Star-News*, 15 March 1941, 16, 21.

"Tavern Topics." *New York Amsterdam Star-News*, 18 April 1942, 16.

Taylor, Joe Gray. "The Food of the New South." *Georgia Review* 20, no. 1 (Spring 1966): 9–28.

Telfair, Georgia. *Georgia Narratives*, vol. 4, pt. 4, 2–10. In Rawick, *American Slave*.

"Texas and Its Capabilities." *New-York Tribune*, 9 November 1854, 6.

"There's Variety in Greens for Salad." *Chicago Defender*, 19 May 1951, 15.

"This Is 'Mancipation Day.'" *Dallas Morning News*, 19 June 1899, 8.

Thompson, Sue Ellen. *Holiday Symbols and Customs: A Guide to the Legend and Lore behind the Traditions, Rituals, Foods, Games, Animals, and Other Symbols and Activities Associated with Holidays and Holy Days, Feasts and Fasts, and Other Celebrations, Covering Calendar, Ethnic, Religious, Historic, Folkloric, National, Promotional, Sporting, and Ancient Events, as Observed in United States and Around the World*. 3rd ed. Detroit: Omnigraphics, 2003.

Thorne, John. *Simple Cooking*. New York: North Point Press, 1996.

"Tines's Troubles." *Atlanta Constitution*, 27 January 1886, 7.

Tobin, Beth Fowkes. "'And There Raise Yams': Slaves' Gardens in the Writings of West Indian Plantocrats." *Eighteenth-Century Life* 23, no. 2 (1999): 164–76.

Toombs, Alonza Fantroy. "He Belonged to Bob Toombs of Georgia." *Alabama Narratives*, 6:383–84. In Rawick, *American Slave*.

To Work and Serve the Home. Dedicated to the New Jersey State Federation of Colored Women's Clubs, Through the Chairman of Ways and Means Department. Ridgewood, N.J., August 1928.

Trillin, Calvin. "An Attempt to Compile a Short History of the Buffalo Chicken Wing." *New Yorker*, 25 August 1980, 82–87.

Turner, Timothy G. "Corn." *Los Angeles Times*, 4 November 1948, A5.

Turner, Janet Driskell. *Through the Back Door: Memoirs of a Sharecropper's Daughter Who Learned to Read as a Great-Grandmother*. 1985. Boulder, Colo.: Creative Press, 2001.

Turner, Lorenzo Dow. *Africanisms in the Gullah Dialect*. Columbia: University of South Carolina Press, 2002.

Turner Broadcasting System website, http://www.tbs.com/stories/story/0,,217 449,00.html. 8 March 2012.

Tyree, Marion Cabell. *Housekeeping in Old Virginia, Containing Contributions from Two Hundred and Fifty of Virginia's Noted Housewives, Distinguished for Their Skill in the Culinary Art and Other Branches of Domestic Economy*. Reprint of 1879 ed., Louisville, Ky.: Favorite Recipes Press, 1965.

Ude, Louis Eustache. *The French Cook*. Facsimile of 1828 ed. New York: Arco, 1978.

"Untitled." *Anderson Intelligencer* (South Carolina), 31 March 1887, image 4, http://chroniclingamerica.loc.gov/lccn/sn84026965/1887-03-31/ed-1/seq-4/;words=sweet+potato+candied?date1=1836&sort=date&date2=1922&searchType=advanced&proxdistance=5&state=&rows=20&ortext=&proxtext=&phrasetext=candied+sweet+potatoes&andtext=&dateFilterType=yearRange&index=0. 12 January 2012.

U.S. One, Maine to Florida. American Guide Series. Compiled and written by the Federal Writers' Project of the Works Progress Administration. Washington, D.C., 1938.

Usner, Daniel H., Jr. "Food Marketing and Interethnic Exchange in the 18th-Century Lower Mississippi Valley." *Food and Foodways* 1 (1986): 279–310.

Vance, Rupert B. *Human Geography of the South: A Study in Regional Resources and Human Adequacy*. Chapel Hill: University of North Carolina Press, 1932.

Van Hook, John F. Georgia Narratives, vol. 4, pt. 4, 72–96. In Rawick, *American Slave*.

Vergil, Emma. Georgia Narratives, vol. 4, pt. 4, 115–22. In Rawick, *American Slave*.

Verrill, A. Hyatt. *Foods America Gave the World: The Strange, Fascinating and Often Romantic Histories of Many Native American Food Plants, Their Origins and Other Interesting and Curious Facts*. Boston: L. C. Page & Co., 1937.

"Vied with Voices in Rival Song." *Atlanta Constitution*, 5 August 1897, 7.

"The Virginians: Extracts from *Letters from the South and West* by Arthur Singleton, Esq." *Hampshire Gazette*, 18 August 1824, 1.

"Visit to a Rice Plantation." *New York Times*, 13 July 1853, 2.

Visser, Margaret. *Much Depends on Dinner: The Extraordinary History and Mythology, Allure and Obsessions, Perils and Taboos of an Ordinary Meal*. New York: Collier, 1986.

Wade, Richard C. *Slavery in the Cities: The South, 1820–1860*. London: Oxford University Press, 1964.

Wagner, Mark. "The Introduction and Early Use of African Plants in the New World." *Tennessee Anthropologist* 6, no. 2 (Fall 1981): 112–24.

Walker, Saunders E. *A Dictionary of the Folk Speech of the East Alabama Negro*. Cleveland: Case Western Reserve University, September 1956.

Watson, Cordie. "Black Chicken King Still Frying." *Chicago Defender*, 11 June 1985, 11.

"The Wealthiest Negro Colony in the World." *New York Times*, 2 September 1917, 58.

Weaver, William Woys. "From Turtle to Tripe: Philadelphia Pepperpot, a Street Food from the West Indies." In *Public Eating: Oxford Symposium on Food and Cookery, 1991*, edited by Harlan Walker, 287–94. London: Prospect Books, 1992.

———. "Pie." In *Encyclopedia of Food and Culture*. Vol. 3, *Obesity to Zoroastrianism, Index*, edited by Solomon H. Katz and William Woys Weaver, 68–73. New York: Scribner, 2003.

Webster, Laura Josephine. "The Operation of the Freedmen's Bureau in South Carolina, Chapters V–VIII." In *Smith College Studies in History* 1, no. 3 (April 1916): 119–63.

Wells, Stanley, and Gary Taylor, eds. *William Shakespeare: The Complete Works*. Oxford: Clarendon Press, 1991.

Westheider, James E. *The African American Experience in Vietnam: Brothers in Arms*. Lanham, Md.: Rowman & Littlefield, 2008.

"What the Cats Do While the Squares Sleep." *Chicago Defender*, 27 August 1958, 18.

"What to Do with Peaches," *New-York Tribune*, 5 September 1897, A7.

"What We Are All Talking About." *New York Sun*, 11 July 1890, 4.

White, A. E. "Fried Fish Joints." *Philadelphia Tribune*, 9 January 1930, 9.

White, Poppy Cannon. "The Soul Food Battle." *New York Amsterdam News*, 29 April 1967, 17.

"White and Yellow Cornmeal." *Macon Telegraph*, 19 May 1909, 4.

Whitlock, Ralph. "Throughout New Year's Day and Night." In *In Search of Lost Gods: A Guide to British Folklore*. Oxford: Phaidon, 1979.

"Why the Hoecake Is Going." *Boston Daily Globe*, 13 February 1898, SM36.

Wiggins, William H., Jr. "Juneteenth: A Red Spot Day on the Texas Calendar." *Juneteenth Texas: Essays in African American Folklore, Publications of the Texas Folklore Society* 54 (1996).

———. *O Freedom! Afro-American Emancipation Celebrations*. Knoxville: University of Tennessee Press, 1987.

Williams, R. O. *Miss Williams' Cookery Book*. 2nd impression. Bristol: Longmans of Nigeria, 1962.

Wilson, C. Anne. *Food and Drink in Britain from the Stone Age to the 19th Century*. Chicago: Academy Chicago Publishers, 1991.

———. "Pottage and Soup as Nourishing Liquids." In *Liquid Nourishment: Potable Foods and Stimulating Drinks*, edited by C. Anne Wilson, 3–19. Edinburgh: Edinburgh University Press, 1993.

Wilson, Ellen Gibson. *A West African Cookbook*. New York: Avon Books, 1971.

Wood, Peter H. *Black Majority: Negroes in Colonial South Carolina from 1670 through the Stono Rebellion*. New York: Norton, 1974.

Woods, Sylvia, and Christopher Styler. *Sylvia's Soul Food: Recipes from Harlem's World-Famous Restaurant*. New York: Hearst Books, 1992.

Woodson, Willis. *Texas Narratives*, vol. 5, pt. 4, 214–15. In Rawick, *American Slave*.

Worden, Helen. *The Real New York: A Guide for the Adventurous Shopper, the Exploratory Eater and the Know-It-All Sightseer Who Ain't Seen Nothin' Yet*. Indianapolis: Bobbs-Merrill, 1932.

"Word Shadows." *Atlantic Monthly*, January 1891, 143–44.

"World's Worst Cuisine." *New York Times*, 14 August 1994, SM13.

Wright, Clifford. "The Medieval Spice Trade and the Diffusion of the Chile." *Gastronomica: The Journal of Food and Culture* 7, no. 2 (Spring 2007): 35–43.

Yeoman, "The South: Letters on the Productions, Industry, and Resources of the Southern States—Number 5." *New York Times*, 10 March 1853, 2.

Index

Abernathy, J. Carle, 235

Abolitionists, 23, 192–93. *See also* Slaves

Abrahams, Roger, 190

Adair, James, 72, 189

Adams, Bob, 106

Adams, Ezra, 151

Addums, Mozis, 116

Advertisements, 1, 38 (ill.), 65 (ill.), 85

Aframomum melegueta. *See* Grains of paradise

Africa. *See* West Africa

African Americans: agricultural jobs for, 32–36, 135; chronic diet-related disease among, 2; civil rights for, in postbellum period, 30; and civil rights movement of twentieth century, 41, 43–45, 255; employment of, in urban areas, 39, 41; in fishing industry, 73; food-related businesses owned by, in postbellum period, 32; housing for, 34, 40, 100–101; middle class of, 41; migration of, to urban areas, 35–40, 260; population statistics on, 35–36; products purchased by, 141–42; and racial caste system, 9, 21–22, 29, 31, 39, 95; segregation of, during postbellum period, 31; food-related stereotypes of, 31, 58, 75, 231; voter registration of, 43–44

Agriculture: and plantation slavery, 16–17, 19, 22–28; and rent farmers, 33; and sharecropping, 32, 33–35, 154, 174–75, 193; Sicilian labor on

sugar plantations, 135–36; statistics on African Americans employed in, 35–36; and sweet potatoes, 178, 182, 183; and white landlords in postbellum period, 30, 32–33, 35, 135–36. *See also* Catfish: farming of

Agua de Jamaica (Jamaica water), 228, 237

Akil, Sababa, 39

Albala, Ken, 121

Alcenia's soul food restaurant (Memphis, Tenn.), 232, 233; Alcenia's Ghetto Aid recipe, 238

Alcoholic beverages: at cornshuckings, 190–91, 230; at fish fries, 81–82; at hog killings, 230; red whiskey, 229–30; at rent parties, 100; in Slave Food period, 229–31; for slaves, 190–91, 229–30; at weddings, 250; in West Africa, 224, 226

Ali, Muhammad, 107

America Eats, 95–96, 101, 116

American Cookery (Simmons), 5, 113, 114–15

American Gangster, 107

America's Next Great Restaurant, 3, 257

Anchor Bar (Buffalo, N.Y.), 220

Ancient world. *See* Greece, ancient; Rome, ancient

Andouillettes, 93

Appalachian cookbooks, 47

Apple cobbler, 244

Apple dumpling, 242

Apple pie, 33, 43, 64, 249

Are We There Yet? (TV sitcom), 1

Army and Lou's restaurant (Chicago), 3
Arrington, Nyesha, 144–45, 256
Arroz con gandules, 118
Ash cake/ash pone, 194–96, 204
Asia (Japan, Vietnam), 106–7
Asian-style hot sauce, 219
Atlantic slave trade, 13–15, 19, 52, 115, 170–71, 188, 212–13, 237
Avirett, James Battle, 27

B. B. King Blues Museum, 77
Baker, Roland, 60
Banana pudding, 4, 241, 243, 246–47; Banana Pudding recipe, 252–53
Barbecue: barbecue stands for black migrants, 38; cornbread with, 191, 199; greens with, 163; for holidays, 231, 234, 242; hot sauce with, 219, 220–21; at L&M Guest House in Vietnam, 107; red drinks with, 231, 234, 237
Bardot, Brigitte, 106
Barker, Karen, 243
Barnes, "Uncle" Henry, 229, 242
Barrow, David, 191
Barton, Chef Scott, 262
Battua, Ibn, 224
Beans. *See specific types of beans*
"Beaten biscuits," 16
Beef. *See* Meats
Bellissimo family, 220
Bell pepper, 211
Bennett, Robert, 103
Berlin, Ira, 15, 32
Bethlehem Bistro (Chattanooga, Tenn.), 140
Bethune, Mary McLeod, 249
Bethune Cookman University, 249
Betty (dessert), 243
Betty's Place (Indianola, Miss.), 77, 83
Betz, Ryan, 161, 162
Beverages. *See* Alcoholic beverages; Milk; Red drinks; Water
Beverly, Robert, 72, 188

Bianco, Marie, 29–30
Big House cooking: of chicken, 54–55, 59; of chitlins, 94–95; of cornbread, 196–97, 200; and cornmeal, 192; of desserts, 241, 248–49; of fish, 74, 89; of greens, 150, 156; and hot sauce, 216; of macaroni and cheese, 134; and racial caste system, 21–22, 29; of red drinks, 230; slaves' sneaking food from, 26; on Sundays and holidays, 27–28; of sweet potatoes, 177; variety and quality of food used in, 21–22. *See also* Slave Food period
Big Red soda, 237
Bilger, Burkhard, 72
Bissap (hibiscus tea), 228
Bitter leaf, 149
Bittman, Mark, 53
Black Belt: cornshuckings in, 191; cuisine of, 17–19, 22; maps and location of, 15–16, 17, 18; migration from, to urban areas, 36, 37; and soul food, 45
Black church: and church suppers, 31, 42–43, 50, 60; communion wine in, 229; emergency food provided by, 39; and fish fries, 83; food businesses run by generally, 39; and fried-chicken-entrepreneur-pastors, 60–62, 64; gardening as health ministry of, 160–62; and preachers' references to fried chicken, 49–50; in rural areas, 31, 39, 42–43; in urban areas, 39, 42–43. *See also* Black preachers; Sunday worship for slaves
Black Culinary History Group (Facebook), 264
Black-eyed peas, 113 (ill.); bias against, 113–14; Black-Eyed Peas recipe, 126–27; compared with other types of beans, 114–15, 119; cooking of, 115; definition of, 112; in Down Home Cooking period,

119; history of, 112–19; and Hoppin' John, 116–19, 121, 124, 126; mashed black-eyed peas, 115–16, 121; as New Year's tradition, 111–12, 119–26, 167, 259; poetry regarding, 120; promotion of, in early twentieth century, 114–15, 123–24; recipes for, 115–16, 124, 126–28; in Slave Food period, 114, 115, 119–20, 259; in Southern Cooking period, 116–17; in West Africa, 12, 112, 115, 118, 121, 163

Blackmon, Douglas, 35–36

Black Muslims. *See* Nation of Islam

Black Panthers, 46–47

Black Power movement, 41, 44–47, 64, 260–61

Black preachers: fried-chicken-entrepreneur-pastors, 60–62, 64; fried chicken for, at Sunday dinners, 56–58; references to fried chicken by, 49–50; in slave communities, 55–56; in urban areas, 58. *See also* Black church; Sunday worship for slaves

Blues (music), 50, 198

Boatright, Donald "Bo," 219

Boghosian, Charlie, 237

Booker, Archie, 73

Boorde, Andrew, 148

Bosman, William, 223

Boston Saloon (Virginia City, Nev.), 218

BP Club (Japan), 106–7

Brassica alba (mustard greens), 147

Brassica campestris (turnip greens), 147

Brassica nigra (mustard greens), 147

Brassica oleracea (cabbage), 147

Brassica oleracea v. acephela (collards), 147

Brassica oleracea v. acephela (kale), 147

Brassica rapa (turnip greens), 147

Brassica spp., 147. *See also* Greens

Bravo Network, 4, 144

Bread. *See* Cornbread; Wheat bread

Briggs, Richard, 172

Britain: carrots in, 171–72; cayenne chilli in, 212; Charita "Momma Cheri" Jones in, 185, 257–58; consumption of beef and pork intestines in, 92–93; deer hunting in, 92–93; fried chicken in, 53; greens in, 148–49, 155; hog killing in, 93; Hopping John in, 117; macaroni and cheese in, 131, 132; New Year's tradition in, 123; pease pottages in, 116; plum cakes in, 250; pottage in, 148; pudding in, 248; soul food restaurant in, 185, 258; sweet potatoes in, 171–72, 248; trifles in, 246

Broccoli, 153, 156

Brooks, Sara, 33, 34, 174, 193

Broom, Mary Lena, 161–62

Brown, Henry, 146

Brown, Ida E., 181

Brown, Warren, 250, 251

Brown, William A., 218

Bryan, Mrs. (Lettice), 5, 96, 176

Bryson, Lew, 230

Buckles (dessert), 243

Buffalo chicken wings, 219–20

Buffalo fish ribs, 77, 83 (ill.)

Bully's Soul Food (Jackson, Miss.), 159, 160

Butchering. *See* Hog killing

Butter beans, 33

Buttermilk, 24, 36, 67–68, 130, 203, 211, 229. *See also* Milk

Byrd, Frank, 100

Byrd, William, II, 54

Cabbage, 34, 147, 148, 150, 153, 155. *See also* Greens

Caesar, Julius, 122

Cain, Louis, 70

Cajun cuisine, 16, 17, 47

Cakelove bakeries (Washington, D.C.), 250. *See also* Brown, Warren

Cakes. *See* Pound cake

Calavances. *See* Black-eyed peas

Calendars, 122–23

Candied yams, 166–67, 176–77, 181, 259; Candied Yams recipe, 184. *See also* Sweet potatoes; Yams

Canning, 159

Capsaicin, 211

Capsicum (chillis), 210. *See also* Chillis

Capsicum annuum (cayenne chillis), 212. *See also* Cayenne chillis

Capsicum baccatum, 212

Capsicum chinense, 212, 214

Capsicum frutescens, 212

Capsicum frutescens var. *tabasco* (Tabasco chilli), 212. *See also* Tabasco chilli

Capsicum pubescens, 212

Caribbean Islands: bananas in, 246; chilli consumption in, 281 (n. 18); hibiscus tea in, 228, 239; hot sauce in, 210; kola nuts in, 226; maize in, 187; *pois à pigeon* (pigeon peas) in, 118; significance of red color for, 224; slavery in, 15, 73, 118, 226; true yam cultivation in, 172; white planters' flight from, due to Haitian Revolution, 117. *See also* West Indies

Carmichael, Stokely, 44–45, 260

Carney, Judith, 149, 172, 226, 228

Carolina Housewife, The (Rutledge), 118, 133–34, 156, 176, 213, 248. *See also* Rutledge, Mrs. (Sarah)

Carolina Rice Kitchen, The (Hess), 117, 118–19

Carr, Lucien, 188–89

Carrots: candied, 176–77; history of, 171–72; Momma Cherri's Candied Carrots recipe, 185

Carver, George Washington, 162–63, 166, 249

Casey, Leon A., 107

Cashion, Ann, 164–65

Cassava, 13, 187

Caste system. *See* Racial caste system

Castle, Sheri, 284 (n. 15)

Catesby, Mark, 172

Catfish, 76 (ill.); African Americans associated with, 74–75; buffalo fish ribs as substitute for, 77, 83; Catfish Curry recipe, 89–90; Creole Broiled Catfish recipe, 88–89; and Down Home Cooking period, 78; farming of, 78–80, 86; and fish fries, 80–83, 259, 260; fishing methods for, 71–75, 80; frying and baking methods for generally, 74; history of, 71–75; hot fish restaurants, 83–86, 219; in Hurston's short story, 70; muddy taste of, 75–76; Nanticoke Catfish recipe, 87–88; Native American attitudes on, 72; prejudices against, 70, 74–76; preparation of, 259; recipes for, 87–90; sin associated with, 70; skinning of, 74; slaves' consumption of, 74–75; and Soul Food period, 70–71, 78–80, 86–87; statistics on African American consumption of, 78; stew with, 74; Vietnamese catfish, 79; in West Africa, 71, 76–77; whites on consumption of, 74–78. *See also* Fish

Catfish Corner (Seattle, Wash.), 77

Catfish Farmers of America, 79

Cayenne chillis, 211–14, 218–19

Centers for Disease Control, 161

Chavis, Shaun, 241, 263

Cheddar cheese, 132. *See also* Macaroni and cheese

Cheddar Waffles and Corn Flake Fried Chicken recipe, 67–69

Cheese. *See* Macaroni and cheese

Chef Hunter (Food Network TV show), 144

Chesapeake Bay cuisine, 15, 16, 17, 22

Chicago: black migration to, 36, 40; chitlins supper in, 101; church suppers in, 43; cornbread in restaurants in, 193; fish consumption in, 78, 85; fried chicken restaurants in, 57, 62, 64; greens eaten in, 155;

housing for black migrants in, 40; Kraft Foods in, 137–38; New Year's traditions in, 120; night spots in, 139; Regal Theater in, 105; soul food restaurants in, 3, 9–10, 193; street vendors in, 198; style of fried chicken in, 57

Chicago Defender, 78, 96, 106, 129, 155, 157

Chicken: buffalo chicken wings, 219–20; domestication of, 51; Henri IV on, 50; in Jewish foodways, 50; meaning of "spring chicken," 54; slaves' associations with, 54, 58, 154; statistics on current consumption of, 53–54; in West Africa, 50–53, 259. *See also* Fried chicken

Chicken and waffles, 16, 53, 59; Corn Flake Fried Chicken and Cheddar Waffles recipe, 67–69

Chicken shacks or chicken houses, 57, 60

Chile. *See* Chillis; Pepper

Chillis (Chile peppers): in Black Belt cuisine, 19; buttermilk chaser after eating chillis, 211; capsaicin in, 211; cayenne chillis, 211–14, 218–19; consumption of, in the Caribbean, 281 (n. 18); folk beliefs on, 214; foraging for, 213; history of, 208–9, 212–18; medicinal uses of, 208, 209, 212–15, 218; peppers as misnomer for, 210, 211; Scoville units of varieties of, 211; in Slave Food period, 208–9, 213–16; species of, 212; spelling of, 280 (n. 1); Tabasco chillis, 208–12, 215–18, 281 (n. 31); in vinegar, 213, 214, 218; in West Africa, 13, 212–13. *See also* Hot sauce

Chilli vinegar. *See* Hot sauce

China and Chinese immigrants, 139, 241; Chinese grocery stores, 139; Chinese noodle dishes, 139; Chinese restaurants, 139

"Chitlin Circuit," 104–5

Chitlins (chitterlings), 93 (ill.); and black GI experience abroad, 105–8; for black migrants, 99–101; and "Chitlin Circuit," 104–5; Chitlins Duran recipe, 108–9; chitlin struts, 96, 100; and chitlin suppers, 101; as controversial food, 91–92, 96, 102, 104, 108; Deep-Fried Chitlins recipe, 110; in Down Home Cooking period, 97, 108; Eldridge Cleaver on, 47; in France, 105–6; history of, 92–96, 108; and hog killing, 93–94, 97–98, 99, 108; as holiday or feast food, 91, 98; Lema's World Famous Chittlins (Knoxville, Tenn.), 103, 104 (ill.); preparation of, 98, 259; recipes for, 108–10; at rent parties, 100–101; in restaurants, 101, 105–8; in Slave Food period, 94–96, 99, 108, 259; smell of, 92, 101–2, 103; in Soul Food period, 102–8; in Southern Cooking period, 99–100, 108; spelling of, 91; techniques for masking smell of, 101–2; whites' consumption of, 94–96, 102; winter sale of, 102

Choice, Jeptha, 172, 174

Cholera, 208–9, 215, 281 (n. 29)

Christmas, 21, 27–28, 129, 130, 140, 228, 246

Churches. *See* Black church

Circus lemonade, 231–32

Civil Rights Act (1964), 255

Civil rights movement, 41, 43–45, 255

Civil War, 28, 29–30, 56, 95, 202, 230

Clams, 73

Classic Macaroni and Cheese recipe, 145

Cleaver, Eldridge, 46–47

Clinton, Catherine, 94

Clyburn, James, 85

Cobblers, 240–46, 252, 260

"Cobblers, Cakes and Cream" dessert-

and-coffee shop (Los Angeles), 241, 244–46
Coca-Cola, 227
Coca plant, 227
Cofer, Willis, 30, 191
Coffee, 30, 35, 36, 84, 230
Cofield, Rod, 197
Cola acuminate (kola), 225
Cola nitida (kola), 225
Colas, 226, 227–28
Collard greens: in Black Belt cuisine, 19; in Britain, 148; canned greens, 159–60; in Harlem, 155; history of, 147; kale compared with, 147; as New Year's tradition, 120; as regular African American dish generally, 153; scientific name of, 147; in sharecroppers' diet, 34; in Slave Food period, 150; in West Africa, 150. *See also* Greens
College of the Virgin Islands Cooperative Extension Service, 239
Collins, Harriet, 120
Collins, Robert, 23
Colquitt, Harriet Ross, 181–82
Columbian Exchange, 13
Columbus, Christopher, 171, 187, 210, 213
Comfort food, 256–57
Commercials. *See* Advertisements
Congo peas, 114
Congress of Racial Equality (CORE), 43
Conwell, Benita, 162–63, 166
Cookbooks. *See specific cookbooks and cookbook authors*
Copeland's restaurant (New York City), 3
CORE. *See* Congress of Racial Equality
Corn, 22, 36, 187–92, 232. *See also* Maize
Cornbread: ash cake/ash pone, 194–96, 204; batter bread, 199; buttermilk with, 203–4; crackling bread, 199; in Down Home Cook-

ing period, 202; egg bread, 199; for festive occasions, 199–200; green cornbread, 199, 201; history of, 187–204; Minnie Utsey's "Never Fail" Cornbread recipe, 207; and Native Americans, 187, 188–89, 194; and pot likker, 203, 205; recipes for, 199, 206–7; in sharecroppers' diet, 34–35; skillet cornbread, 199; in Slave Food period, 22, 24, 59, 114, 150, 190–94, 196–200, 241, 259; Soul Food Cornbread Family Stalk, 195; in Soul Food period, 186–87, 203; southern versus northern versions of, 186–87, 200–202; spider cornbread, 199; sugar in, 200–202, 204, 206–7; Twain on, 186; varieties of, 194–200, 204; in "Virginia Breakfast," 59; white versus yellow cornmeal for, 186–89, 193, 198–202, 204. *See also* Hoe cake; Hot water cornbread; Hushpuppies; Spoonbread
Cornfield peas. *See* Black-eyed peas
Corn grinding, 191–93, 198, 201–2
Cornmeal, 19, 22, 186–89, 192–93, 198–202, 204. *See also* Cornbread
Cornshuckings, 190–91, 230, 259
Corson, Juliet, 156
Covey, Herbert, 95
Cowpeas: and cornbread, 203; and Hoppin' John, 116–19, 121, 124, 126; in sharecroppers' diet, 34; in West Africa, 12, 112, 115, 118, 121. *See also* Black-eyed peas
Cracker Barrel, 257
Crackling bread, 199
Craig, Farris, 32
Cream peas, 114
Creole cuisine, 16, 17, 118
Crisps, 243, 254
Crosby, Alfred, 13
Crowder peas, 112, 114. *See also* Black-eyed peas

Crunches and crumbles, 243
Crysichthys spp. (catfish), 71. *See also* Catfish
Cuba, 118
Cutler, Rev. Mannaseh, 132

Dalziel, J. M., 120
Dangerfield, Rodney, 111
Date with a Dish, A (DeKnight), 78, 96, 138, 157, 183, 204, 244, 249. *See also* DeKnight, Freda
Davidson, Alan, 280 (n. 1)
Davis, Clara, 74
Daytona, Fla., Educational and Industrial Training School for Girls, 249
Deborah's Kitchen (Philadelphia), 62, 63
Deep-dish pie, 243
Deep-Fried Chitlins recipe, 110
DeKnight, Freda, 5–6, 78, 96, 111, 138, 157, 183, 204, 244, 249
Delights of the Garden restaurants, 158
Delta Health Alliance, 161
Denver: New Year's Day at local shelter for distressed families in, 111; restaurants in, 3, 38; Savory Spice Shop, Inc.,in, 88; soul food in generally, 261; West African grocery in, 71
Depression. *See* Great Depression
De Soto, Hernando, 72
Desserts: apple pie, 33, 43, 64, 249; banana pudding, 4, 241, 243, 246–47, 252–53; betty, 243; at black church gatherings, 31; buckles, 243; cobblers, 240–46, 252, 260; crisps, 243, 254; crunches and crumbles, 243; grunts and slumps, 243; history of, 240–44, 246–50; in landowners' diets in postbellum South, 33; peach cobbler, 240–42, 244–45, 252, 260; peach crisp, 254; pound cake, 4, 241, 249–52, 259; pudding, 247–48; recipes for,

247, 252–54; in sharecroppers' diet, 36; in Slave Food period, 241, 242–43, 246, 250, 252; in Southern Cooking period, 252; sweet potato pie, 31, 240, 241, 248–49, 252, 259
Devine, Major Morgan J. *See* Divine, Father
DeWitt, Dave, 209
Dickins, Dorothy, 138, 140, 180, 201
Diner, Hasia, 134–35
Dirks, Robert T., 36, 180, 203
Divine, Father, 60–61, 64
Dodson, Jualynne, 56
Down Home Cooking period (1890s–1970s): and barbecue, 220; beginning of, 36; and black-eyed peas, 119; and canning, 159; and catfish, 78; and chitlins, 97, 108; and cornbread, 202; definition of, 7; fish fries during, 82; and fried chicken, 49–50, 60–62, 64; and gardening, 154–55; and Great Migration to urban areas, 36, 38–39; and greens, 153, 155–57; and macaroni and cheese, 138; restaurants for, 38–39, 41; soul food and down home cooking used for same food, 42; and Sunday dinner tradition, 58; and yams, 182
Down Home Healthy cooking, 256
Dried beans, 34, 36
Drinks. *See* Alcoholic beverages; Milk; Red drinks; Water
Drish, Mrs. Marshall, 119
Dull, Mrs. (S. R.), 96
Durant, Sylvia, 250

Eastside Fish (Nashville, Tenn.), 219
Edge, John T., 236
Edna Lewis Foundation, 255–56
Edna's restaurant (Chicago), 3
Edwards, Gary, 99
Egerton, John, xiii
Eisnach, Dwight, 95
Elderbush tea, 229

Elie, Lolis Eric, 7
Elizabeth I, Queen, 131, 247
Ells, Steve, 4
Emancipation celebrations, 31, 80,
  233–35
Emancipation Proclamation, 234
England. See Britain
Ethiopian restaurant, eating experience in, 11
Ethnic immigrant cuisines. See Immigrants and immigrant foodways;
  and specific ethnic groups
Europeans: and beans, 113–14; and
  black-eyed peas, 112; and carrots,
  167; and chillis, 210–12, 214; colonization of West Africa by, 13–14,
  19, 150, 166, 169–71, 187–88; and
  fish and fishing, 71, 72; and fried
  pies, 243; and greens, 147–48, 150,
  156; influence of, on Big House
  cooking, 21; and kola nuts, 225,
  227; and macaroni and cheese,
  130–31, 134, 142; and New Year's
  Day, 122–26; notions of good food
  from, 259; significance of red color
  for, 223; and soul food restaurants in France, 105–6; soul food's
  meaning for, 42; and sweet potatoes, 166, 167, 170, 171, 172, 176;
  trade between West Africans and,
  71; and true yams, 170; and wheat
  bread, 187–88, 189. See also Atlantic
  slave trade; and specific European countries and immigrant groups
Evans, Mrs. Chas. L., 247
Ezell's fried chicken chain (Seattle),
  62

Falconbridge, Alexander, 14
Fanta (red) soda, 234
Farming. See Agriculture; Catfish:
  farming of
Federal Writers' Project (FWP), 5,
  73–74, 95, 190–91, 198, 229, 249
Ferguson, Sheila, 173

Field peas. See Black-eyed peas
Fifteenth Amendment (U.S. Constitution), 30
Fish: at black church gatherings in
  postbellum period, 31; buffalo fish
  ribs, 77, 83; early white Americans'
  negative attitude toward, 72; hot
  fish restaurants, 83–86, 219; hot
  sauce for fried fish, 219; in landowners' diets in postbellum South,
  33; popularity of, in Chicago and
  New York City, 78; preservation of,
  73–74; in sharecroppers' diet, 36;
  in Slave Food period, 72–75, 151,
  259; in slaves' diet, 73–75; in West
  Africa, 70, 71–72, 74, 76–77, 80,
  187; whiting fish, 85. See also Cat-
  fish
Fisher, Abby, 5, 96, 156, 213, 244, 249
Fisher, M. F. K., 6
Fish fries, 80–83, 199, 259, 260
Fishing industry, 73
Fishing methods, 71–75, 80
Fish 'n' braid, 80
Flay, Bobby, 4
Florida Avenue Grill (Washington,
  D.C.), 158
Folse, John, 135–36
Food assistance programs, 35, 41, 44,
  141
Food Network, 4, 144, 250
Food rationing. See Rations
Food-related business. See Grocery
  stores; Restaurants; Street vending
Foodways, definition of, 4
Foraging, 155, 213
Forme of Cury, 130–31
Fossett, Edith, 131–32
Foster, Mac, 107
Fountain, Della, 120, 123
Fourteenth Amendment (U.S. Consti-
  tution), 30
Fourth of July celebrations, 80, 229,
  242
Fowler, Lee, 29

France. *See* French foodways

Franchising of soul food restaurants, 257–58

Freedmen's Bureau (Bureau of Refugees, Freedmen, and Abandoned Lands), 30French foodways, 8, 50, 93, 105–6, 112, 117, 131, 150, 176–77, 208, 228, 241

French's fried chicken chain (Houston), 62

Fried chicken, 63 (ill.); at black church gatherings, 31; for black preachers at Sunday dinners, 56–58; black preachers' references to, 49–50; in Britain, 53; Chicago-style fried chicken, 57; from fried chicken chains, 57, 60–65; history of, 52–54; for honored guests, 56–57; lard versus vegetable oil for, 53, 55; Marta's Oven-Fried Chicken recipe, 66; Maryland-style fried chicken, 53; in nineteenth-century cookbooks, 53; possible African provenance for, 51–52; "preacher's parts" of, 57; preparation process for, 54–55, 56; recipes for, 66–69; in restaurants, 57, 60–65; as secular convenience food, 65; in sharecroppers' diet, 36; in Slave Food period, 54–56, 58, 59; from street vendors, 58, 60; at Sunday dinner, 49–50, 55–60; for Union soldiers during Civil War, 56; in "Virginia Breakfast," 54, 59; Virginia-style fried chicken, 53, 54, 55; with waffles, 53, 59, 67–69

Fried chicken chains, 57, 60–65

Fried fish. *See* Catfish; Fish

Fried pies, 64, 65, 243

Funky jazz (music), 42, 50; and food descriptors, 42

FWP. *See* Federal Writers' Project

Gaige, Crosby, 89

Galen, 210

Galloway, Lula Briggs, 234

Gallus domesticus, 51

Garcia, Lorena, 4

Gardens: and black church, 160–62; in colonial period, 150; decline of, for African Americans, 154–55; greens in, 146, 154–55, 159, 160–63; heirloom vegetable gardens, 266; of plantations, 22, 23, 151, 153; slave gardens as provision grounds, 23, 24, 151, 152–54, 172, 259; of yeoman farms, 21

Gaskins, Ruth, 53, 58, 83, 250

Gem Restaurant (New Orleans), 216

Genovese, Eugene, 21

Gerlach, Nancy, 209

German immigrants and foodways, 8, 59, 101, 124–25, 168, 171

Gilkes, Cheryl Townsend, 56

Gladys' Luncheonette (Chicago), 3

Glasse, Hannah (*The Art of Cookery Made Plain and Easy*), 5, 53, 93, 156, 172, 248

Glory Foods, 111, 159–60, 257, 261

Goldberg, Whoopi, 223

Golden Bird fried chicken chain (Los Angeles), 62

Goober peas, 114

Good Heart and a Light Hand, A (Gaskins), 58, 83, 250

Goodwin, Mary, 181

Gore, Al, 197

"Gospel Bird," 49. *See also* Fried chicken

Gospel music, 62, 63

Grace, Bishop Charles Manuel "Sweet Daddy," 61–62, 64

Grains of paradise, 228, 280–81 (n. 8)

Granger, Gordon, 234

Grant, Ulysses S., 28

Grape drinks ("purple drank"), 236, 238

Great Britain. *See* Britain

Great Depression, 41, 59, 84, 96, 137–38, 222

Great Migration, 36–40, 260

Greece, ancient, 113, 147

Greek immigrants and foodways, 84, 105

Green, Aliza, 114

Greens: bacon and, 147–48; bitterness of, 149, 151; in Black Belt cuisine, 19; canned greens, 159–60; class distinctions regarding, 150; cleaning of, 159, 160; and cornbread, 203; in Down Home Cooking period, 153, 155–57; eating raw greens, 148, 157; foraging of, 155; frozen, pre-washed, and packaged greens, 159; in gardens, 154–55, 159, 160–63; history of, 147–57; Johnetta's Mixed Greens recipe,163–64; in landowners' diets in postbellum South, 33; with meats other than pork, 147, 149, 156, 157–58, 163–64; "motherless greens," 146, 158; as New Year's tradition, 120, 163; with pork, 146–48, 151, 155, 156, 157–58, 163–64; pot likker from, 151–52, 156, 157, 203, 205; preparation methods for, 148–51, 155–58, 259; recipes for, 163–65; in sharecroppers' diet, 34, 36; in Slave Food period, 150–54, 156, 259; in Soul Food period, 146–47, 157–58, 163; in spoonbread recipe, 164–65; sweet potato greens, 153, 162–63; types of, 147, 153; uses of, by slaves, 151; in West Africa, 149–50, 157, 166; without meat, 147, 156, 158

Grits, 4, 16, 22, 192, 193

Grocery stores: of black entrepreneurs in postbellum period, 32; Chinese immigrants as owners of, 139; cost of soul food in, 47; during Great Migration, 38, 39; greens in, 159

Growing Together project, 161–62

Grunts (dessert), 243

Guinea fowl, 33, 51

Guinea pepper, 280–81 (n. 8), 281 (n. 12)

Gulf South cuisine, 16, 17

Gullah people, 167, 227

Gumbo, 16

Habanero chillis, 211, 214, 219

Haitian Revolution, 117

Hale, Sarah J., 156

Halsey, Joyce, 98

Harlem: Apollo Theater in, 105; black-eyed peas in, 119; chitlins in, 101; greens in, 155, 157; New Year's traditions in, 120; relief distribution in, 141; rent parties in, 100–101; restaurants in, 38, 59, 84, 92, 113, 137, 256–57; spaghetti houses in, 137; sweet potatoes in, 180–81

Harlem Macaroni Co., 137

"Harlem Menu," 38

Harold's Chicken Shacks (Chicago), 57, 62

Harris, Chef Hardette, 127–28, 262

Harris, Jessica, 7–8

Harrison, William H., 150

Hawkins, Sir John, 171

Hayes, Mrs. (W. T.), 5, 96, 156, 200, 244

Haynes, Leroy, 105–6

Health: and alternatives to fried fish, 86; conventional wisdom on, 284 (n. 15); and garden projects, 161–63; and health-focused soul food, 145, 254, 256, 257, 264–65; unhealthy image of soul food, 1–2, 5, 263; and vegetable oil for fried chicken, 53; and vegetarian or vegan restaurants, 256

Heatter, Maida, 252

Height, Dorothy, 249

Hemings, James, 131

Hemings, Peter, 131

Hemings, Sally, 131

Henderson, Fergus, 92

Hendrix, Jimi, 104

Henri IV, King, 50
Hern, Frances, 131–32
Hess, Karen, 117, 118–19, 189, 281
 (n. 21)
Hibiscus: Hibiscus Aid recipe, 239;
 Hibiscus sabdariffa, 228; hibiscus tea,
 224, 225, 228
Highland oysters, 95. *See also* Chitlins
Hip hop culture, 263
Historia Naturalis (Pliny the Elder),
 113–14
Hodges, Smity, 250
Hoe cake, 195, 196–98, 203, 204
Hog killing, 93–94, 97–98, 99, 108,
 190, 191, 230, 259
Holidays: chitlins for, 91; Christmas,
 21, 27–28, 129, 130, 140, 228, 246;
 cornbread for, 199–200; Emancipa-
 tion celebrations, 31, 80, 233–35;
 Fourth of July, 80, 229, 242; June-
 teenth, 233–35; New Year's Day,
 111–12, 119–26, 163, 167, 229, 237,
 259; in postbellum period, 31, 80;
 red drinks for, 228, 229, 230, 233–
 35, 237; in Slave Food period, 21,
 27–28, 242; Thanksgiving, 91, 93,
 102, 129, 163, 167
Holmes, Joseph, 94
Holt, Jane, 138
Hominy, 22, 192
Hooks, Benjamin, 64, 65
Hoppin' John, 116–19, 121, 124, 126
Hot fish, 83–86, 219
Hot peppers. *See* Chillis
Hot sauce: Asian-style hot sauce, 219;
 for barbecue, 219, 220–21; for
 buffalo chicken wings, 219–20;
 in Caribbean, 210; with cayenne
 chillis, 218–19; definition of, 209;
 definition of "hot," 210; formula
 for, 213, 214; for fried fish, 219;
 history of, 208–9, 213–18; ingredients of Louisiana-style hot
 sauce, 210; medicinal uses of, 208,
 209, 213–15, 218; Mexican-style

hot sauce, 219; and Native Americans, 213; in postbellum period,
 218; in Slave Food period, 208–9,
 213–16; for space food, 258; with
 Tabasco chillis, 208–9, 215–18, 281
 (n. 31); vinegar-based, 213, 214,
 218; in West Africa, 210; White's
 hot sauce, 208–9, 213, 215–17, 281
 (n. 31). *See also* Chillis
Hot water cornbread, 195, 197 (ill.),
 203, 204; Hot Water Cornbread
 recipe, 206
Housing, 34, 40, 100–101
Howard, O. O., 30
Hubbell, Sue, 123
Hudgins, Tom, 211
Hughes, Louis, 242–43
Humble pie, 93
Hunger: of black migrants in urban
 areas, 40; during Civil War, 28, 29;
 following Civil War, 30; and food
 assistance programs, 35, 41, 44,
 141; of rural blacks in postbellum
 period, 35. *See also* Rations
Hunt, Charley, 191
Hunt, Sharon, 159, 183
Hurston, Zora Neale, 70
Hushpuppies, 81, 195, 198–99
Hutchins, Imar, 158

Ibo (or Igbo) creation myth, 168–69,
 175
Ictiobus spp. (buffalo fish), 77
Immigrants and immigrant foodways,
 8, 38, 46, 59, 78, 134–35, 258, 261.
 See also specific immigrant groups
Indian corn, 187, 189–90, 194. *See also*
 Maize
Indians. *See* Native Americans
Indigo, 15, 16
Ipomoea batata (sweet potato), 167.
 See also Sweet potatoes
Irish immigrants and foodways, 13,
 39, 101, 152, 168, 215
Irish potatoes, 152, 177, 178, 180

Italian Americans and foodways, 13, 39, 46, 78, 130, 133–37, 142, 220, 257, 266

Izola's Family Dining (Chicago), 3, 193

Jack's American Star Bar Bangkok, 107

Jackson, Andrew, 216

Jackson, Janet, 247

Jackson, Mahalia, 62–65

Jackson, Millie, 104

Jalapeño chillis, 211

Jamaica: cayenne chilli in, 213; hibiscus tea in, 228; hot sauce in, 213; Jonkonnu festival in, 170; kola nuts in, 226, 227; peas and rice dish in, 118; pigeon peas in, 118; slaves' informal economy in, 152

Jambalaya, 16

Jambalaya au congri, 118

Japan, 106–7

Jazz, 42, 45, 50, 59, 251

Jefferson, Thomas, 73, 114, 131–32, 214

Jewish foodways, 50, 78, 92

Jim Crow. *See* Racial caste system

Joffe, Natalie, 40, 43, 58, 137, 155, 175, 180, 203

Johnny's Half Shell Restaurant (Washington, D.C.), 164

Johnson, Lyndon, 141

Johnson, Robert, 198

Johnson, Wayne, 262

Johnson, William, 101

Johnson and Wales University, 8

Jones, Charita "Momma Cherri," 185, 257–58

Jones, LeRoi, 240, 241

Jones, (Chef) Sonya, 262

Jonkonnu festival, 170

Judaism. *See* Jewish foodways

Julien, Honoré, 131

July Fourth celebrations, 80, 229, 242

Juneteenth, 233–35

Jus de bissap (hibiscus tea), 228

Kale, 147, 148, 150, 153, 155. *See also* Greens

Kari, Isaac "Sax," 104

Kemble, Lillian, 124

Kentucky Cook Book, 137. *See also* Hayes, Mrs.

Kentucky Fried Chicken (KFC), 64, 65

Kentucky Housewife, 156, 175–76, 248. *See also* Bryan, Mrs.

Kidney beans, 119

King, B. B., 104

King, Rev. Martin Luther, Jr., 44

Kingsley, Mary H., 71, 72, 271 (n. 4)

Kitchen Nightmares, 185

Klein, Preston, 191

Kola tea and kola nuts, 224–28

Kool-Aid, 222, 226, 235–38

Kool-Aid pickles ("Koolickles"), 236

Kraft Foods, 137–38, 235

LaBan, Craig, 62

Lady peas, 114

L&M Guest House (Saigon), 107

La Rochefoucauld, François de, 189

Laudan, Rachel, 132

Le Jau, Dr. Francis, 55

Lema's World Famous Chittlins (Knoxville, Tenn.), 103, 104 (ill.)

Lemonade (red), 224, 230, 231–33

Leslie, Austin, 50

Leslie, Eliza, 156

Lewicki, Tadeusz, 11, 12, 112, 224

Lewis, Edna, 6–7, 31, 53, 234, 250–51, 255, 264

Lewis, John, 44

Lima beans, 114, 119, 203

Lincoln, Abraham, 234

Liquor. *See* Alcoholic beverages

Lloyd, Duran, 98, 101, 108–9

Long, Huey, 205

Lopez, Odoardo, 225

Louisiana State University, 182

Lowcountry cuisine, 16, 17

Lundy, Ronni, 112

Macaroni and cheese, 140 (ill.); boxed dinners of, 137–38; casserole method for, 133, 144–45; cheese sauce method of, 133–34, 143; as Christmas dish, 129, 130, 140; Classic Macaroni and Cheese recipe, 145; in Down Home Cooking period, 138; etymology of word "macaroni," 275 (n. 3); for European aristocracy, 130–31, 134; in Harlem, 137; history of, 130–41; home economists' recommendations on, 136–37, 140–41; and Italian foodways, 130, 133–37, 142; and Kraft Foods, 137–38; low-class status of, 141–42; lower-fat version of, 145; Mac 'n' Cheese recipe, 143; multiple identities of, 130, 142; in New Orlean, 136; Nyesha Arrington's Mac and Cheese recipe, 144–45; parmesan vs. cheddar cheese in, 132–34; recipes for, 133–34, 143–45; in rural areas, 138, 140; in Slave Food period, 131–34; in Soul Food period, 141–42; in urban areas, 135–38, 140–41

Magnolia Grill (Durham, N.C.), 243

Mahalia Jackson's fried chicken chain, 62–65

Maize, 13, 19, 169, 187–90. See also Corn

Malone, Samuel, 235

Mambo sauce, 219–20

M&D's Cafe restaurant (Denver), 3

Mangam, Charles, 122

Martin, Dulcina Baker, 119–20

Masada Kitchen (Savannah, Ga.), 62

Mason, John, 99

Massey, Mary Elizabeth, 230

Maybell, Hubert, 9, 43

Mayer, Jean, 36, 38

Mayo's and Mahalia Jackson Fried Pies & Chicken (Nashville, Tenn.), 64, 65

McCullough, Lucy, 94

McDonald's, 85

McGee, Harold, 280 (n. 1)

McGlothin, Victor, 222

McGovern, Barney, 82

McIlhenny family, 215, 217, 281 (n. 31)

McIntyre, Constance Fuller, 94–95

Meats: cost of fresh red meat in urban areas in 1890s, 36; with greens, 147, 149, 156, 157–58, 163–64; in landowners' diets in postbellum South, 33; in Slave Food period, 22; statistics on current consumption of, 53–54; steak as metaphor for achievement, 47, 263. See also specific meats

Medicinal uses: of chillis, 208, 209, 212–15, 218; of elderbush and sassafras teas, 229; of kola nuts, 225, 226, 227–28

Mel's Fish Shack (Los Angeles), 85–86

Mendelson, Anne, 133

Mendes, Helen, 45

Mert's restaurant (Charlotte, N.C.), 217

Metamorphoses (Ovid), 147–48

Mexican food, 2, 150, 198

Mexican-style hot sauce, 219

Mexico, 187, 212, 215, 216, 219

Mickler, Ernest Matthew, 47–48, 140, 173

Middle Passage. See Atlantic slave trade

Miege, Jacques, 169

Migration of African Americans. See Great Migration

Milk: buttermilk, 24, 36, 67–68, 130, 203, 211, 229; evaporated milk, 140; in landowners' diets in postbellum South, 33; in sharecroppers' diet, 35, 36; in West Africa, 224, 228

Miller, Anna, 189

Miller, April, 239

Miller, Hyman (father), 72

Miller, Johnetta, 126–27, 163–64, 206, 252–53
Miller, Julian, 182
Miller, Samuel (paternal grandfather), 33
Millet, 12–13, 187, 224–25
Minor, William, 24
Mississippi Health Department, 161
Mitchell, Andrew, 107
Molasses, 19, 22, 200, 229, 232, 241
Molasses and water, 229, 232
Momma Cherri's Soul Food Shack (United Kingdom), 185, 258
Money, Hernando (U.S. senator), 224
Montana Federation of Negro Women's Clubs Cook Book, 137, 181, 213, 247
Moore, Michael, 160, 257, 261
Morgan, Phillip, 74, 172
Moros y cristianos (black beans and rice), 118
Moses, Bob, 44
Moss, Claiborne, 95
Mother African Methodist Episcopal Zion Church, 60
Moxon, Elizabeth, 148
Moxostoma carinatum (Red Horse fish), 199
Mules and Men (Hurston), 70
Music. *See* Blues; Jazz
Muslims. *See* Nation of Islam
Mussels, 73
Mustard greens, 147, 150, 153, 155. *See also* Greens

National Aeronautics and Space Administration (NASA), 258
National Association of Juneteenth Lineage, 234
National Cancer Institute, 254
National Cookery Book, The, 133
National Council of Negro Women, 249
National Heart, Lung, and Blood Institute, 145
Nation of Islam, 46, 70, 85, 92, 158
Native Americans: and black-eyed peas, 113; and chitlins, 105; and cornbread, 187, 188–89, 194, 198; corn cultivation by, 188; fish consumption by, 72; and greens, 150; influence of, on Slave Food period, 16, 19, 45, 188–89, 259, 265; Nanticoke tribe of, 87; and peaches, 242; as slaves, 15; slaves compared with, 229; trade between slaves and, 24
Navy beans, 114–15, 119
Neal, Bill, 199
Neal, Mark Anthony, 104
Negro spirituals, 146
Nehi soda, 234
Nelson, Therese, 264
Neo-Soul period (1990s–present), 7, 256
Newell, "Sir Geechie" Jamara, 251
New Jersey State Federation of Colored Women's Clubs, 181, 213. *See also To Work and Serve the Home*
New Orleans: Chef Leslie's fried chicken in, 50; Chinese noodles eaten in, 139; chitlins eaten in restaurants in, 96; cooking school in, 136; fish fries in, 82; fried catfish eaten in, 75, 85; hot sauce in, 217, 220; Italian population of, 135; macaroni and cheese eaten in, 136; oyster saloons in, 216, 217; red beans and rice in, 118
New Year's Day, 111–12, 119–26, 163, 167, 229, 237, 259
New York Amsterdam News, 120, 137, 141, 155, 157
New York City: black migration to, 36, 37; broccoli's popularity in, 156; food habits study in 1930s in, 78; Italian population of, 135; red lemonade in, 232; restaurants featuring "nose-to-tail cooking" in, 92; sale of black-eyed peas in, 113; soul food restaurants in, 3, 4; street vendors in, 198, 232. *See also* Harlem

New York Times, 1–2, 23, 44–45, 53, 58, 80, 92, 108, 138, 236
Norris, Mr., 95
Nose-to-tail cooking, 92, 266
Nunn, Jefferson Davis, 151

Okigbo, Bede Nwoye, 168
Okra, 4, 33, 149, 163, 228
Oliver, Sandy, 72, 242
Onje Fun Orisa (Food for the Gods) (Edwards and Mason), 99
Oryza glaberrima (rice), 12–13
Ovid, 147–48
Owens, Janis, 160
Oyster saloons, 216, 217

Paddleford, Clementine, 182
Paprika, 211
Park, Frank, 179
Parkes, Anna, 74
Parmesan cheese, 132–33. See also Macaroni and cheese
Paschal's restaurant (Atlanta), 257
Payne, Larkin, 229
Peach cobbler, 4, 240–42, 244–45, 252, 260; Summer Peach Crisp recipe, 254
Peaches, 241–42, 244–45
Peanuts (pinda), 24
Pearl, Minnie, 63
Peas, 33, 114. See also Black-eyed peas; and other types of peas
Pease pottages, 116
Pemberton, Dr. (John), 227
Pennsylvania Dutch cuisine, 59
Pepper, 210. See also Chillis
Pepper relish, 213
Pepper sauce. See Hot sauce
Pepper vinegar. See Hot sauce
Pepsi-Cola, 228
Perkins, Edwin, 222
Philadelphia: French chefs in, 176–77; Italian population of, 135; Jefferson's residence in, 131; restaurants in, 41, 62, 63, 84, 158; soul food in

generally, 261; sweet potatoes in, 176–77, 180
Picante sauces, 209
Picayune Creole Cook Book, The, 118, 136, 217
Pierce, Harold (Harold's Fried Chicken in Chicago), 57
Pies: apple pie, 33, 43, 64, 249; deep-dish pie, 243; fried pies, 64, 65, 243; history of, 248–49; in landowners' diets in postbellum South, 33; popularity of, 247; sweet potato pie, 4, 31, 240, 241, 248–49, 252, 259; terms used for, 247–48. See also Desserts
Pigeon peas (pois à pigeon), 116, 117, 118
Pinckney, Eliza Lucas, 248
Piper nigrum (pepper), 210
Pirtle, Jack, 64, 65
Plantains, 13, 169
Plantations. See Slave Food period; Slaves
Pliny the Elder, 113–14
Plotkin, Mitch, 220
Plum cakes, 250
Pois à pigeon. See Pigeon peas
Pork: Carmichael and SNCC's association of soul food with, 45; as flavoring in fried chicken recipes, 53; greens with, 146–48, 151, 155, 156, 157–58, 163–64; in Hoppin' John, 116–19, 121, 124, 126; as New Year's tradition, 120, 124–25; in sharecroppers' diet, 34–35, 36; as standard southern food, 4, 19, 22, 114; statistics on current consumption of, 53–54; as taboo, 149, 158, 263. See also Hog killing
Possum 'n' taters, 172–74
Post-blackness, 263
Potatoes. See Irish potatoes; Sweet potatoes; Yams
Pot likker, 151–52, 156, 157, 203, 205. See also Greens
Pottage, 148, 152

Pound cake, 4, 241, 249–52, 259
Powell, Georgette (Mel's Fish Shack, Los Angeles), 85–86
Preachers. *See* Black preachers
Prince (Rogers Nelson), 223
Provision grounds. *See* Gardens
Prunus persica (peach tree), 241
Puckett, Newbell Niles, 214, 223
Pudding, 247–48
Puerto Rico, 118
Purple hull peas, 114; Purple Hull Peas recipe, 127–28

Racial caste system: of black migrants in urban areas, 39; meaning of, 9; and segregation, 31; and Slave Food period, 21–22, 29, 95; and stereotypes of African Americans, 31, 58, 75, 231
Radio, and African American marketing study, 141–42
Ramsay, Chef Gordon, 185
Randall, Chef Joe, 110, 255–56
Randolph, Mrs. Mary, 5, 53, 55, 74, 89, 96, 115, 133, 150, 156, 175, 213, 248. *See also Virginia Housewife, The*
Rations (of food): by Freedmen's Bureau, 30; for slaves, 19, 20, 22–24, 30, 73, 191–93, 218; during World War II, 138. *See also* Hunger
Ravnel, Henry, 74
Rawick, George, 15, 24
Rawls, Lou, 104, 107
Recipes: banana pudding, 247, 252–53; black-eyed peas, 126–27, 124, 126–28; candied carrots, 185; catfish, 87–90; chitlins, 108–10; cornbread, 199, 206–7; fried chicken, 66–69; greens, 163–65; macaroni and cheese, 133–34, 143–45; peach crisp, 254; purple hull peas, 127–28; red drinks, 238–39; sweet potatoes/yams, 181, 184
Red beans and rice, 118
Red drinks: alcoholic beverages, 229–31; at black church gatherings, 31; definition of, 223; generational shifts regarding, 236–37; grape drinks versus, 236, 238; hibiscus tea, 224, 225, 228, 239; history of, 222–35; for holidays, 228, 229, 230, 233–35, 237; kola tea, 224–28; Kool-Aid, 222, 226, 235–38; lemonade, 224, 230, 231–33; Mason jars or jelly jars for, 232, 236, 237; recipes for, 238–39; restaurants and red drink heresy, 232; sassafras tea, 229, 230; in sharecroppers' diet, 36; and significance of red color, 223–24; in Slave Food period, 229–31; soda pop, 224, 232–34, 236, 237; in Southern Cooking period, 231–32; tasting notes on, 237; and Vietnam War servicemen, 235–36; in West Africa, 224–28, 259
Red Kool-Aid, 222, 226, 235–38
Red lemonade, 224, 230, 231–33
Red peas, 118–19
Red peppers. *See* Tabasco chillis
Red Rooster Restaurant (Harlem), 113, 256–57
Red soda pop, 224, 232–34, 236, 237
Red sorrel, 228
Red whiskey, 229–30
Red Zinger tea, 228
Relief (food assistance), 35, 41, 141
Religion. *See* Black church; Black preachers; Sunday worship for slaves
Rent farmers, 33. *See also* Agriculture
Rent parties, 100–101
Restaurants: advertisements of, 38, 65, 85; barbecue stands, 38; of black entrepreneurs in postbellum period, 32; chicken shacks or chicken houses, 57, 60; Chinese restaurants, 139; chitlins in, 101, 105–8; closures of soul food restaurants, 3–4, 193; and down home

cooking, 38–39, 41; during Great Migration, 38–39; franchising of soul food restaurants, 257–58; fried chicken chains, 57, 60–65; of fried-chicken-entrepreneur-pastors, 60–62, 64; Greek seafood restaurants, 84; greens served by, 157–58; in Harlem, 38, 59, 84, 92, 113, 137, 256–57; hot fish restaurants, 83–86, 219; Kool-Aid served by, 222, 232; possibility of national soul food chain, 3–4, 257–58; and red drink heresy, 232; soul food restaurants in Asia, 106–7; start-up costs for, 256; vegetarian or vegan clientele for, 256

Resurrection Pie, 105

Reuss, Henry S. (U.S. representative), 47

Rice: in Black Belt cuisine, 19; in Hoppin' John, 116–19, 121, 124, 126; as iconic soul food item generally, 4; in Lowcountry cuisine, 16, 22; and red beans, 118; in sharecroppers' diet, 34; in West Africa, 12–13

Rice, Condoleezza, 129

Rice plantations, 15

Richard, Lena, 136

Richard II, King, 131

Richardson, Charlie, 197–98

Richman, Phyllis C., 61–62

Rious, Allen A., 106–7

Robertson, Pat, 129–30

Robinson, Zandria, 263

Rome, ancient, 113–14, 122–23, 147–48, 241

Roosevelt, Franklin Delano (governor), 205

Rorer, Sarah, 136–37

Rountree, Henry, 94

Rowland, W. M., 123–24

Roy, Lisa, 88–89

Royal Crown Cola, 228

Royster, Mrs. W. E., 181

Ruby's restaurant (Chicago), 3

Russell, Mrs. Malinda, 5, 78, 96, 156, 199, 213, 230, 244, 246, 249

Rutledge, Mrs. (Sarah), 5, 96, 118, 133–34, 156, 176, 178, 213, 248. See also Carolina Housewife, The

Saints Paradise Café (Washington, D.C.), 61–62

Salads, 157

Salsas, 209

Samuelsson, Marcus, 256–57

Sassafras tea, 229, 230

Savannah Cookbook, The (Colquitt), 181–82

Savannah Cooking School, 110, 255

Savitt, Todd, 73

Savory SpiceShop, Inc., 88

School Lunch Program, 141

Seafood: in Cajun and Creole cuisine, 16, 17; in Chesapeake Bay cuisine, 16; collection of shellfish by slaves, 73; Greek-run seafood restaurants, 84. See also Catfish; Fish

Segregation. See Racial caste system

Sells, Abram, 151–52

Sesame seeds (bene), 24

Seventh-day Adventists, 70, 161–62

Shakespeare, William, 41–42

Sharecropping, 32, 33–35, 154, 174–75, 193. See also Agriculture

Shiloh Seventh-day Adventist Church (Greenwood, Miss.), 161–62

Shrimp and grits, 16

Simmons, Amelia, 113. See also American cookery

Simmons, George, 114

"Slabber sauce," 14

Slave Food period (1619–1865): abolitionist critiques of slave diet, 23, 192–93; and alcoholic beverages, 229–31; beginning of, in Jamestown, Va., 15; Black Belt cuisine during, 19, 22; and black-eyed peas, 114, 115, 119–20, 259; and candied yams, 176; cheese and other dairy products in, 130; Chesapeake Bay cuisine during, 16, 17, 22; and chillis and hot sauce, 208–9, 213–16; and chitlins, 94–96, 99, 108, 259; cooking in slave quarters, 22, 25–26, 29; and cornbread, 22, 24, 59, 114, 150, 190–94, 196–200, 241, 259; and cornshuckings, 190–91, 230; definition of, 7; and desserts, 241, 242–43, 246, 250, 252; and field slave cooks and meals, 22, 24–25, 194; fishing and fish consumption during, 72–75, 80, 89, 151, 259; food storage on plantations, 22; and fried chicken, 54–56, 58; and greens, 150–54, 156, 259; Gulf South cuisine during, 16, 17; and hog killing, 94–95, 190, 230; and holiday and weekend foods for slaves, 21, 26–28, 242; Lowcountry cuisine during, 16, 17; and macaroni and cheese, 131–34; plantation slaves' diet, 22–28, 95, 114; rationing of food for slaves, 19, 20, 22–24, 30, 73, 191–93, 218; and red drinks, 229–31; strategies for supplementing rations by slaves, 21, 23, 24, 73; subregional cuisines during, 16–19; Sunday and holiday meals during, 26–28, 55; and sweet potatoes/yams, 172–77, 259; "3 M's" diet (meat, meal, and molasses) during, 19, 22, 23; and trough feeding, 24–25, 151–52; urban slaves' diet, 19–21; and water consumption, 229; yeoman farm slaves' diet, 21, 192. See also Big House cooking; Slaves

Slaves: in Caribbean Islands, 15, 73, 118, 226; and cornshuckings, 190–91, 230; fishing and fish consumption by, 72–74, 80; gardens of, 23, 24, 151, 152–54, 172, 259; hired-out urban slaves, 19, 20–21; and hog killings, 94–95, 190, 230;

holidays and weekends for, 20, 21, 24, 26–28, 120; in Jamaica, 152, 213; large-scale plantation slaves, 15–17, 19, 22–28, 94; live-in urban slaves, 19–20; medicines for, 208–9, 212–13, 226; Middle Passage food for, 14–15, 170, 188; money-making activities of, 20–21, 54, 154; and New Year's Day contracts, 120; northern non-plantation slaves, 15; physical punishment of, 24, 94; raising of chickens by, 54, 154; small-scale, yeoman farm slaves, 19, 21, 192; statistics on, 15, 16–17; Sunday worship for, 20, 27, 55–56; urban slaves, 19–21, 32; work schedule for, 23–24. See also Abolitionists; Atlantic slave trade; Slave Food period (1619–1865)

Slumps (dessert), 243
Smith, Andy, 28
Smith, Gus, 250
Smith, Nellie, 250
Smithsonian Institution, 264
SNCC. See Student Nonviolent Coordinating Committee
Society for the Revival and Preservation of Southern Food, 264
Soda pop, 224, 232–34, 236, 237
Sokolov, Raymond, 50, 93, 187
Solanum tuberosum (potato), 167
Sorghum, 12–13, 224–25, 241
Sorrel tea, 228. See also Hibiscus
"Soul Daddy" healthy soul food, 3–4, 257
Soul food: and Black Power, 41, 44–45, 260–61; blacks' critiques of, 46–47, 260–61, 263; in Britain, 185, 258; closures of soul food restaurants, 3–4, 193; comfort food compared with, 256–57; criticisms of, 1–4, 46–47, 260–61, 263; definitions of, 1, 256–57, 262, 265, 266; different names for, xiii; in France, 105–6; future of, 255–66; health-

focused soul food, 145, 254, 256, 257, 264–65; history of term, 41–45; home cooking of, 264–65; invisibility of, 2–3; and questions of post-blackness, 263; regional differences in, 261–62; restaurants in Asia, 106–7; southern food distinguished from, 6–7, 262; traditional wisdom of, 9–10; typical items on plate of, 4, 264–65; unhealthy image of, 1–2, 5, 46, 263; white responses to, 47–48; White Trash food compared with, 47–48. *See also* Restaurants; Soul Food period; *and specific types of soul foods*

Soul Food: Classic Cuisine from the Deep South (Ferguson), 173

Soul Food Cornbread Family Stalk, 195

Soul Food period (1950s–present): and catfish, 70–71, 78–80, 86–87; and chitlins, 102–8; and cornbread, 186–87, 203; definition of, 7; down home cooking and soul food used for same food, 42; and fish fries, 83; and greens, 146–47, 157–58, 163; history of term "soul food," 41–45; and macaroni and cheese, 141–42; and racial identity politics, 41, 44–45, 260. *See also* Soul food

Soul music, 42

Soul Queen restaurant (Chicago), 3

South America, 122, 167, 168, 212, 226

Southern checker peas, 114

Southern Cooking period (1865–present): and agricultural jobs for African Americans in postbellum period, 32–35; black church gatherings during postbellum period, 31; and black-eyed peas, 116–17; black food habits in urban North in early 1940s, 40; and chitlins, 99–100, 108; church gatherings during, 31; definition of, 7; and desserts, 252; and diet

of black migrants after 1910, 36, 38, 259–60; and diet of black migrants during 1890s, 36; Emancipation celebrations and holidays in postbellum period, 31, 80, 233–35; and Great Migration to urban areas, 36–40, 260; and "Harlem Menu," 38; and hunger following Civil War, 30; landowners' diets in postbellum South, 33; and red lemonade, 231–33; and relief distribution for the hungry, 35, 41; and rent farmers, 33; and sharecroppers' meal pattern, 34–35; soul food distinguished from southern food, 6–7, 29–30, 262; stereotypes of African Americans during, 31, 231; strategies for supplementing food during, 40–41; subregional cuisines within southern cooking, 16–19, 261–62; "3 M's" diet of, 19, 22, 23; urban blacks in postbellum period, 32

Southern Foodways Alliance, 164, 264

Southern Kitchen (Tacoma, Wash.), 232

Southern Rural Black Women's Initiative for Economic and Social Justice, 162–63

Soyer, Alexis, 241

Spain, 112, 171, 172, 176, 210, 242, 248

Spices, 212

Spinach (*Spinacia oleracea*), 150, 153, 155–56, 157, 164

Spoonbread, 194, 199–200; Sweet Potato Greens Spoonbread, 164–65

Stanley, Rev. Walter P., 42

Starr, Kathy, 129, 140

Stereotypes of African Americans, 31, 58, 75, 125, 231

Stern, Jane and Michael, 219

Stier, Isaac, 28

Stone, Curtis, 4

Street vending: of black-eyed pea fritters (*acara*) in Nigeria, 121; for black migrants, 38, 259; demise of, 260; formerly enslaved cooks and, 32; of fried chicken, 58, 60; of macaroni, 134, 135; of red lemonade, 232; of sweet potatoes, 180, 232; of tamales, 198

String beans, 203

Student Nonviolent Coordinating Committee (SNCC), 43–44

Sugar in cornbread, 200–202, 204, 206–7

Sugar plantations, 15, 208–9

Sugar Rush (TV program), 250

Sullivan, Caroline, 227, 246

Sullivan, Herman, 161–62

Summer, William, 174, 175

Summer Peach Crisp recipe, 254

"Sunday cluck," 49. *See also* Fried chicken

Sunday dinner: cooking skills displayed at, 43; desserts for, 251, 252; in Down Home Cooking period, 58; fried chicken for, 49–50, 55–60; macaroni and cheese for, 129, 138, 140, 142; with preacher, 56–58; for slaves, 26–27, 28, 55; for urban blacks, 260

Sunday worship for slaves, 20, 27, 55–56

Sweet Auburn Bread Company (Atlanta), 262

Sweet potatoes, 179 (ill.); baked sweet potatoes, 166; in Black Belt cuisine, 19; carrots compared with, 171–72; Carver on, 162–63, 166, 249; curing/storing of, 174–75; in Down Home Cooking period, 182; farming of, 178, 182, 183; as fries or tater tots, 183; greens of, 162–65, 166; as health food, 183; history of, 167, 171–82; in landowners' diets in postbellum South, 33; Louisiana Creole proverb on, 166; in the North, 176–78, 180–81; possum and, 172–74; preparation

methods for, 175–77; recipes for, 181–82; roasted sweet potatoes, 25, 168, 176–78, 180–81; scientific research on, 182, 258; in sharecroppers' diet, 34, 36; in Slave Food period, 22, 172–77, 259; "Spanish potato" as nickname for, 176; street vending of, 180, 232; as survival food for sharecroppers, 174–75; varieties of, 178, 183; in West Africa, 170–71; yams distinguished from, 167–68, 170–71, 183; yellow-fleshed vs. orange-fleshed yams, 178–83. *See also* Candied yams; Yams

Sweet potato greens, 162–65, 166

Sweet Potato Greens Spoonbread, 164–65

Sweet potato growers' cooperative, 162–63

Sweet potato pie, 4, 31, 240, 241, 248–49, 252, 259

Sweet Stuff (Barker), 243

Sweet tea, 4

Sydnor, Charles, 21

Szathmary, Louis, 8, 258

Tabasco Brand Pepper Sauce, 215, 217, 218, 281 (n. 31)

Tabasco chillis, 208–12, 215–18, 281 (n. 31)

Tamales, 150, 198

Tamayo, B. J., 232

Taste of Country Cooking, The (Lewis), 250–51

Taters. *See* Sweet potatoes

Taylor, Joe Gray, 76–77

TBS. *See* Turner Broadcasting System

Teas. *See* Elderbush tea; Hibiscus tea; Kola tea and kola nuts; Sweet tea

Television: *Are We There Yet?* on Turner Broadcasting System, 1; Bravo Network on, 4, 144; commercial on, about soul food, 1; Food Network on, 4, 144, 250; food programs on,

3, 4, 144, 185, 250, 257; interview with Condoleezza Rice on, 129; *Treme* series on HBO, 7

Telfair, Georgia, 152

Thanksgiving, 91, 93, 102, 129, 163, 167

Theory of Special Edibility, 8, 258. *See also* Szathmary, Louis

"They're Red Hot," 198

Thirteenth Amendment (U.S. Constitution), 30

"This Is It" Restaurant (Atlanta), 91

Thomas, Allen, 235

Thornwell, Rev. Dr. James Henley, 20

"3 M's" diet (meat, meal, and molasses), 19, 22, 23

Through the Back Door (Turner), 97–98

Tibet, 241

Tilapia, 80

Tillman, Ben, 224

Tines, Elizabeth, 232

Tobacco, 13, 15, 16

Tobin, Beth Fowkes, 152–53

Tolbert, Willie, 39

Tomatoes, 34

Top Chef: Texas, 144

Toting, 40–41

Toure, Kwame, 44

To Work and Serve the Home (New Jersey State Federation of Colored Women's Clubs), 181

Treme series, 7

Trifles, 246

Trillin, Calvin, 219–20

Triticum aestivum (wheat), 189

Triticum vulgare (wheat), 189

Turkey: with black-eyed peas, 126–27; with greens, 147, 157–58, 163–64; in landowners' diets in postbellum South, 33

Turner, Janet Driskell, 97–98, 102

Turner, Lorenzo Dow, 167, 227

Turner Broadcasting System (TBS), 1

Turnip greens: in Black Belt cuisine, 19; in Harlem, 155; in mixed greens recipe, 163–64; as regular African American dish generally, 153; scientific name of, 147; in sharecroppers' diet, 34; in Slave Food period, 150; in West Africa, 150

Turnips, 34

Tuskegee diet, 180

Twain, Mark, 186

Two Gentlemen of Verona, The (Shakespeare), 41–42

Ude, Louis Eustache, 176–77

UHOPFAP. *See* United House of Prayer for All People

"Umbles," 92–93. *See also* Chitlins

United House of Prayer for All People (UHOPFAP), 61–62

U.S. Department of Agriculture, 115

U.S. Sweet Potato Council, 183

University of Mississippi, 263

Urban League, 141

Urban slavery, 19–21, 32. *See also* Slaves

Usner, Daniel, 188

Utsey, Minnie, 207

Vance, Rupert, 34–35

Van Hook, John, 190–91, 196

Vegan, 146, 158, 256, 257

Vegan Soul, 256

Vegetarianism, 46, 158, 257

Velveeta cheese spread, 137

Vernonia amygdalina (bitter leaf), 149

Vergil, Emma, 249

Verrill, A. Hyatt, 171

Vietnam, 107; catfish from, 79; Vietnam War, 235–36

Vigna unguiculata (black-eyed peas), 112, 119. *See also* Black-eyed peas

"Virginia Breakfast," 54, 59

Virginia Housewife, The (Randolph), 53, 74, 115, 133, 150, 156, 175, 213, 248. *See also* Randolph, Mrs. Mary

Virgin Islands, 239

Voodoo, 122, 223

Wade, Richard, 21
Waffles and chicken, 16, 53, 59, 67–69
Wagner, Mark, 112–13, 170
Walker, Alice, 223
Wallace, Marta, 66
Washington, George, 114, 227
Washington, Martha, 89
Washington Post, 61–62, 84, 107, 118, 124, 224
Water: molasses and water, 229, 232; sharecroppers' drinking water, 35; slaves' drinking water, 229; West Africans' drinking water, 25, 224
Watermelon, 31, 80, 231
Watts, Kristi, 129
Weaver, William Woys, 59, 219, 248
Weinzweig, Ari, 211
Wells, Joe, 59
West Africa: alcoholic beverages in, 224, 226; black-eyed peas/cowpeas in, 12, 112, 115, 118, 120, 121, 163; chickens in, 50–53, 259; chillis in, 212–13; colonial diet of, 13–14, 19, 150, 166, 169–71, 187–88; cooking of chickens in, 52–53; corn in, 187; culinary carbohydrate zones in, 12–13; culinary connection between African diaspora and, 7–8, 24, 25, 28, 74, 99, 258–59; drinking water in, 25, 224; eyes' folkloric meaning in, 120; fish and fishing in, 70, 71–72, 74, 76–77, 80, 187; folklore and religious systems of, 51–52, 99, 120–21, 259; greens in, 149–50, 157, 166; hibiscus tea in, 224, 225, 228; hot sauce in, 210; Ibo (or Igbo) creation myth from, 168–69, 175; kola tea and kola nuts in, 224–26; maize in, 13, 19, 169, 188; map of, 12; milk in, 224, 228; millet in, 12–13, 187; New World plants in, 13–14, 19, 150, 166, 169–71, 187; oral tradition of, 5, 12; precolonial diet of, 12–13, 168; red drinks in, 224–28, 259; slavery in,

13; spices in, 212; street vendors in, 121; sweet potatoes in, 170–71; true yam festival in, 169–70; and wheat bread, 187–88; yams in, 12, 13, 167–70, 174, 175, 183; Yoruba people of, 51, 99, 108, 121
Westheider, James E., 235
West Indies, 15, 227
Wheat bread, 187–88, 189, 202–3, 204
Wheeler, Joseph, 95
Whippoorwill peas, 114
Whiskey. *See* Alcoholic beverages
White, Barry, 209
White, Izola, 193
White, Maunsel, 208–9, 213, 215–17, 281 (n. 31)
White trash cooking, 47–48
White Trash Cooking (Mickler), 47–48, 140, 173
Whiting fish, 85
Williams, Bill, 159
Williams, Eugene "Hot Sauce," 220
Wilshire Restaurant (Santa Monica, Calif.), 144–45, 256
Wilson, C. Anne, 148, 250
Wilson, Ellen Gibson, 167–68, 170–71
Wilson, Justin, 47
Wilson, Woodrow, 179
Winfrey, Oprah, 223
Women in Agriculture, 162–63
Woods, Jamawn, 257
Woods, Sylvia, 79
Woodson, Willis, 95
World War I, 115, 179, 182
World War II, 138, 182
Wright, Clifford, 212
Wright, Pam, 241, 244–46

Yams: in Down Home Cooking period, 182; history of, 171–82; Ibo (or Igbo) creation myth on, 168–69, 175; and possum, 172–74; preparation methods for, 168; recipes for,

181–82; in Slave Food period, 22, 172–77, 259; sweet potatoes distinguished from, 167–68, 170–71, 183; true yams in West Africa, 12, 13, 167–70, 174, 175, 183; varieties of, 168; yellow-fleshed vs. orange-fleshed yams, 178–83. *See also* Candied yams; Sweet potatoes

Yeoman farm slavery, 19, 21, 192. *See also* Slaves

Yoruba people, 51, 99, 108, 121. *See also* West Africa

Young, John, 219–20

Zingerman's Deli (Ann Arbor, Mich.), 211